IT COMES WITH THE TERRITORY

IT COMES WITH THE TERRITORY

An Inquiry Concerning Work and the Person

A. R. GINI
Loyola University of Chicago

T. J. SULLIVAN

RANDOM HOUSE   NEW YORK

First Edition
987654321
Copyright © 1989 by Random House, Inc.

All rights reserved under International and Pan-American Copyright Conventions. No part of this book may be reproduced in any form or by any means, electronic or mechanical, including photocopying, without permission in writing from the publisher. All inquiries should be addressed to Random House, Inc., 201 East 50th Street, New York, N.Y. 10022. Published in the United States by Random House, Inc., and simultaneously in Canada by Random House of Canada Limited, Toronto.

LIBRARY OF CONGRESS
Library of Congress Cataloging-in-Publication Data

It comes with the territory: an inquiry concerning work and the person/[edited by] A. R. Gini, T. J. Sullivan.
    p.   cm.
  ISBN 0-394-38298-6
  1. Work. 2. Work—Psychological aspects. 3. Work ethic.
I. Gini, A. R. II. Sullivan, T. J.
HD4904.I75 1989
158.7—dc19   88-18505
                                     CIP

Manufactured in the United States of America

Cover & Book Design by Lisa Polenberg

Preface

Like many textbooks, this book comes out of my needs and wants in the classroom. For the last twenty years or so I have watched class after class of entering freshmen select a major on the basis of two criteria: (1) What is in demand in the marketplace? and (2) What are my personal talents and gifts and how can I best utilize them in the job market? These are, admittedly, good criteria. It is my experience, however, that only a small percentage of these individuals have a goal or a career that they want to pursue because they find it attractive or because they think it important to do so, regardless of the state of the economy and the earning power of the job in question. Sadly, I have seen some of the best minds pursue competency in fields that I know will soon bore them or that will shortly limit their creative potential.

During this time I have been searching for a book that deals with the puzzling phenomenon of "how what people do for a living influences and affects their public and private lives." I agree with E. F. Schumacher that the academic disciplines of economics, sociology, social theory, personnel management, philosophy, and psychology do not sufficiently discuss and examine the problems, purpose, and function of work in our daily lives, especially as it affects our character development. While some texts touch on various aspects of the phenomenon of work, no book to my knowledge handles the topic from the point of view of "what work does to us and what work can do for us." This book is organized as a guide for both graduate and undergraduate students. What it offers is an overview of work, with a focus on "what work does to the person."

I think it is essentially correct to state that, outside of time spent sleeping, most adults spend the largest portion of their lives working, either at a paying job or doing domestic chores. Work is one of the formative activities of life, and as such it can be a source of satisfaction or dissatisfaction, a boon or a burden. Work can be either the expression of human creativity or the bearer of human alienation. But what is clear is that most lives are built upon work; for most people to live is to work. Briefly stated, it is my contention that we become what we do. So we must be very careful what we choose to do and therefore become. Work molds us, and our occupational choices directly influence the formation of our characters. In philosophical terms, at the normative/evaluative level, work has a profound effect on the development of human nature.

It is also my contention that we literally *need* to work in order to fulfill and define ourselves as human beings, and that we cannot endure without it, either physically or psychologically. Work is the means by which we become persons; we create our own history through work. Work allows us to obtain the basic goods and services necessary for survival. Work enables us to perfect our skills and talents, allowing us to expand our areas of expression and control of life. Work affords us the opportunity to be with others, establishing at least the rudimentary requirements for a community. Work is that which forms us, gives us a focus, gives us a vehicle for personal expression, and offers us a means for personal definition. Work is the *sine qua non* condition for human existence as individuals and as a species.

While it is my thesis that "we create ourselves in our work," conventional wisdom has it that at best work is a burden or a duty to be borne. In our society the Protestant work ethic is still revered by many, and even though more people than ever are working long and hard, work is, for the most part, negatively perceived. Studies show that contemporary workers (blue-, pink-, and white-collar) are in general agreement with the classical Greek position that one works in order to avoid further work and to have leisure. For most people work is a task, a condition of life. Few people believe that work is in and of itself ennobling or enlightening. Having said this, however, we see an immediate paradox when looking at the statistics and surveys on work: people view the experience of work and the meaning or significance of work very differently. What is clear is that although people dislike and often reject the experience of work itself, they embrace and actively seek out work to give direction to their lives. As we shall see in both narrative and statistical form, while people more often than not dislike their jobs, they almost universally express a desire *to* work. It is only the lucky few who find both the performance and the purpose of their jobs absorbing, engaging, and worthwhile. The task of this text is to examine the phenomenon of work in order to reconcile this seeming paradox. A secondary task will be to address the question: "Can work be remade, so as to remake people?" Or to state it yet another way: "How can jobs be fashioned so as to allow more if not all of the working force to join the ranks of the lucky few?"

A.R.G.
T.J.S.

Acknowledgments

This book had its beginnings in conversations with John Shack, my colleague and friend. The book saw its completion because of the assistance of Terry Sullivan, my co-author, editor, and friend. Neither phase could have been accomplished without their efforts.

Many other people also deserve to be mentioned. Special thanks go to Steven Pensinger for his help and criticism throughout the development of this text. My secretary, Cynthia Rudolph, deserves praise and possibly canonization for typing and retyping this text seemingly dozens of times. Many thanks to Ray Benton for our conversations and his unending series of suggestions and sources. Profound thanks must be offered to John Bannan, chairman of the Department of Philosophy, for his support and his help in getting Loyola University to grant me a leave so that I could work on this text. My thanks also to the extraordinary staff at the Oak Park Public Library for their help and assistance.

And of course, unending thanks to Mary Ann and Monica, Jason and Carla and John and James.

A.R.G.

Contents

Introduction

We begin in Chapter One with "Work: The Process and the Person" because it is the very thesis of this book. People wish to be happy and they see work as part of a happy life. Whether this is because of an intrinsic need for work, or because work—and the need to work—are so pervasive, is one of the questions that gave rise to this book. That people wish for good, fulfilling work, and must have it in order to be healthy human beings, is the thesis of the book. The paradox confronting most people is at the core of their working lives: most people must work and most believe they want to work, and yet most dislike the jobs they have.

The first section of Chapter One, "Conventional Wisdom," looks at the common view of work—that it is necessary and, because of this, a burden. This is also the traditional view, and the section offers an historical background from Genesis to genetic engineering. Work is seen as a yoke, the price of original or some other sin. One can convert work to virtue, but only insofar as one offers labor as a sacrifice to a higher good. The section concludes with a long look at the Protestant ethic and sees in it an apologia for work as a means to an end. Nowhere in this history is work itself of value; nowhere is the process seen as one which people can address as worth the effort for its own sake or theirs. The conventional view of work relies upon an a priori position, an argument from the assumed depravity of humankind.

The second section, "Statistical Wisdom," is a look at the paradox itself: that people report both a desire to work and an aversion to the work they do. Finally, the third section, "Philosophical Wisdom," is an a posteriori analysis of work; that is, a look at the world as encountered, with no assumed or theological position on the nature of man. This is an attempt to understand the paradox in section two (Statistical Wisdom). This is the longest of the three divisions, and it looks first at what is good work and what is bad. It then looks at how people react to each kind and, finally, what there is *about* good work that makes it desirable. What becomes clear in this section is that people will do good work or bad. What emerges is what good and bad work will do to the person.

Chapter Two, "Some Historical Perspectives on Work," is an attempt to offer a limited historical perspective on what some of the most influential classical/modern thinkers have had to say about work.

The pieces by Adam Smith and Frederick Winslow Taylor describe how work has been seen from the point of view of the mechanics of production and the techniques of workshop efficiency. The goal of both writers was to increase productivity. Their concern with the worker as person was, at best, limited. The Max Weber selection is offered as a clear and succinct statement of perhaps the best known tradition in regard to work, the Protestant work ethic. Although social scientists have long disputed the precise contribution of the Protestant work ethic to the genesis of capitalism, they generally agree that thrift, hard work, and a capacity for deferring gratification are beneficial and necessary ingredients for the success of capitalism.

The readings from Karl Marx and Pope John Paul II present different but nevertheless allied perspectives on how workers are perceived and treated in the workplace. For Marx, workers in a capitalistic system are too often treated as object rather than subject, as simply one of the material factors that enter into the production process. As such, workers are seen as complicated anatomical tools. The effect of how they work, or what they work at, on their lives, values, and world views is seen as irrelevant.

For John Paul II, work, as a function of life, must always treat the worker as subject rather than object. Work is done for the individual, to enhance his or her state and status; it is the means by which one fulfills oneself and becomes whole. Work is for the individual, not the individual for work.

Chapter Three, "The 'Work Ethic' in Transition," examines basic changes in the traditional view of the work ethic. These changes are due in part to a number of causes: the rapid expansion of technology and modern industrialization; the movement of people out of agriculture; the increased percentage of the labor force engaged in service industries; the rapid growth in the number of white-collar workers; the emergence in the workplace of the post-World War II "baby boom" generation; increased life expectancy in the population of the work force; a better educated work force; the increase of blacks and Hispanics in the work force, the revolutionary expansion of the numbers of women in the workplace. All of these factors have qualitatively changed the behavior and expectations of the work force as a whole.

The selection by Michael Maccoby and Katherine A. Terzi, "What Happened to the Work Ethic?", addresses the issues of how the classic model has been changed by the social, scientific, and demographic influences of the twentieth century. The articles by Daniel Yankelovich, "The New Psychological Contracts at Work" and Patricia A. Renwich and Edward E. Lawler, "What You Really Want from Your Job," speak to the expectations that the new wave of workers brings with it to the workplace. The article from *U.S. News and World Report* describes and defines the new rising majority in the workplace, "The New-Collar Class."

In January of 1985, in their "Sixth Annual Salary Survey of Women," the magazine *Working Woman* announced a major shift in the composition of the work force. According to the U.S. Census Bureau, 1984 was the first year that the white male (the prototype of the American worker) did not make up the majority of the labor force. Women and minority-group men now hold 50.7 percent of all jobs. More women are now working than ever. Fifty-three percent of all adult females now hold full-time positions, which means that women represent 44 percent of the entire work force. As recently as fifty years ago, the notion of an unfulfilled housewife was, for most women, unheard-of. Prior to World War II, the managing of a house and the attendant tasks, were, if not always fulfilling, at least a full-time occupation and a demonstrably necessary one. Only in recent years, when the quotidian tasks of meal-making, cleaning, and clothing maintenance have become less than full-time occupations, do we see women not merely bored by housekeeping but viewed by large segments of the population as underemployed. For these women, fulfillment in work outide the home was for the first time possible and, for many, necessary. Besides making up 44 percent of the work force, women hold two-thirds of the 20 million jobs created in the past ten years. For the first time the majority of women are seeking jobs not simply for personal "pin money" nor for the exclusive purpose of supplementing family income, but rather for the purpose of pursuing careers. These new careerists are now beginning to define their worth and status by their degree of success in the workplace. Perhaps for the first time, men and women are defining their identity and sense of self-worth according to the same ground rules. A brief review of the literature indicates that the most compelling evidence about the centrality of work in life comes from the recent efforts of women to fill a void in their lives with a sense of identity derived from work. As some social critics have noted, the desire for what work brings to the individual is at the foundation of the women's liberation movement.

Clearly the advent of women in the workplace is one of the most critical factors in the changing of the work force and the work ethic. The entrance of women into the work force has necessitated a fundamental reevaluation of our ideas regarding sexual equality, sexual role modeling, the purpose and function of marriage, the responsibility of parenthood, and the logistics of child-rearing. In effect, a major revolution has been taking place in American society, one that can affect virtually all of our domestic, social, and economic arrangements. As a result of all these issues and questions, Chapters Three, Four, and Five contain readings on the various new roles of women in the changing work force. These readings are not about the issue of sex differences in the workplace, vis-à-vis the question of differing physical abilities and skills. Rather, they are primarily about how women define themselves in their new roles and new identities in the work force.

Chapter Four, "Theory Building: A Search for a New Ethic," looks at some attempts to arrive at a contemporary ethic for the meaning of work. I think it is appropriate to state that as workers we are living in a post-Protestant era and that we are now searching for an as yet unnamed replacement for these traditional values. Whether or not the Protestant work ethic is a valid theory is not at issue. What is at issue is that it did in fact serve as an "action guide" for generations of working individuals. Some of the authors in this chapter are attempting to define and describe an ethic that people now have or are developing in relation to their work. I think that some of these authors are plainly "theory building," that is, searching for an ethic that will explain the phenomenon of work today as satisfactorily as the Protestant work ethic did in the past.

The first two essays, T. Sullivan, "What Do We Mean When We Talk about Work?" and Daniel Bell, "Work and Its Discontents," try to examine and depict what work is like and how it is viewed after, and sometimes in spite of, the critique of the Protestant work ethic. Sullivan's essay is a commonsense language analysis of what we mean by the word "work." He looks at work and how we talk about work in order to arrive at a definition that is applicable and common to all forms of work. Bell's essay, which is drawn from his now classic book of the same title, tries to examine once again the question "Why do people work?" More particularly he asks why people accept harsh, monotonous, repetitive jobs that tie them so painfully to the wheel of life.

Gus Tyler's article, "The Work Ethic: A Union View," is an examination of work not from the theorist's point of view but from the shop-floor practitioner's. Tyler's prime concern is the worker, rather than the work. According to Tyler, unionists are not opposed to either "work" or "ethics." They favor both: work to stay alive and ethics for fair treatment at the workplace. The unionist is not interested in the ideology of work but rather in "working conditions," "fringes," and "hours and wages." Unionists believe that there is an ethical obligation to recognize the worker as a person, and therefore everything possible must be done to make the worksite safer for the body and saner for the psyche. For Tyler it is the unionist view of the work ethic that strengthens and solidifies the social, economic, and political life of America. Harry Magdoff, the Marxist scholar, in "The Meaning of Work: A Marxist Perspective," also takes the position of the worker over work when he states that for Marx a prime aim of socialism is to eliminate the miseries of work and the way of life arising from capitalism. This necessarily implies, in a Marxist framework, the dissolution of all forms of the division of labor that were created by and are integral to the existence of private property and structured economic classes. According to Magdoff, Marx believed that the workers of the world would be able to cast off their chains when they recognized that human nature and the patterns of economic existence are not constant for all time. For Marx the structure of work will change only if we come to realize that acquisitive drives, individualism, and competition are not biological givens but acquired traits of capitalism. Marx wrote, in *The Poverty of Philosophy*, that "all of history is but the continuous transformation of human nature."

The three articles listed under the subtopic of "Meaningful Work" all deal with suiting work to fit the needs and wants of people and not simply harnessing people to the requirements of the worksite. These authors maintain that this society needs good work, i.e., work that produces a good product and a good worker. Good work is, for them: (1) work in which people can become involved, committed, and interested; (2) work that is a challenge to one's capabilities; and (3) work with some form of worker participation in decision making. Irving Bluestone, in "Worker Participation in Decision Making," argues that in a society that prides itself on its democratic system of freedom for the individual and rejection of dictatorial rule, the work place still stands as an island of authoritarianism. A democratic society, says Bluestone, should and must ensure each individual the dignity, respect, and liberty worthy of a free person. It must afford the opportunity for self-expression and participation in the shaping of one's own life culturally, politically, economically, and professionally. Work and the complexity of the workplace cannot be used as excuses to radically curtail the rights and freedoms of an employee. Adina Schwartz, in "Meaningful Work," contends that many people are caught in low-skill, routinized jobs, and that they all too often find both their jobs and their off-the-job lives dissatisfying and unfulfilling. According to Schwartz, interesting work is a requirement of adult life. When people work for considerable lengths of time at jobs that invovle mainly mechanical, repetitive activity, they tend to be made less capable of, and less interested in, rationally and independently pursuing their own plans during the rest of their nonwork time. For Schwartz they are made to lead less autonomous, less interesting, less fulfilling lives.

Theodore Roszak, in "Work: The Right to Right Livelihood," maintains that ongoing industrial progress is predicated upon maximizing labor-saving technology. The justification is that "labor-saving" equals "leisure-making," and that leisure is what life is for. Roszak, however, argues that our personhood is realized in responsible work. The true direction of progress, therefore, is not to save labor, but to preserve it from indiscriminate technological advance. If anything must be saved, it is the concept that work is a necessity of the human condition—not a mere means of survival, but a paramount means of self-discovery. We have a need to work; we have a right to work; and neither the need nor the right has to be justified by proving its profitability or productivity, any more than our need to love, play, or grow should be subjected to its cost-benefit analysis. Our work is our life, and we cannot exercise our right to self-discovery in a world that deprives us of our natural vocation.

Chapter Five, "Work and the Self," represents the central thesis of this text. Work is, finally, the ultimate personal experience. It occupies our bodies and minds at least forty hours of each week, and it both reveals who we are and determines who we become. How we approach our work, the way we organize it, our ability to cope with its structures and demands, are all telling; to observe ourselves at work is to hold up a mirror to the psyche. If the "unexamined life is not worth living," perhaps the "unexamined job is not worth having." The tragedy of our times may well be that so few jobs allow for self-examination, and so many, when examined, prove empty.

The articles in the subsection "Work and Self-Definition" all deal with the notion that we become and define ourselves by what we do. Lee Braude, in "Work and the Self," contends that a person's work is one of the more important parts of his or her social identity. Indeed, Braude claims that there is something almost as irrevocable about our choice of an occupation as there is about our choice of a mate. John Shack's article, "Toward a Dynamic-Interactionalist Taxonomy of Work Style," explores how personal work style and work satisfaction result from the complex interaction of temperament and environmental experience. The article by Frederick Herzberg, "One More Time: How Do You Motivate Employees?" somewhat elliptically addresses the issues of work and self-identity and work and self-esteem by reiterating the major thesis of "his life's work." For true satisfaction and for self-identity to be sustained and augmented, the worker must feel a genuine sense of achievement and accomplishment on the job. To permit human growth, work must be responsible, worthwhile, and challenging. For Herzberg, the hygienic palliatives of a clean and bright workplace, satisfactory tools, and decent pay may make the work environment more tolerable but may not raise motivation, increase productivity, or enrich the worker's professional and personal sense of self. For Abraham Maslow, "Human Needs and Work," work is both a "basic need" and a "growth need" in our lives. For Maslow, work allows us to develop self-esteem ("basic need"), which can lead to feelings of self-confidence, worth, strength, capability, and adequacy—of being useful and necessary in the world. However, says Maslow, adults who do not have work often experience profound feelings of inferiority, weakness, and helplessness. Maslow claims that the only truly happy people he knows (self-actualized, actualized, growth-motivated individuals) are those who are working at something they consider important.

Melvin Kohn's article, "Job Complexity and Adult Personality," is a distillation of his important work with Carmi Schooler, *Work and Personality: An Inquiry into the Impact of Social Stratification.* Kohn claims that the intrinsic meaning and psychological impact of a job result not just from the status or income or interpersonal relationships that the job provides but also from the meaningful challenges the work itself poses. The most important challenge is that of mastering complex tasks—that is, the substantive complexity of the work. The data indicate that substantial complexity affects psychological functioning regardless of needs, values, personal capacities, or social class. What matters most about work is not its attendant rewards, but the work itself. Moreover, Kohn claims that the relationship between work and psychological functioning is reciprocal. There is, in effect, an ongoing process throughout all of adult life whereby the occupational conditions we encounter mold our psychological processes and in turn are molded by our personalities and behavior.

The articles in the subsection "Work and Well-Being" deal with the converse of work as healthful, growthful, and resulting in self-identity. Work can be an affliction and an addiction as well as a beneficial fulfillment. The H.E.W. Task Force report, "Work and Health," is an overview of the maladies that can occur in the workplace and be induced by the stress of a job: e.g., heart disease; mercury poisoning; the melancholia of sailors; the alienation and mental health problems of many factory workers; alcoholism; drug abuse;

suicide. Patricia E. Benner, in "Stress and Satisfaction on the Job," examines patterns of work-related stress. Her study is especially interested in how one's perception of the meaning of work affects his or her reaction to stress. The study seeks to show that these meanings determine a person's perception of a stressful episode and the subsequent response or patterns of coping behavior. Marilyn Machlowitz's essay, "Workaholism: What Is It?" claims that for a workaholic the meaning and purpose of work are distorted, and life is out of balance. Workaholics come from both sexes and all classes and occupations; they share one overriding passion—work. Work becomes an uncontrollable compulsion. If there is no productive work to do, work will be created to fill the available time. Thus the person works long hours at the job, brings work home in the evenings, and dislikes taking a vacation, not because of a desire to create a meaningful product but because of an inner need to work. Deriving extreme pleasure from work does not make a workaholic. It is the compulsion to work that identifies the disorder. Without work the compulsive feels nervous and guilty. If their work schedule is interrupted, they become irritable and cross. The rewards of work are the removal of guilt, fear, and personal uncertainty, and work becomes a way to avoid confronting other concerns in life. In an unstructured social situation, workaholics feel unsure of themselves and uncertain of their abilities; on the job, they know what to do and can bury themselves in their work. In the end, being a workaholic may simply be a socially acceptable way of coping with life when other ways are unavailable or uninteresting.

IT COMES WITH
THE TERRITORY

1

A Critical Overview

WORK: THE PROCESS AND THE PERSON ....

INTRODUCTION

"Work is usually seen as an obstacle to endure, not as an opportunity to expand one's life."

—*A.R.G.*

TOADS

Why should I let the toad work
   Squat on my life?
Can't I use my wit as a pitchfork
   And drive the brute off?

Six days of the week it soils
   With its sickening poison—
Just for paying a few bills!
   That's out of proportion.

Lot of folk live on their wits:
   Lecturers lispers,
Losels, loblolly-men, louts—
   They don't end as paupers;

Lots of folk live up lanes
   With fires in a bucket,
Eat windfalls and tinned sardines—
   They seem to like it.

Their nippers have got bare feet,
   Their unspeakable wives
Are skinny as whippets—and yet
   No one actually *Starves*.

"Toads" by Philip Larkin is reprinted from *The Less Deceived* by permission of the Marvell Press, England.

1

Ah, were I courageous enough
  To shout *Stuff your pension*!
But I know, all too well, that's the stuff
  That dreams are made on:

For something sufficiently toad-like
  Squats in me, too
Its hunkers are heavy as hard luck,
  And cold as snow,

And will never allow me to blarney
  My way to getting
The fame and the girl and the money
  All at one sitting.

I don't say, one bodies the other
  One's spiritual truth;
But I do say it's hard to lose either,
  When you have both.

—Philip Larkin

Folk wisdom has it that the main problem with work is that so few people are able to avoid it. For the vast majority work is an inescapable and irreducible fact of existence. Work is a necessary evil, an activity that is required to sustain and justify the hours between sleeping, eating, and attempting to enjoy ourselves. It is, for most of us, like Larkin's toad: we cannot "drive the brute off." In its very worst light, work is seen as "something evil, a punishment, the great and grindingly inevitable burden of toil and mortality laid upon the human situation."[1] Studs Terkel's book *Working* has become the bible for those who feel that work is by definition degrading, debilitating, and dehumanizing. True believers need only open this text at random to find documented proof that work is one, if not the major, cause of "economic unfreedom," "physical debasement," "personal alienation," and "social ennui." At best, work looms so large and problematic in the lives of most of us that we tend to take it for granted and either calmly forget about it or actively suppress the full significance of its effect on our lives. It is simply *there*, as illness, death, taxes, and mortgage payments are there, something to be endured.[2] From this perspective such statements as "Work is love made visible" (Kahlil Gibran) and "To work is to pray" (St. Benedict) are saccharine palliatives which in no way reflect the reality of the situation. The cynical response to such platitudes is, "If work has so many benefits why is it that so many people spent so much of their lives trying to avoid it?" *Chicago Tribune* columnist Mike Royko accurately encapsulates the spirit of the "common man's" feelings about work when his alter ego in the column, Slats, says:

    . . . why do you think the lottery is so popular? Do you think anybody would play if the super payoff was a job on the night shift in a meat packing plant?

People play it so if they win they can be rich and idle . . . like I told you years ago—if work is so good, how come they have to pay us to do it?[3]

The data being generated in academic circles support this commonsense portrait of work. Since the mid-1950s a horde of sociologists and industrial psychologists have descended upon the workplace in a frenetic attempt to probe, measure, and analyze how workers relate to work, what they feel about work, and how it affects personal values, private lives, and general world-views. The reports from these investigations are not far removed from the "barroom grumblings" most of us are familiar with. The surveys indicate that when asked the question, "Are Americans less motivated to work now?" employees answer both yes and no. The results indicate that some workers are satisfied with certain aspects of their work and others are not. The important point to keep in mind, however, is that for most people the critical issue is not, "Do I still want to work?" as much as "Does my job turn me off?" Surveys show a consistently strong reaffirmation of the value of work for three-quarters of the population. Even more surprising, when asked if they would choose to continue to work even if they could live comfortably for the rest of their lives without doing so, most people say they would choose to work. A seeming contradiction appears when workers are asked: "If you were free to go into any type of job you wanted, what would your choice be?"

The job he or she now has:	38.1
Retire and not work at all:	1.9
Prefer some other job to the job he or she has now:	60.4[4]

The paradox here is that, in general, people want to work but dislike their present jobs; they do not find the work fulfilling or expansive. Perhaps one of the characters in Studs Terkel's book most eloquently stated the predicament in which many workers find themselves:

I think most are looking for a calling not a job. Most of us, like the assembly line worker, have jobs that are not big enough for people.[5]

I believe that work is the means by which we become and complete ourselves as persons; we create ourselves in our work. To restate the old Italian proverb "You are what you eat" in regard to work "You are the work you do." We must be very careful, therefore, in the work we choose. Work is a necessary and defining activity in the development of the human personality. Work is the mark of man and work molds man, or, as Gregory Baum has stated, "labor [work] is the axis of human self-making."[6] All of us need work, work that ennobles the product and ennobles the producer as well. This is what E. F. Schumacher has called "good work."

While many people do not like their work, they need it to help them focus on reality, find a creative outlet, and define themselves as individuals.

Finances aside, the main reason people don't like their work is that their jobs don't match their skills, interests, or talents. It isn't that all work is bad; it is rather that some work is bad for some people at some times. Ideally, the goal of work should be analogous to the Greek definition of happiness: "the use of all of one's powers to achieve excellence."

CONVENTIONAL WISDOM

KAFKA'S WATCH

"I have a job with a tiny salary of 80 crowns, and
an infinite eight to nine hours of work.
I devour the time outside the
office like a wild beast . . .
I don't complain about the work so much
as about the sluggishness of swampy time."

—*Raymond Carver*

For most of us, working is an entirely nondiscretionary activity. We must work in order to survive, certainly to survive with a modicum of security and comfort.[7] Historically, work has carried with it a certain coercive quality; one is forced to work, to do something in order to carry on. In primitive, subsistence societies there was no distinction between working and not working. To be awake was to be working. A person was born, worked, and died. To work was the law of life. Frank Tannenbaum in his text *A Philosophy of Labor* updated and reaffirmed this thesis for the contemporary American working force when he stated:

> We have become a nation of employees. We are dependent upon others for our means of livelihood, and most people have become completely dependent upon wages. If they lose their jobs they lose every resource, except for the relief supplied by the various forms of social security. Such dependence of the mass of the people upon others for all of their income is something new in the world. For our generation, the substance of life is in another man's hands.[8]

I take it to be the case, however, that the common laments against work are not simply based on the fact that most of us are part of the captive work force and hence accept work as inevitable. In well over one hundred studies in the last twenty-five years, workers have regularly depicted their jobs as physically exhausting, boring, psychologically diminishing, or personally humiliating and unimportant.[9] In the opening lines of *Working*, Terkel compellingly exemplifies this point of view:

> This book, being about work is, by its very nature, about violence—to the spirit as well as to the body. It is about ulcers as well as accidents, about shouting

matches as well as fist fights, about nervous breakdowns as well as kicking the dog around. It is above all (or beneath all) about daily humiliations. To survive the day is triumph enough for the walking wounded among the great many of us.[10]

The poor reputation that work currently enjoys has a long and convoluted history. The image of the "negative-necessity" of work seems to have partial origins in the various etymologies of the word itself. The Greek word for "labor" (work), *ponos*, also means "sorrow."[11] In Latin the word *labor* also means "extreme effort associated with pain." According to Hannah Arendt, "labor" has the same etymological root as *labare* ("to stumble under a burden"), signifying "trouble, distress, difficulty." The French word *travail* connotes "a heavy burdensome task." It likewise is of Latin origin and it originally denoted the *tripalium*, a three-pronged instrument of torture used by the Roman legionnaires, hence the suggestion of "sorrow and pain." In medieval German the word *Arbeit* ("to labor") can also be translated to signify "tribulation, persecution, adversity, or bad times." Finally, the word "occupation" emerges from the Latin *occupare*, connoting the adversarial posture "of seizing hold of or grappling with a task." Clearly, these etymologies leave little doubt about antiquity's association of work with pain or irksomeness.[12]

The common perception of work as a "negative and ignoble" activity can also be traced to classical sources. The Bible tells us that originally there was no work to be done in the Garden of Eden; toil was described as a curse imposed by God to symbolize humankind's banishment. After the Fall, work became a necessary activity. For Milton "man's first disobedience" resulted in the curse of work.[13] Genesis graphically expresses the curse that sin brought with it: "Cursed is the ground because of you; in toil you shall eat of it all the days of your life. . . . In the sweat of your face you shall eat bread till you return to the ground, for out of it you were taken."[14] One interpretation of the Jewish tradition perceives work as "painful drudgery" to which we are condemned by sin. It is accepted as an expiation through which one can atone for sin and prepare for the arrival of Messiah. Work is a "heavy yoke" that is "hard to bear," and Ecclesiastes can be heard to sigh: "The labor of man does not satisfy the soul."[15] Primitive Christianity, like Judaism, regarded work as a punishment from God. But work was not only seen as a result of original sin, but also as a means to redemption by sharing the goods of one's labor with those who were in greater need. Thus work, as a means of charity, was a source of grace. Yet work is never exalted as anything in itself, but only as an instrument of purification, charity, or expiation.

By the time of Thomas Aquinas in the thirteenth century, work was being considered a necessity of nature. According to Aquinas, each of us must use our God-given talents ("stewardship") in the service of both ourselves and others. In fulfilling the duty of work, we acquire skill, fulfill our obligations of charity, and pay homage to our creator. With the Scholastic synthesis, work became a natural right and duty, the sole legitimate basis for society, the foundation for property and profit, as well as the means for personal salvation.[16] Nonetheless, the work of this life was still thought to be of little consequence compared to the spiritual work of preparing to face God. By itself work had no purpose, for only the contemplation of God could redeem life.[17]

To the ancient Greeks, whose physical labor was done by slaves, work brutalized the mind and made men unfit for the practice of the gentlemanly virtues. The Greeks regarded work as a curse, a drudgery, and a heavy-hearted activity. Plutarch in his chapter on Pericles remarks that no well-born man would want to be the craftsman Phidias. Because while a gentleman enjoys the contemplation of the sculptor's masterpieces, he himself would never consider using a hammer and chisel and being covered with dust, sweat, and grime.[18] The Greeks felt that work enslaved the worker, chained him to the will of others and corrupted his soul. Work by its very nature inhibited the use of reason and thereby impeded the search for the ultimate ends of life. Work was accepted not as an end in itself but as a means by which some might be freed to pursue higher goals. Aristotle declared that just as the goal of war was peace, so the object of work was leisure. Leisure meant activity pursued free of compulsion or desire for gain, free for the contemplation of philosophical issues and truths. Aristotle saw work as a burden which he had no duty to bear. He himself never worked, accepting the slavery of others because it freed him for leisure.[19]

Work both as a private activity and as a way of life began to take on a less onerous nature during the Renaissance and the Reformation. It was during this period that work, no matter how high or low the actual task, began to develop—at least at the theoretical level—a positive ethos of its own. Most historians credit the origin of the work ethic to Martin Luther. According to Luther, one was summoned by God to a secular "calling" which today we would call a job.[20] Luther stressed that all callings were necessary to life; no one calling was to be recognized as more necessary or blessed than another, and, therefore, all callings had equal worth in the sight of God. For Luther, work was a form of serving God: "There is just one best way to serve God— to do most perfectly the work of one's profession." Thus the only way to live acceptably before God was through devotion to one's calling. However, God demanded more than occasional good works. He demanded a methodical life of good works in a unified pattern of work and worship.[21]

With John Calvin in the sixteenth century, we find Luther's ideas extended, systematized, and institutionalized. Work was divine, a way of serving God. Work was the will of God and even ceaseless "dumb toil" sufficed to please Him. Calvin preached the "predestination of the elect." He believed that the elect could be recognized by certain outward signs, which included self-denial and devotion to duty, and that God caused the elect to prosper. "To prosper" or "to succeed" meant to enjoy not only wealth and happiness on earth, but eternal salvation. "Success" was the symbol of "selective salvation."

Calvin managed, no matter how indirectly, to provide a rationale linking work and the Divine with material success and comfort.

In *The Protestant Ethic and the Spirit of Capitalism* (1905), Max Weber observed that the rise of Protestantism and the rise of capitalism generally coincided in England and throughout most European countries. Weber's explanation was that many basic Protestant ideas encouraged capitalistic activities. For example, the Reformation taught that each person would be individually judged by God, and that judgment would be based on one's whole life's work or "calling." The reformers also taught that the fruits of one's "calling"—money—should not be spent frivolously or unnecessarily. According to Weber, these ideas led to a life of hard work, self-discipline, asceticism, and concern with achievement. This ethic helped advance the rise of the private entrepreneur in that it led to the accumulation of money which could not be spent on luxuries, but which could and should be put into one's own business.[22]

Labor analyst Michael Cherrington maintains that the work ethic typically embraces one or more of the following beliefs:

1. People have a moral and religious obligation to fill their lives with heavy physical toil. For some, this means that hard work, effort, and drudgery are to be valued for their own sake; physical pleasures and enjoyments are to be shunned; and an ascetic existence of methodical rigor is the only acceptable way to live.
2. Men and women are expected to spend long hours at work, with little or no time for personal recreation and leisure.
3. A worker should have a dependable attendance record, with low absenteeism and tardiness.
4. Workers should take pride in their work and do their jobs well.
5. Workers should be highly productive and produce a large quantity of goods or services.
6. Employees should have feelings of commitment and loyalty to their profession, their company, and their work group.
7. Workers should be achievement-oriented and constantly strive for promotions and advancement. High-status jobs with prestige and the respect of others are important indicators of a "good" person.
8. People should acquire wealth through honest labor and retain it through thrift and wise investments. Frugality is desirable; extravagance and waste should be avoided.[23]

For Weber the work ethic seems to mean a commitment to work beyond its utility in providing a living. It is "a conviction that work is a worthwhile activity in its own right, not merely . . . the means to material comfort or wealth."[24]

The direct theological descendants of the Reformation, and of John Calvin in particular, were the dour Puritans who migrated to New England. Citing the parable of the talents (Matthew 25), Calvin urged the Puritans to prosper: "You may labor to be rich for God, though not for the flesh or sin."[25] The gospel of work in America was preached from many other pulpits: William Penn constantly reminded the Quakers of Philadelphia that "diligence is a virtue useful and laudable among men. . . . Frugality is a virtue too, and not of little use in life. . . . It is proverbial, 'A Penny sav'd is a Penny got.' "[26] Perhaps the real solidification of the work ethic in America occurred with its practical translation and secularization by Benjamin Franklin. In his various publications Franklin taught that wealth was the result of virtue and the proper display of character. In his *Autobiography* he defines the work ethic in his list of ideal traits: "Temperance, Silence, Order, Resolution, Frugality, Industry, Sincerity, Justice, Moderation, Cleanliness, Tranquility, Chastity, Humility."[27] With Franklin, the work ethic shifted from a direct form of worshiping God to an indirect way of rendering service to God by developing one's character and doing good to others.[28] Unlike the Puritans, Franklin's craftsman no longer worked for God's glory, but for himself. He maintained that "God helps those who help themselves." Nevertheless, hard work remained the only standard for private success and social usefulness.

By the nineteenth century the Protestant ethic in America had changed its name at least three times, but its essential focus had not changed at all. Whether it was called the Protestant ethic, the Puritan ethic, the work ethic, or the immigrant ethic, hard work was seen as good in and of itself, the only ticket to survival and the possibility of success. According to the noted labor historian Daniel T. Rogers, the central premise of the work ethic is that work is the core of the moral life. "Work made men useful in a world of economic scarcity. It staved off the doubts and temptations that preyed on idleness; it opened the way to deserved wealth and status; it allowed one to put the impress of mind and skill on the material world."[29] In many ways the work ethic posited one's very right to existence; one achieved worth through work.

During the nineteenth century, we see the first stirrings of dissatisfaction with this ethic. These came not from churches, employers, or even workers themselves, but from artists. The popularity of Dickens's novels and of plays such as Gerhart Hauptmann's 1893 drama about cottage industries, *The Weavers*, were foreshadowings of a discontent which would manifest itself only in the mid-twentieth century. Until that time the moral preeminence of work stood essentially unchallenged as an accepted social value. C. Wright Mills pointed out that "the gospel of work has been central to the historic tradition of America, to its image of itself, and to the images the rest of the world have of America."[30] There can be little question that this reverence for work, along with an abundance of natural resources and human capital, was an important determinant of America's material success.[31] Moreover, because of this need for a pool of diligent laborers, every agent of authority and education proclaimed the merits of work. From Luther to Franklin to Horatio Alger, workers received a steady diet of exhortation and incantation from press, pulpit, and primer.

All work was worthwhile and laudable; work well done would inevitably bring reward, and work avoided led to degradation and ruin.[32]

It is, however, important to keep in mind that tracing the idea of work through history is difficult, and the record is inconsistently one-sided. As Barbara Tuchman pointed out in *A Distant Mirror* (1978), the history of an ancient society is usually limited to the record keeping of the nobility and the intelligentsia. Few or no records are to be found depicting what the lower classes actually thought or felt about any momentous occurrence of their age. For example, we have no record of what a Greek slave, a medieval peasant, a Reformation craftsman, or a New England Puritan farmer had to say about the day-to-day experiences of work. We do however have the philosophical speculations of Aristotle, Aquinas, Calvin, and Jonathan Edwards.[33] We infer, therefore, that the proposition of the "nobility of work" is not a working-class concept, but a middle-class one. We do not, however, embrace the cynical view that has labeled the Protestant work ethic as pure "ideological subterfuge" geared to maximizing the workers' efforts and thereby increasing the owners' pool of capital. Rather, we maintain that the Protestant work ethic has often been used as a means of masking the drudgery and necessity of work. We accept the notion that true believers were in fact theologically motivated in their actions and achieved a great deal of personal solace as well as material reward and comfort from their work. Moreover, we take it to be the case that those who subscribed to the more secularized version of the work ethic did so with the faithful expectation that their efforts would reap personal and social gain. Nonetheless, part of the overall effect of the work ethic was to acclimate the individual worker to the inevitable. We want to contend that the tradition of the work ethic glorified and legitimized work and gave it a teleological orientation—a sense of purpose or design—which helped to both sustain individual effort and ameliorate its temporal brutishness. Perhaps former President Richard Nixon's often quoted 1971 Labor Day speech best exemplifies our point. He said: "Scrubbing floors and emptying bedpans have just as much dignity as there is in any work done in this country—including my own. . . ." We suggest that while both jobs must be done and done well, these jobs are too disparate in their impact and import to warrant serious comparison.

Daniel Yankelovich, in *New Rules: Searching for Self-Fulfillment in a World Turned Upside Down*, contends that the post-World War II formulation of the "work ethic myth" is the "giving/getting compact."

- Even though we no longer had anything in common we stayed together. We didn't break up our marriage even when the children were grown.
- We lived on his salary even though I was making good money at the time. He said he would not feel right if we spent the money I earned for food and rent.
- I never felt I could do enough for my parents, especially my mother. She sacrificed a promising career as a singer to take care of us. I realize

now that she must have been miserable most of the time. (Why?) Because she said so. She kept reminding us what she was giving up, but we didn't take her seriously.

- It never occurred to me not to have children. Now I realize I'd have felt less put upon if I had freely chosen that destiny and not had it chosen for me.

- I've worked hard all my life, and I've made a success out of it for myself and my family. We have a nice home. We have everything it takes to be comfortable. I've been able to send my kids to good schools, and my wife and I can afford to go anywhere we want. Yes, I have a real sense of accomplishment.

- Sure it was a rotten job. But what the hell. I made a good living, I took care of my wife and kids. What more do you expect?

The old giving/getting compact might be paraphrased this way:

I give hard work, loyalty and steadfastness. I swallow my frustrations and suppress my impulse to do what I would enjoy, and do what is expected of me instead. I do not put myself first; I put the needs of others ahead of my own. I give a lot, but what I get in return is worth it. I receive an evergrowing standard of living, and my family life with a devoted spouse and decent kids. Our children will take care of us in our old age if we really need it, which thank goodness we will not. I have a nice home, a good job, the respect of my friends and neighbors, a sense of accomplishment at having made something of my life. Last but not least, as an American I am proud to be a citizen of the finest country in the world.[34]

For Yankelovich, no matter what the source or accuracy of this compact, it is difficult to exaggerate how important it has been in supporting the goals of American society in the postwar period. It lies at the very heart of what we mean by the "American dream." Right or wrong, the "giving/getting compact" has helped to sustain and direct the efforts of millions over the years.

The work ethic in all its various formulations contains elements of both myth and reality. In essence, it is a view of the world which promotes and helps to perpetuate a certain perspective on reality that might not otherwise exist. The work ethic is a myth in the sense that nineteenth-century philosopher Georges Sorel used the word; that is, that the truth of the myth is relatively unimportant as long as it furthers the end in view.[35] In general it must be remembered that the work ethic is a product of an era of scarcity and deprivation, when one either worked or starved. It made the negative aspects of work bearable by giving work a moral quality. The conclusion remains that the work ethic was and is an ideology propagated by the middle classes for the working classes with just enough plausibility to make it credible.[36]

According to labor and cultural historian Herbert Gutman, until quite recently few historians questioned as fact the ease with which most past

Americans affirmed the Protestant work ethic. He points out, however, that many prominent Americans have made it clear that the Protestant work ethic was not as deeply ingrained in our nation's social fabric as some today would have us think. Alexander Hamilton and Benjamin Franklin worried about the absence of such virtues within the working classes. When Hamilton proposed his scheme to industrialize the young republic, an intimate commented, "Unless God should send us saints for workmen and angels to conduct them, there is the greatest reason to fear for the success of the plan." Franklin too had such fears. He condemned relief for the poor in 1768 and lamented the absence among English workers of regular work habits. "Saint Monday," he said, "is as duly kept of our working peoples as Sunday; the only difference is that instead of employing their time cheaply at church they are wasting it expensively at the ale house." Franklin believed that if poorhouses were shut down, "Saint Monday and Saint Tuesday" would "soon cease to be holidays."[37] In effect what Hamilton and Franklin were lamenting was the absence of a code of work values. They were advocating the imposition of some sort of myth which could instill a productive focus to the working habits of an emerging nation. Obviously, they were more than a little successful in their endeavors.

For all of its glorification, and no matter how many honorifics we attach to it, work remains, in the eye of the common man, a task to be endured. As trade unionist Gus Tyler has stated, "There are at least two work ethics: that of the overseer and that of the overseen." He claims that workers are not opposed to the work ethic in any literal sense. "But work per se as an ethical imperative gets little, if any, attention because to union people work is such a necessity that it is almost unnecessary to construct a system of values, with theologic overtones, to justify labor. If American unionists have an ethic, it is probably best summed up in the old slogan: 'a fair day's pay for a fair day's work.' "[38] From the unionist point of view, therefore, the proper and only response possible to Max Weber's question "Do we work to live or live to work?" is "We work to live." Most unionists are not so much guilty of working to live as they are guilty of being asked a question to which the answer is moot. If they are *compelled* to work in order to live, why bother asking? Recent appraisals of work and the worker by such scholars as Daniel Bell, Clark Kerr, Robert Strauss, and Daniel Yankelovich have confirmed the suspicion long held by most workers that dull, hard work is not necessarily ennobling and does not produce cultural heroes and role models. Working hard is a basic dimension of human existence; it is a duty. From this point of view, working is obligatory and, while it may at times well warrant a gray—if not red— badge of courage, it is basically a requirement of existence and only a means toward an end. As a character in a popular series of detective mysteries has put it: "If work was [such] a good thing the rich would have it all and not let you do it."[39] Unquestionably my favorite anecdote on this topic is the story of the rich man's response to his daughter's question "Is sex fun or work?"

"Sex must be fun for women," he replied, "because if it were work, your mother would have the maid do it."

Nonetheless, the country's classic work ethic is by no means dead. The mythology lingers on and is perpetuated by diverse sources. The good word on work can now be heard from Jesse Jackson, Lee Iacocca, George Gilder, Ronald Reagan, and certain prime-time television beer commercials.

Jesse Jackson's interpretation of the work ethic stays, perhaps, closest to one of the original tenets of the doctrine; i.e., "how to get more and do better." For Jackson, "black power" is economic success, and this is achieved by getting a piece of the action, working hard, saving, starting one's own business, being innovative, and/or constantly extending the scope and market of one's business. For Jackson the black community will only achieve equality with the white community when it successfully emulates Benjamin Franklin's model. He has spent the last fifteen years exhorting blacks to take pride in who they are, to finish school, to work hard, to be, in short, Puritan. In many ways his message and that of Operation PUSH is a restatement of immigrant work ethic exhortations to get a job, do well, work hard, and things will necessarily be better than they were before.

In recent years Lee Iacocca has emerged not only as the chief spokesman for Chrysler but also, indirectly, as the spokesman for the entire American automobile industry and the sanctity of the American worker's ability. Iacocca's commercial presentations have the emotional punch of a Knute Rockne half-time pep talk. In general, the commercials deliver a message that can be paraphrased as follows: So the foreign cars have been made better! So they have given you better value! So they have on percentage outsold us in the last seven years! OK, we were wrong! We weren't listening to what you wanted! But we hear you now! We're sorry, we forgot what got us to where we are today! Americans can outbuild any car maker in the world! We can build cars that out-perform, outlast and out-distance all our competitors! American "know-how" created the auto industry! We've proven our abilities in the past, we'll prove them to you again! American ingenuity is based on the American worker! I believe in the American worker and so do you! Buy our cars, I personally guarantee them for five years and/or 50,000 miles! Buy American!

On a more academic level, George Gilder, former economist and Nixon White House speech writer, has put together a series of books and articles on the entrepreneurial ethic as the cornerstone of capitalistic prosperity.[40] For Gilder it is the entrepreneur who creates the "trickle-down effect," which in turn stimulates the "invisible hard mechanism," thereby creating "the greatest possible good for the greatest possible number." For Gilder the farsighted, risk-taking, hardworking, self-sacrificing businessman is the catalyst propelling the entire laissez-faire economic system.

Ronald Reagan has consciously attempted to resuscitate the Jeffersonian model of the "rugged individual." This classic model is the individual who is able, by hard work, individual know-how, and personal ingenuity, to create and maintain most if not all of the necessities of life. This is the model of the self-sufficient "agrarian atomist" who first conquered this country by farming the shores of the East Coast and then proceeded during the next 200 years to follow the challenge of our Western expansion. It is not altogether surprising that Reagan's image of the "rugged individual" closely resembles many of the main characters in novelist Louis L'Amour's Western sagas. L'Amour's heroes are self-directed individuals who came into a new region, pacified it, cultivated it, and made it a safe place to rear a family. For Reagan, this country's "manifest destiny" became a fact and not a slogan because of the vision, courage, and hard work of our pioneer ancestors. These are, he believes, the virtues that have made us strong and prosperous and that must be maintained and fostered if the dream of America is to be continued and fulfilled for those who come after us. And these are virtues strongly embodied in the traditional Protestant work ethic.

Prime-time beer commercials are mythic playlets, romanticizing and idealizing the Herculean efforts of men at work.[41] They depict men pouring molten ingots in factories, spanning huge chasms with cables of steel, cutting down tall trees in the mist of a rain forest, blasting tunnels through mountains of solid granite, sailing ancient square-riggers through tempestuous seas, skiing the Tetons to check for avalanche faults, and staging a multi-vehicle highway crash for the concluding scene of a Clint Eastwood film. And through all the grit of these various scenarios the participants are, to a man, grinning from ear to ear at both their accomplishments and their camaraderie. After all of this the worker-warriors retire to a local saloon where they consume large quantities of iced beer and debrief one another in a warm sundown glow of work well done and worth doing.

For all of the hoopla and popular promotion, we feel that the general work force remains unconvinced and unmoved. No matter what the gimmicks, slogans, and logos, too much of the work of life remains uninteresting, unenjoyable, and without obvious purpose and distinction. For too many of us, work is the "curse of Adam," and to be relieved of it would be counted a boon and a blessing. The term "Protestant work ethic," which began as an explanation for the economic behavior of an historical people, exists today almost solely as a pejorative phrase.[42] According to social critic Michael Harrington, whatever value it may have had, the Protestant work ethic has devolved to the notion that "a man establishes his worth in the eyes of his neighbor and his God, . . . by doing drudgery and engaging in savings."[43]

STATISTICAL WISDOM

"The daily life of man is composed of things whose meaning is hidden in the mystery of their familiarity. Work is one of these."

—Y. Simon

Over 109 million people constitute the American work force. This vast army of workers fills 25,000 different full-time occupations, with often overlapping categories of income, education, social status, living standards, and life-style.[44] During the 1970s a great deal of attention was given to "workers' dissatisfaction," i.e., "white-collar woes" and "blue-collar blues." The late 1970s also saw the beginnings of a serious analysis of "pink-collar woes and blues." Specifically, the sudden emergence of women in the workplace forced a re-evaluation of the effects of work on women, women in the workplace, and work in the family.

Indications are that the problems enumerated in the 1970s will not simply go away in the 1980s and 1990s. Indeed, recent surveys indicate a trend of increasing job dissatisfaction as well as a direct increase in the commonality of complaints from members of the rank and file. The lament of uninteresting, unchallenging, nonstimulating, noncreative work is no longer heard exclusively from the assembly-line, lower-status, blue-collar worker. Managers and laborers, office workers and mechanics can now be heard to chorus their disapproval of their nonexpansive occupations. Stanley E. Seashore and J. Thad Barnowe in their article "Collar Color Doesn't Count" perhaps put it most succinctly when they state: "Vulnerability to blue-collar blues is endemic to the whole workforce and rests only slightly on the stereotyped attributes of the middle-class worker."[45] This does not mean, however, that the "hierarchy gap" between managers and clerical workers, hourly employees and piecework employees, does not still exist. But while managers are generally more satisfied than clerical, hourly, and piecework employees, the distinctions and specific issues that once clearly separated management from all other types of employees are becoming blurred.[46] One of the main sources of the indictment of work and the state of worker satisfaction is the 1972 publication *Work in America* by the Upjohn Institute for Employment Research, a study financed by the then Department of Health, Education and Welfare. It revealed widespread dissatisfaction with work among contemporary blue- and white-collar workers and their supervisors in every division of the workplace.

Ironically, these cries of dissatisfaction come from a relatively well-treated and even pampered work force. In an article commemorating Labor Day in 1979, *U.S. News & World Report* claimed that "never before in history have American workers been so well paid, so privileged and yet so discontented in their jobs as they are today." The report went on to claim that as a group the American labor force has made real and significant progress in the last twenty to twenty-five years.

> Today's workers are more affluent. Despite inflation, real spendable earnings have stayed apace and exceeded cost-of-living increases. Moreover, while real individual income has increased, median family income has also increased primarily due to the fact that 63% of all families now have two wage earners.
>
> Today's workers enjoy fringe benefits beyond the wildest dreams of previous generations, everything from dental care to pre-paid fitness club dues.
>
> Today's workers are better educated. Over forty percent of the work force are high school graduates and well over seventeen percent are college graduates.
>
> For the first time half of all workers now hold white-collar jobs. As Daniel Bell has correctly pointed out, we now live in a post-industrial society and the human service industries are destined to become the main mode of employment.

Today's workers have more leisure time. Hours of work have declined; vacations are more generous. Today the average office worker enjoys eleven to twelve paid holidays a year, versus seven to eight days in 1960.

Today's workers are more mobile. The typical worker in 1963 kept a job for 4.6 years. Now he or she changes jobs every 3.6 years.[47]

Nonetheless, with all of these improvements many workers report that they are discontent. The results of a 1979 survey published by the University of Michigan indicated that worker dissatisfaction was at its highest point in over a decade. Sixty percent of the workers surveyed wanted new jobs. Thirty-nine percent thought they were underpaid. Thirty-six percent said they had unused skills. Thirty-six percent felt overqualified for their jobs, and fifty-five percent wanted more time off. Unlike their parents, contemporary workers do not see their jobs in terms of a simple contract: a day's work for a day's pay. As labor-relations analyst John R. Browning has stated, "Today's workers want much more. They want nothing less than eight hours of meaningful, skillfully guided, personally satisfying work for eight hours' pay and that's not easy for most companies to provide.[48] In 1974 Daniel Yankelovich offered a limited but staggering statistic in regard to satisfaction of work when he claimed that only one out of every five men feels that his work fills his psychological as well as his economic needs.[49]

These claims of disappointment and distress seem to fly in the face of a study published in the mid-1950s and frequently replicated since then. In 1955 two sociologists, Nancy Morse and Robert S. Weiss of the University of Michigan's Survey Research Center, published the results of a study of more than 400 men. They asked the question, "If by chance you inherited enough money to live comfortably without working, do you think you would work anyway?" The vast majority (80 percent) of all respondents replied positively, even though the percentages were slightly higher for professional and lower white-collar workers (86 percent) than for the blue-collar workers (76 percent).[50]

At regular intervals over the next twenty-eight years this survey was expanded (both in numbers surveyed and the inclusion of women) and repeated by various research organizations. The results of these follow-up surveys essentially reaffirmed the original survey results: the percentage of those choosing to work ranged from 67.4 percent (1969, University of Michigan), 71.5 percent (1977, University of Michigan), 73 percent (1974, Yankelovich, *The New Morality*), to 75 percent (1978, Renwich and Lawler).[51]

The most recent and perhaps most comprehensive findings on this topic come from a group of researchers at the University of Kentucky in 1983. Of the 7,281 adults polled nationwide, 74 percent of the men and 64 percent of the women surveyed said they would continue to work. While married men were more inclined than married women to say they would keep working, single men and women were equally likely to report that they would stick with it. Younger, better educated respondents with more prestigious jobs were more inclined to say that they would stay employed, compared with older individuals and less educated respondents. But the majority of all groups still reported that they would stay at work.[52]

Perhaps these statistics are not really at odds with the claims of discontent in the workplace if we ask the question "Would you keep doing the work that you now do?" According to the report *Work in America*, one of the most reliable indicators of job dissatisfaction is the response received to the question "What type of work would you try to get into if you could start all over again?" Significantly, of a cross section of white-collar workers (including professionals), only 43 percent would voluntarily choose the same work that they were doing, and only 24 percent of a cross section of blue-collar workers would choose the same kind of work if given another chance.

Percentages in Occupational Groups Who Would Choose Similar Work Again[53]

PROFESSIONAL AND LOWER WHITE-COLLAR OCCUPATIONS	PERCENT	WORKING-CLASS OCCUPATIONS	PERCENT
Urban university professors	93	Skilled printers	52
Mathematicians	91	Paper workers	42
Physicists	89	Skilled autoworkers	41
Biologists	89	Skilled steelworkers	41
Chemists	89	Textile workers	31
Firm lawyers	85	Blue-collar workers, cross section	24
Lawyers	83	Unskilled steelworkers	21
Journalists (Washington correspondents)	82	Unskilled autoworkers	21
Church university professors	77		
Solo lawyers	75		
White-collar workers, cross section	43		

Three separate University of Michigan surveys also produced statistics to indicate that although many people maintain a high motivation to work, fewer and fewer people want to stay with the work that they do. Question: "If you were free to go into any type of job you wanted, what would your choice be?"

	1969	1973	1977
The job he or she now has:	48.2%	43.7%	38.1%
Retire and not work at all:	6.3%	4.6%	1.9%
Prefer some other job to the job he or she has now:	44.4%	51.7%	60.0%[54]

Clearly, the attachment to work is stronger and more general than the attachment to specific jobs. Only as we turn to jobs well up in the preferential ranking of occupations do we find a majority of people saying that they would choose to continue at the kind of work they are now doing. People whose jobs are low in the preferential listing of occupations want to continue working, but not at the jobs they have. When the choice is between the present job or out, they choose out.[55] Another fairly accurate yardstick of job satisfaction is to ask the question: "What would you do with the extra two hours if you had a 26-hour day?" Not so surprisingly, two out of three college professors and one out of four lawyers say they would use the extra time in work-related activity.[56] Strikingly, only one out of twenty nonprofessional workers would make use of the extra time in work-related activity. For many, of course, this statistic is skewed in that they do work which cannot be done outside of a factory or office.

What are the reasons people choose to work? As expected, the main reason white-collar and professional workers would continue working is for "interest or accomplishment," but for the blue-collar worker the main reason given for continuing to work is "to keep occupied."

	WHITE-COLLAR, PROFESSIONAL CLASS	BLUE-COLLAR CLASS
Would continue working, even if inherited enough not to:	86.7%	76%
Reasons for so doing:		
Interest or accomplishments:	44.0%	10%
To keep occupied:	37.0%	71%[57]

Without work, significant numbers of both blue- and white-collar workers said that they would "feel lost, go crazy" and "not know what to do with my time, I can't be idle." Generally, they would most miss the "feeling of doing something," and specifically, they would regret the absence of the "people I know through work, the friends, the contacts." Morse and Weiss concluded: "For many of those in the middle-class (white-collar, professional) occupations working means having something interesting to contribute. [However] those in working-class (blue-collar) occupations view working as virtually synonymous with activity, the alternative to which is to lie around and be bored and restless. . . . Life without working becomes life without anything to do."[58]

In effect, what many workers are now saying is that work is not an activity that is enjoyable in itself. Even though they are paid, work is scheduled and required of them by others. Yet they would continue to work even if they had no need for the pay. What we think these data mean is that for most men and for an increasing number of women there is no alternative to work, no other activity that absorbs time, uses energy, taps creativity, demands attention, provides regular social interaction, and is a source of status, identity, self-respect, and financial remuneration.[59] For whatever reasons, the essential and perhaps unanswerable paradox of the workplace is that although most people don't like their jobs, they do want to work. While most workers accept the necessity of work, and most wish for meaningful jobs, few expect fulfillment from their specific jobs.

PHILOSOPHICAL WISDOM

"Without work, all life goes rotten, but when work is soulless, life stifles and dies."

—*Albert Camus*

The poet W. H. Auden was probably correct when he said that "numbers numb" and that statistics can be manipulated to bolster any thesis. Nonetheless, the surveys discussed in the last section do seem to reinforce much of the conventional wisdom about work. That is, many people are unhappy in their work, but they nevertheless want to go on working.

First, why are so many people so unhappy? Few people have work that engages them and engenders real fulfillment and growth. Most jobs are dull, repetitive, and seemingly meaningless, offering little challenge. Simply put, the reason people don't like their jobs is that they have bad jobs, or, to use E. F. Schumacher's term, they have "bad work."

According to Schumacher, bad work is

mechanical, artificial, divorced from nature, utilizing only the smallest part of man's potential capabilities; it sentences the great majority of workers to spending their working lives in a way which contains no worthy challenge, no stimulus to self perfection, no chance of development, no element of Beauty, Truth, or Goodness. . . .[60]

For Schumacher one of the darkest aspects of contemporary work life is the existence of an appalling number of men and women who are condemned to work that has no connection with their inner lives, no spiritual meaning for them whatever. Bad work for Schumacher offers no opportunity for the individual to become more than he or she already is. By this he means that bad work offers no potential for growth, no sense of beauty and delight, no feelings of completeness, and no sense of well-being in knowing that a job is contributing to the growth of oneself and others.

Work for too many is perceived as "downtime," something that has to be done, but the doing of which does not add to who they are. Too many workers accurately talk about their jobs as if these jobs had nothing to do with their inner sense of self. Studs Terkel reminds us again and again that work for many is a purely alien occupation. One of the people he interviewed remarked, "Unless a guy's a nut, he never thinks about or talks about it. Maybe about baseball or about getting drunk the other night or he got laid or he didn't get laid. I'd say one out of a hundred actually get excited about work."[61] Simply, most work does not engage the person.

To put Schumacher's argument into a more classical perspective, bad work alienates the worker both from himself and from his work. An alienated worker is one who engages in activities that are not rewarding in themselves, that might be demanding in some respects but permit little or no originality, latitude, discretion, or sense of fulfillment and completion. For our purposes the central point of Schumacher's notion of bad work is encapsulated in one of Karl Marx's earlier descriptions of alienation.

> What constitutes the alienation of laboring? That working is external to the worker, that it is not part of his nature and that, consequently, he does not fulfill himself in his work, but denies himself, has a feeling of misery rather than well-being, does not develop freely his mental and physical energies but is physically exhausted and mentally debased . . . its alien character is clearly shown by the fact that as soon as there is no physical or other compulsion it is avoided like a plague . . . it is not his own work but work for someone else.[62]

A clearer, more concise twentieth-century updating of Marx's description can be found in Robert Blauner's work *Alienation and Freedom*:

> Alienation exists when workers are unable to control their immediate work processes, to develop a sense of purpose and function which connects their jobs to the over-all organization of production, to belong to integrated industrial communities, and when they fail to become involved in the activity of work as a mode of personal self-expression.[63]

Social scientists have expanded the concept of alienation, and three kinds are now generally recognized: (1) *powerlessness*—lack of control over management policy and/or over the conditions of employment or the immediate work process; (2) *meaninglessness*—the inability to see the purpose of one's work or how it fits into the whole production process; and (3) *self-estrangement*—the failure to regard work as a central life interest or a means of self-expression; feeling depersonalized and detached while at work.[64] According to the H.E.W. Task Force Report, alienation, thus understood, is an inherent aspect of pyramidal, bureaucratic management patterns that divide and subdivide work into minute, monotonous elements. Frederick Winslow Taylor's effort to systematize and streamline work has made the worker's alienation an integral part of the process.[65]

What Schumacher, and by implication Marx, Blauner, and the H.E.W. Task Force, are contending is that most workers do routine jobs in an adequate fashion even though their tasks are neither stimulating nor innovative. Even when work is not intrinsically rewarding, pay and job security offer a modicum of satisfaction. This critical distinction is nicely illustrated by an interview sociologist George Strauss had with a blue-collar worker on a fairly routine job. The worker told Strauss, "I got a pretty good job." "What makes it such a good job?" Strauss asked. The worker responded somewhat quizzically:

> Don't get me wrong. I didn't say it is a *good* job. It's an O.K. job—about as good a job as a guy like me might expect. The foreman leaves me alone and it pays well. But I would never call it a good job. It doesn't amount to much, but it's not bad.[66]

This is what Strauss calls worker apathy. The worker's expectations are low but he accepts the situation because of the pay or because it's the best he can get. The worker is unhappy, but his unhappiness does not lead to troublesome on-the-job behavior.

Sociologist Robert Kahn suggests that for most workers the only choice is between no work (usually accompanied by severe economic penalties as well as a conspicuous lack of meaningful alternatives) or a job burdened with negative qualities (routines, compulsory scheduling, dependency, etc.). In these circumstances, says Kahn, the individuals have no difficulty with their choice. They choose work as the only viable alternative, and they then pronounce themselves moderately satisfied if not stimulated, enraptured, or excited with what they do.[67] Some workers adjust to their job by viewing work in purely instrumental terms or as a means to other ends. George Strauss has pointed out that a significant number of workers deliberately take on high-paying but boring jobs in order to support their real interests.[68] This is the kind of compromise that many people make. In essence what they say is: "I don't like what I do, but it allows me to do what I like."

We must now address the second part of our thesis: "Given all of the above, why, other than from necessity, do people express a desire to work?" A practical response to this question is that one wants to work to occupy time, to have something, anything, to do to avoid the greater burden and stress of "deadtime" versus "downtime." People want to work because they are intuitively aware that work, be it "bad" or "good," helps to shape them. It gives them a sense of direction and it allows them at least the possibility of personal creativity and fulfillment.

The personal meaning of work is as important as its economic and social meaning. Where we live, how well we live, whom we see socially, what and where we consume and purchase, how we educate our children—all of these factors are dominated by the work we do to make a living.[69] While many people don't like their jobs, they want to work because they are aware at some level that work plays a crucial and perhaps unparalleled psychological role in the formation of human character. Work is not just a livelihood, it is also one of the most significant contributing factors to one's inner life and development. And yet, as Schumacher has indicated, considering the centrality of work in human life, one might have expected that every textbook on economics, political theory, sociology, and philosophy would have presented a theory of work as a foundation for all further considerations. At the very least, work does occupy most of the energies of the human race, and what people actually do is usually more important for understanding them than what they say. This is at the core of American philosophy. The truth of the matter is that discussions of the specific personal impact and import of work are hardly ever to be found in these kinds of texts. Sadly, the question "What does the work do to the worker?" is seldom asked.[70] It is precisely this question on which we would like to focus attention. We want to examine what work does to and for us no matter what the nature of the product we produce by our labors.

We take it to be the case that most scholars, no matter what their ideological frame of reference (Marxist, fascist, capitalist, monarchist), concur in the proposition that human culture is the outcome of the capacity for conceptual thought and work. As the contemporary Marxist labor historian Harry Braverman has stated, all forms of life strive to sustain themselves. Plants absorb moisture, minerals, and sunlight; animals feed on plant life or prey on other animals. But to use the materials of nature as they are given is not work. Work, says Braverman, is an activity that alters the materials of nature to improve on their usefulness. Thus the human species shares with many of the animals the process of acting upon nature in a manner that changes its forms to make them more suitable for its needs.[71] People, however, differ from other animals because their work is grounded in freedom and reason. That is, animals follow their instincts (which may include episodes of logical reflection); human beings alone freely engage themselves, following the designs of their reasoning, in creating the conditions necessary for survival, growth, and development. More than mere survival, we create our history in our work.[72]

We need to work in order to finish and define our natures. Work makes us human because we make something of ourselves through work. In saying this, however, we do not want to embrace totally either the teaching of Catholicism or the spirit of traditional Protestantism in regard to the work ethic. Although viewing it from different perspectives, both Christian traditions contend that people are specifically made and ordained for work. While we do not feel qualified or comfortable enough to debate this theological vision of homo-faber (man the toolmaker) as well as the formal notion of predestination implied at the core of such a belief statement, we do agree with these traditions that we are made by our work. As sociologist Peter Berger has stated, "To be human and to work appear as inextricably intertwined notions."[73]

In his earliest philosophical writings in the 1840s, Karl Marx defined the individual as a worker. For Marx, one acquired self-definition through labor. Work is the means by which we become persons.[74] In Marx we can find a full-scale analysis of the meaning of work in human development as well as what he saw as the distortion of this development in capitalistic society.

Marx analyzed factory work in the early years of industrialization and concluded that factory work had alienated man from the rightful integral relationship of work and meaning. Marx analyzed the conditions of production that prevent workers from being subjects, that remove responsibility and creativity from them. According to his analysis, the objective side of labor, the product and the machinery of the industrial process have been allowed to take over and become all important. The owners and managers of industries look upon workers not as subjects but as objects, as one of the material factors that enter into the productive process. And because they are regarded as objects and treated as objects, workers easily experience themselves as objects. They lose the sense that they are subjects, or at least meant to be subjects.[75]

In the Western world, Marx's critique of the workplace and its effect on people gets lost in his overall analysis of capitalism and his attacks on bourgeois society. While many scholars feel that his writings are extremely critical of late–nineteenth-century capitalism as a social and political system, his real focus was the effect of work on the individual and of the individual upon work. A significant portion of his doctrine of historical materialism is devoted to his belief that the "material conditions of life" and, specifically, "the mode of production of the material means of existence," determine much else in human life, consciousness, and society. For Marx the essence of the human being rests upon one's work:

> As individuals express their life [sic], so they are. What [individuals] . . . are . . . coincides with their production, both with what they produce and with how they produce. The nature of individuals thus depends on the material conditions determining their production.[76]

As Schumacher has pointed out in Marx's regard, it is a great error to overlook or to underestimate the effects of the "modes of production" upon people's lives. How people work and what they produce necessarily affect what they think and their own personal sense of freedom and independence.[77] In other words, both the process and the product of our work help us to know who and what we are.

A somewhat unexpected but nevertheless important ally to Marx's overall thesis on work is Pope John Paul II's 1981 encyclical *Laborem exercens* (*On Human Work*):

> Man is made to be in the visible universe an image and likeness of God Himself, and he is placed in it in order to subdue the earth. From the beginning he is called to work. . . . Only man is capable of work, and only man works, at the same time by work occupying his existence on earth. Thus work bears a particular mark of man and of humanity, the mark of a person operating within a community of persons.[78]

That by labor or work one "occupies his existence on earth" means that we literally create our own reality by virtue of work. In work we create and define the world, and in the process we become more human. According to the encyclical, the human world is not a simple given or a fixed thing. It is rather a "fact" continuously being produced by human labor. Work, the encyclical claims, is a good thing, in the sense that it is useful or something to enjoy and expresses and expands our dignity. Through work, one not only transforms nature, adapting it to his or her own needs, but one also achieves fulfillment as a human being and in a sense becomes "more a human being."[79] For Pope John Paul II it is through work that people see themselves individually as directing their own lives, and collectively as taking part in a common history. He further emphasizes that what happens to the "subject of work" at work is more important than "what the work produces." The dignity and honor that work communicates to people are derived not from the "object achieved" but from one's "actual engagement" in the process, that is, from the labor of one's hands and mind. In labor the transformation experienced by the subject is of greater value and importance than the object produced. "The preeminence of the subjective meaning of work over the objective one" is a principle that plays an important part in the reasoning of the entire encyclical. However true it may be that we are "destined for work" and "called to work," what must always be kept in clear perspective is that "work is for man and not man for work."[80]

Sigmund Freud has written that at the very least work gives one "a secure place in the human community."[81] Work also helps establish the regularity of life, its basic rhythms and cycles of day, week, month, and year. Without work, days and time patterns become confused.[82] Further, work organizes, routinizes, and structures our lives. It allows a safe outlet for our competitive strivings and often helps to keep us sane. More than this, as the German philosopher Martin Heidegger stated, "You are your projects."[83] To use the vocabulary of metaphysics, Heidegger is implying that through "projects" (work) and the projection and continuation of these projects into the future, one posits, establishes, and acknowledges his or her "being" in the world. Heidegger is suggesting that "You are what you do." Identity is largely a function of determined action or productive achievement. We are known by others and we know and define ourselves primarily by the projects we devise, by the products we create, and by the occupations we hold. A person who cannot point to any achievements does not and cannot feel like a full person. Subjective experience is simply too diffuse for self-identity. To say "I feel it" is not as definitive as to say "I did it." Nothing else in our lives can give us the sense of objective identity that work can.[84]

When psychiatrists and psychologists talk of "ego boundaries" they mean that well-balanced people have clear perspectives on the limits and outlines of their own identities. They do not suffer from "boundary diffusion" and possess a clear sense of integrity and continuity. For most of us the primary source of life's labels and ego boundaries is our work. In work we come both to know ourselves and orient ourselves to the external world. Work allows us to establish a "coherent web of expectations" of the rhythm, direction, and definition of our lives.[85] Self-definition implies the ability to feel contained within precise outlines: "I'm a doctor" or "I'm a cardiovascular surgeon"; "I'm a lawyer" or "I'm a litigator in my firm's antitrust division"; "I'm in advertising" or "I'm the artistic director for Leo Burnett"; "I'm an educator" or "I'm a professor of physics at MIT"; "I'm a carpenter" or "I'm a cabinetmaker." The more descriptive we can be about ourselves the greater our sense of self-definition. Nothing is so uniquely personal, so active a representation of individuals as their skills and works.[86] According to Robert Kahn:

> When people ask that most self-identifying of questions—Who am I?—they answer in terms of their occupation: toolmaker, press operator, typist, doctor, construction worker, teacher. Even people who are not working identify themselves by their former work or their present wish for it, describing themselves as retired or unemployed. And work that is not paid lacks significance, much as we might wish it otherwise. Many people who are usefully occupied, but not paid, respond to questions in ways that deprecate both their activities and themselves. A woman who takes care of a home and several small children and is engaged in a wide range of community activities may answer with that tired and inaccurate phrase, "just a housewife. A retired man equally busy with an assortment of projects, is likely to say, "Oh, I'm retired; I don't do anything."[87]

To reiterate Gregory Baum's handsome phrase, "Labor is the axis of human selfmaking," we contend that work is a necessary attribute of the human personality. To work is an act of personal freedom, self-assertion, self-fulfillment, and self-realization. The relationship between work and self-identity is well summarized by Elliot Jacques:

> . . . working for a living is one of the basic activities in a man's life. By forcing him to come to grips with his environment, with his livelihood at stake, it confronts him with the actuality of his personal capacity—to exercise judgment, to achieve concrete and specific results. It gives him a continuous account of his correspondence, between outside reality and the inner perception of that reality, as well as an account of the accuracy of his appraisal of himself. . . . In short, a man's work does not satisfy his material needs alone. In a very deep sense, it gives him a measure of his sanity.[88]

Clearly underlying this position is a modification of the classical Cartesian formula: "Laboro, ergo sum"—"I work, therefore I am."

If, for good or ill, work shapes and defines people, what is needed are forms of work which will help rather than impede the attainment of self-realization and self-actualization. What is needed is the establishment of what Schumacher called "good work." Schumacher is convinced that we are not separate from our work. Because of the time spent at a job we need to ensure that it is time well spent. "Good work," says Schumacher, is "work that ennobles the product as it ennobles the producer."[89] Schumacher believes that good work is part of the "university of life." Good work should offer us the opportunity to develop our potential and explore our creativity. At the very least work should not diminish the spirit so that other avenues for growth are unavailable to the worker. Schumacher is convinced that good work is one of the joys of life and is an absolute requirement for our development, but meaningless work is an abomination and seriously detrimental to our well-being.[90] The spirit of Schumacher's message is, again, analogous to the Greek definition of happiness: "Good work is the use of all of one's powers to achieve excellence."

Practically speaking "good work" means "meaningful work." According to Karl Marx all citizens have a right to meaningful work—opportunities for employment in which the work for which pay is received is interesting, calling for intelligence and initiative, and in which the worker has considerable freedom to determine how the work is to be done and some say in the character and policies of the process.[91] For Daniel Yankelovich, people want "(1) work in which they can become involved, committed, and interested; (2) work that challenges them to the utmost of their capabilities; and (3) participation in decision making."[92] According to W. H. Auden three things are needed for meaningful work: the person must be fit for it; must not do too much of it; and must have a sense of success in doing it.[93] Finally, according to the H.E.W. Task Force, "When it is said that work should be 'meaningful,' what is meant is that it should contribute to self-esteem, to a sense of fulfillment through the mastering of one's self and one's environment, and to a sense that one is valued by society."[94] The fundamental question the individual worker asks is, "What am I doing that really matters?"

A meaningful job is one that the employee enjoys and excels in, feeling in control of the work activity. It is a job that fits the worker rather than having the worker re-made to fit the job. It is a job that makes the worker feel that he or she makes a difference. It is a job in which the incentive to work is not fear or compulsion but rather a search for fulfillment. Most important, as ethicist Patricia Werhane has pointed out, meaningful jobs require that one have information about one's work; otherwise job decisions cannot be intelligently made. According to Werhane, since work enjoyment can develop from involvement in business decisions, meaningful employment requires some form of participation in the decision-making process in the workplace. This participation can be as minimal as choosing one's work hours or may include taking responsibility as part of a team for the production of a particular product. Participation can also extend to full participation in the management of the entire business.[95] As one commentator has indicated, the single most significant new element in labor negotiating since the 1970s can be summarized in the phrase: "They used to want more pay, now they want more say."[96]

Robert Kahn claims that if we select those items that were rated as very important by more than 60 percent of the men and women throughout the United States, we emerge with a profile of a good job. Our composite respondent tells us:

A good job is one in which the work is interesting, I have a chance to develop my own special abilities, and I can see the results of my work. It is a job where I have enough information, enough help and equipment, and enough authority to get the job done. It is a job where the supervisor is competent and my responsibilities are clearly defined. The people I work with are friendly, and helpful, the pay is good, and so is the job security.[97]

This position is further reinforced by the ever-useful statistics compiled by the University of Michigan's Survey Research Center in 1973. When workers were asked how important they regarded some twenty-five different aspects of work, they ranked the following eight in order of importance:

1. Interesting work
2. Enough help and equipment to get the job done
3. Enough information to get the job done
4. Enough authority to get the job done
5. Good pay
6. Opportunity to develop special abilities
7. Job security
8. Seeing the results of one's work[98]

A somewhat different argument that nevertheless reinforces this general position can be found in the theory of one of the pioneer researchers in the allied fields of "meaningful work" and "satisfaction in the workplace," clinical psychologist Fredrick Herzberg.[99] Herzberg's research led him to conclude that job satisfaction and dissatisfaction are not simply opposite points on a continuum but actually two separate dimensions. Herzberg's findings led him to believe that motivation is composed of two factors: (1) Those issues and activities that prevent dissatisfaction but do not propel workers to grow—extrinsic factors; (2) Those factors that directly motivate workers to grow and excel—intrinsic factors. Extrinsic factors, such as company policy, incompetent supervision, or unsatisfactory working conditions, often lead to dissatisfaction. This dissatisfaction may be reduced by such "hygienic measures" as higher pay, increased fringe benefits, better working conditions, "human relations" training for foremen, or improved company policies. However, such measures will not make workers satisfied. For true satisfaction to be obtained, intrinsic factors must be provided, such as achievement, accomplishment, responsibility, and challenging work. Satisfaction, then, is a function of the content of work; dissatisfaction, of the environment or the context of work. For Herzberg, satisfaction alone leads to increased productivity. The presence of dissatisfaction may lead to low morale or absenteeism, but its elimination will not raise motivation or productivity. Therefore, while traditional hygienic, extrinsic improvements may make the work environment more tolerable, they will not necessarily raise motivation or productivity. The latter depends on enriching jobs to make them more interesting and important.[100]

If there is a congruence between personality and work, then a partial explanation of why people need good work can be found in how people respond psychologically to the stimuli of work. It is well established that work stress can lead to physical illness, especially heart disease, ulcers, and arthritis, as well as alcoholism, drug addiction, and a host of psychosomatic ailments. However, the impact of routine or boring work is less clear and somewhat difficult to measure. A high percentage of people who do routine work report having happy and uncomplicated home lives, but there are enough who do not that statistical studies indicate a direct correlation between routine, low-skilled work and off-the-job dissatisfaction. These studies imply that at the level of mental health, interesting work is a requirement of adult life. The underlying thesis here is one borrowed from the philosopher Adina Schwartz. According to Schwartz, when persons work for considerable lengths of time at jobs that involve mainly mechanical repetitive activity, they tend to be made less capable of, and less interested in, rationally and independently framing, pursuing, and adjusting their own plans during the rest of their nonwork time. They thereby lead less autonomous, less interesting, and less fulfilling lives.[101]

Although Adam Smith praised the factory arrangements described in the first chapter of *The Wealth of Nations*, he was under no illusions about the dehumanizing effects of the "mode of production" on the worker:

> The understandings of the great part of men are necessarily formed by their ordinary employments. The man whose whole life is spent in performing a few simple operations . . . has no occasion to exert his understanding. . . . He naturally loses, therefore, the habit of such exertion and generally becomes as stupid and ignorant as it is possible for a human creature to become. . . . His dexterity at his own particular trade seems . . . to be acquired at the expense of his intellectual virtues.[102]

This thesis is echoed in recent longitudinal studies. In one such study Melvin L. Kohn and Carmi Schooler argue that there is a reciprocal relationship between the substantial complexity of work and intellectual flexibility. Their data indicate that "current job demands affect current thinking processes. . . . If two men of equivalent intellectual flexibility were to start their careers in jobs differing in substantive complexity, the man in the more complex job would be likely to outstrip the other in further intellectual growth."[103] A direct implication of Kohn and Schooler's research is that routine jobs do not simply prevent persons from acting autonomously while at work. They also hinder them from developing the intellectual abilities that they must have if they are to rationally frame, adjust, and pursue their own plans during their nonwork time. Routine jobs cause persons to be less inclined, in all aspects of their lives, to engage in the purposeful striving that is characteristic of autonomous individuals. Kohn and Schooler conclude that jobs tend to determine personalities more than personalities determine jobs.

Arthur Kornhauser's classic *Mental Health of the Industrial Worker: A Detroit Study* speaks to this point:

> . . . factory employment, especially in routine production tasks, does give evidence of extinguishing workers' ambition, initiative, and purposeful direction towards life goals. . . . The unsatisfactory mental health of working people consists in no small measure of their dwarfed desires and deadened initiative, reduction of their goals and restriction of their efforts to a point where life is relatively empty and only half meaningful. [104]

Kornhauser's study of the Detroit automobile worker concludes that mental health at work, like job satisfaction, varies according to status. "Mental health is poorer among factory workers as we move from skilled, responsible, varied types of work to jobs lower in those respects." [105] Kornhauser also concluded that mental health was low among those workers who felt that they had no chance to use their abilities. It was suggested that low-grade work caused lowered self-esteem, discouragement, futility, and feelings of failure and inferiority in contrast to a sense of personal growth and self-fulfillment resulting from more varied, responsible, challenging undertakings that afford opportunity to develop and use one's ideas and skills.

We can also assess mental health by looking at recreation and the use of leisure time. Question: "Do those with unchallenging jobs make up for this with challenging recreation and the creative use of leisure time?" One imaginative study, by Martin Meissner, concluded that workers tend to engage in leisure-time activities that reflect the nature and complexity of their jobs. Those workers whose jobs permit active discretion tend to spend more time in leisure-time pursuits that also involve discretion, such as participating in organizations, sports, or home improvements. Those whose jobs permit social activity but not discretion have as their main forms of recreation visiting, group outings, and "beer-and-talk." Finally, those workers whose jobs permit neither discretion nor social activity engage in fishing, religious activities, going for a drive, watching television, and similar activities. As George Strauss has pointed out, we must be careful not to generalize too much from a single study such as this. Certainly there are individuals who are able to compensate for a boring job through creative activity off the job whether it be at home or in the community. Nevertheless the Meissner study suggests that this sort of an adjustment is indeed a rare phenomenon. The simple fact is that the vast majority of workers are unable to counteract the effects of dull work through active recreation. [106]

It seems that only a statistical minority of the work force finds meaning in work beyond the basic reward of the paycheck. [107] In our industrial society the very notion of good work exists as a possible option only for the artist and certain professional classes of workers. Satisfaction with life seems to be related to satisfaction on the job. Those who are unhappy with their jobs are also likely to be unhappy with life in general. While it is possible that this means that some people are perpetual malcontents, there is some evidence that workers with objectively less challenging jobs have less satisfying lives, and that unskilled workers suffer from poorer mental health than do those involved in more skilled work.[108]

Good work is the ideal, but clearly good work is hard to find. Perhaps the only realistic compromise available to most of us is to find and make the most of whatever good is possible in our work. The conclusion remains Marx's dictum, "As individuals express their life, so they are." As individuals we must find work that is good for us; as a society we must create work that is good for individuals. No matter how optimistic the technological forecasts for the future, there is no real possibility that work itself will become obsolete and unnecessary. The challenge will be to make it available and fulfilling.[109] In the following quotation, educator and essayist Joseph Epstein nicely summarizes what I have been trying to communicate about good work and the well-balanced personality.

> I sometimes think that the world is divided between those who work so they can live and those who live chiefly so they can work. I make this sound more black-and-white, either-or, one-way-or-the-other than it truly is. But the fact is, in my experience, some of the most forlorn people I know are those who haven't found their work: people of artistic temperament who have no art to practice, leaders without followers, serious men and women with nothing serious to do. On the other side, people who have found their work can seem, while at work, creatures of great dignity, even beauty. "A man blowing a trumpet successfully is a rousing spectacle," noted the Welsh writer Rhys Davies in one of his short stories. And so, too, is a man or woman working at anything he or she loves.[110]

CONCLUSION

"Our work keeps us free of the three great evils: boredom, vice and poverty."

—*Voltaire*

Work is one of the central activities of life and as such it is both a source of satisfaction and dissatisfaction, a boon and a burden, a cause of mental health or mental illness. Work can be either the expression of our creativity or the bearer of alienation. But what is clear is that our self-creation occurs through work. Our lives are built up every day from work and we literally create our own history through work.[111] The encyclical *Laborem exercens* goes so far as to contend that "man's self-constitution through labor" is a moral imperative which one is required to fulfill by divine law. Without engaging in theological reasoning, it is possible to concur with the notion that work is our "moral task" in life and that the quality of our lives is directly dependent upon the quality of the work we do. The point is that given what you do, you cannot avoid being who you are. Each person, having chosen a job, shapes its content. And to a greater or lesser extent the content of the job shapes the person. Not only are we affected by what we do; we tend to become what we do. A person's activities determine his or her self-identity, and in Western culture paid employment is, rightly or wrongly, the main activity by which we define and assess ourselves and others.[112]

The phrase "quality of work" is one we most commonly associate with the quality of the outcome or the final product. Quality of work has, however, an additional meaning. It also can refer to the quality of the work experience itself. Both meanings are important, but they are not the same, as having a good job is not the same as doing a good job.[113] A good job is one that: (1) allows us to provide the necessary goods and services required for a decent existence; (2) enables us to utilize and develop our individual gifts and abilities; (3) enables us to work in service and cooperation with others, so as to liberate ourselves from our inborn egocentricity.[114] The most fortunate people are of course those for whom the line between work and play is rubbed out. These are the people for whom work is pleasure and pleasure is in work.[115] John Dewey said: "Work which remains permeated with the play attitude is art—in quality if not in conventional designation."[116]

> She is a sculptor. Stress and pleasure
> For her thus perfectly combined,
> The boundaries of toil and leisure
> By definition ill-defined.
> Her work time doubles as her play time.[117]

Having said all of this about the problems, pitfalls, maddening monotony, and deprivations of some forms of work, we must, however, try to avoid the arrogance of critics who discourse on the "brutalization of work" simply because they cannot imagine themselves performing the job.[118] While we do not embrace the thesis that, with certain obvious exceptions, the vast majority of jobs are value-neutral and that their value is entirely dependent upon the attitude that the individual worker brings to the task, we do believe that within tolerable limits the workers can influence the job and its effect on themselves and others. There are, after all, individuals who can make the creation of poetry or the leadership of a large corporation seem loathsome and boring. There are also people who can make the job of a porter or a waitress seem good, useful, and exciting.[119] It is also important to keep in mind that although work is central to the lives of most people, there is a small minority for whom a job is merely a means to a livelihood. For these individuals a job is an activity that they would gladly forgo if a more acceptable option for earning a living were available. What little evidence there is on this point suggests that for most of these individuals the kinds of jobs available to them do little to provide the sense of self-esteem, identity, and direction that genuinely meaningful work can provide. These individuals turn to other activities (music, hobbies, sports, crime) and other institutions (family, church, community, gangs) to find the psychological rewards that they do not find in their jobs. In effect, these activities for those individuals become their real work and the primary means by which their identity is formulated and directed.[120]

In the end, this essay has simply been an attempt to examine closely the stated purpose of a nationally recognized graduate school of industrial relations: "the Fulfillment of the Human Person through Work."[121] Clearly the notion that we are made and defined by work is not a thesis of classical antiquity. It is, however, a thesis that is growing in currency in some of the literature in psychology, sociology, personnel management, and philosophy. We need work; we are formed by work. To be denied work is to be denied far more than the things that work can buy; it is to be denied the ability to define and respect one's self; and it is to be denied a basic and primary organizing principle in life. As Theodore Roszak quite correctly points out in regard to work, "The doing is as important as what gets done, the making as valuable as the made."[122]

At the beginning of this piece, Philip Larkin asked why the toad work must "squat on" his life. He answered the question as we have, because it *must*. Years later, Larkin, in "Toads Revisited," comes to terms with this dilemma of his youth. Faced with the alternative of empty days, of a life without meter or rhyme, he accepts the toad. As well he might, for the toad is better than no work at all. People have always struck this bargain. The task facing our culture is to transform the toad, to make of work a thing we can embrace rather than an encumbrance we must bear.

TOADS REVISITED*

Walking around in the park
Should feel better than work;
The lake, the sunshine,
The grass to lie on,

Blurred playground noises
Beyond black-stockinged nurses—
Not a bad place to be.
Yet it doesn't suit me,

Being one of the men
You meet of an afternoon:
Palsied old step-takers,
Hare-eyed clerks with the jitters,

Waxed-fleshed out-patients
Still vague from accidents,
And characters in long coats
Deep in the litter-baskets—

*"Toads Revisited" is reprinted by permission of Faber and Faber Ltd from *The Whitson Weddings* by Philip Larkin.

All dodging the toad work
By being stupid or weak.
Think of being them!
Hearing the hours chime,

Watching the bread delivered,
The sun by clouds covered,
The children going home;
Think of being them,

Turning over their failures
By some bed of lobelias,
Nowhere to go but indoors,
No friends but empty chairs—

No, give me my in-tray,
My loaf-haired secretary,
My shall-I-keep-the-call-in-Sir:
What else can I answer,

When the lights come on at four
At the end of another year?
Give me your arm, old toad;
Help me down Cemetery Road.

—*Philip Larkin*

NOTES

[1] "What Is the Point of Working?" *Time*, May 11, 1981, pp. 93–94.

[2] Lee Braude, *Work and Workers: A Sociological Analysis* (New York: Praeger Publications, 1975), p. 3.

[3] Mike Royko, "Silver Spoon Fits, Why Not Wear It?" *Chicago Tribune*, November 11, 1985, Sec. 1, p. 3.

[4] Michael Maccoby and Katherine A. Terzi, "What Happened to the Work Ethic?" in W. Michael Hoffman and Thomas J. Wyly (eds.), *The Work Ethic in Business* (Cambridge, Mass.: Oelgeschlager, Gunn, and Hain, Publishers, 1981), pp. 31–34.

[5] Studs Terkel, *Working* (New York: Pantheon Books, 1974), p. 521.

[6] Gregory Baum, *The Priority of Labor* (New York: Paulist Press, 1982), p. 10.

[7] Jay B. Rurlich, *Work and Love: The Crucial Balance* (New York: Summit Books, 1980), p. 29.

[8] Frank Tannenbaum, *A Philosophy of Labor* (New York: Knopf, 1951), p. 9.

[9] *Work in America: Report of a Special Task Force to the Secretary of Health, Education and Welfare* (Cambridge, Mass.: MIT Press, 1980), p. 13.

[10] Terkel, *Working*, p. xi.

[11] Hannah Arendt points out that the words "labor" and "work" are really two different words, and for Arendt they connote two different but not disparate meanings.

The Latin work is *ponos*, the French *travail*, and the German *Arbeit*. The word "work" has different etymological roots. In Latin "to work" is *facere* or *fabricari*, in Greek it is *ergazesthai*, in French it is *ouvrer*, and in German *werken*. For Arendt "labor" is the "toil of life," that "drudgery" that must be done to minister to the necessities of existence. To labor is to use one's body to achieve a task. "Work," she feels, has a higher significance. It connotes "to make," "to do with intention," "to accomplish as task"; it refers to craftsmanship. Granting Professor Arendt these real and implied differences, we shall nevertheless use these terms as if they were synonymous.

[12] Hannah Arendt, *The Human Condition* (Chicago: University of Chicago Press, 1958), pp. 48 n., 80 n., 110 n.

[13] Braude, *Work and Workers*, p. 5.

[14] *The New Oxford Annotated Bible* (New York: Oxford University Press), Gen. 3:17b–19.

[15] Adriand Tilgher, *Homo Faber: Work Through the Ages*, trans. Dorothy Canfield Fisher (Chicago: Henry Regnery, 1965), pp. 11–12.

[16] *Ibid.*, pp. 29–40.

[17] Sar A. Levitan and Wm. B. Johnston, *Work Is Here to Stay, Alas* (Salt Lake City: Olympian Publishing Co., 1973), p. 28.

[18] *Plutarch's Lives* (New York: Modern Library, 1932), p. 183.

[19] Levitan and Johnston, *Work Is Here to Stay, Alas*, p. 28.

[20] Tilgher, *Homo Faber*, p. 49.

[21] Michael Cherrington, *The Work Ethic: Working Values and Values that Work* (New York: AMACOM, 1980), pp. 20–33.

[22] Michael Argyle, *The Social Psychology of Work* (New York: Taplinger Publishing, 1972), pp. 22–23.

[23] Cherrington, *The Work Ethic*, p. 20.

[24] Gerhard E. Lewski, *The Religious Factor: A Sociological Study of Religious Impact on Politics, Economics and Family Life* (New York: Doubleday, 1961), pp. 4–5.

[25] Maccoby and Terzi, "What Happened to the Work Ethic?" p. 22.

[26] Cherrington, *The Work Ethic*, p. 35.

[27] Jesse L. Lemisch, *Benjamin Franklin: 'The Autobiography' and Other Writings* (New York: New American Library, 1961), p. 95.

[28] Cherrington, *The Work Ethic*, p. 35.

[29] Daniel T. Rodgers, *The Work Ethic in Industrial America, 1850–1920* (Chicago: University of Chicago Press, 1978), p. 14.

[30] C. Wright Mills, "The Meaning of Work Throughout History," in Fred Best (ed.), *The Future of Work* (Englewood Cliffs, N.J.: Prentice-Hall, 1973), p. 6.

[31] Joseph F. Quinn, "The Work Ethic and Retirement," in *The Work Ethic—A Critical Analysis* (Madison, Wisc.: Industrial Relations Research Association, 1983), p. 87.

[32] Levitan and Johnston, *Work Is Here to Stay, Alas*, p. 31.

[33] *Ibid.*, p. 27.

[34] Daniel Yankelovich, *New Rules: Searching for Self-Fulfillment in a World Turned Upside Down* (New York: Bantam Books, 1982), p. 7.

[35] Jack Barbash, "Which Work Ethic?" in *The Work Ethic—A Critical Analysis*, p. 258.

[36] *Ibid.*, p. 232.

[37] Herbert G. Gutman, *Work, Culture and Society* (New York: Vintage Books, 1977), pp. 3–5.

[38] Gus Tyler, "The Work Ethic: A Union View," in *The Work Ethic—A Critical Analysis*, pp. 197–198.

[39] Elmore Leonard, *Split Images* (New York: Avon, 1981), p. 13.

[40] George Gilden, *Wealth and Poverty* (New York: Bantam Books, 1982); also *The Spirit of Enterprise* (New York: Simon and Schuster, 1984).

[41] "What Is the Point of Working?" pp. 93–94.

[42] Joseph Epstein, "Work and Its Contents," *The American Scholar*, Summer 1983, p. 307.

[43] Eric Larrabee, "Time to Kill: Automation, Leisure and Jobs," in Robert V. Guthrie (ed.), *Psychology in the World Today* (Reading, Mass.: Addison-Wesley, 1968), p. 312.

[44] Melvin Kranzberg and Joseph Gies, *By the Sweat of Their Brow—Work in the Western World* (New York: G. P. Putnam's, 1975), p. 4.

[45] Stanley E. Seashore and J. Thad Barnowe, "Collar Color Doesn't Count," *Psychology Today*, August 1972, p. 80.

[46] One of the most important surveys to directly deny this contention is M. R. Cooper, B. S. Morgan, P. M. Foley, and L. B. Kaplan, "Changing Employee Values: Deepening Discontent?" *Harvard Business Review*, Jan./Feb. 1979, pp. 117–125.

[47] "New Breed of Workers," *U.S. News & World Report*, Sept. 3, 1979, p. 35.

[48] *Ibid.*, pp. 35–36.

[49] Daniel Yankelovich, "The Meaning of Work," in Jerome M. Rosow (ed.), *The Worker and the Job: Coping with Change* (Englewood Cliffs, N.J.: Prentice-Hall, 1974), pp. 44–45.

[50] Nancy Morse and Robert Weiss, "The Function and Meaning of Work," *American Sociological Review*, 20 (April 1966): 191–198.

[51] Maccoby and Terzi, "What Happened to the Work Ethic?" p. 33.

[52] Wm. B. Lacy, J. L. Bokemeier, and J. M. Shepard, "Job Attribute Preferences and Work Commitment of Men and Women in the United States," *Personnel Psychology*, 3 (1983): 315–329.

[53] *Work in America: HEW Task Force Report*, pp. 15–17.

[54] Maccoby and Terzi, "What Happened to the Work Ethic?" p. 34.

[55] Robert L. Kahn, *Work and Health* (New York: Wiley, 1981), p. 27.

[56] *Work in America: HEW Task Force Report*, pp. 15–17.

[57] Morse and Weiss, "The Function and Meaning of Work," pp. 191–198.

[58] *Ibid.*

[59] Kahn, *Work and Health*, p. 69.

[60] E. F. Schumacher, *Good Work* (New York: Harper Colophon Books, 1980), p. 27.

[61] Terkel, *Working*, p. xxxiv.

[62] Karl Marx, "Estranged Labor," in Dirk Struik (ed.), *The Economic and Philosophic Manuscripts of 1844*, trans. Martin Milligan (New York: International Publishers, 1964), pp. 110–111.

[63] Robert Blauner, *Alienation and Freedom, the Factory Worker and His Industry* (Chicago: University of Chicago Press, 1964), p. 15.

[64] Argyle, *The Social Psychology of Work*, pp. 225–226.

[65] *Work in America: HEW Task Force Report*, pp. 22–24.

[66] George Strauss, "Workers: Attitudes and Adjustments," in *The Worker and the Job: Coping with Change*, pp. 86–87.

[67] Robert L. Kahn, "The Meaning of Work: Interpretations and Proposals for Measurement," in Angus Campbell and Philip Converse (eds.), *The Human Meaning of Social Change* (New York: Basic Books, 1972).

[68] Strauss, "Workers: Attitudes and Adjustments," p. 83.

[69] Yankelovich, "The Meaning of Work," p. 19.

[70] Schumacher, *Good Work*, pp. 2–3.

[71] Harry Braverman, *Labor and Monopoly Capital* (New York: Monthly Review Press, 1974), p. 45.

[72] Baum, *The Priority of Labor*, p. 9.

[73] Bernard Lefkowitz, *Breaktime* (Hawthorn Books, 1979), p. 14.

[74] Baum, *The Priority of Labor*, p. 12.

[75] *Ibid.*, p. 15.

[76] Karl Marx, "The German Ideology," ed. and trans. Loyd Easten and Kurt Guddat, in *Writings of the Young Marx on Philosophy and Society* (New York: Doubleday, 1967), p. 409.

[77] Schumacher, *Good Work*, pp. 41–42.

[78] *Laborem exercens*, Encyclical Letter of Pope John Paul II, in Baum, *The Priority of Labor*, p. 95.

[79] *Ibid.*, p. 112.

[80] *Ibid.*, pp. 104–106.

[81] Nathan Hale, "Freud's Reflections on Work and Love," in Neil J. Smelser and Erik H. Erikson (eds.), *Themes of Work and Love in Adulthood* (Cambridge, Mass.: Harvard University Press, 1980), p. 30.

[82] *Work in America: HEW Task Force Report*, p. 8.

[83] Martin Heidegger, *Being and Time*, trans. John Macquarrie and Edward Robinson (New York: Harper and Row, 1962), pp. 102–186. Also Martin Heidegger, *The Basic Problems of Phenomenology*, trans. Albert Hofstadter (Bloomington, Ind.: University of Indiana Press, 1982), pp. 168–171.

[84] Erik A. Erikson, "Themes of Adulthood in the Freud-Jung Correspondence," in *Themes of Work and Love in Adulthood*, pp. 43–74.

[85] Lefkowitz, *Breaktime*, pp. 16–17.

[86] Erikson, "Themes of Adulthood in the Freud-Jung Correspondence," pp. 55–58.

[87] Kahn, *Work and Health*, p. 11.

[88] *Work in America: HEW Task Force Report*, p. 6.

[89] Schumacher, *Good Work*, p. 122.

[90] *Ibid.*, pp. 118–119.

[91] Richard J. Arneson, "Meaningful Work and Market Socialism," The Eastern Division of American Philosophical Association, Dec. 1984, p. 1.

[92] Yankelovich, "The Meaning of Work," pp. 35–36.

[93] W. H. Auden, *A Certain World: A Commonplace Book* (New York: Viking Press, 1970), p. 407.

[94] *Work in America: HEW Task Force Report*, pp. 4–5.

[95] Patricia H. Werhane, *Persons, Rights & Corporations* (Englewood Cliffs, N.J.: Prentice-Hall, 1985), p. 134.

[96] Kranzberg and Gies, *By the Sweat of Their Brow*, p. 9.

[97] Kahn, *Work and Health*, p. 48.

[98] *Work in America: HEW Task Force Report*, pp. 12–13.

[99] F. B. Herzberg, *Work and the Nature of Man* (Cleveland: World Publishing Co., 1966). Also F. B. Herzberg, B. Mausner, and B. Synderman, *The Motivation to Work* (New York: Wiley, 1959).

[100] Strauss, "Workers: Attitudes and Adjustments," p. 86.

[101] Adina Schwartz, "Meaningful Work," *Ethics* 92 (July 1982): 634–646.

[102] Adam Smith, *An Inquiry into the Nature and Causes of the Wealth of Nations*, Edwin Cannan (ed.) (Chicago: University of Chicago Press, 1976), 2: 302–303.

[103] Melvin L. Kohn and Carmi Schooler, "The Reciprocal Effects of the Substantive Complexity of Work and Intellectual Flexibility: A Longitudinal Study," *American Journal of Sociology*, 84 (1978): 43, 48.

[104] Arthur Kornhauser, *Mental Health of the Industrial Worker: A Detroit Study* (New York: Wiley, 1964), pp. 252–270.

[105] *Ibid.*, p. 263.

[106] George Strauss, "Is There a Blue-Collar Revolt Against Work?" in Roy P. Fairfield (ed.), *Humanizing the Workplace* (Buffalo, N.Y.: Prometheus Books, 1974), p. 32.

[107] Terkel, *Working*, p. xi.

[108] Strauss, "Is There a Blue-Collar Revolt Against Work?" p. 31.

[109] Kahn, *Work and Health*, p. 16.

[110] Epstein, "Work and Its Contents," p. 299.

[111] Baum, *The Priority of Labor*, p. 66.

[112] Kahn, *Work and Health*, p. 11.

[113] *Ibid.*, p. 13.

[114] Schumacher, *Good Work*, pp. 3–4.

[115] Epstein, "Work and Its Contents," p. 308.

[116] John Dewey, "Democracy in Education" (1916), Vol. 9 of *The Middle Works of John Dewey, 1899–1924* (Carbondale: Southern Illinois University Press), p. 219.

[117] Vikram Seth, *The Golden Gate* (New York: Random House, 1986), p. 9.

[118] "What Is the Point of Working?" pp. 93–94.

[119] Epstein, "Work and Its Contents," p. 306.

[120] *Work in America: HEW Task Force Report*, p. 10.

[121] The Institute of Industrial Relations, Loyola University, Chicago.

[122] Theodore Roszak, *Person/Planet* (New York: Doubleday, 1979), p. 227.

2

....

Some Historical Perspectives on Work

INTRODUCTION

This chapter presents a short survey of some historical positions on work ranging from the late nineteenth century to the present, and from Marxist to religious perspectives.

Adam Smith, writing in 1776, explains the division of labor as the consequence of our natural inclination to barter—itself an outgrowth of self-interest. From the perspective of the times, the division of labor was responsible for the creation of wealth for nations and individuals, and as such could hardly be seen as negative. Laborers' lots are improved by increased income earned by the increased production that results when "the whole attention of their minds is directed toward [a] single object." From our more recent perspective, it may seem naïve to overlook the effect on the mind of such a narrow focus of attention.

More than a hundred years and an entire industrial revolution later, Frederick Winslow Taylor reached some startling conclusions, many of which still seem revelatory today in the reincarnation of "Theory Z" management and its reliance on worker involvement. Taylor was an engineer—actually a machinist—who applied scientific methods to the management of a steel mill. While the effort smacks of the transference that gave birth to Social Darwinism, his conclusions speak of the involvement of workers in task analysis, cooperation, democratic plant management, and the use of incentives. The section concerning the "Science of Shoveling," despite sounding like a Woody Allen title, is a study in the involvement of labor in management decisions and displays a rare respect for manual labor. Taylor is sometimes thought—generally by people who have not actually read him—as a time-and-motion-study expert attempting to manipulate laborers as an engineer manipulates machine tools. He gives us, rather, a look at management several generations ahead of his time.

The Weber selection, perhaps the best known of the group, is an analysis of the Puritan underpinnings of industrial capitalism. Relatively evenhandedly, he looks at asceticism—the condemnation of dishonesty and the dedication to simplicity—as the base upon which Victorian capitalism was founded. He speaks of the death of Puritan asceticism but correctly predicts that the industrial model it abetted would carry on without its support. The attitudes of the Protestant ethic live on today in the deification of a lifetime of hard work, no matter how stupefying the work may be.

The Marx piece is the first selection that deals directly with the notion of alien work—work which is done not to satisfy needs, but as a "means for satisfying other needs." He speaks of the near universal avoidance of this type of labor as the proof of alienation. The extent to which the contemporary mind accepts the notion that work is both necessary and distasteful may make Marx's position more difficult to see, or it may point to the near universally alienating nature of contemporary work.

Finally, Pope John Paul II writes on the ninetieth anniversary of *Rerum Novarum*, Leo XIII's encyclical on work. This piece can be seen in counterpoint to Marx, although they speak from the same perspective of work as necessarily subjective. While Marx looks at what work has become and at what it should not be, John Paul II addresses what it might become. This is more a prescription than a lament. He describes a model of work as focusing on the worker, as basic to human needs, while perhaps suggesting that the laborer must make meaning from the work if the work itself appears to be without meaning.

Together, these five selections represent a fair history of the development of modern work attitudes and a look at some dissatisfactions with it. While they are far from comprehensive, they will do for a starting point before we look at some contemporary, and changing, viewpoints of work.

ADAM SMITH
THE DIVISION OF LABOR ....

The greatest improvement in the productive powers of labour, and the greater part of the skill, dexterity, and judgment with which it is any where directed, or applied, seem to have been the effects of the division of labour. . . .

. . . To take an example . . . the trade of the pin-maker; a workman not educated to this business (which the division of labour has rendered a distinct trade), nor acquainted with the use of the machinery employed in it (to the invention of which the same division of labour has probably given occasion), could scarce, perhaps, with his utmost industry, make one pin in a day, and certainly could not make twenty. But in the way in which this business is now carried on, not only the whole work is a peculiar trade, but it is divided into a number of branches, of which the greater part are likewise peculiar

Adam Smith, *The Wealth of Nations*, Edwin Cannan, ed. (New York: The Modern Library, 1937). Published by Random House, Inc.

trades. One man draws out the wire, another straights it, a third cuts it, a fourth points it, a fifth grinds it at the top for receiving the head; to make the head requires two or three distinct operations; to put it on, is a peculiar business, to whiten the pins is another; it is even a trade by itself to put them into the paper; and the important business of making a pin is, in this manner, divided into about eighteen distinct operations, which, in some manufactories, are all performed by distinct hands, though in others the same man will sometimes perform two or three of them. I have seen a small manufactory of this kind where ten men only were employed, and where some of them consequently performed two or three distinct operations. But though they were very poor, and therefore but indifferently accommodated with the necessary machinery, they could, when they exerted themselves, make among them about twelve pounds of pins in a day. There are in a pound upwards of four thousand pins of a middling size. Those ten persons, therefore, could make among them upwards of forty-eight thousand pins in a day. Each person, therefore, making a tenth part of forty-eight thousand pins, might be considered as making four thousand eight hundred pins in a day. . . .

In every other art and manufacture, the effects of the division of labour are similar to what they are in this very trifling one; though, in many of them, the labour can neither be so much subdivided, nor reduced to so great a simplicity of operation. The division of labour, however, so far as it can be introduced, occasions, in every art, a proportionable increase of the productive powers of labour. The separation of different trades and employments from one another, seems to have taken place, in consequence of this advantage. This separation too is generally carried furthest in those countries which enjoy the highest degree of industry and improvement; what is the work of one man in a rude state of society, being generally that of several in an improved one. In every improved society, the farmer is generally nothing but a farmer; the manufacturer, nothing but a manufacturer. The labour too which is necessary to produce any one complete manufacture, is almost always divided among a great number of hands. . . .

This great increase of the quantity of work, which, in consequence of the division of labour, the same number of people are capable of performing, is owing to three different circumstances; first, to the increase of dexterity in every particular workman; secondly, to the saving of the time which is commonly lost in passing from one species of work to another; and lastly, to the invention of a great number of machines which facilitate and abridge labour, and enable one man to do the work of many.

First, the improvement of the dexterity of the workman necessarily increases the quantity of the work he can perform; and the division of labour, by reducing every man's business to some one simple operation, and by making this operation the sole employment of his life, necessarily increases very much the dexterity of the workman. . . .

Secondly, the advantage which is gained by saving the time commonly lost in passing from one sort of work to another, is much greater than we should at first view be apt to imagine it. It is impossible to pass very quickly from one kind of work to another, that is carried on in a different place, and with quite different tools. A country weaver, who cultivates a small farm, must lose a good deal of time in passing from his loom to the field, and from the field to his loom. When the two trades can be carried on in the same workhouse, the loss of time is no doubt much less. It is even in this case, however, very considerable. A man commonly saunters a little in turning his hand from one sort of employment to another. When he first begins the new work he is seldom very keen and hearty; his mind, as they say, does not go to it, and for some time he rather trifles than applies to good purpose. The habit of sauntering and of indolent careless application, which is naturally, or rather necessarily acquired by every country workman who is obliged to change his work and his tools every half hour, and to apply his hand in twenty different ways almost every day of his life; renders him almost always slothful and lazy, and incapable of any vigorous application even on the most pressing occasions. Independent, therefore, of his deficiency in point of dexterity, this cause alone must always reduce considerably the quantity of work which he is capable of performing.

Thirdly, and lastly, every body must be sensible how much labour is facilitated and abridged by the application of proper machinery. . . . The invention of all those machines by which labour is so much facilitated and abridged, seems to have been originally owing to the division of labour. Men are much more likely to discover easier and readier methods of attaining any object, when the whole attention of their minds is directed towards that single object, than when it is dissipated among a great variety of things. But in consequence of the division of labour, the whole of every man's attention comes naturally to be directed towards some one very simple object. It is naturally to be expected, therefore, that some one or other of those who are employed in each particular branch of labour should soon find out easier and readier methods of performing their own particular work, wherever the nature of it admits of such improvement. . . .

It is the great multiplication of the productions of all the different arts, in consequence of the division of labour, which occasions, in a well-governed society, that universal opulence which extends itself to the lowest ranks of the people. Every workman has a great quantity of his own work to dispose of beyond what he himself has occasion for; and every other workman being exactly in the same situation, he is enabled to exchange a great quantity of his own goods for a great quantity, or, what comes to the same thing, for the price of a great quantity of theirs. He supplies them abundantly with what they have occasion for, and they accommodate him as amply with what he has occasion for, and a general plenty diffuses itself through all the different ranks of the society. . . .

This division of labour, from which so many advantages are derived, is not originally the effect of any human wisdom, which foresees and intends that general opulence to which it gives occasion. It is the necessary, though very slow and gradual, consequence of a certain propensity in human nature which has in view no such extensive utility; the propensity to truck, barter, and exchange one thing for another.

Whether this propensity be one of those original principles in human nature, of which no further account can be given; or whether, as seems more probable, it be the necessary consequence of the faculties of reason and speech, it belongs not to our present subject to enquire. It is common to all men, and to be found in no other race of animals, which seem to know neither this nor any other species of contracts. . . .

In almost every other race of animals each individual, when it is grown up to maturity, is entirely independent, and in its natural state has occasion for the assistance of no other living creature. But man has almost constant occasion for the help of his brethren, and it is in vain for him to expect it from their benevolence only. He will be more likely to prevail if he can interest their self-love in his favour, and shew them that it is for their own advantage to do for him what he requires of them. Whoever offers to another a bargain of any kind, proposes to do this. Give me that which I want, and you shall have this which you want, is the meaning of every such offer; and it is in this manner that we obtain from one another the far greater part of those good offices which we stand in need of. It is not from the benevolence of the butcher, the brewer, or the baker, that we expect our dinner, but from their regard to their own interest. We address ourselves, not to their humanity but to their self-love, and never talk to them of our own necessities but of their advantages. . . .

As it is by treaty, by barter, and by purchase, that we obtain from one another the greater part of those mutual good offices which we stand in need of, so it is this same trucking disposition which originally gives occasion to the division of labour. . . .

Among men . . . the most dissimilar geniuses are of use to one another; the different produces of their respective talents, by the general disposition to truck, barter, and exchange, being brought, as it were, into a common stock, where every man may purchase whatever part of the produce of other men's talents he has occasion for.

FREDERICK WINSLOW TAYLOR
THE PRINCIPLES OF SCIENTIFIC MANAGEMENT ....

By far the most important fact which faces the industries of our country, the industries, in fact, of the civilized world, is that not only the average worker, but nineteen out of twenty workmen throughout the civilized world firmly

Frederick W. Taylor, "The Principles of Scientific Management." Reprinted by permission, *Bulletin of the Taylor Society*, 1916, Society for Advancement of Management.

believe that it is for their best interests to go slow instead of to go fast. They firmly believe that it is for their interest to give as little work in return for the money that they get as is practical. The reasons for this belief are twofold, and I do not believe that the workingmen are to blame for holding these fallacious views.

If you will take any set of workmen in your own town and suggest to those men that it would be a good thing for them in their trade if they were to double their output in the coming year, each man turn out twice as much work and become twice as efficient, they would say, "I do not know anything about other people's trades; what you are saying about increasing efficiency being a good thing may be good for other trades, but I know that the only result if you come to our trade would be that half of us would be out of a job before the year was out." That to the average workman is an axiom, it is not a matter subject to debate at all. And even among the average business men of this country that opinion is almost universal. They firmly believe that that would be the result of a great increase in efficiency, and yet directly the opposite is true.

THE EFFECT OF LABOR-SAVING DEVICES

Whenever any labor-saving device of any kind has been introduced into any trade—go back into the history of any trade and see it—even though that labor-saving device may turn out ten, twenty, thirty times that output that was originally turned out by men in that trade, the result has universally been to make work for more men in that trade, not work for less men.

Let me give you one illustration. Let us take one of the staple businesses, the cotton industry. About 1840 the power loom succeeded the old hand loom in the cotton industry. It was invented many years before, somewhere about 1780 or 1790, but it came in very slowly. About 1840 the weavers of Manchester, England, saw that the power loom was coming, and they knew it would turn out three times the yardage of cloth in a day that the hand loom turned out. And what did they do, these five thousand weavers of Manchester, England, who saw starvation staring them in the face? They broke into the establishments into which those machines were being introduced, they smashed them, they did everything possible to stop the introduction of the power loom. And the same result followed that follows every attempt to interfere with the introduction of any labor-saving device, if it is really a labor-saving device. Instead of stopping the introduction of the power loom, their opposition apparently accelerated it, just as opposition to scientific management all over the country, bitter labor opposition to-day, is accelerating the introduction of it instead of retarding it. History repeats itself in that respect. The power loom came right straight along.

And let us see the result in Manchester. Just what follows in every industry when any labor-saving device is introduced. Less than a century has gone by since 1840. The population of England in that time has now more than doubled. Each man in the cotton industry in Manchester, England, now turns out at a restricted estimate ten yards of cloth for every yard of cloth that was turned out in 1840. In 1840 there were 5,000 weavers in Manchester. Now there are 265,000. Has that thrown men out of work? Has the introduction of labor-saving machinery, which has multiplied the output per man by ten-fold, thrown men out of work?

What is the real meaning of this? All that you have to do is to bring wealth into this world and the world uses it. That is the real meaning. The meaning is that where in 1840 cotton goods were a luxury to be worn only by rich people when they were hardly ever seen on the street, now every man, woman and child all over the world wears cotton goods as a daily necessity.

Nineteen-twentieths of the real wealth of this world is used by the poor people, and not the rich, so that the workingman who sets out as a steady principle to restrict output is merely robbing his own kind. That group of manufacturers which adopts as a permanent principle restriction of output, in order to hold up prices, is robbing the world. The one great thing that marks the improvement of this world is measured by the enormous increase in output of the individuals in this world. There is fully twenty times the output per man now that there was three hundred years ago. That marks the increase in the real wealth of the world; that marks the increase of the happiness of the world, that gives us the opportunity for shorter hours, for better education, for amusement, for art, for music, for everything that is worth while in this world—goes right straight back to this increase in the output of the individual. The workingmen of today live better than the king did three hundred years ago. From what does the progress the world has made come? Simply from the increase in the output of the individual all over the world.

THE DEVELOPMENT OF SOLDIERING

The second reason why the workmen of this country and of Europe deliberately restrict output is a very simple one. They, for this reason, are even less to blame than they are for the other. If, for example, you are manufacturing a pen, let us assume for simplicity that a pen can be made by a single man. Let us say that the workman is turning out ten pens per day, and that he is receiving $2.50 a day for his wages. He has a progressive foreman who is up to date, and that foreman goes to the workman and suggests, "Here, John, you are getting $2.50 a day, and you are turning out ten pens. I would suggest that I pay you 25 cents for making that pen." The man takes the job, and through the help of his foreman, through his own ingenuity, through the help of his friends, at the end of the year he finds himself turning out twenty pens instead of ten. He is happy, he is making $5, instead of $2.50 a day. His foreman is happy because, with the same room, with the same men he had before, he has doubled the output of his department, and the manufacturer himself is sometimes happy, but not often. Then someone on the board of directors asks to see the payroll, and he finds that we are paying $5 a day where other similar mechanics are only getting $2.50, and in no uncertain terms he announces that we must stop ruining the labor market. We cannot pay $5 a day when the standard rate of wages is $2.50; how can we hope to compete with surrounding towns? What is the result? Mr. Foreman is sent for, and he is told that he has got to stop ruining the labor market of Cleveland. And the foreman goes back to his workman in sadness, in depression, and tells his workman, "I am sorry, John, but I have got to cut the price down for that pen; I cannot let you earn $5 a day; the board of directors has got on to it, and it is ruining the labor market; you ought to be willing to have the price reduced. You cannot earn more than $3 or $2.75 a day, and I will cut your wages so that you will only get $3 a day." John, of necessity accepts the cut, but he sees to it that he never makes enough pens to get another cut.

CHARACTERISTICS OF THE UNION WORKMAN

There seem to be two divergent opinions about the workmen of this country. One is that a lot of the trade unions' workmen, particularly in this country, have become brutal, have become dominating, careless of any interests but their own, and are a pretty poor lot. And the other opinion which those same trade unionists hold of themselves is that they are pretty close to little gods. Whichever view you may hold of the workingmen of this country, and my personal view of them is that they are a pretty fine lot of fellows, they are just about the same as you and I. But whether you hold the bad opinion or the good opinion, it makes no difference. Whatever the workingmen of this country are or whatever they are not, they are not fools. And all that is necessary is for a workingman to have but one object lesson, like that I have told you, and he soldiers for the rest of his life.

There are a few exceptional employers who treat their workmen differently, but I am talking about the rule of the country. Soldiering is the absolute rule with all workmen who know their business. I am not saying it is for their interest to soldier. You cannot blame them for it. You cannot expect them to be large enough minded men to look at the proper view of the matter. Nor is the man who cuts the wages necessarily to blame. It is simply a misfortune in industry.

THE DEVELOPMENT OF SCIENTIFIC MANAGEMENT

There has been, until comparatively recently, no scheme promulgated by which the evils of rate cutting could be properly avoided, so soldiering has been the rule.

Now the first step that was taken toward the development of those methods, of those principles, which rightly or wrongly have come to be known under the name of scientific management, the first step that was taken was taken in an earnest endeavor to remedy the evils of soldiering; an earnest endeavor to make it unnecessary for workmen to be hypocritical in this way, to deceive themselves, to deceive their employers, to live day in and day out a life of deceit, forced upon them by conditions—the very first step that was taken toward the development was to overcome that evil. I want to emphasize that, because I wish to emphasize the one great fact relating to scientific management, the greatest factor, namely, that scientific management is no new set of theories that has been tried on by any one at every step. Scientific management at every step has been an evolution, not a theory. In all cases the practice has preceded the theory, not succeeded it. In every case one measure after another has been tried out, until the proper remedy has been found. That series of proper eliminations, that evolution, is what is called scientific management. Every element of it has had to fight its way against the elements that preceded it, and prove itself better or it would not be there to-morrow.

All the men that I know of who are in any way connected with scientific management are ready to abandon any scheme, any theory in favor of anything else that could be found that is better. There is nothing in scientific management that is fixed. There is no one man, or group of men, who has invented scientific management.

What I want to emphasize is that all of the elements of scientific management are an evolution, not an invention. Scientific management is in use in an immense range and variety of industries. Almost every type of industry in this country has scientific management working successfully. I think I can safely say that on the average in those establishments in which scientific management has been introduced, the average workman is turning out double the output he was before. I think that is a conservative statement.

THE WORKMEN THE CHIEF BENEFICIARIES

Three or four years ago I could have said there were about fifty thousand men working under scientific management, but now I know there are many more. Company after company is coming under it, many of which I know nothing about. Almost universally they are working successfully. This increasing of the output per individual in the trade, results, of course, in cheapening the product; it results, therefore, in larger profit usually to the owners of the business; it results also, in many cases, in a lowering of the selling price, although that has not come to the extent it will later. In the end the public gets the good. Without any question, the large good which so far has come from scientific management has come to the worker. To the workman has come, practically right off as soon as scientific management is introduced, an increase in wages amounting from 33 to 100 per cent, and yet that is not the greatest good that comes to the workmen from scientific management. The great good comes from the fact that, under scientific management, they look upon their employers as the best friends they have in the world; the suspicious watchfulness which characterizes the old type of management, the semi-antagonism, or the complete antagonism between workmen and employers is entirely superseded, and in its place comes genuine friendship between both sides. That is the greatest good that has come under scientific management. As a proof of this in the many businesses in which scientific management has been introduced, I know of not one single strike of workmen working under it after it had been introduced, and only two or three while it was in process of introduction. In this connection I must speak of the fakers, those who have said they can introduce scientific management into a business in six months or a year. That is pure nonsense. There have been many strikes stirred up by that type of man. Not one strike has ever come, and I do not believe ever will come, under scientific management.

WHAT SCIENTIFIC MANAGEMENT IS

What is scientific management? It is no efficiency device, nor is it any group or collection of efficiency devices. Scientific management is no new scheme for paying men, it is no bonus system, no piece-work system, no premium system of payment; it is no new method of figuring costs. It is no one of the various elements by which it is commonly known, by which people refer to it. It is not time study nor man study. It is not the printing of a ton or two of blanks and unloading them on a company and saying, "There is your system, go ahead and use it." Scientific management does not exist and cannot exist until there has been a complete mental revolution on the part of the workmen working under it, as to their duties toward themselves and toward their employers, and a complete mental revolution in the outlook of the employers, toward their duties, toward themselves, and toward their workmen. And until this great mental change takes place, scientific management does not exist. Do you think you can make a great mental revolution in a large group of workmen in a year, or do you think you can make it in a large group of foremen and superintendents in a year? If you do, you are very much mistaken. All of us hold mighty close to our ideas and principles in life, and we change very slowly toward the new, and very properly too.

Let me give you an idea of what I mean by this change in mental outlook. If you are manufacturing a hammer or a mallet, into the cost of that mallet goes a certain amount of raw materials, a certain amount of wood and metal. If you will take the cost of the raw materials and then add to it that cost which is frequently called by various names—overhead expenses, general expense, indirect expense; that is, the proper share of taxes, insurance, light, heat, salaries of officers and advertising—and you have a sum of money. Subtract that sum from the selling price, and what is left over is called the surplus. It is over this surplus that all of the labor disputes in the past have occurred. The workman naturally wants all he can get. His wages come out of that surplus. The manufacturer wants all he can get in the shape of profits, and it is from the division of this surplus that all the labor disputes have come in the past—the equitable division.

The new outlook that comes under scientific management is this: The workmen, after many object lessons, come to see, and the management come to see that this surplus can be made so great, providing both sides will stop their pulling apart, will stop their fighting and will push as hard as they can to get as cheap an output as possible, that there is no occasion to quarrel. Each side can get more than ever before. The acknowledgement of this fact represents a complete mental revolution.

INTELLIGENT OLD-STYLE MANAGEMENT

There is one more illustration of the new and great change which comes under scientific management. I can make it clearer, perhaps, by contrasting it with what I look upon as the best of the older types of management. If you have a company employing five hundred or a thousand men, you will have in that company perhaps fifteen different trades. The workmen in those trades have learned absolutely all that they know, not from books, not by being taught, but they have learned it traditionally. It has been handed down to them, not even by word of mouth in many cases, but by seeing what other men do. One man stands alongside of another man and imitates him. That is the way the trades are handed down, and my impression is that trades are now picked up just as they were in the Middle Ages.

The manufacturer, the manager, or the foreman who knows his business realizes that his chief function as a manager—I am talking now of the old-fashioned manager—ought to be to get the true initiative of his workman. He wants the initiative of the workman, their hard work, their good will, their ingenuity, their determination to do all they can for the benefit of his firm. If he knows anything about human nature, if he has thought over the problems, he must realize that in order to get the initiative of his workman, in order to modify their soldiering, he must do something more for his men than other employers are doing for their men under similar circumstances. The wise manager, under the old type of management, deliberately sets out to do something better for his workmen than his competitors are doing, better than he himself has ever done before. It takes a good while for the workmen to stop [being suspicious] . . . but if the manager keeps at them for a sufficiently long time he will get the confidence of the men, and when he does workmen of all kinds will respond by giving a great increase in output. When he sets out to do better for his men than other people do for theirs, the workmen respond liberally when that time comes. I refer to this case as being the highest type of management, the case in which the managers deliberately set out to do something better for their workmen than other people are doing, and to give them a special incentive of some kind, to which the workmen respond by giving a share at least of their initiative.

WHAT SCIENTIFIC MANAGEMENT WILL DO

I am going to try to prove to you that even that type of management has not a ghost of a chance in competition with the principles of scientific management. Why? In the first place, under scientific management, the initiative of the workmen, their hard work, their good-will, their best endeavors are obtained with absolute regularity. There are cases all the time where men will soldier, but they become the exception, as a rule, and they give their true initiative under scientific management. That is the least of the two sources of gain. The greatest source of gain under scientific management comes from the new and almost unheard-of duties and burdens which are voluntarily assumed, not by the workmen, but by the men on the management side. These are the things which make scientific management a success. These new duties, these new burdens undertaken by the management have rightly or wrongly been divided into four groups, and have been called the principles of scientific management.

The first of the great principles of scientific management, the first of the new burdens which are voluntarily undertaken by those on the management side is the deliberate gathering together of the great mass of traditional knowledge which, in the past, has been in the heads of the workmen, recording it, tabulating it, reducing it in most cases to rules, laws, and in many cases to mathematical formulae, which, with these new laws, are applied to the co-operation of the management to the work of the workmen. This results in an immense increase in the output, we may say, of the two. The gathering in of this great mass of traditional knowledge, which is done by the means of motion study, time study, can be truly called the science.

Let me make a prediction. I have before me the first book, so far as I know, that has been published on motion study and on time study. That is, the motion study and time study of the cement and concrete trades. It contains everything relating to concrete work. It is of about seven hundred pages, and embodies the motions of men, the time and the best way of doing that sort of work. It is the first case in which a trade has been reduced to the same condition that engineering data of all kinds have been reduced, and it is this sort of data that is bound to sweep the world.

I have before me something which has been gathering for about fourteen years, the time or motion study of the machine shop. It will take probably four or five years more before the first book will be ready to publish on that subject. There is a collection of sixty or seventy thousand elements affecting machine-shop work. After a few years, say three, four or five years more, some one will be ready to publish the first book giving the laws of the movements of men in the machine shop—all the laws, not only a few of them. Let me predict, just as sure as the sun shines, that is going to come in every trade.

Why? Because it pays, for no other reason. That results in doubling the output in any shop. Any device which results in an increased output is bound to come in spite of all opposition, whether we want it or not. It comes automatically.

THE SELECTION OF THE WORKMAN

The next of four principles of scientific management is the scientific selection of the workman, and then his progressive development. It becomes the duty under scientific management, of not one, but of a group of men on the management side, to deliberately study the workmen who are under them; study them in the most careful, thorough and painstaking way, and not just leave it to the poor, overworked foreman to go out and say, "Come on, what do you want? If you are cheap enough I will give you a trial."

That is the old way. The new way is to take a great deal of trouble in selecting the workmen. The selection proceeds year after year. And it becomes the duty of those engaged in scientific management to know something about the workmen under them. It becomes their duty to set out deliberately to train the workmen in their employ to be able to do a better and still better class of work than ever before, and to then pay them higher wages than ever before. This deliberate selection of the workmen is the second of the great duties that devolve on the management under scientific management.

BRINGING TOGETHER THE SCIENCE AND THE MAN

The third principle is the bringing together of this science of which I have spoken and the trained workmen. I say bringing because they don't come together unless some one brings them. Select and train your workmen all you may, but unless there is some one who will make the men and the science come together, they will stay apart. The "make" involves a great many elements. They are not all disagreeable elements. The most important and largest way of "making" is to do something nice for the man whom you wish to make come together with the science. Offer him a plum, something that is worth while. There are many plums offered to those who come under scientific management—better treatment, more kindly treatment, more consideration for their wishes, and an opportunity for them to express their wants freely. That is one side of the "make." An equally important side is, whenever a man will not do what he ought, to either make him do it or stop it. If he will not do it, let him get out. I am not talking of any mollycoddle. Let me disabuse your minds of any opinion that scientific management is a mollycoddle scheme.

I have a great many union friends. I find they look with especial bitterness on this word "make." They have been used to doing the "making" in the past. That is the attitude of the trade unions, and it softens matters greatly when you can tell them the facts, namely, that in our making the science and the men come together, nine-tenths of our trouble comes with the men on the management side in making them do their new duties. I am speaking of those who have been trying to change from the old system to the new. Nine-tenths of our troubles come in trying to make the men on the management side do what they ought to do, to make them do the new duties, and take on these new burdens, and give up their old duties. That softens this word "make."

THE PRINCIPLE OF THE DIVISION OF WORK

The fourth principle is the plainest of all. It involves a complete redivision of the work of the establishment. Under the old scheme of management, almost all of the work was done by the workmen. Under the new, the work of the establishment is divided into two large parts. All of that work which formerly was done by the workmen alone is divided into two large sections, and one of those sections is handed over to the management. They do a whole division of the work formerly done by the workmen. It is this real co-operation, this genuine division of the work between the two sides, more than any other element which accounts for the fact that there never will be strikes under scientific management. When the workman realizes that there is hardly a thing he does, that does not have to be preceded by some act of preparation on the part of the management, and when that workman realizes when the management falls down and does not do its part, that he is not only entitled to a kick, but that he can register that kick in the most forcible possible way, he cannot quarrel with the men over him. It is team work. There are more complaints made every day on the part of the workmen that the men on the management side fail to do their duties, than are made by the management that the men fail. Every one of the complaints of the men have to be heeded, just as much as the complaints from the management that the workmen do not do their share. That is characteristic of scientific management. It represents a democracy, co-operation, a genuine division of work which never existed before in this world. . . .

MAX WEBER
THE SPIRIT OF WORK ....

Let us now try to clarify the points in which the Puritan idea of the calling and the premium it placed upon ascetic conduct was bound directly to influence

Max Weber, *The Protestant Ethic and the Spirit of Capitalism*, Talcott Parsons, trans. (New York: Charles Scribner's Sons, 1958, and London: Allen and Unwin). Reprinted with permission of the publisher.

the development of a capitalistic way of life. . . . This asceticism turned with all its force against one thing: the spontaneous enjoyment of life and all it had to offer. This is perhaps most characteristically brought out in the struggle over the *Book of Sports* which James I and Charles I made into law expressly as a means of counteracting Puritanism, and which the latter ordered to be read from all the pulpits. The fanatical opposition of the Puritans to the ordinances of the King, permitting certain popular amusements on Sunday outside of Church hours by law, was not only explained by the disturbance of the Sabbath rest, but also by resentment against the intentional diversion from the ordered life of the saint, which it caused. And, on his side, the King's threats of severe punishment for every attack on the legality of those sports were motivated by his purpose of breaking the anti-authoritarian ascetic tendency of Puritanism, which was so dangerous to the State. The feudal and monarchical forces protected the pleasure seekers against the rising middle-class morality and the anti-authoritarian ascetic conventicles, just as to-day capitalistic society tends to protect those willing to work against the class morality of the proletariat and the anti-authoritarian trade union.

As against this the Puritans upheld their decisive characteristic, the principle of ascetic conduct. For otherwise the Puritan aversion to sport, even for the Quakers, was by no means simply one of principle. Sport was accepted if it served a rational purpose, that of recreation necessary for physical efficiency. But as a means for the spontaneous expression of undisciplined impulses, it was under suspicion; and in so far as it became purely a means of enjoyment, or awakened pride, raw instincts or the irrational gambling instinct, it was of course strictly condemned. Impulsive enjoyment of life, which leads away from work in a calling and from religion, was as such the enemy of rational asceticism, whether in the form of seigneurial sports, or the enjoyment of the dance-hall or the public-house of the common man. . . .

The theatre was obnoxious to the Puritans, and with the strict exclusion of the erotic and of nudity from the realm of toleration, a radical view of either literature or art could not exist. The conceptions of idle talk, of superfluities, and of vain ostentation, all designations of an irrational attitude without objective purpose, thus not ascetic, and especially not serving the glory of God, but of man, were always at hand to serve in deciding in favour of sober utility as against any artistic tendencies. This was especially true in the case of decoration of the person, for instance clothing. That powerful tendency toward uniformity of life, which to-day so immensely aids the capitalistic interest in the standardization of production had its ideal foundations in the repudiation of all idolatry of the flesh. . . .

This worldly Protestant asceticism . . . acted powerfully against the spontaneous enjoyment of possessions; it restricted consumption, especially of luxuries. On the other hand, it has the psychological effect of freeing the acquisition of goods from the inhibitions of traditionalistic ethics. It broke the bonds of the impulse of acquisition in that it not only legalized it, but (in the sense discussed) looked upon it as directly willed by God. The campaign against the temptations of the flesh, and the dependence on external things, was, as besides the Puritans the great Quaker apologist Barclay expressly says, not a struggle against the rational acquisition, but against the irrational use of wealth.

But this irrational use was exemplified in the outward forms of luxury which their code condemned as idolatry of the flesh, however natural they had appeared to the feudal mind. On the other hand, they approved the rational and utilitarian uses of wealth which were willed by God for the needs of the individual and the community. They did not wish to impose mortification on the man of wealth, but the use of his means for necessary and practical things. The idea of comfort characteristically limits the extent of ethically permissible expenditures. It is naturally no accident that the development of a manner of living consistent with that idea may be observed earliest and most clearly among the most consistent representatives of this whole attitude toward life. Over against the glitter and ostentation of feudal magnificence which, resting on an unsound economic basis, prefers a sordid elegance to a sober simplicity, they set the clean and solid comfort of the middle-class home as an ideal.

On the side of the production of private wealth, asceticism condemned both dishonesty and impulsive avarice. What was condemned as covetousness, Mammonism, etc., was the pursuit of riches for their own sake. For wealth in itself was a temptation. But here asceticism was the power "which ever seeks the good but ever creates evil"; what was evil in its sense was possession and its temptations. For, in conformity with the Old Testament and in analogy to the ethical valuation of good works, asceticism looked upon the pursuit of wealth as an end in itself as highly reprehensible; but the attainment of it as a fruit of labour in a calling was a sign of God's blessing. And even more important: the religious valuation of restless, continuous, systematic work in a worldly calling, as the highest means to asceticism, and at the same time the surest and most evident proof of rebirth and genuine faith, must have been the most powerful conceivable lever for the expansion of that attitude toward life which we have here called the spirit of capitalism.

When the limitation of consumption is combined with this release of acquisitive activity, the inevitable practical result is obvious: accumulation of capital through ascetic compulsion to save. The restraints which were imposed upon the consumption of wealth naturally served to increase it by making possible the productive investment of capital. How strong this influence was is not, unfortunately, susceptible of exact statistical demonstration. In New England the connection is so evident that it did not escape the eye of so discerning a historian as Doyle. But also in Holland, which was really only dominated by strict Calvinism for seven years, the greater simplicity of life in the more seriously religious circles, in combination with great wealth, led to an excessive propensity to accumulation. . . .

As far as the influence of the Puritan outlook extended, under all circumstances—and this is, of course, much more important than the mere encouragement of capital accumulation—it favoured the development of a rational bourgeois economic life; it was the most important, and above all the only consistent influence in the development of that life. It stood at the cradle of the modern economic man. . . .

A specifically bourgeois economic ethic had grown up. With the consciousness of standing in the fullness of God's grace and being visibly blessed by Him, the bourgeois business man, as long as he remained within the bounds of formal correctness, as long as his moral conduct was spotless and the use to which he put his wealth was not objectionable, could follow his pecuniary interests as he would and feel that he was fulfilling a duty in doing so. The power of religious asceticism provided him in addition with sober, conscientious, and unusually industrious workmen, who clung to their work as to a life purpose willed by God.

Finally, it gave him the comforting assurance that the unequal distribution of the goods of this world was a special dispensation of Divine Providence, which in these differences, as in particular grace, pursued secret ends unknown to men. Calvin himself had made the much-quoted statement that only when the people, i.e., the mass of labourers and craftsmen, were poor did they remain obedient to God. In the Netherlands (Pieter de la Court and others), that had been secularized to the effect that the mass of men only labour when necessity forces them to do so. This formulation of a leading idea of capitalistic economy later emerged into the current theories of the productivity of low wages. Here also, with the dying out of the religious root, the utilitarian interpretation crept in unnoticed, in the line of development which we have again and again observed. . . .

Now naturally the whole ascetic literature of almost all denominations is saturated with the idea that faithful labour, even at low wages, on the part of those whom life offers no other opportunities, is highly pleasing to God. In this respect, Protestant Asceticism added in itself nothing new. But it not only deepened this idea most powerfully, it also created the force which was alone decisive for its effectiveness: the pyschological sanction of it through the conception of this labour as a calling, as the best, often in the last analysis the only means of attaining certainty of grace. And on the other hand it legalized the exploitation of this specific willingness to work, in that it also interpreted the employer's business activity as a calling. It is obvious how powerfully the exclusive search for the Kingdom of God only through the fulfilment of duty in the calling, and the strict asceticism which Church discipline naturally imposed, especially on the propertyless classes, was bound to affect the productivity of labour in the capitalistic sense of the word. The treatment of labour as a calling became as characteristic of the modern worker as the corresponding attitude toward acquisition of the business man. It was a perception of this situation, new at his time, which caused so able an observer as Sir William Petty to attribute the economic power of Holland in the seventeenth century to the fact that the very numerous dissenters in that country (Calvinists and Baptists) "are for the most part thinking, sober men, and such as believe that Labour and Industry is their duty towards God. . . ."

The Puritan wanted to work in a calling; we are forced to do so. For when asceticism was carried out of monastic cells into everyday life, and began to dominate worldly morality, it did its part in building the tremendous cosmos of the modern economic order. This order is now bound to the technical and economic conditions of machine production which to-day determine the lives of all the individuals who are born into this mechanism, not only those directly concerned with economic acquisition, with irresistible force. Perhaps it will so determine them until the last ton of fossilized coal is burnt. In Baxter's view the care for external goods should only lie on the shoulders of the "saint like a light cloak, which can be thrown aside at any moment." But fate decreed that the cloak should become an iron cage.

Since asceticism undertook to remodel the world and to work out its ideals in the world, material goods have gained an increasing and finally an inexorable power over the lives of men as at no previous period in history. To-day the spirit of religious asceticism—whether finally, who knows?—has escaped from the cage. But victorious capitalism, since it rests on mechanical foundations, needs its support no longer. The rosy blush of its laughing heir, the Enlightenment, seems also to be irretrievably fading, and the idea of duty in one's calling prowls about in our lives like the ghost of dead religious beliefs. Where the fulfilment of the calling cannot directly be related to the highest spiritual and cultural values, or when, on the other hand, it need not be felt simply as economic compulsion, the individual generally abandons the attempt to justify it at all. In the field of its highest development, in the United States, the pursuit of wealth, stripped of its religious and ethical meaning, tends to become associated with purely mundane passions, which often actually give it the character of sport.

No one knows who will live in this cage in the future, or whether at the end of this tremendous development entirely new prophets will arise, or there will be a great rebirth of old ideas and ideals, or, if neither, mechanized petrification, embellished with a sort of convulsive self-importance. For of the last stage of this cultural development, it might well be truly said: "Specialists without spirit, sensualists without heart; this nullity imagines that it has attained a level of civilization never before achieved. . . ."

KARL MARX
ALIENATED LABOUR ....

We shall begin from a *contemporary* economic fact. The worker becomes poorer the more wealth he produces and the more his production increases in power and extent. The worker becomes an ever cheaper commodity the more goods he creates. The *devaluation* of the human world increases in direct relation with the *increase in value* of the world of things. Labour does not only create goods;

Karl Marx: Early Writings, The Economic and Philosophical Manuscripts of 1844, T. B. Bottomore (trans.) (New York: McGraw-Hill Co., 1963). Reprinted by permission of the publisher.

it also produces itself and the worker as a *commodity*, and indeed in the same proportion as it produces goods. . . .

All these consequences follow from the fact that the worker is related to the *product of his labour* as to an *alien* object. For it is clear on this presupposition that the more the worker expends himself in work the more powerful becomes the world of objects which he creates in face of himself, the poorer he becomes in his inner life, and the less he belongs to himself. It is just the same as in religion. The more of himself man attributes to God the less he has left in himself. The worker puts his life into the object, and his life then belongs no longer to himself but to the object. The greater his activity, therefore, the less he possesses. What is embodied in the product of his labour is no longer his own. The greater this product is, therefore, the more he is diminished. The *alienation* of the worker in his product means not only that his labour becomes an object, assumes an *external* existence, but that it exists independently, *outside himself*, and alien to him, and that it stands opposed to him as an autonomous power. The life which he has given to the object sets itself against him as an alien and hostile force.

. . . the worker becomes a slave of the object; first, in that he receives an *object of work*, i.e. receives *work*, and secondly, in that he receives *means of subsistence*. Thus the object enables him to exist, first as a *worker* and secondly, as a *physical subject*. The culmination of this enslavement is that he can only maintain himself as a *physical subject* so far as he is a *worker*, and that it is only as a *physical subject* that he is a worker. . . .

What constitutes the alienation of labour? First, that the work is *external* to the worker, that it is not part of his nature; and that, consequently, he does not fulfill himself in his work but denies himself, has a feeling of misery rather than well-being, does not develop freely his mental and physical energies but is physically exhausted and mentally debased. The worker, therefore, feels himself at home only during his leisure time, whereas at work he feels homeless. His work is not voluntary but imposed, *forced labour*. It is not the satisfaction of a need, but only a *means* for satisfying other needs. Its alien character is clearly shown by the fact that as soon as there is no physical or other compulsion it is avoided like the plague. External labour, labour in which man alienates himself, is a labour of self-sacrifice, of mortification. Finally, the external character of work for the worker is shown by the fact that it is not his own work but work for someone else, that in work he does not belong to himself but to another person. . . .

We arrive at the result that man (the worker) feels himself to be freely active only in his animal functions—eating, drinking and procreating, or at most also in his dwelling and in personal adornment—while in his human functions he is reduced to an animal. The animal becomes human and the human becomes animal.

Eating, drinking and procreating are of course also genuine human functions. But abstractly considered, apart from the environment of human activities, and turned into final and sole ends, they are animal functions.

We have now considered the act of alienation of practical human activity, labour, from two aspects: (1) the relationship of the worker to the *product of labour* as an alien object which dominates him. This relationship is at the same time the relationship to the sensuous external world, to natural objects, as an alien and hostile world; (2) the relationship of labour to the *act of production* within *labour*. This is the relationship of the worker to his own activity as something alien and not belonging to him, activity as suffering (passivity), strength as powerlessness, creation as emasculation, the *personal* physical and mental energy of the worker, his personal life (for what is life but activity?), as an activity which is directed against himself, independent of him and not belonging to him. This is *self-alienation* as against the above-mentioned alienation of the *thing*.

We have now to infer a third characteristic of *alienated labour* from the two we have considered.

Man is a species-being not only in the sense that he makes the community (his own as well as those of other things) his object both practically and theoretically, but also (and this is simply another expression for the same thing) in the sense that he treats himself as the present, living species, as a *universal* and consequently free being.[1]

Species-life, for man as for animals, has its physical basis in the fact that man (like animals) lives from inorganic nature, and since man is more universal than an animal so the range of inorganic nature from which he lives is more universal. . . .The universality of man appears in practice in the universality which makes the whole of nature into his inorganic body: (1) as a direct means of life; and equally (2) as the material object and instrument of his life activity. Nature is the inorganic body of man; that is to say nature, excluding the human body itself. To say that man *lives* from nature means that nature is his *body* with which he must remain in a continuous interchange in order not to die. The statement that the physical and mental life of man, and nature, are interdependent means simply that nature is interdependent with itself, for man is a part of nature.

Since alienated labour: (1) alienates nature from man; and (2) alienates man from himself, from his own active function, his life activity; so it alienates him from the species. It makes *species-life* into a means of individual life. In the first place it alienates species-life and individual life, and secondly, it turns the latter, as an abstraction, into the purpose of the former, also in its abstract and alienated form.

For labour, *life activity, productive life*, now appear to man only as *means* for the satisfaction of a need, the need to maintain his physical existence. Productive life is, however, species-life. It is life creating life. In the type of life activity resides the whole character of a species, its species-character; and free, conscious activity is the species-character of human beings. Life itself appears only as a *means of life*.

[1]In this passage Marx reproduces Feuerbach's argument in *Das Wesen des Christentums*.

The animal is one with its life activity. It does not distinguish the activity from itself. It is *its activity*. But man makes his life activity itself an object of his will and consciousness. He has a conscious life activity. It is not a determination with which he is completely identified. Conscious life activity distinguishes man from the life activity of animals. Only for this reason is he a species-being. Or rather, he is only a self-conscious being, i.e. his own life is an object for him, because he is a species-being. Only for this reason is his activity free activity. Alienated labour reverses the relationship, in that man because he is a self-conscious being makes his life activity, his *being* only a means for his *existence*.

The practical construction of an *objective world*, the *manipulation* of inorganic nature, is the confirmation of man as a conscious species-being, i.e. a being who treats the species as his own being or himself as a species-being. . . .

It is just in his work upon the objective world that man really proves himself as a *species-being*. This production is his active species-life. By means of it nature appears as *his* work and his reality. The object of labour is, therefore, the *objectification of man's species-life:* for he no longer reproduces himself merely intellectually, as in consciousness, but actively and in a real sense, and he sees his own reflection in a world which he has constructed. While, therefore, alienated labour takes away the object of production from man, it also takes away his *species-life*, his real objectivity as a species-being, and changes his advantage over animals into a disadvantage in so far as his inorganic body, nature, is taken from him.

Just as alienated labour transforms free and self-directed activity into a means, so it transforms the species-life of man into a means of physical existence.

Consciousness, which man has from his species, is transformed through alienation so that species-life becomes only a means for him. (3) Thus alienated labour turns the *species-life of man*, and also nature as his mental species-property, into an *alien* being and into a *means* for his *individual existence*. It alienates from man his own body, external nature, his mental life and his *human* life. (4) A direct consequence of the alienation of man from the product of his labour, from his life activity and from his species-life, is that *man* is *alienated* from other *men*. When man confronts himself he also confronts *other* men. What is true of man's relationship to his work, to the product of his work and to himself, is also true of his relationship to other men, to their labour and to the objects of their labour.

In general, the statement that man is alienated from his species-life means that each man is alienated from others, and that each of the others is likewise alienated from human life.

Human alienation, and above all the relation of man to himself, is first realized and expressed in the relationship between each man and other men. Thus in the relationship of alienated labour every man regards other men according to the standards and relationships in which he finds himself placed as a worker.

We began with an economic fact, the alienation of the worker and his production. We have expressed this fact in conceptual terms as *alienated labour*, and in analysing the concept we have merely analysed an economic fact. . . .

The *alien* being to whom labour and the product of labour belong, to whose service labour is devoted, and to whose enjoyment the product of labour goes, can only be *man* himself. If the product of labour does not belong to the worker, but confronts him as an alien power, this can only be because it belongs to *a man other than the worker*. . . .

Thus, through alienated labour the worker creates the relation of another man, who does not work and is outside the work process, to this labour. The relation of the worker to work also produces the relation of the capitalist (or whatever one likes to call the lord of labour) to work. *Private property* is, therefore, the product, the necessary result, of *alienated labour*, of the external relation of the worker to nature and to himself.

Private property is thus derived from the analysis of the concept of *alienated labour;* that is, alienated man, alienated labour, alienated life, and estranged man.

We have, of course, derived the concept of *alienated labour (alienated life)* from political economy, from an analysis of the *movement of private property*. But the analysis of this concept shows that although private property appears to be the basis and cause of alienated labour, it is rather a consequence of the latter, just as the gods are *fundamentally* not the cause but the product of confusion of human reason. At a later stage, however, there is a reciprocal influence.

Only in the final state of the development of private property is its secret revealed, namely, that it is on one hand the *product* of alienated labour, and on the other hand the *means* by which labour is alienated, *the realization of this alienation*. . . .

Just as *private property* is only the sensuous expression of the fact that man is at the same time an *objective* fact for himself and becomes an alien and non-human object for himself; just as his manifestation of life is also his alienation of life and his self-realization a loss of reality, the emergence of an *alien* reality; so the positive supersession of private property, i.e. the *sensuous* appropriation of the human essence and of human life, of objective man and of human *creations*, by and for man, should not be taken only in the sense of *immediate*, exclusive *enjoyment*, or only in the sense of *possession* or *having*. Man appropriates his manifold being in an all-inclusive way, and thus as a whole man. All his *human* relations to the world—seeing, hearing, smelling, tasting, touching, thinking, observing, feeling, desiring, acting, loving—in short, all the organs of his individuality, like the organs which are directly communal in form, are in their objective action (their *action in relation to the object*) the appropriation of this object, the appropriation of human reality. The way in which they react to the object is the confirmation of *human reality*. It is human effectiveness and human *suffering*, for suffering humanly considered is an enjoyment of the self for man.

Private property has made us so stupid and partial that an object is only *ours* when we have it, when it exists for us as capital or when it is directly eaten, drunk, worn, inhabited, etc., in short, *utilized* in some way. But private property itself only conceives these various forms of possession as *means of life*, and the life for which they serve as means is the life of *private property*—labour and creation of capital.

The supersession of private property is, therefore, the complete *emancipation* of all the human qualities and senses. It is such an emancipation because these qualities and senses have become *human*, from the subjective as well as the objective point of view. The eye has become a *human* eye when its *object* has become a *human*, social object, created by man and destined for him. The senses have, therefore, become directly theoreticians in practice. They relate themselves to the thing for the sake of the thing, but the thing itself is an *objective human* relation to itself and to man, and vice versa. Need and enjoyment have thus lost their *egoistic* character and nature has lost its mere *utility* by the fact that its utilization has become *human* utilization. . . .

LABOREM EXERCENS (*ON HUMAN WORK*) ENCYCLICAL LETTER OF POPE JOHN PAUL II ....

Through work man must earn his daily bread and contribute to the continual advance of science and technology and, above all, to elevating unceasingly the cultural and moral level of the society within which he lives in community with those who belong to the same family. And work means any activity by man, whether manual or intellectual, whatever its nature or circumstances; it means any human activity that can and must be recognized as work, in the midst of all the many activities of which man is capable and to which he is predisposed by his very nature, by virtue of humanity itself. Man is made to be in the visible universe an image and likeness of God himself, and he is placed in it in order to subdue the earth. From the beginning therefore he is called to work. Work is one of the characteristics that distinguish man from the rest of creatures, whose activity for sustaining their lives cannot be called work. Only man is capable of work, and only man works, at the same time by work occupying his existence on earth. Thus work bears a particular mark of man and of humanity, the mark of a person operating within a community of persons. And this mark decides its interior characteristics; in a sense it constitutes its very nature. . . .

"Laborem Exercens," Third Encyclical of Pope John Paul II, September 15, 1981.

Man's life is built up every day from work, from work it derives its specific dignity, but at the same time work contains the unceasing measure of human toil and suffering and also of the harm and injustice which penetrate deeply into social life within individual nations and on the international level. While it is true that man eats the bread produced by the work of his hands— and this means not only the daily bread by which his body keeps alive but also the bread of science and progress, civilization and culture—it is also a perennial truth that he eats this bread by "the sweat of his face," that is to say, not only by personal effort and toil, but also in the midst of many tensions, conflicts and crises, which in relationship with the reality of work disturb the life of individual societies and also of all humanity. . . .

The Church finds in the very first pages of the Book of Genesis the source of its conviction that work is a fundamental dimension of human existence on earth. An analysis of these texts makes us aware that they express—sometimes in an archaic way of manifesting thought—the fundamental truths about man, in the context of the mystery of creation itself. These truths are decisive for man from the very beginning, and at the same time they trace out the main lines of his earthly existence, both in the state of original justice and also after the breaking, caused by sin, of the Creator's original covenant with creation in man. When man, who had been created "in the image of God . . . male and female," hears the words: "Be fruitful and multiply, and fill the earth and subdue it," even though these words do not refer directly and explicitly to work, beyond any doubt they indirectly indicate it as an activity for man to carry out in the world. Indeed, they show its very deepest essence. Man is the image of God partly through the mandate received from his Creator to subdue, to dominate, the earth. In carrying out this mandate, man, every human being, reflects the very action of the Creator of the universe.

Work understood as a transitive activity, that is to say, an activity beginning in the human subject and directed toward an external object, presupposes a specific dominion by man over "the earth," and in its turn it confirms and develops this dominion. It is clear that the term "the earth" of which the biblical text speaks is to be understood in the first place as that fragment of the visible universe that man inhabits. By extension, however, it can be understood as the whole of the visible world insofar as it comes within the range of man's influence and of his striving to satisfy his needs. The expression "subdue the earth" has an immense range. It means all the resources that the earth (and indirectly the visible world) contains and which, through the conscious activity of man, can be discovered and used for his ends. And so these words, placed at the beginning of the Bible, never cease to be relevant. They embrace equally the past ages of civilization and economy, as also the whole of modern reality and future phases of development, which are perhaps already to some extent beginning to take shape, though for the most part they are still almost unknown to man and hidden from him.

While people sometimes speak of periods of "acceleration" in the economic life and civilization of humanity or of individual nations, linking these periods to the progress of science and technology and especially to discoveries which are decisive for social and economic life, at the same time it can be said that none of these phenomena of "acceleration" exceeds the essential content of what was said in that most ancient of biblical texts. As man, through his work, becomes more and more the master of the earth, and as he confirms his dominion over the visible world, again through his work, he nevertheless remains in every case and at every phase of this process within the Creator's original ordering. And this ordering remains necessarily and indissolubly linked with the fact that man was created, as male and female, "in the image of God." This process is, at the same time, universal: It embraces all human beings, every generation, every phase of economic and cultural development, and at the same time it is a process that takes place within each human being, in each conscious human subject. Each and every individual is at the same time embraced by it. Each and every individual, to the proper extent and in an incalculable number of ways, takes part in the giant process whereby man "subdues the earth" through his work. . . .

Man has to subdue the earth and dominate, because as the "image of God" he is a person, that is to say, a subjective being capable of acting in a planned and rational way, capable of deciding about himself and with a tendency to self-realization. As a person, man is therefore the subject of work. As a person he works; he performs various actions belonging to the work process. Independently of their objective content, these actions must all serve to realize his humanity, to fulfill the calling to be a person that is his by reason of his very humanity. The principal truths concerning this theme were recently recalled by the Second Vatican Council in the Constitution "Gaudium et Spes," especially in Chapter 1, which is devoted to man's calling.

And so this "dominion" spoken of in the biblical text being meditated upon here not only refers to the objective dimension of work, but at the same time introduces us to an understanding of its subjective dimension. Understood as a process whereby man and the human race subdue the earth, work corresponds to this basic biblical concept only when throughout the process man manifests himself and confirms himself as the one who "dominates." This dominion, in a certain sense, refers to the subjective dimension even more than to the objective one. This dimension conditions the very ethical nature of work. In fact there is no doubt that human work has an ethical value of its own, which clearly and directly remains linked to the fact that the one who carries it out is a person, a conscious and free subject, that is to say, a subject who decides about himself.

This truth, which in a sense constitutes the fundamental and perennial heart of Christian teaching on human work, has had and continues to have primary significance for the formulation of the important social problems characterizing whole ages.

The ancient world introduced its own typical differentiation of people into classes according to the type of work done. Work which demanded from the worker the exercise of physical strength, the work of muscles and hands, was considered unworthy of free men and was therefore given to slaves. By broadening certain aspects that already belonged to the Old Testament, Christianity brought about a fundamental change of ideas in this field, taking the whole content of the Gospel message as its point of departure, especially the fact that the one who, while being God, became like us in all things devoted most of the years of his life on earth to manual work at the carpenter's bench. This circumstance constitutes in itself the most eloquent "gospel of work," showing that the basis for determining the value of human work is not primarily the kind of work being done, but the fact that the one who is doing it is a person. The sources of the dignity of work are to be sought primarily in the subjective dimension, not in the objective one.

Such a concept practically does away with the very basis of the ancient differentiation of people into classes according to the kind of work done. This does not mean that from the objective point of view human work cannot and must not be rated and qualified in any way. It only means that the primary basis of the value of work is man himself, who is its subject. This leads immediately to a very important conclusion of an ethical nature: However true it may be that man is destined for work and called to it, in the first place work is "for man" and not man "for work." Through this conclusion one rightly comes to recognize the preeminence of the subjective meaning of work over the objective one. Given this way of understanding things and presupposing that different sorts of work that people do can have greater or lesser objective value, let us try nevertheless to show that each sort is judged above all by the measure of the dignity of the subject of work, that is to say, the person, the individual who carries it out. On the other hand, independent of the work that every man does, and presupposing that this work constitutes a purpose— at times a very demanding one—of his activity, this purpose does not possess a definitive meaning in itself. In fact, in the final analysis it is always man who is the purpose of the work, whatever work it is that is done by man— even if the common scale of values rates it as the merest "service," as the most monotonous, even the most alienating work. . . .

God's fundamental and original intention with regard to man, whom he created in his image and after his likeness, was not withdrawn or canceled out even when man, having broken the original covenant with God, heard the words: "In the sweat of your face you shall eat bread." These words refer to the sometimes heavy toil that from then onward has accompanied human work; but they do not alter the fact that work is the means whereby man achieves that "dominion" which is proper to him over the visible world, by "subjecting" the earth. Toil is something that is universally known, for it is universally experienced. It is familiar to those doing physical work under sometimes exceptionally laborious conditions. It is familiar not only to agricultural workers, who spend long days working the land, which sometimes "bears thorns and thistles," but also to those who work in mines and quarries, to steelworkers at their blast furnaces, to those who work in builders' yards and in construction work, often in danger of injury or death. It is also familiar to those at an intellectual workbench; to scientists; to those who bear the burden of grave responsibility for decisions that will have a vast impact on society. It is familiar to doctors and nurses, who spend days and nights at their patients' bedside. It is familiar to women, who sometimes without proper recognition on the part of society and even of their own families bear the daily burden and responsibility for their homes and the upbringing of their children. It is familiar to all workers and, since work is a universal calling, it is familiar to everyone.

And yet in spite of all this toil—perhaps, in a sense, because of it—work is a good thing for man. Even though it bears the mark of a "bonum arduum," in the terminology of St. Thomas, this does not take away the fact that, as such, it is a good thing for man. It is not only good in the sense that it is useful or something to enjoy; it is also good as being something worthy, that is to say, something that corresponds to man's dignity, that expresses this dignity and increases it. If one wishes to define more clearly the ethical meaning of work, it is this truth that one must particularly keep in mind. Work is a good thing for man—a good thing for his humanity—because through work man not only transforms nature, adapting it to his own needs, but he also achieves fulfillment as a human being and indeed in a sense becomes "more a human being. . . ."

3

....

The Work Ethic in Transition

INTRODUCTION

Chapter Three looks at the movement away from the traditional work ethic and toward a new type of worker and workplace. Much of the transition is tied to two major changes. The first is the movement of the American economy from a manufacturing base to a service-sector economy, and the second is the enormous post–World War II increase in the standard of living and affluence.

The opening selection examines relative rates of job satisfaction and concludes with the observation that self-fulfillment is becoming a major goal of today's worker. While much of this can be attributed to a culture that affords the luxury of self-fulfillment, the authors also credit the decline of Puritan asceticism and the rise of technology, urbanization, and secularization with contributing to the need for a new work ethic. They suggest a choice between a "new work ethic of self-fulfillment and service" and a solipsistic search for fulfilling work.

The second piece—"The Survival of Work"—deals with the persistence of paid employment, even in the face of reduced need. While the work hours necessary for the purchase of goods and services have consistently declined, the percentage of the population employed has risen. Rather than not work, the population seeks ever increased standards of living. The authors predict no revolution in the workplace but an increased demand for vacation, holidays, and flex-time to allow for increased leisure-time use of increased income.

Daniel Yankelovich, in "The New Psychological Contracts at Work," and Renwick and Lawler in "What You Really Want from Your Job," point to new value structures—born of a generation raised in the sixties—which require of work a whole new set of psychological satisfactions. Again, the rise of standards of living and the growth of a generation raised in relative affluence have added issues of self-esteem and well-being to the equation of work and income. While this may or may not be a temporary phenomenon, tied to a

64

healthy economy, it is an important consideration even if seen only as a major influence on job satisfaction.

U.S. News & World Report's "The New-Collar Class" is a report on the largest segment of the baby-boom generation. As the economy has moved from manufacturing to service-based, the attitudes and dispositions of the employed have remained relatively stable. The lunch pail has been replaced by the styrofoam cheeseburger box—just as the punch press has been replaced by the CRT (cathode ray tube)—but the nature of the new working class is a reincarnation of blue-collar concerns.

Our own article—"Woman's Work"—is an analysis of women's attitudes toward work and the workplace's attitudes toward them. We examine the notion of occupation as a source of identity and the conflict between work and the family.

Finally, Pomer's "Mobility of Women into the Economic Mainstream" is a statistical look at low-level, low-paying jobs and the avenues of upward mobility that men have traditionally used to leave them. While women have entered directly into professional ranks in increasing numbers, they have only 40 percent as many channels for upward mobility as men if they begin in low-paying jobs.

This chapter is about change and transition. It leads logically to the next—a search for new ways of making sense of work.

Changing Attitudes Toward Work

MICHAEL MACCOBY AND KATHERINE A. TERZI
WHAT HAPPENED TO THE WORK ETHIC? ....

Are Americans less motivated to work now? What is the evidence of a decline in motivation to work? One approach to answering this question is to examine changes in attitudes to work. Another is to examine objective indicators of motivation, such as absenteeism and turnover. Studies over the last quarter century share one conclusion: the issue is complex and confusing. Some groups are satisfied with certain aspects of work and not others. Some groups report high levels of satisfaction and others low levels. From our point of view this is not surprising. For example, we would expect individuals with a strong

Michael Maccoby and Katherine A. Terzi, "What Happened to the Work Ethic?" in W. Michael Hoffman and Thomas J. Wyly (eds.), *The Work Ethic in Business* (Cambridge, Mass.: Oelgeschlager, Gunn, and Hain, Publishers, 1981). Reprinted by permission of the publishers.

career ethic to be satisfied with work if they felt they were moving up organizational hierarchies, and dissatisfied if stuck, but not really greatly concerned about the substance or meaning of the work itself or its social value. We would expect those with the craftsman's ethic to be satisfied, if they had the opportunity to perform skilled work with good pay, and dissatisfied, if they did not. But surveys do not provide information on the fit between work ethics and social character in relation to job characteristics. Rather, we can only infer these relationships by focusing on distinctions between different socioeconomic, occupational, and cultural subgroups in relation to work attitudes and satisfaction. . . .

For most people the issue is not: Do I still want to work? as much as: Does my job turn me off? Surveys show a consistently strong affirmation of the value of work for three-quarters of the population. When asked if they would continue to work even if they could live comfortably for the rest of their lives without working, most people choose to work. This holds constant throughout several surveys, the percentage choosing to work ranging from 67.4 percent (1969, University of Michigan), 71.5 percent (1977, University of Michigan), 73 percent (1974, Yankelovich, *The New Morality*), to 75 percent (1978, Renwick & Lawler).[1] About the same proportion don't think they would be happier if they "didn't have to work at all": 76.3 percent (1977, University of Michigan). A full 84 percent of college-age youth in 1973 believed it was "very important to do any job (one was doing) well. . . ."

If we accept the premise that Americans still believe in the value of work well done and most want the chance to work, how can we understand indications of dissatisfaction? The first explanation is that while working remains important, other arenas of life—leisure, family—are also gaining in importance. The second explanation, which we will explore now, concerns dissatisfaction, not with work per se, but with the actual jobs that people hold and the nature of supervision. Do existing work patterns, rewards, and incentives engage and motivate employees? Or, do they cause people to withdraw, disaffected, perhaps focusing their productive energies outside of work? One observer put it well:

> That the work ethic—that collection of beliefs, attitudes and aspirations about work—is changing, I have no doubt. Whether it is eroding—in the sense that individuals are losing the commitment to, and pride and satisfaction in, work—remains to be seen. . . . If in the face of changing work values, employers attempt to continue the traditional patterns and habits of organizing, managing and motivating people, they will be on a collision course with the future and the work ethic will most surely be eroded.[2]

There is evidence to suggest some jobs are less satisfying despite a still high motivation to work. One item on the University of Michigan survey supports this view. When asked: "If you were free to go into any type of job you wanted, what would your choice be?" the results were:

	1969	1973	1977
The job he or she now has:	48.2	43.7	38.1%
Retire and not work at all:	6.3	4.6	1.9%
Prefer some other job to the job he or she has now:	44.4	51.7	60.0%

15.6% increase. . . .

JOB SATISFACTION: DEMOGRAPHIC DIFFERENCES

Who is most dissatisfied? Who is most satisfied? Whose attitudes are changing most? Do we know why? There is general agreement that the most dissatisfied sectors of the labor force are young (under 30), black, and low income (under $10,000). The most satisfied are older (over 50), in professional/managerial occupations or self-employed. Dissatisfaction has been increasing most for those with some high school education or a college degree, those in the 21–29 age bracket, the wage and salaried, men, professional/administrative/managerial employees, operatives, and nonfarm laborers.

Beyond these sketchy generalizations, the picture gets cloudy. Different studies report contradictory conclusions, which is not surprising since demographic categories lump together different types of people in terms of character and competencies. Despite these limitations . . . the categories most often referenced and used for drawing distinctions in terms of work attitudes are:

age
income level
race
sex
educational attainment
occupation (particularly blue-collar—white-collar, and nonmanagerial—
    professional/managerial differences). . . .

1. **Age:** Numerous reports in newspapers, journals, and television programs have alerted us to a growing unrest of young workers, and surveys support these reports. It is generally agreed that the young (under 30) are among the most dissatisfied workers, while older people (over 50) are among the most satisfied.[3]

What contributes to this widespread malaise? Is it really a new phenomenon? Now, as always, the young begin their working lives in entry-level jobs which are usually less interesting, less responsible, and lower-paid than the jobs reserved for those with more experience and training. They are apprentices who are expected to follow orders. However, today more than ever before, young people resent autocratic authority.

What is new is that today's youth have grown up in a socioeconomic context significantly different from that of their parents and grandparents. Most are not immigrants, either from foreign lands, or newly arrived from rural areas to cities almost as alien to them as to their foreign-born counterparts. Unions and government have established basic conditions of employment as rights incorporated into law. Affirmative action and equal access have become rights. The shadow of a major economic depression does not linger in the memories of young workers, and most grew up in a period when rising living standards from year to year came to be taken more and more for granted. With the exception of pockets of hopelessness in the inner cities and rural outposts, few people live with the expectation of long periods of unemployment and hardship. Thanks to government programs, such as unemployment and workmen's compensation, and unions' negotiated supplementary benefits, most workers and their families are protected against at least the worst effects of joblessness. These changes have, of course, had an impact on the population as a whole. But the young, with no other experience, have been most affected by these conditions, which they take as a matter of course and a matter of right. Changes in society have changed the social character so that it is less frightened and submissive, more self-affirmative and critical of inequity. There is no evidence that large numbers of young people are trying to avoid work. However, their reasons for working and the terms on which they will work show changing values. If these values are frustrated at work, young workers may increasingly seek to disengage themselves from their jobs.

2. **Income:** Of course, low income contributes to job dissatisfaction.[4] The growing concern for nonmaterial rewards at work does not replace the wish for material rewards. Concern for good pay, job security, a decent living, and the opportunities it affords does not exclude a concern for interesting, self-fulfilling work. Those who feel their compensation is inequitable or who feel stuck in low-paying jobs are dissatisfied.

3. **Race:** Blacks are consistently less satisfied with their jobs than are whites. This is true of all categories except one: neither white nor black workers over 44 are comparatively dissatisfied.[5] Young blacks are especially unhappy about their employment situation, their work *and* lack of it. Estimates of black youth unemployment range from 46–60 percent.[6] When they manage to find a job, it tends to be both low-paid and low in intrinsic rewards. When young blacks find employment, it is usually in jobs noted for high job dissatisfaction: as unskilled laborers or as operatives. It is not surprising, then, to learn that this group—young, low-paid, black workers—reports the "highest levels of depression," gauged from questions such as "How often do you feel down-hearted and blue?"[7] The revitalization of these down-hearted, written-off sectors of the population is one of the most complicated and serious challenges facing America. It requires understanding the social character of these young people

in relation to their opportunities, and developing social policy which brings out the best in them.

4. Occupation: Operatives and nonfarm laborers are the two least satisfied occupational groups by most accounts. They are also the groups with the sharpest *declines* in satisfaction between 1969 and 1977.[8] Service workers and clerical workers are the next most dissatisfied groups. In general, blue-collar workers appear more dissatisfied than white-collar workers, but when professional/managerial white-collar employees are excluded, the rest (the clerks, typists, etc.) increasingly resemble blue-collar workers. Professional and managerial employees, in contrast, are among the most satisfied groups, but they are also becoming more dissatisfied.[9]

Overall, professional, managerial, highly skilled, or self-employed workers are most satisfied, while the unskilled, clerical, sales, or service workers are least so. A recent *Harvard Business Review* article calls this the "hierarchy gap," and points to an increasing similarity of attitudes between lower-level employees regardless of collar color, when compared to their professional and administrative higher-ups. They conclude:

> The distinctions that once clearly separated clerical and hourly employees are becoming blurred. Both groups value and expect to get intrinsic satisfactions from work (e.g., respect, equity, and responsiveness), which were formerly reserved for managers. The work force itself and what it demonstrably values are indeed changing: all parts of the work force are beginning to overtly articulate their needs for achievement, recognition, and job challenge.[10]

5. Educational Attainment: Level of formal education by itself does not appear to appreciably determine job satisfaction. On the whole, those with most (graduate level) and least (8 years or less) schooling are more satisfied than the vast majority who have some high school education up through an undergraduate degree.[11] Satisfaction has dropped in all categories (except graduate level). The largest numerical increases in the labor force come in precisely those groups who are comparatively less satisfied; that is, those with some high school up to college graduates. This category is growing: between 1948 and 1972, the average educational attainment of the labor force increased from 10.6 years to just beyond high school (12.4 years). The increase in education of the American population is striking. Between 1950 and 1975, the percent of Americans aged 25 and over with a high school diploma almost doubled, from 34 percent to 63 percent.[12] As we have noted, many of these people are experiencing dissatisfaction with work that does not ask enough of them. The combination of low income and some college is a sure formula for discontent.

Daniel Yankelovich's comparative studies of youth (noncollege, college, some college education) offer evidence for the view that a general change in social character (and the work ethic) is occurring. He concludes that young people without a college education want the same sorts of personal satisfactions and opportunities in their work as do their college-educated peers, but they have little hope of attaining them in a labor market where *one-third* already say they are overeducated for their jobs. [13]

6. Sex: Differences between men and women regarding job satisfaction are not conclusive. Some studies report higher satisfaction on the part of men; some by women; and some no significant differences. [14] Although there was not much difference between men's and women's attitudes in the 1977 University of Michigan Survey, male job satisfaction did show a significantly greater *decline* between 1969 and 1977 than did that of women. [15] Most observers agree that the increase of women in the work force has profound consequences for the organization of work, but there is less agreement on the nature of these consequences. Clearly the desire for flexible working hours was initiated and fueled by the entry of women into the workplace. Still primarily responsible for home and children but anxious to work outside the home, women are seeking flexible hours in hopes of balancing demands of family and work.

What do we know about why women are seeking paid employment in unprecedented numbers? What satisfies and dissatisfies them? And, how does work compare in importance to home and family?

Clearly there are many reasons why women take jobs. First, economic needs. Many married women consider a second income necessary to maintain their standard of living. In 1977, 21 percent of those surveyed said their family income was inadequate for meeting monthly expenses. For 57 percent of those same respondents, this posed a "sizeable" or "great" problem. [16] Also, as divorce becomes commonplace, women can no longer depend on their husbands for support.

The combination of inflation's erosion of household income, expectations of a comfortable standard of living, and changing attitudes of women and men towards working mothers, as well as availability of child care, have contributed to a dramatic change in the American household. According to Rosabeth Moss Kantor: "The traditional nuclear family—husband as breadwinner, wife not in the paid labor force—now accounts for *fewer than 20 percent of all American families*. The number of single-parent households has risen dramatically" (our emphasis). [17]

Second, independence and self-development are goals which some women try to achieve by taking paid employment. Desiring more egalitarian relationships with their husbands, they want to contribute directly to their family income; or they want their own income separate from their husbands', and not subject to male control.

When they take a job, are they likely to find it satisfying? On a number of counts, they may find it wanting: pay, status, intrinsic interest, responsibility, authority.

Despite affirmative action programs and gains by women in recent years in advancing to managerial levels and in entering occupations formerly the sole province of men, women remain concentrated in lower-level, lower-paid, and lower-status jobs in a few sectors, mainly clerical and services (52.9 percent in 1974). In 1970, over a third of working women were concentrated in only seven occupations: secretary, retail saleswoman, household worker, elementary schoolteacher, bookkeeper, waitress, or nurse. Half of all women workers were concentrated in only twenty-one occupations, in contrast to a much broader distribution of men over sixty-five occupations. The segregation of women into relatively few sex-specific jobs is further illustrated by the fact that in 1960 over half of working women held jobs where 70 percent or more of their co-workers were also women.[18]

These are also sectors where dissatisfaction is concentrated and increasing. However, most surveys do not find significantly greater dissatisfaction on the part of women over men. The exception is women with preschool children (under 6 years old). They register higher job dissatisfaction for reasons which we can only speculate about: perhaps juggling child-rearing responsibilities with a job; perhaps they have lower-paying jobs;[19] or perhaps they would prefer to spend more time with their children.[20] More in-depth studies are needed to understand the causes of such reported dissatisfaction and to understand the goals of women at work.

Summary: Sorting out reports of demographic characteristics, a general profile emerges of the most and least satisfied sectors of the labor force:

MOST SATISFIED	LEAST SATISFIED
Middle-aged or older	Under thirty years
White	Black
Graduate education	Some high school through college degree, especially if overeducated for jobs
Professionals/managers/administrators	Unskilled laborers or operatives Low income (under $10,000)

Declines in job satisfaction, however, are reported across-the-board for most sectors of the labor force. Demographic differences show some trends, but many researchers consider that they are "not generally the best indicators of job satisfaction."[21] How else can we understand differences between groups of people? Very few studies are available that focus on understanding differences in job satisfaction based on character and culture.[22] Yet many reports allude to such differences. All descriptions of a "new breed" of worker, the "new narcissism," the "me generation," and so on refer to a change in the American character. Following these observers, we find evidence of such an attitudinal change emerging, from the career ethic to the self-fulfillment, self-development ethic.

No work ethic fits all Americans, but most Americans are motivated to work. For some, work is an expression of religious belief. For some, it is craftsmanship. Some are driven by entrepreneurial dreams. Some strive to climb the corporate ladder to success or at least to a position of "status." Some seek a form of self-fulfillment through service.

A great many individuals who are motivated to work are dissatisfied with employment that blocks their strivings for self-fulfillment and that does not fit their work ethic. The frustrated craftsman forced into monotonous work may become angry and careless. The hard-working careerist "stuck" in a dead-end job that allows neither learning nor promotion may become bitter. Many of those who feel bored and powerless at work lose interest and look for satisfactions outside. These can be either self-developing activities—childrearing, community service, gardening, crafts, sports—or activities that support an escapist, consumer attitude, encouraged by television images of enjoyment. The evidence from studies indicates, however, that unfulfilling work stimulates escapist, rather than self-developing leisure, and that it is difficult to develop and maintain an active attitude to life when one is continually turned off at work.[23] This issue of human productivity is not limited to the workplace. Rather, it is an issue of national character and national vitality. Unless leadership in business, government, and unions understands what motivates people, it is likely to bring out the worst rather than the best in a changing national character.

CONCLUSION: THE CHANGING AMERICAN CHARACTER

To understand the changes in the American character that have caused increased dissatisfaction with work, we need to examine two broad interrelated historical currents.

One current is the transformation of traditional rural to modern urban values based on innovations in technology, increased education, and the disappearance of a sense of independence rooted in self-employment and the entrepreneurial ethic. The other is the decline of patriarchal authority based on new demands for human rights and the changed role of women, such as equality in the workplace. These are, of course, trends. Although some people, especially in rural areas, are still rooted in the older patterns, and different social character types (e.g., craftsmen and careerist) express these changes differently, the trends affect everyone.

One of the most significant social changes in America in this century has been the migration from farms and small towns to the cities. Traditional rural values included fundamentalist religious belief and an ascetic ethic of self-sacrifice, either for personal salvation or for family welfare. Unlike in farm society, the unity of family and religious community is no longer necessary for survival. The majority today must adapt to a different reality of large organizations, where success depends on technical or professional competence and the ability to cooperate with different types of people. Although Americans are still more religious than many West Europeans, the modern urban individual is more skeptical about religion and beliefs that separate people than his rural counterpart, and more oriented to self-fulfillment rather than to God or family. Technological advances have lessened the need for hard physical work and stimulated new desires for entertainment. Technology for the home as well as telecommunications and personal transportation have freed women from housework and isolation in the household. Education has encouraged more people to aspire to higher status. Freed somewhat by technology and affluence from the tyranny of necessity, individuals of all classes have broken old taboos and sought experiences that in the past were the exclusive property of the rich. From a psychoanalytic point of view, both sexual liberation (based on new contraceptive technology and the erosion of traditional values) and the media's message to consume rather than save, which in the expansive 1950s and 60s appeared economically positive, has undermined the main mechanisms of the traditional, up-tight, hoarding character. The negative traits of the new character are narcissistic modes of self-fulfillment, self-centeredness, greediness, and lack of concern for others. The positive traits are increased concern and personal responsibility for self-development and personal health, freedom to learn and experiment.

The disappearance of self-employment is, in large measure, a result of the demise of the family farm and the small town services that supported it, and the growth of corporate forms of organization, aided by innovations in telecommunication and data processing. Gone with self-employment is the comforting idea that if one does not like work in the organization, he can always go out and start his own business. Increasingly, the sense of independence is rooted in technical, professional, and managerial skills, rather than ownership of a farm or a business. The negative traits that have resulted are those of careerist self-marketing, the need to sell oneself, to become an attractive package at the expense of integrity. The positive traits are those of flexibility and tolerance, and the need to understand and cooperate with strangers.

The decline in patriarchy has resulted both from urban values, from a science and information based technology, and from many challenges to the domination of the father and the boss. Unions, welfare and unemployment payments, the civil rights movement, the women's movement, and protest against the great wars of the twentieth century have enlarged the concept of human rights and destroyed the automatic respect for authority traditionally held by the autocratic patriarchal figure in both business and government. The decline of patriarchy results in the demand for rights, as opposed to protection by a powerful figure (although, like adolescents, some people want both).

For organizations, the negative side of this trend has been the crisis of authority. Lacking respect for traditional bosses and institutions, employees become cynical, rebellious, and expert at beating the system. The positive side is a critical, questioning attitude. This is combined with the wish for mutual respect and involvement in an organization run on principles of equity and concern for individual development that is based on voluntary cooperation rather than submission.

In other words, the rebellious spirit can either undermine authority or transform the authority structure. How will this transformation take place? Union-Management Cooperative Projects to change work in Bolivar, Tennessee (Harman-UAW) and Springfield, Ohio (city management-AFSCME) have been achieved through collective bargaining, but they have required managers able to act as resources rather than bosses.

These projects and others have demonstrated that the primary tasks of leadership at work are to understand different attitudes, different strivings for self-fulfillment, and to establish operating principles that build trust, facilitate cooperation, and explain the significance of the individual's role in the common purpose. What brings out the worst in employees, including middle and lower levels of management, is a sense of powerlessness due to size and anonymous authority that treats everyone like a part in a large machine and denies individuality. Insecurity, suspicion, rumor, and a sense of injustice grow in organizations where employees do not understand the reasons for decisions and do not have a say in how work is organized and evaluated.

Our experience in projects to improve work in both industry and government is that only a small minority of workers have a negative character structure that is immune to good leadership and the resulting peer pressure to cooperate. This is a generation prepared to communicate, and responsive to reasonable explanations. Leadership will bring out the best in the emerging American character only by welcoming the positive aspects of that character, the needs for involvement, personal development, including life-long learning at work and equity. This becomes a necessity in an era of limits when concern for the common good must temper the career ethic.

How will future technology affect these changes? Changing technology in both industry and offices provides possibilities for involving employees in the organization of work, but only if leadership is able to develop the trust and involvement necessary.[24] In an information-based society, there are increasing needs for service, but again, the quality of service will depend on the quality of leadership. Some of the most talented college graduates seek self-fulfillment by making a meaningful social contribution through public service, believing that business is not an institution that serves society. Often, they are disappointed by the lack of orientation to service in government as opposed to policing and control. Real opportunities for service are, in fact, great in both government and business, but again, this requires leadership sensitive to bringing out the best in people by a commitment to ethical as well as economic values.

Is this leadership a new form of benevolent patriarchal authority? That is unlikely, since in most large organizations, managers are employees also. Trust depends, not on the owner's good faith, but on a "constitutional" system of rights and obligations. However, even within such a system managerial leadership concerned about people as well as profit is necessary to bring out the best in people.

If leadership in business, unions and government does not help to establish a new work ethic of self-development and service by appealing to the positive elements in the American character, it is likely that the traditional work ethics will be replaced by a negative search for "self-fulfillment." This ambiguous ethic can mean either greedy cravings to have more for oneself, or it can mean demands for employment that serves both personal growth and social welfare. It can mean development of one's authentic interests in the arts, sciences, and professions; or it can mean a drive to win at any price.[25] As long as we do not distinguish ethically based self-development from other modes of self-fulfillment, and organize work to support what is most productive in the American character, the new ethic may contribute to undermining the motivation to work.

NOTES

[1] Daniel Yankelovich, *The New Morality* (New York: McGraw-Hill Book Co., 1974), surveyed college-age youth only; Renwick and Lawler surveyed readers of *Psychology Today* (May 1978); the University of Michigan Survey of Working Conditions was a nationwide statistical sampling of all employed persons.

A 1955 study suggests this may have declined. In 1955, between 58 percent (unskilled workers) and 91 percent (sales workers) of employed men studied chose to continue working. Figures are not available as totals, only detailed by occupation and class. Comparability with the more recent studies is further reduced since they surveyed both men and women while the 1955 study included only men. However, additional evidence of a decline comes from the University of Michigan 1969 Survey which reports that a 1960 sample of employed men responded 80 percent in favor of working, up from 78 percent in 1950 (Weiss and Kahn). The 1969 Michigan Survey reported only 73.3 percent of men would continue working, a decline of about 7 percent (University of Michigan Survey, 1969, p. 45), in male workers' attraction to work in general. N. C. Morse and R. S. Weiss, "Function and Meaning of Work and the Job," *American Sociological Review*, vol. 20, no. 2, April 1955, p. 197. Cited in: Robert S. Weiss and David Reisman, "Social Problems and Disorganization in the World of Work," *Contemporary Social Problems*, Robert K. Merton and Robert A. Nisbet, eds. (New York: Harcourt, Brace & World, 1961).

[2] Ian H. Wilson, "Here Comes Change, Ready Or Not," *Mainliner Magazine*, vol. 23, no. 5, 1979.

[3] It is interesting to note the University of Michigan (1977) reports that workers under 21 showed no increase in dissatisfaction between 1973 and 1977. Their dissatisfaction was already among the highest in the labor force. It would be interesting to trace the satisfaction of a cohort of workers through several years, especially if such a study included social character and type of work.

[4] Considered as under $5,000 or between $5,000 and $10,000, depending on the survey used. Patricia A. Renwick and Edward E. Lawler, "What You Really Want from Your Job," *Psychology Today*, May 1978. Sar A. Levitan and William B. Johnston, *Work Is Here to Stay, Alas* (Salt Lake City, Ut.: Olympus Publishing Company), 1973.

[5] Levitan and Johnston, *op. cit.* It is interesting to note that although their dissatisfaction is lower than blacks, white workers' dissatisfaction is increasing at about the same *rate* as that of black workers.

[6] Daniel Yankelovich, "The New Psychological Contracts at Work," *Psychology Today*, May 1978, p. 47.

[7] Renwick and Lawler, "What You Really Want from Your Job." Granted readers of *Psychology Today* are a very specialized sample, this finding is also supported by Gallup poll and other reports, indicating that general life satisfaction and job satisfaction go hand-in-hand.

[8] Blue-collar craft workers are also reported as becoming more dissatisfied, although still basically satisfied.

[9] Robert P. Quinn and Graham L. Staines, The 1977 Survey, p. 306. *The Harvard Business Review* article cited below, however, finds that managerial discontent is not increasing.

[10] Michael R. Cooper, *et al.*, "Changing Employee Values: Deepening Discontent?" p. 118.

[11] Robert P. Quinn and Graham L. Staines, *The 1977 Quality of Employment Survey* (hereafter *The 1977 Survey*) (Ann Arbor, Michigan: Survey Research Center, Institute for Social Research, University of Michigan, 1977), p. 306.

[12] George Strauss, "Workers: Attitudes and Adjustments," in Jerome Rosow (ed.), *The Worker and the Job* (Englewood Cliffs, N.J.: Prentice-Hall, Inc., 1974). Bill Cunningham, "Bringing Productivity Into Focus," *The AFL-CIO American Federationist*, May 1979, vol. 86, no. 5, p. 6.

[13] Daniel Yankelovich, in Rosow, "The Workplace," p. 41.

[14] Renwick and Lawler, "What You Really Want from Your Job," p. 55.

[15] Why is open to speculation in the absence of studies on the question. Daniel Yankelovich foresees an erosion of male job satisfaction as a consequence of the increased female labor force participation rate as the male role as family provider undergoes change. "If . . . the man's role as he-who-makes-sacrifices-for-his-kid's-education-and-his-family's-material-well-being grows less vital, the whole fragile bargain threatens to break down. . . . One unanticipated and unwanted by-product of the women's movement may be to intensify men's disaffection with their work . . . (and) puts at risk a fragile psychosocial balance which has supported men's job satisfaction for many years." Daniel Yankelovich, in Rosow, "The Workplace: A Changing Scene," p. 45.

[16] Robert P. Quinn and Graham L. Staines, *The 1977 Survey*, p. 48.

[17] Rosabeth Moss Kantor, "A Good Job Is Hard To Find," *Working Papers*, May–June 1979, p. 45.

[18] Carolyn J. Jacobson, "Women Workers: Profile of a Growing Force," *AFL-CIO American Federationist*, July 1974. Also, Eli Ginzberg, "The Changing American Economy and Labor Force," in Rosow, "The Workplace."

[19] Robert P. Quinn and Graham L. Staines, *The 1977 Survey*, pp. 10–11.

[20] There is some evidence to suggest that many women still prefer to stay home rather than work for pay: . . . the percentage of wives who work outside the home declines, as family income rises, from nearly half whose husbands earn $3,000–$7,000, to less than 20% whose husbands earn $25,000. Levitan and Johnston, *Work Is Here to Stay, Alas*, p. 78.

[21] Levitan and Johnston, *op. cit.*, p. 73.

[22] Charles F. Sabel, "Marginal Workers in Industrial Society," *Challenge*, March-April 1979, is an exception.

[23] There are two theories concerning the effects of the quality of working life on the quality of leisure. One is called "the tradeoff hypothesis" and the other, "the spillover argument." The spillover argument maintains that the way people feel about their jobs will "spillover" into their life outside work. People with uninteresting, dissatisfying jobs can't be expected to lead productive, active lives after they punch out. Preliminary studies seem to confirm this view. But caution (and further study) is needed on this point. It could also be that dissatisfying homelife and leisure "spillover" into work.

According to the tradeoff or compensatory hypothesis, people dissatisfied at work turn to their life outside for their satisfaction and development. Of course this happens. What is at issue is the quality of nonwork activities. Is it possible to sustain an active challenging, leisure time when work is dull and boring? The limited evidence available suggests it's not likely. However, research on this topic is not conclusive, and much more study is needed to understand the ways in which different people adapt to unsatisfying work life, home life, free time and the changes in work and culture needed to stimulate human development. Robert P. Quinn, Graham L. Staines, and Margaret R. McCullough, *Job Satisfaction: Is There a Trend?* Manpower Research Monograph no. 30, document no. 2900-00195 (Washington, D.C.: U.S. Government Printing Office, 1974). George Strauss, "Workers: Attitudes and Adjustments," in Jerome Rosow (ed.), *The Worker and the Job* (Englewood Cliffs, N.J.: Prentice-Hall, Inc., 1974).

[24] See the work of Richard Walton on the office of the future.

[25] The work of Abraham Maslow, so often quoted by managers, has contributed to this confusion, with an amoral concept of "self-actualization" as the highest level of human development. Maslow implies that when "lower needs" for survival, security, belongingness, status, and self-esteem are met, individuals automatically seek self-actualization. He fails to distinguish between self-actualization as an expression of self-indulgence and that which expresses an ethically based striving to overcome greed and egocentrism through the development of both head and heart. For a critique of Maslow's concept, see Michael Maccoby, *The Gamesman*, chapter 8.

SAR A. LEVITAN AND CLIFFORD M. JOHNSON
THE SURVIVAL OF WORK ....

THE GROWING LABOR FORCE

. . . Rather than abandoning work, Americans have sought it in unprecedented numbers. The U.S. labor force has more than tripled in size since the turn of the century, and the relative percentage of the population that works has crept steadily upwards since World War II. The slow growth in the ratio of workers to the working-age population is particularly significant when viewed in light of gains in productivity. Despite an enormous decrease during this century in the amount of human labor required to produce given quantities of goods, no

Sar A. Levitan and Clifford M. Johnson, "The Survival of Work," in J. Barbash *et al.* (eds.), *The Work Ethic—A Critical Analysis* (Madison, Wis.: Industrial Relations Research Association, 1983). Reprinted by permission of the publisher.

corresponding decrease in the number or relative proportion of workers has taken place. Driven by rising expectations and an abiding interest in relative income gains, individuals have continued their work effort and sought to maintain their share of society's increasing wealth. . . .

Societal gains in wealth have been mirrored in a gradual rise of real earnings since the Great Depression. By impressive margins, American workers have more money than ever before, and until the mid-1970s average real wages moved upward in an unbroken record of annual gains. The disastrous setbacks of the 1930s arrested temporarily the growth of real personal income, but failed to alter the long-term pattern of improved economic status of employed workers. While these average real wage increases have not solved the problems of relative poverty and unequal distribution of wealth, they have represented great gains for the majority of workers.

Workers *have* responded to the potential freedoms of rising productivity and affluence, but not in the manner feared by some. Instead of abandoning work, workers have opted for greater amounts of paid leisure to complement their rising incomes in traditional 40-hour-per-week jobs. Factories have not stood idle, but employers have been faced with demands for more paid holidays and longer vacations as part of the "fringe benefits" of employment. The process is one of gradual evolution, in which individuals continually adjust to rising standards of living and balance further income gains against the utility of additional "free time" away from the workplace. . . .

THE ARRIVAL OF WOMEN AT WORK

The increasing number of people who work each day are a new breed, or at least a distinctly more feminine one. At the turn of the century, the vast majority of workers were men. In the social order of that day, the man was the breadwinner and the woman was the homemaker. Eighty years later, the distribution of labor between the sexes has changed radically—women have joined men at the workplace in record numbers, more than doubling their share in the labor force since 1900 (Figure 1). In more than 60 percent of all marriages today, the husband is not the sole provider for his family. For the first time in history, working wives outnumber housewives. . . .

Why have women rushed with such vigor into the labor force in the course of just a few decades? Some social scientists turn to changing technology— in the bedroom as well as the kitchen—in their attempts to explain the labor market behavior of women. Housekeeping consumes less time today than a few decades ago and the number of children in the home has also declined, leaving more time for work. In addition, a woman now can virtually determine the number of children she will have and when she will have them. As a result of this increasing control, the average number of children per family dropped from 2.3 to 1.9 during the 1970s, with the fertility rate reaching a historic low of 15.3 births per thousand people by 1980. . . .

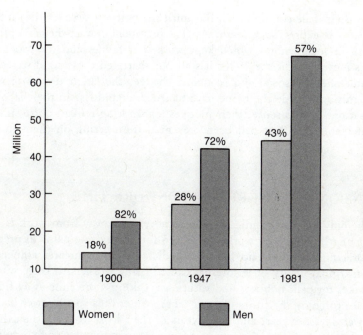

FIGURE 1 Women Comprise Twice as Large a Share of the Labor Force
Source: U.S. Bureau of Labor Statistics.

Traditional economic incentives also can account for only part of the growing labor force participation of women. For some women, economic needs do play a significant role in stimulating work effort—in the aggregate, white wives account for one-quarter of their family income and black wives provide one-third of family income. Without this work effort, many American families could not maintain their middle-class status. Yet the strong inverse relationship between a husband's income and the labor force activity of his wife which once dominated women's work roles has weakened considerably amidst growing affluence. The Bureau of the Census reported that almost 60 percent of the women in families with annual incomes of $25,000 or more worked in 1980. According to a 1980 opinion poll, less than 50 percent of working women took their jobs to support themselves or their families (Roper Organization 1980, p. 36). For most women, only the pursuit of relative income gains provides an economic incentive for working. Many families simply are unwilling to settle for the standard of living their parents enjoyed in the 1950s, and so women continue to enter the labor market.

The rapid movement of women into the workforce has derived its strength and permanence from the same sociological needs for a sense of community, identity, and self-esteem which drive the work efforts of men in an affluent society. Some women no doubt always envied the work roles and related social status of their male counterparts, but until the past few decades they have had little chance to express such yearnings. The precedent of wartime labor provided the crack in social mores which kept women at home, and the more recent women's movement of the 1970s has all but shattered these rigid stereotypes. Once unleashed by social and economic change, the latent desires of women for recognition outside the home have fueled the rapid rise in their labor force participation. In this sense, their motives for working remain quite similar to those of men—they just had been prevented from acting on them in earlier times. . . .

EXPANSION OF LEISURE AND NONWORK TIME

. . . The only pervasive indications of a movement away from work is a slow but growing tendency for workers to forgo further income gains in preference for greater amounts of paid leisure. Predictably, with greater affluence the higher marginal utility of leisure has caused many workers to trade wage and salary hikes for paid holidays and vacations. Taking more time away from the workplace to enjoy the fruits of their labor, Americans spend fewer hours per day, fewer days per year, and fewer years of their lives working than they did in the past. It is this trend, stemming not from any weakening commitment to work but from rational economic judgments of the relative value of income and leisure, which is reshaping the nature of work in the 1980s.

The shift toward greater leisure in itself is not a new phenomenon. In fact, the most spectacular shrinkage in worktime came in the early part of this century from sharp reductions in the length of the average workweek. However, since 1940, much of the gain in free time has been achieved through both paid vacations and paid holidays. Before 1940, few nonmanagerial workers received paid vacations. By 1970, virtually all plant workers and office workers in metropolitan areas worked in establishments that provided paid vacations, with the average full-time worker receiving two full weeks. Similarly, the number of paid holidays more than quadrupled between 1940 and 1980, growing from an average of two to nine days annually. Perhaps the most telling sign of workers' continuing appetite for leisure is that full-week vacations taken without pay rose between 1968 and 1979 from 14 to 20 percent of all vacations for men and from 34 and 39 percent for women (Hedges and Taylor 1980, p. 9). This push for vacations and holidays (plus an increase in the number of part-time workers) has reduced the average annual hours of work by nearly one-fifth during the past four decades.

The rise in the number of families with two or more wage earners may add to the pressure for more time away from the workplace in the years ahead. This push for greater leisure will be partially an outgrowth of the relative affluence of multiple income households, but it may also reflect an increasing pattern of husbands and wives sharing family responsibilities. This mutual acceptance of both provider and parenting roles would require an added measure of flexibility in work hours, and these emerging needs in the modern family may well be translated into future demands for paid leisure and shorter or more personalized work schedules. . . .

NEW SERVICES AND OCCUPATIONS

Even as Americans continue to work, their jobs are constantly changing. Today's jobs are considerably different from those of a century or a few decades ago, with some work roles dwindling as new ones emerge. By weight of numbers, secretaries now deserve more scrutiny than auto workers. Public schoolteachers outnumber all the production workers in the chemical, oil, rubber, plastic, paper, and steel industries combined. The office is replacing the factory as the most common workplace, and employment is shifting to the service sector of the economy with ever-increasing speed.

A sizable and growing segment of the population no longer has even a secondary relationship to the production or distribution of goods, instead providing an array of services of unprecedented scope and diversity. Agriculture, manufacturing, and mining, which once dictated the basic structure of the labor market, are increasingly anachronistic—in the same manner that the industrial revolution reduced the portion of American workers laboring on farms from over 40 percent to less than 3 percent, a contemporary transformation of work is steadily undermining the relative importance of manufacturing as a generator of jobs. In the United States, growth in the service sector accounted for 84 percent of all additional jobs created in the three decades following 1950, and virtually every major industrial country in the world now has at least half its labor force in this tertiary sector (OECD 1978).

The shift toward service employment is in many ways a direct result of rising affluence and technological advance. With machine-supported manufacturing requiring a declining share of the nation's overall work effort, Americans have been able to purchase and to provide services that earlier generations never contemplated. No doubt the surge of women into the labor force has strengthened this demand for personal services, but increasing affluence alone would have aroused a growing appetite for the many amenities of a service economy. Aided by technological advances in fields ranging from health care to home entertainment, the growth of the service sector is now altering our most basic concepts of work and destroying traditional links between work and physical effort. Increasingly, we engage in "abstract" work with symbols instead of tools, producing annual research volumes rather than baking bread. Only an affluent society could afford the luxury of freeing so many of its workers from the production process.

Along with the shift from the manufacturing to the service sector, a parallel transformation of the labor market can be seen in the movement from blue-collar to white-collar employment. Farming was the most common occupation in 1900 and blue-collar workers were most numerous in 1940, but by 1982 slightly more than half of the workforce held white-collar jobs. In 1900, unskilled laborers outnumbered managers and professionals, household servants were more common than professionals, and unskilled workers filled one-third of all blue-collar jobs. In contrast, managers and professionals today outnumber unskilled laborers by more than six to one, professionals are 17 times more prevalent than household servants, and craftsmen and semiskilled workers comprise 85 percent of the blue-collar workforce. The long-term trend is clear—white-collar employment has grown dramatically at the expense of farm and unskilled blue-collar work. . . .

EDUCATED WORKERS: A MIXED BLESSING?

The possibility of future discontent at the workplace emerges not from changes in work, but rather from the educational gains of American workers. Through major public investments in a comprehensive educational system spanning from kindergarten to postgraduate programs, the United States has achieved impressive advances toward the goal of a universally educated population. The median educational attainment of 8.7 years that a worker brought to the job in 1940 rose in four decades to 12.7 years. The greatest gains in education have accrued to those who formerly had the least schooling, and the segment of the labor force with less than three years of high school is expected to continue its sharp decline throughout the 1980s.

Typically, we view education as an unqualified good, and from a societal viewpoint these rising education levels may indeed bode well for our cultural development and for the vitality of our democratic system—at least that's the hope. Yet in a narrower sense, more schooling does not necessarily foster greater contentment among workers. As Americans in all occupations enter the labor market with more education than ever before, the prospect of educational gains outpacing skill requirements becomes more threatening. If the rising educational attainment of workers were accompanied by an increase in the number of demanding and challenging jobs, there would be cause for optimism. Unfortunately, the evidence suggests that the extra certificates and diplomas may produce little more for modern workers than higher goals and more frequent disappointments. . . .

Signs that labor market requirements have not kept pace with the expectations of an educated workforce abound. In a landmark study, Ivar Berg (1970) estimated that in 1970 one-fifth of all college graduates held jobs that did not require their level of educational attainment. Workers' own assessments of the match between their academic credentials and actual job requirements have reinforced that finding; the University of Michigan's 1970 *Survey of Working Conditions* (Survey Research Center 1971, p. 406) found that more than one in three workers believed they had more education than their jobs required. Finally, the data on initial job placements of college graduates in more recent years suggest that the correlation between educational attainment and jobs has not improved—almost 90 percent of college graduates entering the labor force between 1962 and 1968 assumed professional, technical, managerial, or administrative roles, while less than two-thirds of those entering between 1969 and 1976 succeeded in obtaining similar positions.

The potential for a growing mismatch between skill requirements and workers' educational attainment is a source of increasing concern among labor market analysts. According to one estimate, college graduates entering the labor force are likely to exceed job openings in professional and managerial categories by some 2.7 million over the next decade, leaving two and one-half graduates to compete for every choice job (O'Toole 1979, p. 9). A detailed study of the slow change in general skill requirements and rising educational attainment among workers during the period from 1960 to 1976 confirmed that these trends had combined to increase the incidence of "overeducation" in the labor market (Rumberger 1981, p. 97). With employment growth likely to occur primarily in low-skilled clerical, retail trade, and service jobs, this pattern of widening disparities between job opportunities and worker education and expectations seems certain to persist. . . .

The problems arising from the "overeducation" of the workforce are not easily catalogued, but the potential for worker dissatisfaction with jobs that fail to utilize their education is disturbing. The consequences of a mismatch between education and jobs may reach much farther to include deteriorating mental and physical health, falling productivity, and rising frequency of disruptive behavior among workers. The current trends in turnover, absenteeism, and other outward manifestations of worker attitudes are as yet unconvincing in this regard, but our apparent inability to provide suitable opportunities for more educated workers must be a source of serious concern. Collectively at least, we may not be doing our children any favors by sending them off to college and graduate school unless labor market conditions improve in the years ahead.

WHAT THE FUTURE HOLDS

No revolution at the workplace is in the offing. Americans are continuing to work, and in much the same manner as their forefathers. Movement away from work has occurred very slowly in the form of increased leisure and earlier retirement, while overall labor force participation rates have actually climbed in recent years. Workers are more affluent and better educated than ever before, and yet these trends have not triggered any exodus from the workplace. Even if they are indifferent about their jobs, today's workers have not shunned the attachment to work that we associate with the work ethic. . . .

In general, the fear that Americans will abandon work has no rational basis. People work for many different reasons, and even when growing affluence enables workers to obtain more leisure, such gains are taken in gradual increments of paid holidays and vacations. Labor force data suggest that increasing proportions of Americans are working more, not less, opting for leisure only when that step is consistent with a continuing identification with established work roles. While the absolute economic need to work may diminish over time, the desire for relative income gains and the social and psychological functions of work persist. Those who anticipate the demise of work are likely to be disappointed—even as both jobs and workers change, the great majority of Americans no doubt will continue to find reasons to work.

REFERENCES

Berg, Ivar. *Education and Jobs: The Great Training Robbery.* New York: Praeger, 1970.

Hedges, Janice Neipert, and Daniel E. Taylor. "Recent Trends in Worktime: Hours Edge Downward." *Monthly Labor Review* 103 (March 1980), pp. 3–11.

Kreps, Juanita, ed. *Women and the American Economy: A Look to the 1980s.* Englewood Cliffs, N.J.: Prentice-Hall, 1976.

Liebow, Elliot. *Tally's Corner.* Boston: Little, Brown and Co., 1967.

Organisation for Economic Cooperation and Development. *A Medium Term Strategy for Employment and Manpower Policies.* Paris: OECD, 1978.

O'Toole, James. "Education Is Education and Work Is Work—Shall Ever the Twain Meet?" *Teachers College Record* (Fall 1979).

The Roper Organization. *The 1980 Virginia Slims American Women's Opinion Polls.* New York: 1980.

The New Worker

DANIEL YANKELOVICH
THE NEW PSYCHOLOGICAL CONTRACTS AT WORK ....

A new breed of Americans, born out of the social movements of the 60s and grown into a majority in the 70s, holds a set of values and beliefs so markedly different from the traditional outlook that they promise to transform the character of work in America in the 80s. . . .

In the last half century, the field of psychology has added greatly to our understanding of what contributes to people's feelings of well-being. A variety of studies have demonstrated that psychological well-being is a complex structure. Among its chief building blocks are: a sense of self-esteem and conviction of one's worth as an individual; a clear-cut sense of identity; the ability to believe that one's actions make sense to others as well as to oneself;

Daniel Yankelovich, "The New Psychological Contracts at Work," *Psychology Today*, May 1978. Reprinted by permission.

a set of concrete goals and values; feelings of potency and efficacy; enough stimulation to avoid boredom; a feeling that one's world is reasonably stable; and an overall sense of meaning and coherence in one's life. People for whom these needs are met often experience a joy in living and a conviction that they are successful as human beings. Their lives may be marked by suffering and frustration—such is the human condition—but, psychologically speaking, they are the fortunate ones.

Because psychologists focus so sharply on the *individual*, their writings imply that it is up to each person to achieve his or her psychological well-being through inner resources. Unfortunately, psychologists fail to appreciate how dependent all of us are on the ability of the society and culture to create the conditions—social, economic, political, and cultural—in which personal ego strengths can be nurtured.

For most of this century, and in particular in the quarter century following World War II (roughly up to 1970), the value system of most Americans centered around a number of powerful, culturally derived symbols that drew their strength from their ability to "deliver" at least some of the essentials of psychological well-being. In particular, they proved capable of giving people a sense of self-esteem, a clear identity, concrete, well-defined goals and values, a sense of effectiveness, and a conviction that one's private goals and behavior also contributed to the well-being of others.

Most of these symbols are strikingly middle-class in character. They became dominant values in the 1950s and 1960s as more people were able to move into the middle class through education, a booming economy, and a steady rise in the median income of all but the poorest 20 percent of the population.

Some of the consequences of the old value system for the world of work can be summed up as follows:

- If women could afford to stay home and not work at a paid job, they did so.
- As long as a job provided a man with a decent living and some degree of economic security, he would put up with all its drawbacks, because it meant that he could fulfill his economic obligations to his family and confirm his own self-esteem as breadwinner and good provider.
- The incentive system—mainly money and status rewards—was successful in motivating most people.
- People were tied to their jobs not only by bonds of commitment to their family, but also by loyalty to their organizations.
- Most people defined their identity through their work role, subordinating and suppressing most conflicting personal desires.
- For all practical purposes, a job was defined as a paid activity that provided steady full-time work to the male breadwinner with compensation adequate to provide at least the necessities, and, with luck, some luxuries, for an intact nuclear family.

Under the onslaught of a new value system, all these consequences of the old value system have already changed or are in the process of changing. The New Breed values are expressed in the world of work in some ways that are obvious and others that are quite subtle. Three of the more striking manifestations of New Breed work-related values are (1) the increasing importance of leisure, (2) the symbolic significance of the paid job, and (3) the insistence that jobs become less depersonalized.

THE PURSUIT OF LEISURE

Along with family life, work and leisure always compete for people's time and allegiance. One or the other is usually the center of gravity; rarely does the individual strike an equal balance among all three. For the New Breed, family and work have grown less important and leisure more important. When work and leisure are compared as sources of satisfaction in our surveys, only one out of five people (21 percent) states that work means more to them than leisure. The majority (60 percent) say that while they enjoy their work, it is not their major source of satisfaction. (The other 19 percent are so exhausted by the demands work makes of them that they cannot conceive of it as even a minor source of satisfaction.) . . .

THE PAID JOB AS A SYMBOL

If leisure grows more important for men in the pursuit of self-fulfillment, for New Breed women the symbolic significance of a paid job has greatly intensified. Let us acknowledge at once that most women work for money: many women have no other source of economic support but their own work, and increasing numbers support their dependent children through paid work. Even when the burden of making a living falls mainly on the man, the money earned by the woman in most families has proven indispensable to maintaining a standard of living the family considers satisfactory. Yet, even though work is often an economic necessity for women, one of the essential points of the women's movement is the symbolic meaning of a paid job.

In recent years, unpaid housework has suffered a severe loss in social status. For women today, being "just a housewife" is a poor means of maintaining self-esteem. For New Breed women, exclusive confinement to the unpaid work of homemaker and mother somehow implies being cut off from the full possibilities of self-fulfillment. A paid job has become a badge of membership in the larger society and an almost indispensable symbol of self-worth. It is also a means of achieving autonomy and independence.

The woman with a paid job, however menial or poorly paid, feels that she no longer has to be totally dependent on the will and whim of a man. No longer is she obliged, when trapped in total dependency, to stay with an unsatisfactory marriage. Divorce rates have shot up because divorce is now a practical option for millions of women. They now have, or can acquire, the "price of admission" to independence in our society—a paid job. This does not mean that only women are choosing divorce and are solely responsible for high divorce rates. Many women do not choose divorce because they are able to find work—but find work because they are forced to support themselves after their men leave to "fulfill themselves."

To observers, and indeed to many women who work, exchanging the security of homemaker for a poorly paid job seems like a bad bargain. Often it *is* a bad bargain. Probably, therefore, women in the 1980s will grow more discriminating about the jobs they take. But even when this occurs—as seems inevitable—the pendulum will not swing all the way back. Unfortunately, many women seem to have accepted unquestioningly the male-dominated values of the old era; instead of bringing men to a greater appreciation of the values of home, family, and child care, women have endorsed the male values associated with paid work.

THE PERSON COMES FIRST

More complex and intangible is the New Breed's refusal to subordinate their personalities to the work role. To understand this refusal is to grasp the essence of the New Breed's quest for self-fulfillment.

One of the most striking characteristics of the old value system was the tendency for people to identify themselves with their work role. European visitors to the United States are often startled when Americans introduce themselves by saying, "I am a car dealer"; "I'm assistant manager of the local bank"; "I'm a housewife"; "I manage the personnel department at J.C. Penney's."

Today, there is no greater source of discomfort to the New Breed than this traditional equation of identity with work role. In their eyes, when an individual is subordinated to his role, he somehow is turned into an object, and his humanity is reduced in some indefinable but all-important sense. In the new value system, the individual says, in effect, "I am more than my role. I am myself." The New Breed person demands that his or her individuality be recognized.

When we ask people in our surveys which aspects of their work are becoming more important to them, they stress, above all else, "being recognized as an individual person." They also stress "the opportunity to be with pleasant people with whom I like to work." Significantly, for the majority of people these demands come ahead of the desire that the work itself be interesting and nonroutine.

SEEKING NEW BREED INCENTIVES

Perhaps no question will dominate the workplace in the 1980s more than how to revamp incentives to make them a better match for the work motivations of the New Breed. One might assume that because so many people want paid jobs, they are therefore motivated to work hard. This is true for some people, but the desire for a paid job and the motivation to work hard are independent factors. Just *having* a paid job meets important human needs: for income, independence, self-respect, belonging to the larger society. In principle, a person might be satisfied merely by holding a job without working at it seriously.

And, in practice, this is what a great many do. People will often start a job willing to work hard and be productive. But if the job fails to meet their expectations—if it doesn't give them the incentives they are looking for—then they lose interest. They may use the job to satisfy their own needs but give little in return. The preoccupation with self that is the hallmark of New Breed values places the burden of providing incentives for hard work more squarely on the employer than under the old value system.

Unaccustomed to this burden, employers are angry and frustrated. Under the old value system, they relied on the carrot-and-stick approach, the carrot being money and success, the stick being the threat of economic insecurity. This combination still works, but not as well as in the past. With the advent of New Breed values, the motivational context has changed drastically. . . .

As long as the traditional carrot-and-stick worked well, those at the top could afford to pay less attention to the human side of the organization. Perhaps the chief lesson we should draw from the changes shaped by the new values is that concern with the human side of the enterprise can no longer be relegated to low-level personnel departments. In the 1980s, knowledge of how the changed American value system affects incentives and motivations to work hard may well become a key requirement for entering the ranks of top management in both the private and public sector. If this occurs, we shall see a New Breed of managers to correspond to the New Breed of employees. . . .

PATRICIA A. RENWICK AND EDWARD E. LAWLER
WHAT YOU REALLY WANT FROM YOUR JOB ....

Toward the end of the 19th century, when trade unionism and radical socialism were competing for the soul of the American worker, the country was asking what labor wanted. Samuel Gompers' simple answer was *"more."* . . .

Psychology Today's survey of our readers' work satisfaction reveals that you, too, want *more.* But not simply more money and benefits—you were raised in affluence and tend to take these for granted. Instead, you want more psychological satisfactions. More opportunities to learn and grow. More chance

Patricia A. Renwick and Edward E. Lawler, "What You Really Want from Your Job," *Psychology Today*, May 1978. Reprinted by permission from *Psychology Today Magazine*. Copyright © 1978 American Psychological Association.

to exercise to the fullest your talents and skills. More possibility of accomplishing something worthwhile.

Like your parents, you are willing to work hard and even put in long hours. Although you value your leisure, our survey suggests (in contrast to some other national studies on broader populations) that you still find much of your identity in work. But you want more control over the decisions in the workplace, especially those that affect your own jobs. And you want more freedom to set the pace of your own work, to control your own hours and schedules, to get in an hour of tennis before work or take a long skiing weekend. You have a whole hierarchy of needs, which you see as necessary for what Abraham Maslow called self-actualization. . . .

A total of 23,008 readers returned the 77-item questionnaire in our September issue that asked, "How Do You Like Your Job?" From the survey results and the letters that many of you who wanted to comment in detail sent in, we conclude that most of you are generally satisfied with your jobs for now, but that there is an unmistakable undercurrent of restlessness that may well create problems for your employers as the American economy rambles toward the 1980s. You are potentially quite a mobile generation, with only loose loyalties to a particular corporation or a particular occupation.

The questionnaire, developed jointly by the authors and the *PT* staff, also tells us where you stand on a number of social issues related to jobs, ranging from whose career comes first in dual-career families; to who feels discriminated against on the job, and why; to how men and women are dividing the household tasks these days; and how people regard the ethical standards of their companies. Since we drew some questions from items in previous surveys by the Institute for Social Research at the University of Michigan, we can compare what you think with the opinions of other Americans.

Among the more intriguing results of the *PT* survey:

- 43 percent of *PT* readers felt that they had been victims of job discrimination in the past five years. Yet 82 percent oppose programs of affirmative action to make up for past discrimination against women and members of minorities.
- 78 percent would like to be able to set the hours that they start and leave work—suggesting strong support for plans such as "flextime."
- 44 percent feel "locked into," or trapped in, their jobs.
- Most people would continue working even if they could live comfortably for the rest of their lives without doing so.
- The most popular method of relieving tension from the job was not alcohol or drugs but physical exercise.
- Despite the influence of the women's movement, men's careers still come first in two-career families, and women are still stuck with most of the housework. . . .

As a group, *Psychology Today*'s readers are closer in composition to Daniel Yankelovich's New Breed than to the country as a whole. They tend to be younger, better educated, and higher paid, with a heavy concentration of professionals (43.4 percent vs. a national average of 15.1 percent). In the sampling of questionnaires we analyzed, almost half earned between $10,000 and $20,000 a year. About 44 percent were 25 to 34 years old, which means this group was overrepresented in comparison to the nation.

There were more women than men (52 percent vs. 48 percent), reflecting the population as a whole but not the labor force, which has approximately 12 percent fewer women than the *PT* sample. The racial composition was 92 percent white and 8 percent nonwhite, similar to the ratio in the national labor force. . . .

The majority of our sample had fairly positive attitudes toward their present jobs and were notably free of depression. Their reports on how satisfied they were break down much like the results of the myriad other large-scale national studies of work satisfaction done in recent years: 21 percent said they were *very* satisfied, 20 percent registered some dissatisfaction, and, of these, 6 percent were *very* dissatisfied.

Not surprisingly, managers, executives, and professionals were more satisfied, less often depressed by their work, and less likely to feel trapped in their jobs than semiskilled, unskilled, and clerical workers. The most dissatisfied workers were the young (under 24), blacks, and those with an annual income between $5,000 and $10,000. These groups also reported the highest levels of depression. . . .

Women generally tended to be as satisfied as men, which contradicts some other studies that show them to be more dissatisfied; the evidence from various studies on this point is inconsistent. By the same token, women did not report more depression than the men in our sample.

But men report higher levels of satisfaction than women in five aspects of their work: the opportunities it offers them to learn new things; the freedom they have on the job; the degree of participation in decision-making; their chances of promotion; and monetary rewards. . . .

In general, *PT* readers were dissatisfied with the way rewards are distributed and their performances evaluated in their organizations. As might be expected, they ranked pay and lack of advancement as chief causes of dissatisfaction, but they frequently complained as well about the share of praise they receive for doing a good job and the amount of information they are given about their job performance. . . .

Cynicism about corporate processes was also apparent in the response to a question about how people get promoted. Almost half the people in the survey think that getting ahead in an organization depends more on whom you know than job performance. . . .

Some writers have argued that most workers have about as much say in decision-making as they really want, and that only social scientists are concerned with giving them more. What did *PT* readers think? Overall, they tended to agree that such influence was desirable and that they wanted more of it. The majority said they had most influence on decisions directly related to their own work—but wanted more. They also said they had relatively little influence on corporate policy in general and on the division of work in their organization. Here, too, they wanted more say. Finally, they reported having the least say in personnel matters, such as firing and promoting others, but they were ambivalent about whether they wanted more influence in those decisions.

Men also reported having more say than women in every area of decision-making except in the scheduling of their own work routines. Women seemed less interested in opportunities to make decisions than the men in our sample, for reasons we could not determine.

PT readers seem to make a sharp distinction between what they liked about their jobs and what they thought was most important about work in general. When asked how satisfied they were with various aspects of their jobs, the thing that pleased the largest number was the friendliness of their fellow workers.

But when asked to rate the things they felt were most important in work, they told another story. It was the possibilities for self-growth that crowded the head of the list, including opportunities to develop their skills and abilities, to learn new things, and to accomplish something that would make them feel good about themselves. Among the least important things (though not necessarily unimportant) were fringe benefits, chances for promotion, the physical surroundings at work—and the friendliness of coworkers.

Was self-actualization really more important than money? We pressed people on the issue by asking them if they would accept a higher-paying job if it meant less interesting work. Almost two-thirds of the sample were unwilling to do so.

On the other hand, 46 percent said they would not accept a *more* interesting job if it paid less than their present one (41 percent were willing to make such a tradeoff). Those least likely to take a pay cut for more interesting work were divorced women (55 percent), widows (47 percent), women living with someone (47 percent), and married men (49 percent).

The data suggest that people have in mind a level of compensation that they consider adequate for them. If their pay falls below this level, then money becomes more important than interesting work. If wages or salary are above this level, then whether they consider their job interesting assumes more importance.

The majority of *PT* readers in our sample appear to be having second thoughts about their occupations. Many of those who think they might make a change in the next five years are, of course, the same people who express overall dissatisfaction with their jobs. Though women seem to be no more dissatisfied than men, they are more inclined to make a change in the next five years.

People are restless for a number of reasons that we can only speculate about. Some go through a mid-career crisis and are forced to reevaluate their previous values and goals. Others discover that because of changes in the economy, their skills are simply no longer in demand and they must learn new ones.

The *PT* survey suggests another reason may be that their choice of career was poorly thought-through in the first place. Almost 40 percent of the reader sample said they had happened into their occupation by chance, without much deliberation. Still another 16 percent reported that they had settled for their present occupation because they couldn't get a job in another one they preferred. Only 23 percent were working in their occupation of choice.

As for the 44 percent who feel "locked in," most of them may think the time isn't right to take a risk or that they have too much at stake in the present job to move. Pay plans, seniority advantages, and fringe benefits are powerful incentives for staying with a company—even if an employee isn't happy there. A tight labor market and high unemployment may contribute to nervousness about a hasty move.

More than half of our sample (54 percent) were optimistic about their ability to find another job at about the same level of pay and benefits as their present one. Managers and executives felt most keenly that they had too much at stake to leave their present positions now. However, it was the semiskilled and unskilled who expressed the strongest feelings about being trapped and thought it would be very difficult to find a job equal to their present one.

The data on job mobility only affirm that work is to this generation of adults more than an economic necessity to be avoided if at all possible. Only 9 percent said they would stop working if they could live as comfortably as they liked for the rest of their lives. Almost 75 percent reported that they would continue to work; and women were as likely as men to want to continue, which suggests, in part, that work now is as important to their identities as it is to men's.

The average *PT* reader spends between nine and $10\frac{1}{2}$ hours a day on work and work-related activities. To be sure, attitudes toward work have changed. For the most part, this generation agrees with Douglas McGregor, author of *The Human Side of Enterprise*, that "work is as natural as play." But work also causes pressures and tensions. How do our readers cope with them?

They appear to make a conscious attempt to separate home and work. Almost 70 percent in our survey said they like to keep the two separate. But the attempt to compartmentalize doesn't always succeed. Three-fourths of those in the sample said they brought their work, troubles, and frustrations home with them.

For our survey members, work was rewarding, but not when it cut into leisure or time with family. About 24 percent of them complained about excessive hours. Another 28 percent felt they had to start work too early or leave too late. Some 20 percent found it difficult to complete assigned work during office hours; 13 percent objected to excessive overtime. And 21 percent reported that their work schedules interfered with their family lives. (Executives and managers complained most about long hours and the impact on their families.) . . .

Although women as well as men seek the psychological satisfactions of work nowadays, this apparently does not spare women from the housekeeping chores. The reports of both men and women on how they divide household tasks indicate that women still do most of the grocery shopping, cleaning, cooking, and clearing away after meals. When there are children, women generally take care of them, including driving them to activities, or, they share the responsibilities with their mates. The younger the woman, the more likely she was to report that the household work is shared equally—a sign that changes may be coming, though slowly.

As for household finances, most people reported that they handled the bills themselves or shared the task with their mates. It seems likely that in most cases each partner managed different aspects of the family budget.

The men and women in our sample also displayed traditional attitudes on the issue of whose career comes first when both partners work. Almost all the women in the survey (93 percent) and most of the men (59 percent) were in the dual-career category. About 65 percent of the men said that their careers came first in decisions affecting both parties, while only 9 percent of the women said theirs came first.

Similarly, when we asked men and women whether they would move if their partner were offered a better job in another city—even if it meant that they might be initially unemployed or underemployed—women were much more likely to pick up stakes and follow their men (64 percent of the women vs. 19 percent of the men would move). The higher a man's income, the more resistant he was to moving under these circumstances. His mate's income had absolutely nothing to do with what he said he would do. It seems that reports of the death of traditional sex roles are greatly exaggerated. . . .

Many of the views of *PT* readers seem to represent a healthy new commitment to the importance of work. But it would be wrong to conclude that their attitudes represent a return to traditional feelings about job values. Healthy, yes; traditional in the spirit of the 40s and 50s, probably not. *PT* readers do not have the strong commitment to working for a particular organization or in a particular occupation that was characteristic of the old days. They appear to be very willing to change jobs if they can better themselves. They also seem very concerned about the decision-making opportunities, interest, and challenge in their jobs. Further, they seem to have little of the social consciousness that was so important to young people in the 60s.

It seems to us that the best term to describe our respondents' approach to work is "self-oriented." The phrase expresses a turning inward that is taking place in the nation as a whole. Americans today seem to have less interest in social reform than they do in securing a satisfying job for themselves.

This high self-orientation should, in some ways, make management of organizations easier than it was in the rebellious 60s and early 70s. People seem to believe again in the value of hard work and in developing themselves at the workplace. On the other hand, they are not likely to be easy to satisfy or retain as employees. They are likely to demand a great deal, and, if they don't receive it, will look elsewhere. . . .

K. T. WALSH, G. BRONSON, J. THORNTON, AND
M. WALSH
THE NEW-COLLAR CLASS ....

Out of the masses of the baby-boom generation is emerging a new class of individuals who are challenging the politicians and peddlers of the American dream.

Some 22 million strong, they are the young-to-middle-age adults who program America's computers, manage its fast-food stores, type its letters, drive its trucks, teach its children and find community in the gritty populist anthems of singer Bruce Springsteen.

These are the "new-collar" workers—the latest target of politicians, social scientists, advertisers and merchandisers who are trying to tap into their life-styles, their dreams and their pocketbooks.

They are important because they are so many—comprising one third of the biggest generation in American history. And they are different because they represent a new kind of worker, holding positions in a gray area between professional and laboring ranks—many in service jobs.

"In our postindustrial economy, they are successors to the traditional blue-collar workers," says Ralph Whitehead, public-service professor at the University of Massachusetts. "They continue that work-horse role, but culturally and to a significant degree politically, they are just a different breed."

Whitehead's observations help to form a portrait of the new-collar group assembled by *U.S. News & World Report* from talks with a host of sociologists, business analysts and political scientists, as well as from government and private studies. Their demographic profile is simple: 21 to 40 years old, incomes between $15,000 and $30,000 a year. Though individually not well-to-do or powerful, altogether they are enormously appealing. American business eyes their 327 billion dollars in annual spending power, and politicians covet their clout as 13 percent of the electorate.

"They are the single biggest group of boomers and therefore are very important," says Joe Trippi, a top strategist for the Democratic Party. "If we can start moving those voters into the Democratic column, we're back in the saddle."

In essence, the new collars are the middle class of the baby-boom generation and until now have gotten scant notice because their lives lack the glamour and free-spending ways of young urban professionals, or "yuppies," the most recent targets of upscale merchandisers.

Sometimes this newly discovered class is referred to as "Rinso-blue collars"—a phrase coined by Deputy Treasury Secretary Richard Darman, who describes them as "forgotten white-collar workers," the nonyuppies who have made it to white-collar clothes but not to yuppie power or position.

"I prefer to think of us as the backbone of the country," says Mary Cunningham, a 30-year-old Houston nurse. "We carry about the daily business of living but not with a great deal of flair."

What makes them so challenging to purveyors of everything from candidates to cosmetics is that they are "the most deeply individualistic generation in American history," according to Whitehead, a Democratic Party strategist.

"It's a new kind of conservatism," reports Peter Kim of the J. Walter Thompson advertising agency, which has just finished an extensive study of adults born between 1946 and 1964. "It's more a resurgence of individualism, being pragmatic and solution oriented, and a reluctance to accept cliché liberalism of the 1960s. It would be a mistake to say these groups were returning to strict, traditional values as earlier defined by the Republican vs. the Democratic parties."

Economically, they are between the poor and the affluent, yet their values are by no means traditionally middle class. Most aren't TV addicts, though they are devoted to certain shows. They make purchases primarily for need rather than whim. They are skeptical about government, corporations, indeed all institutions.

To business, because they bargain shop for quality, new collars are an elusive and not fully exploited market. James McKinnon, director of market planning in the U.S. for Nissan Motor Corporation, says, "Demographic projections tell us they are going to be more pragmatic buyers than their parents."

In politics, because they grant little allegiance to politicians or parties, they are a crucial swing bloc that can decide elections. Republican political consultant Lee Atwater notes: "What I'm seeing is a new kind of trapped American in this age group. This generation was basically brought up at a time when there was unprecedented optimism. But many so-called new-collar voters are finding out for the first time that the American dream will not work out the way they thought it would." Atwater predicts that rising frustration among the new working class—"the populists of tomorrow"—eventually will produce an antiestablishment rebellion and a tax revolt, perhaps as soon as 1988.

Labels

Now, this group of Americans is up for grabs. And everybody's grabbing, reaching for handles such as "new collar" and "would-bes" for those who aspire to be yuppies. Sticking labels on this generation has been intensifying ever since people realized their numbers—and then tried to figure out what to do with them.

"Yuppie," that ubiquitous acronym for young, upwardly mobile professionals, grew out of the 1984 presidential campaign as politicos attempted to identify and reach well-educated younger people—a social stratum that once had liberal leanings but is more conservative in this generation.

It is a peculiarity of labels that they are perishable. But while they last, they can have profound impact, as has been seen throughout the country's history. Tories, Mugwumps, Know-Nothings. In a nation of nations, Americans have labeled each other by ethnic group, political stripe or economic status ever since the Revolution.

In this century, Franklin D. Roosevelt decried the "economic royalists" who opposed his policies. And for a time, the idea that there existed a coterie of selfish millionaires gave a sense of brotherhood to the have-nots during the Great Depression. In the early 1970s, Richard Nixon and Spiro Agnew spoke to the "silent majority," giving feelings of pride and purpose to those alienated by civil disturbances of the times.

Today, the focus on the yuppie brackets is waning as the experts realize that those young strivers may be outnumbered by about 3 to 1 by the new collars.

Class Portrait

Theories about the new-collar workers by Whitehead of the University of Massachusetts have provoked widespread interest in Washington's political community. As he explains, "The new collars aren't so much the young people in the baby-boom generation who put on the show we call the Sixties; they're the people who were at home watching it on television. But they were picking up its influences and acting on them at a later time, maybe several years later. What you see is the slow but steady penetration of Sixties values into the new collars."

These young Americans are society's mainstays in virtually every city, town and hamlet across the country. They account for 51 percent of all clerical workers, 52 percent of all blue-collar workers and secretaries, 54 percent of truckers, 57 percent of computer operators and 63 percent of technicians, according to government statistics.

Researchers say these new middle Americans accept many traditional values held by their parents, such as a commitment to family and a patriotic attitude toward the nation. "I have no goals of obtaining a certain level of wealth except basic needs of having a house and providing for my family," says Bill Franchini, a 38-year-old teacher in Torrance, Calif.

But they blend such precepts with contemporary realities, including a high divorce rate, a more permissive sexual climate and skepticism toward their leaders. Many have more sophisticated tastes than their parents and are in a hurry to achieve the good life. Madison Avenue has found, too, that they sometimes are the arbiters of tastes and styles for the older generation.

They are patriotic and respect authority, but they are more liberal than their parents on issues such as abortion, premarital sex and marijuana use.

The new-collar workers frequently find that their financial well-being is precarious. William McCready, director of the cultural-pluralism research center at the University of Chicago, observes: "Being middle class has meant you had some property and some degree of financial security. But this new generation of the middle class is learning that they have to worry about jobs. They have trouble paying their bills, and they can go broke. Many have trouble seeing how things are going to get better. They are on the edge."

"In my income bracket, without a credit card there's no hope of getting even the basics," says Darlene Jenkins, a Chicago hospital clerk. "I have to budget everything down to the penny."

They work hard but are not as obsessed with careers as are the yuppies— and they relish their leisure time. At the top of their reading lists are *People* magazine and *TV Guide*. They often save their hard-earned dollars to buy videocassette recorders and use them regularly at home to watch rented movies such as "Raiders of the Lost Ark," "The Terminator" or "Flashdance." Favorite TV shows include "Cheers," "Hill Street Blues," "The Bill Cosby Show" and "Monday Night Football."

Many of these young Americans have been disappointed to find that a college degree and a white-collar job do not guarantee affluence or even financial security. About 55 percent of them have some higher education, but many find that their college training has little application to their current jobs.

"There are just so many of them that they are always competing with each other," sociologist McCready says. "And it eats up a lot of time, so they are looking for people who can do something for them—serve them fast food, do their bookkeeping, do their financial planning."

They don't have the money to dine very often at upscale bistros or to drink multicolored concoctions at yuppie-style bars. Instead, they pick up a burger and fries at a fast-food restaurant with the family or down a few beers with friends at a local saloon. Or they have a health drink after a jog.

Despite their economic problems, most of the new-collar class seem to remain optimistic. Says Sylvia Busha, a 24-year-old clerical worker from Yale, Mich.: "I've had the opportunity to learn word processing and a little bit about computers. I hope this job will be the steppingstone to a better one."

Frank Naglieri, a 28-year-old New York firefighter, says, "I think things are going to go well for us. I've worked hard for everything that I've gotten, and unlike some people, I think the opportunities are there."

Harvard sociologist Daniel Bell notes that these workers are raising families, making major purchases such as houses or cars and in general "settling down." But their notions of family are markedly different from those of their parents.

While the older generation tended to shun divorce, the breakup of marriages is common among younger middle Americans. Today, half of all first-time marriages will end in divorce, compared with only 20 percent 35 years ago. These young adults are much more independent than their parents were. For instance, in 1960, among women age 20 to 24, about 70 percent were married. Now, only 40 percent of them are.

While older couples also adhered to the traditional family model in which the father left for work and the mother stayed home with the children, new collars find that arrangement either financially impossible or personally unacceptable. As a result, more than 60 percent of younger married women are in the work force at any given time today, compared with only 25 percent in 1950.

This means there are many more two-income families with latchkey children who are at home alone until their parents arrive or who are sent to child-care facilities each day. These children tend to be even more questioning than their parents were as youngsters, and this can make parenting difficult, says Graham Spanier, professor of sociology and psychiatry at the State University of New York at Stony Brook.

Another way in which they differ from their parents is that they have more choices in their lives, ranging from whether to have children to where they will live. "They are comfortable dealing with multiple options," says one advertising expert. "The older generations weren't."

Music, especially rock 'n' roll, is a bonding experience for this class. At the top of the new collars' list of stars is Springsteen, whose songs blend new-collar traits such as earnestness, straightforwardness and hard work with the sense that reality may not live up to expectations. In "My Hometown," Springsteen sings, "They're closing down the textile mill across the tracks. Foreman says these jobs are going, boys, and they ain't coming back. . . ."

Business Target

Advertisers wish they had some of the Springsteen magic in order to connect with a group that collectively has hundreds of billions to spend. "There is a real recognition that while some demographic commonalities exist among baby-boomers, you can't think of them as one homogeneous mass in terms of marketing," says Joseph Plummer, executive vice president and research director for the Young & Rubicam advertising agency in New York.

New York's J. Walter Thompson ad agency has come up with a detailed study breaking the post-World War II generation into various segments which agency researchers believe can be specifically targeted.

One segment is called the "would-bes"—baby-boomers who would be yuppies except for the fact that they earn less than $30,000 a year even though they have at least four years of college education. Thompson estimates that there are 11.8 million would-bes, a group that includes teachers, pharmacists and dental hygienists. Another subgroup identified by Thompson consists of "elite workers"—about 2.3 million people, including foremen, plumbers, electricians and some construction workers who earn at least $30,000 without college educations.

Because the many baby-boom groups share many values, the business world's appeal to new collars often is part of an overall pitch to America's young adults. Products such as Miller beer, Coke, Pepsi and Sunkist soft drinks, McDonald's and Wendy's hamburgers all emphasize baby-boomers' rock music in their TV and radio ads. Such commercials often have a 1960s or 1970s sound, sometimes including variations on "golden oldies" such as hits by the Beach Boys. And while marketing strategies differ on how to reach them, the new collars can be found in more and more advertising. Some examples:

- Miller beer's "American Way" TV commercials that combine a patriotic pitch with images of camaraderie, hard work and good times among workers.
- A number of commercials for cosmetics, household goods and other products depicting young, middle-class women struggling to balance careers and family obligations.
- A Subaru ad showing a son surprising his cost-conscious father by buying a sporty—but practical—car.
- A McDonald's commercial showing a young woman who pumps gas in the morning to work her way through college, and barely has enough time to gobble an Egg McMuffin for breakfast.

Among the businesses that have discovered the baby boom's middle class: Discount clothing stores such as T.H. Mandy and Loehmann's; cosmetics companies such as Avon, and a growing number of supermarket warehouse stores. Analysts also see this demographic group as a prime market for used cars and less-expensive new vehicles, such as American-made subcompacts.

The new-collar Americans are a major target for Levitz furniture stores, says company Vice President Robert Gorden. The firm's warehouse-showroom concept represents a big change from the way older generations shopped. This generation wants "instant gratification," Gorden says, and they like the idea of picking out their furniture and taking it right home. "We're geared more toward the younger, freer thinker than the traditionalist who orders and waits three months for it to be delivered," he adds.

Dennis Lynch, a spokesman for the Wendy's hamburger chain, proclaims: "They're our bread-and-butter customers." Bernadette Mansur, who speaks for Avon Products, adds: "We are very actively pursuing them. Not only are they a high-user market, they are also a group of strivers. It's about time we started talking about them." . . .

. . . As more corporate marketers, social scientists and political strategists notice this segment of the population, its own self-awareness is bound to increase. Its tastes, needs, beliefs and aspirations will be analyzed by everybody with something to sell.

Defining, analyzing and labeling the baby-boomer bulge in America's demographic profile—"the pig in the python," as one advertising seer puts it—now is considered good business and good politics. And it makes some so labeled feel good about themselves.

Vance Packard, author of the books *A Nation of Strangers* and *The Hidden Persuaders*, observes: "As the connections between people become tenuous, there is a deeply felt need for more continuity. Basically, our organizations are getting too large for good human relations. People feel left out. So people want to let you know who they are."

Women in Transition

A. R. GINI AND T. J. SULLIVAN
WOMAN'S WORK: SEEKING IDENTITY THROUGH OCCUPATION ....

In a recent issue of *The New Republic*, Barbara Ehrenreich commented that twenty years ago the stereotypical liberated woman was a braless radical, hoarse from denouncing the twin evils of capitalism and patriarchy. Today's stereotype is more often a blue-suited executive carrying an attaché case and engaging in leveraged buyouts—before transmogrifying into a perfect mother and seductive cook in the evenings, e.g., the recent television commercial pitch: "I can bring home the bacon, fry it up in the pan . . . ." (Ehrenreich, p.28.) Neither is or ever was true, but they can tell us a great deal about what women and men would like to believe. What is true, according to David Bloom—a Harvard economist and demographer—is that the single most important change in the American labor market in the twentieth century is the unprecedented entry of large numbers of women into the work force. (*U.S. News & World Report*, p.46.)

At the turn of the century, only 5 million of the 28 million working Americans were women. One-quarter of these were teenagers and only a very few were married. As recently as 1947, women accounted for fewer than 17 million of the 59 million employed. Since that time, however, six of every ten additions to the work force have been women and, in the last ten years, women have entered two-thirds of the 20 million newly created jobs. (Smith, p.1.) The U.S. Census Bureau reports that 1984 was the first year in which the historical prototype of the American worker—the adult male—did not make up the majority of the labor force. Women and minority-group men now hold 50.7 percent of all jobs. Fifty-three percent of all adult women now hold full-time jobs and make up 44 percent of the entire work force.

Demographers estimate that by 1995 the percentage of employed women will rise to between 57 and 60 percent, and that women may represent a simple majority of the work force early in the twenty-first century. (Borman, p.73.)

This extraordinary increase of employed women has been stimulated by the women's movement and its impact on social consciousness, technological advances in the information and communications industries, the conversion to a service economy, increased access to education, and fair-employment and affirmative-action legislation. For these and perhaps other reasons, there are now 49 million women in the American labor market—and the profile of the female employee has changed dramatically.

While single and divorced women have long had relatively high labor-force participation rates, fewer than one in five married women with a child under the age of one was working full-time in 1960. That number is nearly 50 percent today. (*U.S. News & World Report*, p.46.) Of the 26 million married working women, nearly one in five earns more than her spouse. (*Newsweek*, p.72.) Recent estimates also suggest that only 23 percent of all American households now fit the pattern of a father employed outside the home and a mother at home caring for one or more children. (Borman, p.73.) Surveys conducted over a five-year period by *Working Woman* reveal that, in addition to increasing their numbers in the job market, women in significant numbers have begun to find employment outside the occupations traditionally labeled "women's professions." While nurses, teachers, librarians, and clerical workers are still predominantly women, the proportion of female engineers, architects, physicians, and public officials—while still small in whole numbers—has more than doubled since 1960. Typical law school classes are now often composed of 40 percent women, and nearly 50 percent of those working in sales, technical, and administrative jobs are women. The proportion of women in what are classified as management or "management-related" occupations increased from 39 percent to 45 percent in the years 1983 to 1985 alone. (*Working Woman*, Jan. 1985, p.65.) While women are grossly over-represented at the lower-paying end and the entry levels of the professions, it is clear that the once absolute distinctions between "woman's work" and "man's work" have begun to blur.

As we remarked in the preface to this work, the notion of an unfulfilled homemaker was, for most women, unheard of a generation or two ago. Prior to World War II, the maintenance of a house and, often, a large family was—if not every woman's dream of fulfillment—a full-time occupation, acknowledged as such. Only in recent years have the quotidian tasks of meal preparation and house and clothing maintenance become less than full-time jobs. This, and the decrease in family size, have left large numbers of women no longer merely bored by housekeeping but viewed by large segments of the population as underemployed. While contemporary women's grandmothers may or may not have found satisfaction by staying at home, they had little choice and were at pains to find time for employment even had it been possible. Their daughters and granddaughters, however, now find full-time work outside the home to be not only possible, but in most cases, financially necessary. For the first time, women are defining their worth and status by their degree of success in the workplace. For the first time, men and women are beginning to establish their personal sense of identity and self-worth using the same ground rules.

The personal meaning of work is as important is its economic and social meaning. Where we live, how well we live, whom we see, what we purchase and where, how we educate our children—all of these are dominated by the work we do. (Yankelovich, p. 19.) While a great many—perhaps most—people are unhappy with their jobs, virtually all insist that they want to work because they are aware at some level that work plays a crucial and perhaps unparalleled psychological role in the formation of human character. Work is not simply a source of a livelihood but one of the main factors in defining a sense of self. It may very well be that working in the home has, over the course of the past two generations, simply changed until it no longer meets the definition of work to which most people now subscribe. At one time housework was demonstrably necessary and clearly a full-time occupation, and women were able to forge a sense of self-worth from it, regardless of their capacity for more challenging occupations.

People simply need to work. They see in work the outlines of human definition. Sociologist Peter Berger has written that "to be human and to work appear as inextricably intertwined notions." (Lefkowitz, p. 14.)

Rightly or wrongly, work molds our perceptions of ourselves; to work is to be shaped by the job, to become, in some sense, what we do. In America in the last quarter of the twentieth century, paid employment is, rightly or wrongly, the principal activity that is classified as work. And because of this, paid employment is the principal activity by which we define ourselves and others. (Kahn, p. 11.)

Granting the general thesis that work—paid employment—is the primary factor in defining worth and one's sense of self, it's particularly interesting that, at the moment, men and women perceive the importance of work and its impact on personal identity slightly differently. University of Kentucky researchers conducted a series of nationwide surveys to test assumed gender differences in attitudes toward work. (Lacey, pp. 315–328.) Overall, the results showed only minimal differences between women and men in their preference of job attributes. Approximately half of each group named meaningfulness of the work as most important and ranked the other four attributes in the following order: promotion possibilities, annual income, job security, and hours. There were, however, statistically significant differences between men and women in two of the five attributes. Women were more likely than men to select meaningfulness of the work as a first preference, and men were more likely than women to select job security as a first preference. Marital status had no significant impact upon the preferences listed by men. Currently married women, and women who had never been married, however, chose meaningful work as the first choice more often than men or any other marital category of women.

Most interesting, perhaps, was the response to the question: "If by chance you inherited enough money to live comfortably without working, do you think you would work anyway?" Seventy-four percent of the men and 64 percent of the women said they would continue to work even when it had become unnecessary financially. The difference was directly related to marital status. Among unmarried men and women there seemed to be no significant differences. Married men were, however, more likely than married women to continue working, and unmarried women were significantly more likely than married women to continue to work. These responses are consistent with the historical standard that men, single or married, derive primary status and identity from their occupations and that women do not. The most compelling conclusion is that while more and more women are seeking identity through occupation, women retain some avenues of social-cultural identity other than paid employment.

Gloria Emerson has pointed out, in her award-winning *Some American Men*, that every twelve-year-old boy in America knows what must be done to make it as a man: Money must be made—nothing else is as masculine as this. She cites as the major difference between American men and women the expectation that men will work faithfully all of their lives, without interruption or openly wishing otherwise. (Emerson, p.32.) While the "post-feminist" generation of women are now more likely to draw their status from their jobs, this life sentence to career is not yet, at least for married women, as rigid as it has been for men.

This most recent generation of working women has, as male generations have for years, responded to a stereotype—the image of superwoman, working in a psychologically demanding career, maintaining an intimate relationship with a partner, and nurturing children. While many women have won the right to go off to the corporate citadel every morning, they have more often than not retained the obligation to bear most of the responsibility for the home. This may be a case of it being easier to *do* it all than it is to change both corporate life and home life at the same time. Whatever the reason, this attempt to emulate an unattainable stereotype is beginning to cause many women to reappraise their professional victories. (*Newsweek*, pp.58–59.) Women are now being forced to reexamine their roles and newly found public identities— and popular literature is beginning to talk about the new working woman's identity crisis.

Betty Friedan has said that women believe there is something wrong if they are unable to be corporate executives and, simultaneously, perfect wives and mothers. Women in critical numbers are facing this double burden. Women, especially those over thirty, who do not have a family report a sense of unhappiness and frustration stemming from their fear that their careers and the competitive energies necessary to succeed in them have robbed them of the opportunity for marriage and children. Many of these women report that their careers are less fulfilling and more costly than they expected, and that the deficits in their personal relationships in many ways negate the success they have achieved on the job.

Clearly the women of the 1980s are caught between two powerful images that have shaped the notion of what a successful woman should be. *Newsweek* has pointed out that the myth of the Supermom managing a perfectly run home and starring in the office is fading fast, doomed by an anger, guilt, and exhaustion that Bill Cosby's television spouse, Phylissia Rashad, and others like her never seem to feel.

Ideally, postfeminist women would like to strike a balance between the responsibilities of job and home. The reality is that more women are reporting that they are being forced by circumstances to choose between the two. Large numbers of middle-class working women of the baby-boom generation spent years building careers before having children. The birth of the second child is, in the opinion of countless women, the moment when even the most dedicated career woman is frustrated trying to keep everything in motion at once. For most women, the solution is to choose one—to give up the career or to spend far less time than they would like with the children—and neither one is satisfying.

While there are significant numbers of men who are now substantially more committed to sharing the responsibilities of home and children, this alone—even in the unlikely event that it were to become more widespread—will not answer the problem. The fact is that very few organizations operate as if half of their employees were women. Most businesses and government policies are geared toward a family model that has not been dominant since 1945. Tied to this is the limited support available to working women for child care and home maintenance. Secretary of Labor William Brock has said: "It is just incredible that we have seen the feminization of the work force with no more adaptation than we have had. It is a problem of sufficient magnitude that everybody is going to have to play a role: families, individuals, businesses, local government and state government." (*Newsweek*, p.47.) In the newly published *A Lesser Life: The Myth of Women's Liberation in America*, economist Sylvia Hewlett argues: "The lack of any kind of mandated benefits around childbirth is the biggest single reason why women are doing so badly in the workplace. Unless you support women in their role as mothers, you will never get equality of opportunity." (Hewlett, p.113.)

Jobs have always been important for men, and men have seen their work as honorable—even if only as an honorable burden—and as their primary means of acquiring status. Over the past twenty-five years, women have increasingly demanded the right to be measured by these same standards and have, at least to some extent, succeeded. The dilemma in which they now find themselves is that, while they are able to compete with men in the workplace, the presence of children makes demands that in many cases simply cannot be met unless something very firmly entrenched gives way. A poll conducted by the Gallup Organization for *Newsweek* reported that of 1,009 women surveyed, 37 percent say they have changed jobs or working hours after having children and 45 percent that they drastically cut back on career plans. (*Newsweek*, p. 51.) These are career changes that men have never had to consider—in fact men have generally become even more career oriented after the birth of children.

In the beginning, the women's movement simply seemed to ask for a piece of the pie. It now appears that some other pieces of the pie will have to be made smaller, or that the ingredients will have to change, if American society wishes to have both successful, adult women and another generation of children. The ingredients will be flex-time, guaranteed maternity leave, parental leave (without loss of seniority), child-care facilities or allowances, part-time professional employment—for both men and women—and job sharing. While the upkeep of a home has eased enormously, the raising of children has not. And professional women are concluding that almost nobody can sustain a career and a successful family at the same time. If women are to participate fully in corporate life and find meaning in both home and family, work must change and families must be seen by everyone, including corporations, as the responsibility of both men and women. The solution will be nearer when a man can confidently take the morning off to attend a third-grade play.

In an essay in the tenth anniversary issue of *Working Woman*, Betty Friedan stated that the real crisis of the "second stage of the women's movement" stems from a set of political problems, and the only way they can be solved is if some women come together and force change. (*Working Woman*, Nov. 1986, p. 152.) Women now have the right to work, she reports, but at the cost of being penalized by almost every American institution if they choose to work and have a family. Women should have a right to seek identity through work as well as through parenthood—as men have always done. But the fact is that society is not yet structured for women to pursue this right. For the time being, many women resolve the issue by remaining childless and working under rules and expectations set for a work force of men with wives at home, or by opting out of their careers for long periods of time. At the same time, a group of new women entrepreneurs are emerging, seeking professional careers that allow them to manage their own time and commitments in order to balance work and family. Independence is, however, not possible for all women, just as it is not possible for all men. Most people will earn their livings working for organizations. It is those few women who refuse to compromise, who insist on the right to work within the organizational structure and the right to a family, who will have to push for changes in the workplace just as hard as they had to push to gain admittance to jobs in the first place.

From the beginning, feminism declared that the personal is always political. So it is, suggests Friedan, and so it will always remain. But as feminism enters its next stage, it is clear that the political must now accommodate the personal.

NOTES

Kathryn M. Borman, "Fathers, Mothers and Child Care in the 1980's" in K. M. Borman *et al.* (eds.), *Women in the Workplace: Effects on Families* (New Jersey: Ablex Publishing Corp., 1984), p. 73.

Barbara Ehrenreich, "Strategies of Corporate Women," *The New Republic*, January 27, 1986, p. 28.

Gloria Emerson, *Some American Men* (New York: Simon and Schuster, 1985), p. 32.

Betty Friedan, "Where Do We Go from Here?" *Working Woman*, November 1987, pp. 152ff.

Sylvia Ann Hewlett, *The Lesser Life: The Myth of Women's Liberation in America* (New York: William Morrow, 1986), p. 112.

Robert L. Kahn, *Work and Health* (New York: Wiley, 1981), p. 11.

William B. Lacey, J. L. Bokemeier, and J. M. Shepard, "Job Attribute Preferences and Work Commitment of Men and Women in the United States," *Personnel Psychology* 36 (1983): 315–328.

Bernard Lefkowitz, *Breaktime* (Hawthorn Books, 1979), p. 14.

Ralph E. Smith (ed.), *The Subtle Revolution: Women at Work* (Washington, D.C.: The Urban Institute, 1979), p. 1.

Daniel Yankelovich, "The Meaning of Work," in Jerome M. Rosow (ed.), *The Worker and the Job: Coping with Change* (Englewood Cliffs, N.J.: Prentice-Hall, 1979), p. 19.

"Feminism's Identity Crisis," *Newsweek*, March 31, 1986, pp. 58–59.

"A Mother's Choice," *Newsweek*, March 31, 1986, pp. 47, 51.

"The New Pocketbook Issue," *Newsweek*, December 1, 1986, p. 72.

"Changing Profile of the U.S. Labor Force," *U.S. News & World Report*, September 2, 1985, pp. 46–47.

"Sixth Annual Salary Survey," *Working Woman*, January 1985, p. 65.

MARSHALL I. POMER
MOBILITY OF WOMEN INTO THE ECONOMIC MAINSTREAM ....

Increasing demands on the labor market to provide opportunities for women have resulted in more women in the fields of law, medicine and the sciences. At the same time, most women find themselves in non-professional jobs and face traditional barriers. Employers and unions may be motivated by sex bias, and individual male employees may rebel against supervision by women. To enhance awareness of the difficulty that women have in improving their economic positions, it is helpful to investigate upward mobility out of low-paid occupations.

Marshall I. Pomer, "Mobility of Women into the Economic Mainstream," *Journal of Business Ethics*, Vol. 2, No. 3, August 1983, pp. 185–189. Copyright © 1983 by D. Reidel Publishing Company. Reprinted by permission.

Access to the mainstream of American social and economic life depends on a well-paid job (Coleman and Rainwater, 1978). Accordingly, in this analysis upward mobility is defined as movement from a low-paid job to a job in the mainstream stratum, where the mainstream stratum consists of occupations which are at least moderately well-paid. There are two parts to the analysis. First, we shall examine gender differences in the overall rate of upward mobility. Second, we shall identify types of occupational changes which tend to be gender specific.

THE SAMPLE

Data are drawn from the 1970 United States Census of Population. Three percent of the population were required to report not only their occupations at the time of the survey in 1970, but also their occupations in 1965. This unusually large data base makes it possible to analyze upward mobility in terms of very specific occupational categories.

We shall examine the mobility into the mainstream stratum from seventeen low-paid occupations. Each of these seventeen occupations had median earnings below $4000 in 1969. The mainstream stratum consists of all occupations with median earnings of $6000 or more in 1969, and roughly distinguishes workers who earn an income minimally sufficient to maintain a life-style for their families in the social mainstream (Coleman and Rainwater, 1978). Movement from the low-paid stratum to the mainstream stratum constitutes an occupational change of the type that might lift an individual or a family out of poverty.

The occupations in the low-paid stratum are listed in Table I. Ten of the occupations are categories of service workers: cleaners, cooks, dishwashers, fountain workers, waiters and waitresses, food service workers, personal attendants, porters, crossing guards, and household servants. Five of the occupations refer to laborer categories: carpenters' helpers, gardeners, lumberworkers, stockhandlers, and vehicle washers. Finally there are two operative categories: garage workers, and produce graders. In order to reduce variation caused by extraneous factors, the sample is restricted to white and black workers who in 1965 were between the ages of 31 and 54. In all, there are 37,119 women and 17,297 men in the sample.

THE GENDER DIFFERENTIAL

Whereas 25.00% of the low-paid men move into the mainstream, only 9.75% of the women do so.

Thus the rate of upward mobility for men is more than 2.5 times the rate for women. Since women are more likely to leave the labor force, the gender differential would be even higher if the sample were to include persons who left the labor force.

TABLE I Occupations in Low-paid Stratum

Garage Workers (623)

Produce Graders (625)

Carpenters' Helpers (750)

Gardeners (755)

Lumberworkers (761)

Stockhandlers (762)

Vehicle Washers (764)

Cleaners (902)

Cooks (912)

Dishwashers (913)

Fountain Workers (914)

Waiters and Waitresses (915)

Food Service Workers, nec (916)

Personal Attendants (933)

Porters (934)

Crossing Guards (960)

Household Servants (984)

Note: The numbers in parentheses are the census occupational codes.

This differential is very substantial, but perhaps it can be attributed to differences in the characteristics of the sampled men and women? To answer this question, a statistical model was used to adjust for differences in mobility related to age, education, occupation, and industry. Table II presents the adjusted probabilities of upward mobility for white men, white women, black men, and black women.

TABLE II Standardized Probabilities of Upward Mobility

RACE/GENDER CATEGORY	PROBABILITY	DIFFERENCE	RATIO
White Males	22.7%	0%	1.00
Black Males	16.3	− 6.4	0.72
White Females	12.3	− 10.4	0.54
Black Females	8.2	− 14.5	0.36

Based on the adjusted probabilities, being a woman cuts the chances of upward mobility in half. Thus, observed differences in the jobs and personal characteristics of men and women explain only a small portion of the gender differential in upward mobility.

CHANNELS TO WELL PAYING JOBS

Where are the opportunities for low-paid workers? Which occupations serve as openings out of the low-paid stratum—as doorways through which escape is most possible?

OPPORTUNE DESTINATIONS

Table III lists the mainstream occupations most frequently entered by the upwardly mobile workers. At least 1.0% of the occupational changers moved into each of these occupations. Five of these opportune destinations are operative categories: machine operatives (miscellaneous operatives, and checkers. Two are clerical: bookkeepers and secretaries. Two are managerial: managers (not elsewhere classified), and restaurant managers. And two are craft categories: supervisors or foremen (not elsewhere classified), and auto mechanics. There are no professional, sales, service, or laborer occupations among the opportune

TABLE III   Most Common Occupational Destinations of Low-paid Workers Who Move into Mainstream

OCCUPATION	PERCENT
Managers, nec (245)	3.39
Restaurant managers (230)	3.10
Machine operatives, misc. specified (690)	2.12
Assemblers (602)	2.18
Truck drivers (715)	1.87
Bookkeepers (305)	1.33
Foremen, nec (441)	1.29
Miscellaneous operatives (694)	1.25
Checkers (610)	1.12
Secretaries (372)	1.10
Auto mechanics (473)	1.07

Note: Percent is the percentage of those who changed occupations who have the specified occupation as their destination occupation.

destinations. Although only eleven in number, these opportune destinations account for nearly half (45.7%) of the upward mobility from the low-paid stratum to the mainstream.

Channels

Table IV identifies and measures the channels of upward mobility, which are defined by specifying a low-paid occupation and a mainstream occupation. The rate of flow through a mobility channel is measured separately for each race-gender group and is defined to be the proportion of occupational changers initially employed in the low-paid occupation who move to the mainstream occupation. The channels are unevenly distributed: 25 are for white males, 8 for black males, and 11 for white females.

For white men, there are five mobility channels to the supervisor (foremen) destination, whereas there are no such channels for women. Also, white men

TABLE IV   Channels of Upward Mobility

INITIAL OCCUPATION	GROUP	DESTINATION OCCUPATION	P
Garage Workers	WM	Truck Drivers	7.30
″	WM	Auto Mechanics	8.19
″	WM	Managers, nec	14.97
″	BM	Managers, nec	6.62
″	BM	Auto Mechanics	9.27
″	BM	Truck Drivers	7.95
″	WM	Foremen, nec	11.90
Produce Graders	WF	Machine Op's, misc spec	8.75
Carpenters' Helpers	WM	Truck Drivers	4.90
Gardeners	WM	Truck Drivers	7.06
″	WM	Foremen, nec	6.45
Lumberworkers	WM	Managers, nec	5.80
″	WM	Truck Drivers	8.07
″	WM	Machine Op's, misc spec	4.14
″	WM	Foremen, nec	4.35
″	BM	Truck Drivers	11.36
Stock Handlers	WM	Managers, nec	16.93
″	BM	Managers, nec	9.76
″	WF	Managers, nec	4.08
″	WF	Bookkeepers	4.94
″	WM	Foremen, nec	6.94

TABLE IV   Channels of Upward Mobility (*Continued*)

INITIAL OCCUPATION	GROUP	DESTINATION OCCUPATION	P
Vehicle Washers	BM	Machine Op's, misc spec	5.88
"	WM	Machine Op's, misc spec	8.62
Cleaners	WM	Managers, nec	4.29
"	WM	Truck Drivers	4.29
"	WM	Foremen, nec	4.91
"	BM	Truck Drivers	5.20
"	WF	Assemblers	4.15
Cooks	WM	Managers, nec	3.94
"	WM	Restaurant Managers	22.01
"	BM	Machine Op's, misc spec	4.85
"	WF	Restaurant Managers	6.52
Dishwashers	WF	Misc Operatives	6.41
Fountain Workers	WM	Restaurant Managers	16.95
"	WF	Restaurant Managers	5.50
Waiters, Waitresses	WM	Managers, nec	4.13
"	WM	Restaurant Managers	11.98
"	WF	Restaurant Managers	4.97
"	WF	Machine Op's, misc spec	5.05
"	WF	Secretaries	7.07
Food Service Workers	WM	Restaurant Managers	6.59
"	WM	Managers, nec	10.78
"	WM	Machine Op's, misc spec	4.19
Personal Attendants	WF	Secretaries	13.33

Notes: P = Transition probability of mobility channel. To identify the race-gender groups, W = white, B = black, F = female, and M = male.

have relatively very high rates of mobility to the managerial categories. White women often move into well-paid operative jobs, but they do not often become truck drivers, an occupation which is a frequent male avenue into the economic mainstream. The upward mobility of white women is apparently often limited to access to clerical destinations, namely bookkeeper or secretary, neither of which is a frequent destination for men.

CONCLUSION

The findings from our study provide indirect evidence of discrimination and document the inferior position of women in the labor market. For the low-paid occupations examined, upward mobility for men is about two and one half times the rate for women. This differential is scaled down only slightly after taking account of race, age, education, occupation, and industrial sector. Furthermore, the character of mobility out of low-paid occupations differs for women and men. For women, upward mobility is often limited to becoming well-paid factory workers, secretaries or bookkeepers, whereas men frequently move into positions of authority.

Awareness of the situation of women is the first and possibly the most important step toward equalizing rates of upward mobility. Women need to carefully scrutinize their prospects for advancement when deciding on jobs, but it is crucial to broaden the awareness of employers. Sensitized to the restricted opportunities of women, employers are more likely to recognize that women are often underutilized and have potential for advancement.

REFERENCES

Beck, E. M., Patrick M. Horan, and Charles M. Tolbert II: 1980, "Industrial Segmentation and Labor Market Discrimination," *Social Problems* 28, 113–30.

Bergmann, Barbara R. and William Darity, Jr.: 1980, "Social Relations in the Workplace and Employer Discrimination," *Industrial Relations Research Association Series: Proceedings of the Thirty-third Annual Meeting*, 155–62.

Coleman, Richard P., and Lee Rainwater with K. A. McClelland: 1978, *Social Standing in America: New Dimensions of Class*, Basic Books, New York.

Kantor, Rosabeth: 1977, *Men and Women of the Corporation*, Basic Books, New York.

Leigh, Duane E.: 1978, *An Analysis of the Determinants of Occupational Upgrading*, Academic Press, New York.

Rosenfeld, Rachel A.: 1980, "Race and Sex Differences in Career Dynamics," *American Sociological Review* 45, 583–609.

Rosenfeld, Rachel A. and Aage B. Sørensen: 1979, "Sex Differences in Patterns of Career Mobility," *Demography* 16, 89–101.

Sewell, William H., Robert M. Hauser, and Wendy C. Wolf: 1980, "Sex, Schooling, and Occupational Status," *American Journal of Sociology* 86, 551–83.

U.S. Bureau of the Census: 1972, *Public Use Samples of Basic Records from the 1970 Census: Description and Technical Documentation*, Government Printing Office, Washington, D.C.

Wolf, Wendy C. and Neil D. Fligstein: 1979, "Sex and Authority in the Workplace: The Causes of Sexual Inequality," *American Sociological Review* 44, 235–52.

4

....

Theory Building: A Search for a New Ethic

INTRODUCTION

This chapter looks at a cross section of attempts to explain work and its impact on our lives. It is a necessarily varied collection of essays from a number of quite different perspectives—but all are tied together by the common search for a rationale to justify the manner in which most people spend the bulk of their lives.

The first piece is a commonsense look at what the colloquial use of the word "work" implies about our attitude toward work. It attempts to define work in light of what we mean when we talk about work.

Daniel Bell wrote in 1956 with a prescience that the past thirty years have borne out. He said that industrialization, and the later routinization of nonindustrial work, would foster a two-stage change in the way people seek satisfaction. The "human relations" revolution, dating from the Hawthorne studies in 1927, began the "tyranny of psychology" whereby we sought satisfaction not from work itself—which could no longer be said to have the potential to satisfy—but from the ancillary social aspect of the workplace. This is matched, Bell says, by the shift "from authority to manipulation as means of exercising dominion." Second, Bell predicted, and the culture has fully accepted, that work for most people holds no intrinsic satisfaction and that success in life-style is the wellspring of happiness. A relative disappearance of absolute hunger as a motivation to work has resulted in the carrot's displacement by the "candied carrot" of consumer goods. Aided by advertising and consumer credit—the "two most fearsome social inventions since the discovery of gunpowder"—we now accept as a given that work is a tedious means to buy satisfaction elsewhere, and that it cannot be otherwise.

Gus Tyler's address to the ILGWU is a look at the consumer society from the other side. The union position has been—largely of necessity—independent of the nature of jobs, as control over the product and methods of production have been almost universally seen as the property of management. Unions have focused on compensation and hours and have accepted the drudgery of work as necessary. Tyler traces the labor movement as a quest for equity and views the achievement of leisure and a high standard of living as victories. While he does not directly treat what Bell sees as the loss of satisfying work, he makes clear that for the bulk of working people, satisfaction drawn from labor is a myth, a shibboleth traded by nonlaboring classes.

The Magdoff article returns to the notion that work itself ought to be liberating, and is central to human life. He traces the division of labor from a Marxist perspective, concluding that the effort to divide labor into the simplest possible tasks inevitably results in the nearly total degradation of work and alienation of laborers. At the core of the debate is the Marxist refutation of the notion that labor is a curse, that only the force of economic necessity can drive people to work. Magdoff cites other incentives and the adaptability of human nature—and he concludes with a call for the "total departure from the culture of capitalism and consumerism" as the only avenue leading to the return of labor as a central, satisfying human occupation.

The third section of the chapter deals with the search for meaningful work and begins with Irving Bluestone's assertion that the history of the workplace is nothing more or less than the history of mankind. The struggle for freedom from oppression, "between those who govern and those who are governed," is replicated on the job in the effort of workers to influence and direct their working lives. And the progress from feudal to Western democratic society is recapitulated, albeit incompletely, in the history of industrial society. The workplace is still, by and large, the most authoritarian setting most people encounter. Bluestone calls for worker participation in decision making as a necessary step in the "humanizing of the workplace." He ends with a vision of cooperation, an end to the adversarial contest between labor and management, as the hope for the worksite and for society.

Adina Schwartz posits no less a position than that routine, mechanical tasks are at odds with the notion of a just society; that to demand work which offers virtually no autonomy to the worker is to deny liberty. She develops this philosophical position at length and examines some current alternatives to total routinization, rejecting all but the restructuring of the workplace, so that "jobs . . . be democratically redesigned . . . in a way that abolishes the distinction between those who decide and those who execute others' decisions." She concludes that autonomy in a democratic workplace is the only alternative if we hope to be a society of free individuals.

Theodore Roszak expands on the idea that progress is not the saving of labor and the creation of leisure, but the preservation of meaningful work from "indiscriminate technological advance. . . ." This is something of a Luddite argument and is the most romantic of the essays, with Roszak saying that "neither the need nor the right to work has to be justified by proving its profitability or productivity, any more than our need to love, play or grow should be made to present its cost-benefit credentials." He cites some serious irrationalities of consumer excess and asks some probing questions about the impact of this and degrading work upon a culture. He concludes, however, with a series of predictions based upon scant anecdotal evidence. While some of his positions are easily dismissed as futurist bunkum, he is of interest here because he does, indeed, envision what the future *may* hold. Many of the notions that he put forth in *The Making of the Counterculture* proved to be, in fact, bunkum, but many others have been absorbed into what has become conventional wisdom. In any event, romantic notions tell us much of what we would like if not of what we shall have.

Patricia Werhane examines what Judith Rosener has called "sexual static" in the workplace. Men and women in professional settings are interacting in new roles, and in many instances are uncertain of what gender-specific behaviors mean. She looks at how both men and women in professional settings react to these changes in roles and behavior.

Helena Lopata traces the history of paid employment for women in America, with particular attention to the difficulties of compiling statistics from times when definitions and methods of data collection were often unclear at best.

Finally, Donna Green and Thomas Zenisek look at the contemporary issue of dual-career couples. Their work is a survey of current research and provides the most comprehensive view available of what is almost certainly the future for most families in America.

What's to Like?

T. J. SULLIVAN
WHAT DO WE MEAN WHEN WE TALK ABOUT WORK? ....

What is it anyway, this *work?* Is it something, anything, that we do for money? Clearly this works as a definition—that is to say that if we are paid to do something, we generally feel permitted to call that work. This is true for bookbinders, cement finishers, senators, and hit men. What becomes, however, of the sentence "I have so much work to do around the house this weekend"? It is a perfectly sensible thing to say; everyone understands it and accepts it as legitimate, and yet nobody is paying us to clean out the garage. What are we really saying when we say this? How about: "I have actions to perform, which I do not wish to perform and will not enjoy, which I am compelled by necessity to do"? There may be something here. Is not the compulsion, either by the necessity of the work or the necessity of the money which performing a task will earn, at the core of why we use the word work?

Exceptions are good tests for this sort of definition, according to Aristotle. Imagine an experience, usually pleasant, which has become unpleasant, i.e., lunch with an old friend which you know will focus on a discussion of his impending divorce. The sentence "This lunch is going to be work" makes sense, does it not? Compulsion works here as a defining characteristic—we are compelled by the friendship to go to lunch, and we won't make any money at it.

What becomes of the sentence: "I love my work"? This is a problem, because what becomes of work when we are paid to do that which we would do anyway, compelled or not, paid or not? What becomes of the person whose leisure is spent working? For John Dewey, work which becomes play is art. The people whose work is that which they would do anyway are perhaps the fortunate exceptions, and perhaps we should have a different word for what they do, such as "art." But we don't. We still expect them to say, "I'm working on a novel." And, often, they will work on the novel whether they expect to be paid or not, and we will understand that they are working. This appears to be a problem because, since most of us do not enjoy that for which we are paid, we confuse all unwelcome tasks with work and call them work. Conversely, we confuse all things for which people are paid with unwelcome tasks. Hence the temptation to call what the artist does something other than work.

Let's look at this from the standpoint of compulsion. If work is that which we are compelled to do for money, or because it must be done, then cannot artists' work be that which they are compelled to do for some equally strong compulsion, such as the feeling that it has to be done? It seems to me perfectly sensible that artists are people who must do their work in order to achieve a sense of well-being, just as we must clean the garage because we haven't anywhere else to park the car, and we must go to work because we have no other means of paying the mortgage on the house—and cluttered garage.

Most people work. And most of them work for money, at tasks they find at least less than pleasant. The degree to which we call them lucky is the degree to which we perceive their tasks as pleasant. We all accept as luckiest those who are paid to do what we think of as fun. And we are sometimes mystified by people who appear to be happy doing things we find extremely unpleasant—the smiling mortician. Are they simply well-adjusted? Self-deceived? Rousseau thought the happy man was one who had learned to embrace the inevitable, to understand his limitations and accept them. But the inevitable still compels us, does it not? Let's look again at the artists. We've established that they are doing work which they would do paid or not, but have we established that they are happy? Not necessarily. To be compelled to make novels, or to be compelled to make widgets for money, is not to be happy or unhappy. Who then is happy in his work? Must the work be intrinsically satisfying? Not if there are happy assembly-line workers—and there are. Is it *sufficient* that the work be satisfying? Not if there are unhappy novelists—and there certainly are. Work is not, I would argue, possessed of intrinsic value. We assume that working the swing shift at a doorknob factory has no intrinsic worth. We assume that writing plays does. Or that cabinet-making does. Why do we believe this? Why do we believe that whole products are more satisfying to construct than discrete parts? Current management theory would tell us that the team that builds a car from beginning to end is more satisfied, and more useful, than the people on the paint line at another auto plant. We think the piano builder is an artist—or artisan—while the guy who drills the holes in piano hinges is a drone, and miserable. We make these assumptions probably because "we" are composed almost exclusively of people who cannot conceive of working the line at Oldsmobile.

That people can and do manage happy lives working at monotonous jobs is evident—and seems a function of factors not related to the work. Is the pay adequate for perceived needs? Are the conditions reasonably comfortable? Is the work steady and secure and the hours such that there is time for a life outside the job? And, finally, do the people doing the job accept the trade-off as a good bargain?

Work, then, is that which we are compelled to do by some force inside or outside of us—the need for money, for self-expression, for accomplishment, to park the car. The question of which of these compulsions is greater, and who has which, is another issue entirely. The larger question is whether the work ought to be satisfying, ought to make us happy. The answer is, of course, yes, but only because we seek satisfaction, we want to be happy, and we feel we deserve to get that which we seek. We may even *actually* deserve to get what we seek. The work itself, unfortunately, is indifferent to our needs.

Work is what you have to do. For some of us, it is a *particular* thing we must do, and if we're lucky it pays and it makes us happy. For most of us, it is money, a livelihood, that compels us—and that makes the vocational task a matter of trying to find something that pays and is also pleasant. The degree to which we can find this combination is the degree to which work, any work, is satisfying.

DANIEL BELL
WORK AND ITS DISCONTENTS ....

By and large the sociologist, like the engineer, has written off any effort to readjust the work process; the worker, like the mythical figure of Ixion, is chained forever to the endlessly revolving wheel. But the spectacle has its

Daniel Bell, from *Work and Its Discontents* (Boston: Beacon Street, 1956). Reprinted by permission of the publisher.

unnerving aspect, and the sense of dehumanization is oppressive. Industry has been told, therefore, that production may suffer when only the mechanical aspects of production are considered. Hence the vogue in recent years of "human relations." Its rationale is stated by Cornell sociologist William F. Whyte. The "satisfactions of craftsmanship are gone, and we can never call them back," he writes. "If these were the only satisfactions men could get out of their immediate work, their work would certainly be a barren experience. There are other important satisfactions today: the satisfactions of human association and the satisfactions of solving technical and human problems of work."

The statement summarizes the dominant school of thought which has grown out of the work of the late Elton Mayo of the Harvard Business School and his followers. For Mayo, following the French sociologist Emile Durkheim, the characteristic fact about the modern scene is the presence of constant, disruptive change. The family, the primal group of social cohesion, breaks up as a work and educational unit; neighborhood roots are torn up, and social solidarity, the key to human satisfactions, gives way to *anomie*. If solidarity is to be re-established, it will have to be done within the corporation and factory. "The manager," writes Fritz Roethlisberger, Mayo's chief disciple at the Harvard Business School, "is neither managing men nor managing work . . . he is administering a social system."

In this, as in many instances, social engineering imitates art. Twenty years ago the first "solidarity hymn" was penned by Aldous Huxley, in his *Brave New World*, and the refrain voiced by the Alphas and Betas could be the school song for industrial sociology:

> Ford, we are twelve; oh make us one
> Like drops within the social river.
> Oh, make us now together run
> As swiftly as thy shining flivver.

This is not the place to recapitulate the many criticisms that have been made of the Mayo school. The fundamental point, as it affects the worker in his own work environment, is that the ends of production are taken as "given" and the worker is to be "adjusted" to his job so that the human equation matches the industrial equation. As one management consultant, Burleigh Gardner, succinctly phrased it: "The more satisfied [the worker] is, the greater will be his self-esteem, the more content he will be, and therefore, the more efficient in what he is doing." A fitting description not of human, but of cow, sociology.

The source of this interest in "human relations" was the famous experiment during the thirties at the Hawthorne works of the Western Electric Company in Chicago, perhaps the single most painstaking experiment in the history of the social sciences. The question that first interested the researchers was of the relationship of fatigue to output. A group of five girls were subjected to exhaustive study; the methods were the most meticulous in regard to scientific procedure and control. A series of possible "variables" affecting production were listed, e.g. amount of heat, degree of light, variations in menstruation cycles of the workers; and for a period of thirteen weeks at a time, one factor was changed or studied and all others were kept constant. "A skilled statistician," Roethlisberger reports, "spent several years trying to relate variations in the physical circumstances of these five operators. For example, he correlated the hours that each girl spent in bed the night before with variations in output the following day. Inasmuch as some people said the effect of being out late one night was not felt the following day but the day after that, he correlated variations in output with the amount of rest the operators had had two nights before. . . . The attempt to relate changes in physical circumstances to variations in output resulted in not a single correlation of enough statistical significance to be recognized by any competent statistician as having any meaning."

Then came the great *éclaircissement*. In period XII of the experiment, the girls were returned to a bread-and-water diet, so to speak—a 48-hour week without rest breaks, without lunches, the same illumination as when the experiment began. Yet output kept rising. It then became clear that the workers were responding, not to any of the physiological or physical variables, but to the interest and attention centered on them. The experiment itself, not any outside factor, was the missing link, the unknown determinant.

This led to the second phase of the Hawthorne experiment: the introduction of ambulatory confessors, or walking counselors, ready at any moment to stop and listen to a harassed worker air his woes. Counseling for Mayo was meant to be "a new method of human control." But of this, as of all such objectives, one can ask: Control of whom for what purposes? The answer has been given by Roethlisberger: in counseling, one seeks to shift "the frame of reference," so that the worker sees his grievance in a new light. As one Hawthorne counselor described this process: "In the case of the down-graded employee . . . her focus of attention shifts from alleged inequities, transfer and down-grading grievances, etc. . . . to her unhappy home life; then, when she returns to her original grievance, things do not look so bad."[1]

While "human relations," as a result of the tremendous publicity given to the Hawthorne findings and of Mayo's further work, became a great vogue, personnel counseling in the broader sense did not spread widely for a while, even within the Bell Telephone System where it originated. The reason, in large measure, was that management itself did not fully understand its function. There seemed to be no tangible "pay-off" in diminished cost or increased

---

[1] The explanation recalls an old folk tale: A peasant complains to his priest that his little hut is horribly overcrowded. The priest advises him to move his cow into the house, the next week to take in his sheep, and the next week his horse. The peasant now complains even more bitterly about his lot. Then the priest advises him to let out the cow, the next week the sheep, and the next week the horse. At the end the peasant gratefully thanks the priest for lightening his burdensome life.

production that management could point to; moreover, it seemed to some to represent too much "coddling." Since the Second World War, and largely because of the continuing influx of women into the work force, counseling has become more and more an adjunct of a company's medical service to its employees. Some large companies, like DuPont and Eastman Kodak, maintain staff psychiatrists. Many, like Hughes Aircraft and Raytheon, have full-time social workers who advise employees on a multitude of problems, financial and marital.

It was the psychologist in this instance, however, who taxed the manager for not appreciating the benefits of what Huxley called "advanced emotional engineering." And it was the growing prestige of the management consultant that led management to accept these psychological gimmicks.

While counseling lagged, "communication and participation" quickly became great management fads. In theory, "communication" is supposed to open a two-way street whereby those down the line can talk back to those above and thus "participate" in the enterprise. In few instances have such systems become operative. In most cases communication consists simply of employee newsletters or "chain-of-command" conferences in which vice-presidents meet with managers, managers with supervisors, supervisors with foremen, and so on down the line. In some cases, the system operates with a characteristic advertising-agency twist. At Westinghouse, for example, statements of company policy were recorded on tape, and by dialing on the inter-plant telephone system one could listen to the messages given to the hundreds of top supervisors. The dial number ostensibly was a secret, confined to 1,200 supervisory employees. In practice, it was a secret in name only, since supervisors were instructed to "leak" the number "confidentially" to various employees, and these men, gleeful at knowing a secret, quickly spread the information to others. The result was that thousands of workers eagerly rushed to listen to hortatory talks which at other times might have been received with utter indifference.

There are two points to be noted about the vogue of "human relations." One is that, in the evident concern with understanding, communication and participation, we find a change in the outlook of management, parallel to that which is occurring in the culture as a whole, from authority to manipulation as a means of exercising dominion. The ends of the enterprise remain, but the methods have shifted, and the older modes of overt coercion are now replaced by psychological persuasion. The tough brutal foreman, raucously giving orders, gives way to the mellowed voice of the "human-relations oriented" supervisor. The worker doubtless regards this change as an improvement, and his sense of constraint is correspondingly assuaged. In industrial relations, as in large areas of American society, accommodation of a sort has replaced conflict. The second point is that these human-relations approaches become a substitute for thinking about the work process itself. All satisfactions are to be obtained in extracurricular areas: in the group, in leisure pursuits. Thus the problems of work are projected outward and swathed in psychological batting.

This tyranny of psychology has led management into a curious discounting of the "economic man." We are told that what the worker really wants is security, recognition, rewarding personal relations, and that he is more concerned with these than with other "larger, out-of-plant, off-the-job issues." "Labor disputes," writes a Harvard Business School authority, "are often stated in terms of wages, hours of work and physical conditions. Is it not possible that these demands are disguising, or in part are symptomatic expression of, much more deeply rooted human situations which we have not learned to recognize?"

Such a statement suggests more about Harvard Business School than about the workers; it suggests that the academic doesn't know how to talk to a man in the shop. "Now the operators in my shop," reports a sociologist who went into one, "made noises like economic men. Their talk indicated that they were canny calculators and that the dollar sign fluttered at the masthead of every machine."

To say, in fact, that the American worker is not really or primarily interested in money contradicts, in a deep sense, the very motive power of the economic system. Why else would people submit themselves to such a work environment?

Why do people work? More particularly, why do people accept the harsh, monotonous repetitive jobs that tie them to Ixion's wheel? A conventional answer, by now, is the Protestant Ethic. In that respect, Max Weber, with his hypnotic view of man endlessly working, accepting deprivation, minimizing his creature comforts and driving hard against the environment because of his need to prove himself before God, has exercised a beguiling influence in social science.

Perhaps the bourgeois entrepreneur was of this mold. It is doubtful whether the worker was. Certainly the workers in Hogarth's Gin Alley, or the people whom Melville's Redburn saw in the Liverpool slums, were little concerned with the scourging hand of God. What drove them to work was hunger, and much of the early movements of social protest can only be understood with that fact in mind.

Hunger itself was not always the goad. From the time of Elizabeth I, the English poor, and those unable to get work, could live on public relief. In 1795, the government extended this system by passing the famed Speenhamland law, a measure which Canning and other English statesmen felt would stave off the revolution that had already swept France and that now threatened England. As Karl Polanyi points out, the law, in effect, excluded labor from the market economy. If wages fell below a minimum point, the government would make up the difference. In this way a minimum subsistence was guaranteed to each worker. In practice all wages soon fell below the minimum, since the employer expected the government to make up the wage; and no worker had any interest in satisfying the employer. Speenhamland had put a premium on shirking, and thereby increased the attraction of pauperism.

To the Protestant divines (and to the merchant class) the Speenhamland law was a curse. The moralists opened their fire. William Townsend openly extolled the virtues of hunger. "Hunger will tame the fiercest animals, it will teach decency and civility, obedience and subjection to the most perverse. . . . it is only hunger which can spur and goad [the poor] on to labor; yet our laws have said they shall never hunger . . ."

Perhaps the most powerful voice at the time was that of Thomas Malthus. Against the optimism of Godwin and other utopians, he argued that a society could exist only if held under powerful restraints and checks. Without such restraints, licentiousness would reign, populations increase, misery fester. The poor laws, thundered Malthus, simply encouraged vice. "If our benevolence be indiscriminate . . . we shall raise the worthless above the worthy; we shall encourage indolence and check industry; and in the most marked manner subtract from the sum of human happiness. . . . the laws of nature say with St. Paul, 'If a man will not work, neither shall he eat.' " Jeremy Bentham added his voice with such schemes as the *panopticon*. To the question, "What can the law do to raise subsistence?" Bentham answered, "Nothing, directly."

As a result of these many pressures the Speenhamland law was repealed in 1832. And in 1834, with the New Poor Laws, the age of *laissez faire* was abruptly ushered in. (Yet England's *laissez faire*, it should be noted, was planned with "minute utilitarian administration.") Under the new law, a man had to pass a means test before he could get relief, and the poorhouse was invested with a moral stigma. The scorn of the community now drove him to work, but since aid-in-wages was discontinued, a man's wage was what the employer would pay. Henceforth the price of labor would be determined in the fluctuating market, and despite its protestations labor had become a commodity. (After all, a large economy of abundance could not be produced without high instinctual repression, and the harness of regularized work had to be put upon the worker.) "The refractory tempers of work-people accustomed to irregular paroxysms of diligence," of which Andrew Ure wrote a century ago, became tamed, and diligence was regularized. Even the American worker, a man, according to the national stereotype, of boisterousness, individualism and independence, submitted to the tyranny of the clock.

But in our day, surely, it is not physical hunger which is the driving force; there is a new hunger. The candied carrot, the desire for goods, has replaced the stick, the standard of living has become a built-in automatic drive. Aided and abetted by advertising and the installment plan, the two most fearsome social inventions of man since the discovery of gunpowder, selling has become the most striking activity of contemporary America. Against frugality, selling emphasizes prodigality; against asceticism, the lavishness of display. No creature in history is more uxorious than the American consumer, and this submissiveness drives him to buy. The "golden chain" is the deferred payment plan. By mortgaging his future, the worker can buy a house, car, appliances and other comforts. By possession of these products he enters the provinces heretofore tenanted only by the *haut monde*. The aural nerve of *homo*

Americanus has been tightened to the most excruciating pitch. The American citizen, as *Fortune* once noted, lives in a state of siege, from dawn until bedtime. "Nearly everything he sees, hears, touches, tastes, and smells is an attempt to sell him something. . . . to break through his protective shell the advertisers must continuously shock, tease, tickle or irritate him, or wear him down by the drip-drip-drip or Chinese water torture method of endless repetition. Advertising is the handwriting on the wall, the sign in the sky, the bush that burns regularly every night."

If the American worker has been "tamed" it has not been through the discipline of the machine, but by the "consumption society," by the possibility of a better living which his wage, the second income of his working wife, and easy credit all allow. Nowhere is this more evident than in Detroit. In American radical folklore, the auto worker was considered the seedling of the indigenous class-conscious radical—if there was ever to be one in America. Uninhibited, rootless (many were recruited from the Ozark hills), with his almost nihilistic temper he was the raw stuff for revolutionary sentiment—once he realized (or so the Marxists thought) that he was trapped by his job. Few auto workers today have a future beyond their job. Few have a chance of social advancement. But they are not radical. What has happened is that old goals have been displaced, and the American Dream has been given a new gloss. Success at one's job becomes less important than success in one's style of life. A worker sees himself "getting ahead," as Eli Chinoy points out in a recent study, not by promotion in the plant—he knows that *that* ladder has vanished, even though Henry Ford and Walter P. Chrysler began from the mechanics' bench[2]—but because he is working towards a "nice little modern house." These changes in values are reflected most sharply among younger workers. The desire for immediate gratifications—a car, spending money, a girl—burns strong. Rather than spend hard years at study, a man goes immediately into a plant at its attractive starting wage. Once in the plant, he may realize, sickeningly, that he has made a devil's bargain. His advancement depends upon educational training; but this he has foregone. He becomes restless. But dissatisfactions on the job lead not to militancy, despite occasional sporadic outbursts, but to escapist fantasies—of having a mechanic's shop, a turkey farm, a gas station, of "owning a small business of one's own." An idle dream.

This essay has talked by and large about "the" factory worker and the constraints imposed upon him. Certainly any large-scale generalizations become fuzzy if matched against complex and protean reality. And factory work, after all, comprises only a fraction of the kinds of work done in the United States. Other occupational groups have their own work psychology and problems. A

---

[2] So compelling was the old American myth that Chrysler, who built the third largest auto empire in the United States, entitled his autobiography the *Life of an American Workman*. Would a European tycoon ever do likewise?

skilled worker may find his job monotonous, and a chambermaid in a bustling metropolitan hotel may not. Nothing may be more deadly, perhaps, than the isolated, hermetic life of the bank teller in his cage or the elevator operator in his sealed jack-in-the-box. Longshoremen swear by their occupation, gaining satisfactions in the free use of muscle and the varieties of excitement on a big city pier, while scorning those who are tied down to the bench or lathe. Musicians, typographers, miners, seamen, loggers, construction workers all have their special cast of work. Yet the factory is archetypical because its rhythms, in subtle fashion, affect the general character of work the way a dye suffuses a cloth. And, equally, because the rhythms of mechanization spill over into once individualized modes of work. Coal mining, once spoken of as "underground farming," now with mechanization of the cutting and conveying takes on much of the aspects of factory work. In offices the installation of rapid high-speed calculators, tabulators and billing machines turns the white-collar workers into mechanically paced drones. The spread of mechanization into "materials handling" (i.e. warehouses and super-markets) has introduced mechanical rhythms into the distributive sector of the economy.

These changes accentuate, too, the tendencies toward the evasion of work which are so characteristic of the American factory worker and which today obsess all workers. The big lure of escape remains the hope of "being one's own boss." The creed of "the 'individual enterprise' has become by and large a working-class preoccupation," sociologists Reinhard Bendix and S. M. Lipset report. "Though it may have animated both working class and middle class in the past, it is no longer a middle-class ideal today. Instead, people in the middle class aspire to become professionals and, as a second choice, upper-white-collar workers." Of course fewer people actually try to go into business than those who think of it as a goal, "but here again the manual workers report more such efforts than the white-collar group."

How realistic are these aspirations? We know that the labor force of the economy is being transformed. Colin Clark, in his *Conditions of Economic Progress*, long ago pointed out that, as incomes rose and the quantity and quality of goods produced increased, large sections of the economy would shift to service and other "tertiary" occupations. Since 1910, the proportion of farmers, farm owners and unskilled workers in the labor force has decreased sharply as an aggregate; skilled workers have held their own; service workers have increased slightly; professional persons have moved up from 4.4 to 7.5 per cent and proprietors and managers from 6.5 to 8.8 per cent of the work force in that period. The largest increases have come in the categories of semi-skilled labor, and clerks and sales personnel. Between 1910 and 1950 the semi-skilled group increased from 14.7 to 22.4 per cent, the white collar worker from 10.2 to 20.2 per cent.

Followers of Clark, seeking to refine the conceptual scheme, have talked of "quarternary" occupations (communications, finance, transport, commerce) and "quinary" occupations (medical care, education, research, recreation). Certainly the expansion of the American economy has made many new careers possible, and these new occupations are located, on the whole, outside the factory. But the fascination with these *rates* of growth should not mislead us into failing to consider the limited number of such positions available, or the fact that social mobility in the United States is a matter *between* generations— it is the children who may get ahead, not the father; the father reaches a point and usually stays there. The study of occupational mobility by Bendix and Lipset showed that individuals held an average of 4.8 jobs over a 25-year work history. But, while workers do change jobs, "between those who work with their hands and those who do not, there is . . . relatively little shifting." This is perhaps the most fundamental cleavage in American society. All those who work with their hands have spent 80 per cent of their working lives in manual occupations; all who do not work with their hands have spent 75 per cent of their working lives in non-manual occupations.

The sense of having a fixed place is grinding. And even as in the large corporations, if one still thinks of moving up, the escalator-like process is slow. In compensation, there is a considerable—and sometimes pathetic— effort, if not to lift oneself, to lift one's occupation by its bootstraps. A man will do an infinite amount of physically dirty work, says sociologist Everett Hughes, if the status and prestige arrangements are right; the physically unpleasant jobs of the doctor, for example, are legion. The effort to "professionalize" work has become the major means of giving one's job a badge of honorific quality which the nature of the work itself denies. We have schools of hotel management, as well as social work. The garage becomes the "lubritorium"; individuals do not say "I am selling skillets" but "I am in selling"; the janitor becomes the "superintendent"; the hospital superintendent turns into the "administrator"; the secretary becomes the "executive assistant"; and the minister, if he is unable to rise to bishop, measures his success in terms of the social class of his parishioners.

The most significant form taken by the flight from work is the desperate drive for "leisure." Work is irksome, but if it cannot be evaded, it can be reduced. In modern times, the ideal is to minimize the unpleasant aspects of work as much as possible by pleasant distractions (music, wall colors, rest periods) and to hasten away as quickly as possible, uncontaminated by work and unimpaired by its arduousness. A gleaming two-page advertisement in *Life* magazine shows a beautiful Lincoln car in the patio-living room of an elegantly simple house, and the ad proclaims: "Your home has walls of glass. Your kitchen is an engineering miracle. Your clothes and your furniture are beautifully functional. *You work easily; play hard.*"

The themes of play, of recreation, of amusement are the dominant ones in our culture today. They are the subject of the "hard sell." Sports clothes, travel, the outdoor barbecue, the portable TV set all become the hallmarks of the time. In this passivity, there are already the seeds of decay. Yet some serious social critics see in the development of leisure time the potentialities of achieving a spontaneity of spirit, free of the restraints of work and of the older moral injunctions which frowned upon undisciplined expression. David Riesman mocks those who would seek to introduce "joy and meaning" into modern industrialism. "In a fallacy of misplaced participation," he says, they would like to "personalize, emotionalize and moralize the factory and white collar worlds." But "it makes more sense," he argues, "to work with rather than against the grain of impersonality in modern industry: to increase automatization in work—but for the sake of pleasure and consumption and not for the sake of work itself."

What Riesman wants is "freedom in play." "Far from having to be the residue sphere left over from work-time and work-feeling, [play] can increasingly become the sphere for the development of skill and competence in the art of living. Play may prove to be the sphere in which there is still room left for the would-be autonomous man to reclaim his individual character from the pervasive demands of his social character."

Few can quarrel with the ideal, perhaps because it is so amorphous. ("Admittedly we know very little about play," writes Riesman. ". . . research has been concerned mainly with the 'social character' of the producer.") But can "play" be divorced from work? Play, it should be pointed out, is not leisure—at least not in the classical image as it has come down from Plato to T. S. Eliot. A leisure civilization is one with the fixed task of exploring and extending a specific cultural heritage. Leisure is not, as Josef Pieper points out, a dalliance or wanton play, but a full-time cultivation of the gentle arts, a "working at" pursuits which make up the calling of the gentleman. Nor is relaxation play. Relaxation, whether it be puttering or daydreaming, is an interstice between efforts, a trough between peaks. It is not "free time," as any man who takes a "break" from work knows, but lapsed time, an integral part of the rhythms of work.

Play (not leisure or relaxation) is a release from the tension of work, an alternate use of muscle and mind. But a tension that is enervating or debilitating can only produce wildly aggressive play, or passive, unresponsive viewing. To have "free time" one needs the zest of a challenging day, not the exhaustion of a blank one. If work is a daily turn round Ixion's wheel, can the intervening play be anything more than a restless moment before the next turn of the wheel?

Edward Bellamy in his *Looking Backward* foresaw a state wherein an individual spent twenty to twenty-five years of his life in drudging routine for a few hours a day and then was free to pursue his own desires. Here, in the United States in mid-twentieth century, in a curious fashion, Bellamy's vision is being realized. The average work week has been reduced from 70.6 hours (in 1850) to 40.8 (in 1950). The two-day week-end is now standard in American life, and the seven-hour work day is at the threshold. But what workers have been denied in work, they now seek to recapture in manifold ways. Over the past decade there has been a fantastic mushrooming of arts-and-crafts hobbies, of photography, home woodwork shops with power-driven tools, ceramics, high fidelity, electronics, radio "hams." America has seen the multiplication of the "amateur" on a scale unknown in previous history. And while this is intrinsically commendable, it has been achieved at a high cost indeed—the loss of the satisfaction in work. . . .

Two Unorthodox Views

GUS TYLER
THE WORK ETHIC: A UNION VIEW ....

Address to the International Ladies' Garment Workers' Union

Work is a curse, according to Western tradition. The Bible said so. Because Adam had eaten the forbidden fruit, he and his descendants would all have to earn their daily bread in the sweat of their brow. Whether the story of the Fall and the exile of Eden is fact or fiction, it served to set an ethic. Work must be done gladly because it is the penalty man must pay for his sin against God.

For working people, this ethic was always easy to live by. There was no alternative.

For people of means, this ethic was hard to live by because they could luxuriate without laboring. So instead of turning to hard labor, they opted to do good work, to be the Lord's overseers on earth, toiling mightily to see to it that their employees paid proper respect to the divine injunction to sweat their way to the grave and ultimate salvation.

As one Caribbean unionist, oft-quoted of AFL-CIO President Lane Kirkland, put it: "If hard work were really such a great thing, the rich would have kept it all to themselves." Instead, the affluent proffered this privilege to their underlings—a neat division of labor before the eyes of the Almighty.

Hence, there are at least two work ethics: that of the overseer and that of the overseen. In the statements of the former, there is much preaching about the work ethic—as we shall soon note. But, among the millions of resolutions passed by unions over many generations in many countries, there probably is not a single one that refers to the "work ethic." This does not mean that unionists are opposed either to "work" or to "ethics." They favor both: "work" to stay alive and "ethics" for fair treatment at the workplace. But work per se as an ethical imperative gets little, if any, attention because to union people work is such a *necessity* that it is almost unnecessary to construct a system of values, with theologic overtones, to "justify" labor.

Gus Tyler, "The Work Ethic: A Union View," in J. Barbash *et al.*, eds., *The Work Ethic—A Critical Analysis* (Madison, Wis.: Industrial Relations Research Association, 1983). Reprinted by permission of the publisher.

To the typical worker and his or her union, work plays the same role in the laboring universe as Ananke played in the realm of the Greek gods. When Ananke, the God of Necessity, entered, all other gods bowed down, whether Love or Hate, Peace or Discord, or even the sovereign Zeus. To folk who live by their labor, whether self-employed or employee, work is a must, in and of itself, and needs no outside authority to rationalize its importance. Hence, it is no surprise that there are no formal motions "resolving" that work must be performed in response to some ethical injunction handed down from on high.

The nearest thing to a formal *ethic* on the part of American labor was probably summed up in the old slogan: "A fair day's pay for a fair day's work."

The concept is so patently "fair" that there hardly appears occasion for dispute. Yet, over the key word "fair," have many contests been fought. Whatever the outcome, the basic philosophy of organized labor is that wages and salaries are in exchange for work done and that there ought to be some "fair" relationship between input and income—however sloppily the system operates.

Although there is little in labor literature that extols the ethicality of toil, one can find countless statements denouncing the *unethical* behavior of those who live, and live luxuriously, *without working*. The parasitical classes are excoriated repeatedly because they draw their overabundant "profits" from the sweat of those who labor, toil, and create the world's goods. The injustice inherent in the disparate rewards of those who live by labor and those who live in leisure was put grandiloquently by the Philadelphia Mechanics' Union of Trade Associations in 1827. In a compelling ethical appeal to the community for support, the union declared:

> We appeal to the most intelligent of every community and ask—Do not you, and all society, depend *solely* for subsistence on the products of human industry? Do not those who labor, while acquiring to themselves thereby only a scanty and penurious support, likewise maintain in affluence and luxury the rich who *never labor?* Do not all the streams of wealth which flow in every direction and are emptied into and absorbed by the coffers of the *unproductive,* exclusively take their rise in the bones, marrow, and muscles of the *industrious classes?* In return for which, exclusive of bare subsistence (which likewise is the product of their own labor), they receive—not anything! (Italics mine.)

The New England Association of Farmers, Mechanics and Other Workingmen (1831) echoes the plaint, noting "the low estimation in which *useful* labor is held by many whose station in society enable them to give the tone to public opinion." Lashing out at the schemes of their nonproductive critics, the Association declared:

> All who can do so resort to some means of living *without hard work,* the learned professions are crowded, and combinations are formed by that portion of society that have money and *leisure,* or who live by their wits, to maintain and increase their own relative importance, whilst the more *industrious* and *useful* portion of

the community, who are too intent upon their daily occupation to form combinations for mutual advantage, or to guard against the devices of their better informed and enterprising neighbors, are reduced to constant toil, stripped of the better share of their earnings, holding a subordinate if not degraded situation in society, and frequently despised by the very men, and women and children, who live at *ease* upon the fruits of their *labor*. (Italics mine.)

In a circumlocutory way, organized labor was voicing a "work ethic," a sentiment that those who "produced" were the good people and those who did not were the evil—at least the less desirable—personages. The "work ethic"— defined here as the superior moral claims of those who created things—was implicit in the philosophy, stated or unstated, of the early American labor organizations. They repeatedly drew the line between the working poor and the idle rich as a way to unite the various forces, unions, federations of working people.

In doing so, the unions were not at variance with commonly accepted economic theory about the origin of wealth. "Labour," wrote Adam Smith in *The Wealth of Nations,* "is the real measure of the exchangeable value of all commodities. . . . Labour is the only universal, as well as the only accurate measure of value. . . . In this state of things, the whole produce of labour belongs to the labourer." This "labor theory of value" was extended by John Locke to the labor theory of "property" when he wrote *Concerning Civil Government:* "Though the earth and all inferior creatures be common to all men, yet every man has a 'property' in his own 'person.' The 'labour' of his body and the 'work' of his hands are properly his. Whatsoever, then, he removes out of the state that Nature has provided and left it in, he hath mixed his labour with it, and joined to it something that is his own, and thereby makes it his property." At a later time, Karl Marx carried this to what he believed was its logical conclusion: namely, that labor could enjoy the full fruits of its toil only when the capitalist class—those idlers—was eliminated.

But the many statements of unions, claiming "more" for those who worked, were not based on anyone's economic theory, be it Smith, Locke, or Marx. The sentiments flowed quite naturally from people who did not think it fair for a few to reap what the many had sowed.

The employing class, on whom the claims for "more" were made, had its own version of the work ethic. If the poor were poor, it was due to their laziness or drunkenness or to some form of unethical behavior for which God was punishing them. Spokesmen for the economic elite did not deny that the "industrious" deserved the greatest wealth. They merely argued that a man's riches proved his industry. Thus John Hay: "That you have property is proof of industry and foresight on your part or your father's; that you have nothing is a judgment on your laziness and vices, or on your improvidence. The world is a moral world, which it would not be if virtue and vice received the same reward." Hence, riches proved righteousness.

The "vices" of the poor were described in pretty much the same terms as today: "Too many are trying to live without labor . . . and too many squander their earnings on intoxicating drinks, cigars, and amusements who cannot afford it." Also, of course, they suffer from "excessive reproduction, sexually."

Both labor and capital believed in a "work ethic." Labor said that work was good, the creator of all things, and that, therefore, pay should be good for those who worked. Capital said that God decreed that people should be rewarded according to their industry and that, therefore, those who had the most must surely have contributed the most to society. Both agreed that work was good; they disagreed about how to divvy up the goodies.

To unions, one such goodie was *leisure*. First, there was the movement for the ten-hour day, then the eight-hour day, then the five-day week, then vacations, sabbaticals, early retirement. Hours and wages have been cornerstones of labor-management contracts in America.

To many employers, the demand for shorter hours was proof positive that labor was lazy. Why else would they seek to shirk their God-ordained mission on earth by curtailing the hours of toil unless it be to indulge in evil habits? Said the merchants and shopowners of Boston (1832): "The time thus proposed to be thrown away would be a serious loss to this active community" and the "habits likely to be generated by the indulgence of idleness in our summer mornings, and afternoons will be very detrimental to [the employees] individually, and very costly to us as a community." Long workhours were especially important for children because a shorter workday—such as ten hours a day— would exert an "unhappy influence" on the young by "seducing them from that course of industry and economy of time" to which their work should "inure them."

The notion of a ten-hour day—actually 12 hours with a one-hour break for breakfast and another for lunch—was so outlandish that, according to a public advertisement of the Master Carpenters, it could not have "originated with any of the faithful and industrious Sons of New England" but was "an evil of foreign growth." This harsh view of the work ethic—to inure the child and adult to incessant toil so that they would not deprive the community of their labor and would not debauch themselves with leisure—appeared to unions, even at the earliest time, to be unethical, undemocratic, and unnecessary. The response was the demand for a ten-hour day.

Although long labor, from sunup to sunset, sometimes seven days a week, should per se have been reason enough to demand a "ten-hour day" because longer toil was dangerously onerous, dehumanizing, debilitating, deadening, and deathly, the early statements of unions preferred to invoke the egalitarian spirit of the American Revolution, in which their fathers or grandfathers had fought, to provide a popular rationale for their demands. Too much time at work, they proclaimed, deprived them of time to act like free men—to develop their mental faculties and to organize their associations to play the proper role of citizens in a democracy.

Thus the argument of the Philadelphia unions:

Is it equitable that we should waste the energies of our minds and bodies, and be placed in a situation of such increasing exertion and servility as must necessarily, in time, render the benefits of our liberal institutions to us inaccessible and useless, in order that the products of our labor may be accumulated by a few into vast pernicious masses, calculated to prepare the minds of the possessors for the exercise of lawless rule and despotism, to overawe the meager multitude, and fright away that shadow of freedom which still lingers among us?

The same sentiments were echoed in a public declaration of the Boston Carpenters (1835):

We have been too long subjected to the odious, cruel, unjust and tyrannical system which compels the operative mechanic to exhaust his physical and mental powers. We have rights and duties to perform as American citizens and as members of society, which forbid us to dispose of more than ten hours for a day's work.

In a letter to the *Boston Post* (1835), a rank-and-filer said it all in plain talk: "By the old system we have no time for mental cultivation—and that is the policy of the big bugs—they endeavor to keep people ignorant by keeping them always at work."

As unions saw it, the leisure time of their masters was put to use to plot and to politic. To keep workers from doing the same, the masters schemed to keep hands so busy that there would be no time for heads. The long workweek was a way to prolong "tyranny," allowing the leisure class to conspire while making the working class perspire. The ten-hour day would mean not only economic, but also political, liberation.

The unions were prepared to concede that there might be a situation that demanded long, even burdensome, hours of work because society could not survive without such back-breaking exertion. "If unceasing toil were actually required to supply us with a bare, and in many instances wretched, subsistence; if the products of our industry, or an equitable proportion of them, were appropriated to our actual wants and comfort, then would we yield without a murmur to the stern and irrevocable degree of necessity." They were ready to bow before Ananke. "But," continued the Philadelphia resolution, "this is infinitely wide of the fact. . . . At the present period, when wealth is so easily and abundantly created that the markets of the world are overflowing with it, and when, in consequence thereof, and of the continual development and increase of scientific power, the demand for human labor is gradually and inevitably diminished, it cannot be necessary that we, or any portion of society, should be subjected to perpetual slavery."

Long hours and low wages then could no longer be justified by *necessity*, and hence continued exploitation of workers was *unethical*. It was also *uneconomic*, a threat to the entire system.

The line of logic offered by the Philadelphians to show how long hours and low wages were, in the long run, just as injurious to the "capitalist" as to the working man is so modern in its approach that it is incredible that it was set forth in 1827, about a century before John Maynard Keynes espoused the same basic case in profound postulates. In a series of simple syllogisms, the unions explained why it was in the best interests of the capitalist to provide proper compensation to labor:

> The workman is not more dependent upon his wages for the support of his family than they [employers] are upon the demand for the various articles they fabricate or vend. If the mass of the people were enabled by their labor to procure for themselves and their families a full and abundant supply of the comforts and conveniences of life, the consumption of articles, particularly of dwellings, furniture and clothing, would amount to at least twice the quantity it does at present, and of course the demand, by which alone employers are enabled either to subsist or accumulate, would likewise be increased in an equal proportion. . . . The workman need not languish for want of employment, the vender for sales, nor the capitalist complain for want of profitable modes of investment . . . if, therefore, as members of the community, if they [employers] are desirous to prosper, in vain will they expect to succeed unless the great body of the community is kept in a healthy, vigorous, and prosperous condition.

In the absence of adequate *demand,* derived from proper remuneration of labor, all classes will be hurt. First, the workers will "begin to pine, languish, suffer. But the evil stops not here. The middle class next, venders of the product of human industry, will begin to experience its deleterious effects. . . . At last the contagion will reach the capitalist . . . and his capital . . . will become useless, unemployed, and stagnant."

The effects will be social as well as economic. The mighty capitalist "throned as he is in the midst of his ill-gotten abundance" will become "the trembling victim of continued alarms from robberies, burnings and murder."

In this early declaration of American unions is contained a concept of "work" and an ethic revolving around work that flowed from the natural inclinations and daily experiences of working people:

First, man does not live to work; he works in order to live. Communities are composed to protect and promote man's needs and work is an important and necessary way to do so, but only a means toward an end.

Second, since it is man—not work—that is to be served, man should try to produce as much with his labor as possible and should find ways to lighten his burden. To do so, man learns a skill; he also invents wheels, pulleys, and other "tools" to ease his toil.

Third, as leisure becomes possible, man—including the working man—should use that newly found time to develop his mind and to participate more fully in a democratic society.

Finally, if this ethic is denied—if man is subordinated to toil, if the idle grow rich at the expense of those who labor, if leisure is denied the people—then a society will be plagued by crisis and crime.

Ergo, an ethic that sees work serving man, that apportions the community's income justly, that gives humans the time to grow as individuals and as citizens, will serve the purposes of both *equity* and *efficiency* and establish "a just balance of power, both mental, moral, political and scientific, between all the various classes and individuals which constitute society at large."

If I have dealt at some length on the ethical attitudes of laboring people toward work in the first decades of the last century, it was not to get lost in some nostalgic moment in the past. It was an attempt to dig out and describe an attitude that prevailed among unions—may we add, enlightened working people—at a time in our nation's history when, it is generally held, the "work ethic" prevailed. The choice of statements from Philadelphia and Boston suggests that this ethic was also likely to be the "Protestant work ethic," since these communities were so heavily Puritan and Quaker in their commitment. Finally, the statement drawn from our Protestant past, serves still another purpose since it sets forth the basic principles that guide American unions today.

In the century and a half since the Philadelphia and Boston declarations, American labor has hewed fairly tightly to the "work ethic" as defined by those forefather unionists. Work is necessary; the fruits of labor should be shared justly; leisure is imperative so a worker may be a human and a citizen; shorter hours and higher wages are a sine qua non for a market economy that depends upon its wage and salaried employees for its consumers.

The application of this kind of "work ethic" that envisions the economy and its dynamic as intended to elevate, rather than degrade, humans has, when allowed to operate, been responsible for the remarkably strong performance of America among world economies. Consider, briefly, some of the economics of this ethic.

The starting point is the belief among American workers that they are not lesser persons because they belong to a class of employees dependent on the employer for a livelihood. This feeling has always been especially strong among the more skilled who truly felt that there was a dignity in labor. In time, this attitude spread to working people in general as the semiskilled and the unskilled joined the skilled craftsmen in unions.

Where did this notion come from—this concept that a man at work was still "a man for a' that"? There are several interlocking factors encouraging this humanistic view of work among workers.

First, the American worker—barring the blacks of the slavery period—was not raised in a stratified society that had formed its social relations, its attitudinal postures, through generations of feudalism. In the New World, there might be rich and poor, boss and bossed, but there were no formal legal castes. Workers felt they were freemen, equals.

Second, there was a relative shortage of labor in the American colonies. Indeed, the recruitment of blacks from Africa and of indentured servants from Europe were efforts to swell the labor force. Despite this and later operations to bring over contract labor from Asia as well, the labor market was—by and large—tight in early America, pushing wages well above those for comparable jobs in the Old World.

Third, there was the frontier—an abundance of land, allowing the worker to escape the city and to perpetuate the relative shortage of labor.

Fourth, the American Revolution provided a rhetorical and ideological spur for egalitarian ideals.

Finally, the enfranchisement of the unpropertied in the 1820s gave workers a sense that they could and should have a say in the shaping of the world in which they worked and lived.

All these impulses interacted, reinforcing one another: free men reached out for a larger share of the nation's output and for a bigger say in government, emboldened to do so because they knew that their hands were needed and because they or their fathers had risked or given their lives in the war for equality.

The practical consequences of all this was very early organization of workers in unions (with strikes preceding formal organization) and a relatively high wage. This "high" wage, in turn, stimulated the economy to make it more productive—that is, to turn out more per worker-hour.

Confronted with "high" wages, employers quite naturally sought out ways to increase the output per employee. They put their Yankee ingenuity to work to invent "labor-saving" devices that increased worker output per hour.

These devices would have been counterproductive, however, if there were not a mass market to absorb the mass production of workshops equipped with new technologies. Without a market, the costly machines would have been just so much idle overhead. But, fortunately, the market was there because wages were relatively high and because there were many farm families with the income to purchase manufactured goods.

Hence, there was a double spur for employers to introduce new technologies: to get more for the higher wage and to supply a mass market. Both these factors were present because the American worker organized to take advantage of relative labor scarcity to get a greater portion of the fruits of his labor.

Productivity was also spurred by the advance of *science* in the United States and by the *education* of the labor force. Both of these developments owed much to a labor movement committed to an "ethic" that preached the need for both leisure and learning for workers to play their proper role in a democracy. The Working Men's Party of Philadelphia put it elegantly and eloquently in a platform that made education—universal, free, public—its paramount plank (1830):

> All history corroborates the melancholy fact, that in proportion as the mass of people becomes ignorant, misrule and anarchy ensue—their liberties are subverted, and tyrannic ambition has never failed to take advantage of their helpless condition. . . . Let the *productive* classes then, unite, for the preservation of their free institutions, and by procuring for all the children in the Commonwealth Republican Education, preserve our liberties from the dangers of foreign invasion or domestic infringement. . . . This [education] is the rock on which the temple of moral freedom and independence is founded; any other foundation than this will prove inadequate to the protection of our liberties, and our republican

institutions. In order to support the superstructure, the foundation must be broad. Our government is republican; our education should be equally so. [Italics mine.]

To all the workingmen's parties of that time, the democratization of knowledge was essential for the democratization of politics.

The drive for universal, free, public school education at the elementary level was followed by the extension of the same ideal to intermediate education. With the Morrill Act and land grant colleges, the idea was carried to higher education.

The unions that threw themselves into these campaigns did so because, by their "ethic," a worker was not just a clod of clay shaped to toil with some tool. He was a citizen in a democracy, a creature created in the image of his Maker, who had a "right" to schooling to enable him to do better at the workplace and at the voting place. America's broad-based educational system— "the foundation" to "support the superstructure" of democracy—was a concrete result of the "work ethic" as labor saw it.

The consequences of this extension of education were threefold. First, the labor force was *better educated* and, to the extent that such preparation for work makes the worker more productive, education boosted productivity—measured as output per hour per worker. Second, this broad-based educational system, drawing talent from all classes and not simply from the narrow restricted elite, gave America a great reservoir of *trained intellects* to do the research, development, introduction of technology, starting with pure science and ending up with miraculous engineering applications to American industry—and farming.

Third, education did give working people a better capacity to understand the society in which they lived and to use their ballot with greater wisdom. This *political* fact has had its *economic* impact. Workers were able to use their vote not simply to enact labor legislation that affected unions institutionally, to back social legislation to protect themselves against the hazards of work, but also—and most critically—to support programs to *maximize* employment in the nation. Central to labor's role in American politics in the last half century—from FDR on—has been the push for full employment: support for the New Deal, the Employment Act of 1946, the Humphrey-Hawkins Act, and numerous ad hoc laws to make jobs available to all who could and would work.

It is one of the great ironies of capitalism that the capitalists, who were among the most ardent advocates of a "work ethic" that made man's whole existence out to be little more than hard labor, pursued practices that periodically left workers without work. No matter how much the worker needed work, no matter how long he was ready to toil for how little, he was denied the opportunity to work by precisely those people who told him that idleness was evil—for society and for the idler. The Great Depression was America's most dramatic manifestation of this irony.

In the years that followed, American labor pursued policies to promote "full employment," a job for anyone able and willing to work. Essentially, these policies were an extension of the prescription proposed by the Philadelphia unions: expand aggregate demand by allocating to labor a fuller share of the national income. In its Keynesian refinement, "demand" was further to be expanded, when necessary, by government expenditures for socially desirable ends. In this *economic* program—presently the hub of labor's political program— there was an implicit *ethic:* work was not only a "necessity," it was a "right." This "right to work" was enshrined in Roosevelt's 1944 State of the Union Message when in his "Second Bill of Rights" he called for "the *right* to a useful and remunerative job in the industries or shops or farms or mines of the nation."

In those years when our national policies and practices encouraged maximum employment, to make the "right to work" a reality, *productivity* rose—again defining productivity as output per worker; in those years when unemployment rose and workers were denied the "right to work" in larger numbers, *productivity*—output per worker—fell.

The spread of education, stimulated in large part by labor's crusade for schooling, has spurred *productivity* in America by better preparing workers for the job, by creating a great reservoir of scientists and technicians, and by enabling working people to use their vote to further full employment. As a consequence, the United States leads the world in productivity. If we assign an index of 100 to this country, then next in line is Canada with 91.6, France with 84.7, West Germany with 79.1, and Japan with 63.2. If, in recent years, starting with 1970, America has been slipping in its lead, this is primarily due to the depressed state of the economy in that decade.

The many positive economic effects of education on our economy were reinforced by the growth of *leisure.* The hope of the early unions that leisure would provide the time to think, to organize, to get into politics, were not in vain. Unions are in politics deeply and play a role in the shaping of national policy.

But, in time, leisure proved to offer *economic* advantages. The worker on an eight-hour day was, hour for hour, more productive than his brother on a ten- or twelve-hour day, whose output was dragged down by fatigue. The shorter workweek also turned out to be a very direct way to realize the "right to work" by making room for additional employees: instead of one person for 16 hours, it became two persons for eight hours.

Leisure also stimulated leisure-time activities—sports, travel, amusement, restaurants, hunting, fishing, watching TV—and thereby stimulated industries and services. Today, a huge chunk of the American economy is built around "leisure-time" demand. It does seem perverse to suggest that "leisure," usually seen as the opposite of labor, is today a vital part of the "work ethic," but it is. It adds to productivity, to employment, and to the humanization of the worker's life.

Because the worker, rather than the work, is the prime concern of the laborist "work ethic," working conditions and "fringes" are today high on the bargaining agenda along with "hours and wages." Whereas "working conditions" were once limited to items such as lighting, heating, toilet facilities, and fire escapes, at present the term applies to protective devices, dangerous materials, noise level, workload, classroom size. In some cases, working conditions involve muzak, redesign of job, breaks for exercise, rotation of assignments. But whatever is done to make the worksite and the working assignment safer for the body and saner for the psyche, it is widely accepted that there is an "ethical" obligation to recognize the worker as a person. It is this same recognition that has led to the proliferation of fringes such as workers' compensation, unemployment insurance, retirement, health care, personal days, sabbaticals. Many of these "benefits" protect the worker in times of distress, whether injured, out of work, or too old to want to work; others are ways to make life a bit more pleasant. In both cases, they show concern for the worker even when he or she is not in the workplace but is, nevertheless, a soul in our society.

The union view of the "work ethic" has, in many direct and indirect ways, strengthened the economic and political life of America. This fact generally goes unnoted because we are not in a position to see what the country would be like if organized labor had not been there to raise wages, shorten the workday and workweek, and advocate public education. But just suppose that the employer's view of the "work ethic" prevailed: long hours and no leisure, low wages and no fringes, no public schools and no vote for the unpropertied, and—above all—no unions to raise hell about the odious circumstance. Would we not end up entrapped in an oppressive process which— to quote the Philadelphia unionists—"in its ultimate effects, must be productive of universal ruin and misery and destroy alike the happiness of every class and individual in society."

Luckily, for America, labor has offered an alternate work ethic.

HARRY MAGDOFF
THE MEANING OF WORK: A MARXIST PERSPECTIVE ....

. . . Adam Smith, the great theoretician of the capitalist economy . . . is much more explicit when, in a different context, he defines work as an activity requiring the worker to give up "his tranquility, his freedom, and his happiness." Wages, according to Smith, are the reward the laborer receives for his or her sacrifices. How utterly different is the Marxist perspective! Look at the scorn Marx heaps on Smith for this negative attitude to work:

> In the sweat of thy brow shalt thou labor! was Jehovah's curse on Adam. And this is labor for Smith, a curse. "Tranquility" appears as the adequate state, as

Harry Magdoff, "The Meaning of Work: A Marxist Perspective," *Monthly Review,* Vol. 34, No. 5, October 1982. Copyright ©1982 by Monthly Review, Inc. Reprinted by permission of Monthly Review Foundation.

identical with "freedom" and "happiness." It seems quite far from Smith's mind that the individual, "in his normal state of health, strength, activity, skill, facility," also needs a normal portion of work, and of the suspension of tranquility. Certainly, labor obtains its measure from the outside, through the aim to be attained and the obstacles to be overcome in attaining it. But Smith has no inkling whatever that the overcoming of obstacles is in itself a liberating activity— and that, further, the external aims become stripped of the semblance of merely external natural urgencies, and become posited as aims which the individual himself posits—hence as self-realization, objectification of the subject, hence real freedom, whose action is, precisely, labor. He is right, of course, that, in its historic forms as slave-labor, serf-labor, and wage-labor, labor always appears as repulsive, always as *external forced labor;* and not-labor, by contrast, as "freedom and happiness." This holds doubly: for this contradictory labor; and relatedly, for labor which has not yet created the subjective and objective conditions for itself . . . in which labor becomes attractive work, the individual's self-realization, which in no way means that it becomes mere fun, mere amusement. . . . Really free working . . . is at the same time precisely the most damned seriousness, the most intensive exertion. The work of material production can achieve this character only (1) when its social character is posited, (2) when it is of a scientific and at the same time general character, not merely human exertion, as a specifically harnessed natural force, but exertion as subject, which appears in the production process, not in a merely natural, spontaneous form, but as an activity regulating all the forces of nature. Adam Smith, by the way, has only the slaves of capital in mind.*

Marx and Engels saw work as central to human existence. This theme is developed by Engels in his unfinished essay, "The Part Played by Labour in the Transition from Ape to Man," where he maintains that labor "is the prime basic condition for all human existence, and this to such an extent that, in a sense, we have to say that labor created man himself."** This speculation by Engels on the evolution of human beings focuses on the idea that walking on two feet freed the use of the hand and made possible its development for

---

*Karl Marx, *Grundrisse* (Baltimore, Maryland: Penguin Books, 1973), pp. 611–12. Marx is discussing the following statement in Adam Smith's *The Wealth of Nations:* "In his ordinary state of health, strength and spirits; in the ordinary degree of his skill and dexterity, [the laborer] must always lay down the same portion of his ease, his liberty, and his happiness." Marx read the French translation of *The Wealth of Nations.* By the time we get the *Grundrisse* in English, his references to Smith have passed through several languages. In order to make the passage from Marx more understandable, when quoting Smith I used the somewhat inaccurate version that appears in the English translation of the *Grundrisse.*

**The original title of the essay reads, *"Anteil der Arbeit an der Menschwerdung des Affen."* Although the primary meaning of *Mensch* is *human being,* translators have adopted the convention of equating *Mensch* with *man.* The reader should know that in the citations from this essay by Engels and the one from Marx used later in this article, the original text referred to *Mensch* and not *man.*

complex tasks. The specialization of the hand in turn led to labor, the mastery over nature, and the differentiation of the human species. Labor brought people together under conditions "where they had something to say to each other." Thus, with labor came speech and the stimuli under the influence of which the brain of the ape gradually changed into that of human beings. Further evolution along this path led to society:

> By the combined functioning of hands, speech organs, and the brain, not only in each individual but also in society, men became capable of executing more and more complicated operations, and were able to set for themselves and achieve higher and higher aims. The work of each generation itself became different, more perfect and more diversified. Agriculture was added to hunting and cattle-raising; then came spinning, weaving, metal-working, pottery, and naviga-tion . . . trade, industry, art, and science.*

Along with the growing complexity of society, however, came private property, the separation of people into classes, and a social division of labor—all of which deeply altered the meaning of work. Differences in environment led to differences in the way people worked and in the things they made. The type of soil and the availability of animals, fish, forests, ores, coal, waterfalls, etc., influenced the means of production and subsistence of each community. Nature provided both the opportunities and the fetters. Yet within these constraints it was nevertheless the social factor that increasingly determined the organization of work and the distribution of its products.

---

*"The Part Played by Labour in the Transition from Ape to Man," in Frederick Engels, *Dialectics of Nature* (Moscow: Foreign Languages Publishing House, 1954). It is also available as an appendix, along with an interesting introduction by Eleanor Burke Leacock, in F. Engels, *The Origin of the Family, Private Property, and the State* (New York: International Publishers, 1972). Engels' theory of human origins is examined in the light of scientific explorations since the essay was written (1876) in an interesting book by Charles Woolfson, *The Labour Theory of Culture* (London: Routledge and Kegan Paul, 1982).

In addition to discussing the evolution of man, Engels introduces an ecological theme that has a very modern ring: "In short, the animal merely *uses* its environment, and brings about changes in it simply by his presence; man by his changes makes it serve his ends, *masters* it. This is the final, essential distinction between man and other animals, and once again it is labor that brings about this distinction. Let us not, however, flatter ourselves overmuch on account of our human victories over nature. For each such victory nature takes its revenge on us. Each victory, it is true, in the first place brings about the results we expected, but in the second and third places it has quite different, unforeseen effects which only too often cancel the first. . . . Thus at every step we are reminded that we by no means rule over nature like a conqueror over a foreign people, like someone standing outside nature, but that we, with flesh, blood and brain, belong to nature and exist in its midst, and that all our mastery of it consists in the fact that we have the advantage over all other creatures of being able to learn its laws and apply them correctly."

THE FIRST SOCIAL DIVISION OF LABOR

In the earliest forms of social organization, family and kinship relations set the pattern for the way different tasks were undertaken or assigned. There are various theories—or shall we say speculations?—about how this low-technology mode of production based on personal relations and production for use (rather than for exchange) gave way to the dominance of exchange, private property, and an increasingly rigid division of labor. According to Engels, the early "natural" division of labor eventually "undermines the collectivity of production and appropriation, elevates the appropriation of products by individuals into the general rule and thus creates exchange between individuals. . . . Gradually, commodity production becomes the dominating form." (*Origin of the Family, Private Property and the State* [New York: International Publishers, 1972], p. 237) But whatever the precise sequence of these developments, it is clear that the division of labor based on private property and exchange became the dominant characteristic of economic life.

For Marx and Engels the primary, decisive division is that between town and country. As Marx put it:

> The foundation of every division of labor that is well developed, and brought about by the exchange of commodities, is the separation between town and country. It may be said that the whole economic history of society is summed up in the movement of this antithesis. (*Capital,* vol. 1 [Moscow: Progress Publishers], p. 333)

The differentiation of town and country arises of course from the division between agricultural and industrial and commercial labor. Eventually other separations take place, as between industrial, commercial, and financial activities within the cities. But what needs to be understood is that the town-country antithesis encompasses much more than merely city vs. farm. Thus as nations evolve, regional differences emerge and become ossified. Today, even in the most advanced industrial countries, conflicts and contrasts exist between, on the one hand, regions that specialize in industry, commerce, and finance, and, on the other, those that engage primarily in agriculture. Furthermore, with the progress of international trade and empire-building by the industrially and militarily superior capitalist nations, an international division of labor is created and reproduced (by the use of force and the "normal" operations of the market) between the core countries ("town") and those of the periphery ("country").

To be sure, new social formations and advances in productive forces alter particular aspects of the way people become separated by job specialization and life style. Still, there are two features common to all the variations in the social division of labor: (1) It always coincides with a particular set of hierarchical relations between individuals, social groups, and, in certain periods in history, nations—whether associated with patriarchalism, slavery, castes, estates, or modern classes. And (2) it is always taken over, shaped, and reproduced by and for a dominant social group, generally comprising those who own or control the primary means of production. . . .

THE SECOND DIVISION OF LABOR

The hierarchical structures accompanying the town/country antithesis entail a second major division that works to perpetuate differences among people, i.e., the separation of mental and manual labor. The roots of this contradiction and its psychological reinforcement go far back in time. Note, for example, how Socrates views manual work and the manual worker:

> What are called the mechanical arts carry a social stigma and are rightly dishonored in our cities. For these arts damage the bodies of those who work at them or have charge of them, by compelling the workers to a sedentary life, by compelling them, indeed, in some cases to spend the whole day by the fire. This physical degeneration results also in deterioration of the soul. Furthermore, the workers at these trades simply have not got the time to perform the offices of friendship or citizenship. Consequently they are looked upon as bad friends and patriots. And in some cities, especially the warlike ones, it is not legal for a citizen to ply a mechanical trade.*

Socrates clearly reflects the attitudes and ideology of upper-class free citizens in a society where slaves are extensively engaged in manual tasks. But the debasement of physical labor is typical not only of social systems based on various forms of forced labor; it is common to all class societies. As Veblen explained:

> The distinction between exploit and drudgery is an invidious distinction between employments. Those employments which are to be classed as exploit are worthy, honorable, noble; other employments which do not contain this element of exploit, and especially those which imply subservience or submission, are unworthy, debasing, ignoble. The concept of dignity, worth, or honor, as applied either to persons or conduct, is of first-rate consequence in the development of classes and class distinctions. . . . (Thorstein Veblen, *The Theory of the Leisure Class* [New York: Random House, 1934], p. 15)

Veblen's "exploit" differs from Marxist usage of the term. What he is referring to is the wide spectrum of non-manual activities. The thrust of his classification is to identify the "exploit" social groups that emerged as soon as manual workers could produce a surplus of means of subsistence for chieftains, nobles, priests, large landowners, merchants, capitalists, military personnel, rulers of governments, etc. To be sure, the "exploit" category in this sense

---

*Attributed to Socrates by Xenophon in his *Oeconomicus,* as cited in Benjamin Farrington, *Head and Hand in Ancient Greece* (London: Watts & Co., 1947), pp. 28–29.

includes many useful and non-exploitative occupations. But what is important is that the objective elements creating and perpetuating divisions and subdivisions of manual and non-manual workers—private property, exploitative class structures, and the state—are reinforced by a subjective, supportive social psychology and ideology that separates people and their work according to degrees of inferiority and superiority. . . .

DIVISION OF LABOR AND MODERN INDUSTRY

The changeover to wage labor greatly altered the way of life and the meaning of work for formerly independent farmers and craftspeople. In seventeenth-century England work for wages was looked on as a form of enslavement. Not only were many factories constructed like poorhouses and prisons, but the work discipline imposed in these shops also presupposed prison-like practices. In the pre-industrial period the time devoted to work was determined by the task to be performed and by natural conditions (weather for farmers, tides for fishers, etc.). Work, leisure, and religious festivals were intertwined, with little demarcation between "work" and "life."* The factory system, on the other hand, created an entirely new work discipline, with time and task rigidly imposed by overseers.

Capitalism also introduces a new stage in the division of labor. In addition to the earlier social division of labor, the production process is itself fractionalized. The extensive use of machinery routinizes the different segments of manufacturing to which a worker is tied, in effect transforming the worker into an appendage of the machine he or she tends. These changes are brilliantly examined in Harry Braverman's classic, *Labor and Monopoly Capital* (New York: Monthly Review Press, 1974). Bringing Marx's analysis of the labor process in Volume I of *Capital* up to date, Braverman explains:

> Labor power [in a capitalist society] has become a commodity. Its uses are no longer organized according to the needs and desires of those who sell it, but rather according to the needs of its purchasers, who are, primarily, employers seeking to expand the value of their capital. And it is the special and permanent interest of these purchasers to cheapen this commodity. The most common mode of cheapening labor power is exemplified by the Babbage principle: break it up into its simplest elements. And as the capitalist mode of production creates a working population suitable to its needs, the Babbage principle is, by the very shape of this "labor market," enforced upon the capitalists themselves.
>
> Every step in the labor process is divorced, so far as possible, from special knowledge and training and reduced to simple labor. Meanwhile, the relatively few persons for whom special knowledge and training are reserved are freed so

---

*See E. P. Thompson, "Time, Work Discipline, and Industrial Capitalism." *Past and Present* no. 38 (December 1967) and Keith Thomas, "Work and Leisure in Pre-Industrial Society," *Past and Present* no. 29 (December 1964).

far as possible from the obligations of simple labor. In this way, a structure is given to all labor processes that at its extremes polarizes those whose time is infinitely valuable and those whose time is worth almost nothing. This might even be called the general law of the capitalist division of labor. It is not the sole force acting upon the organization of work, but it is certainly the most powerful and general. Its results, more or less advanced in every industry and occupation, give massive testimony to its validity. It shapes not only work, but populations as well, because over the long run it creates that mass of simple labor which is the primary feature of populations in developed capitalist countries. (pp. 82–83)

The apt subtitle of Braverman's book reads: "The Degradation of Work in the Twentieth Century." It is important to understand that it isn't only the alienation and dehumanization of the labor process itself that debases work in a capitalist society. The insecurity, the frequency of unemployment, the demanding aspects of the search for work, the growing employment in wasteful and socially harmful occupations, not to mention the meager rewards for the mass of workers all contribute to the degradation of labor in our time. . . .

MARX AND WORK UNDER SOCIALISM

For Marx, a prime aim of socialism would be to eliminate the miseries of work and the way of life arising from capitalism. But, as is well known, he devised no blueprint for such a society. The future would be shaped in the process of revolution, influenced by historical circumstances and in response to the experience gained by the working classes as they engaged in the revolutionary transformation of state and society. Nevertheless there were features that would be essential to the revolution by the exploited: the abolition of classes and private property in the means of production in favor of social control of production. This necessarily implied, in the Marxist framework, the dissolution of all forms of the division of labor that were created by and integral to the existence of private property and classes. How central this point was to Marx's thinking can be seen in his vision of what could and should be the ultimate aim of a communist society:

In a higher phase of communist society, after the enslaving subordination of individuals under the division of labor, and therewith also the antithesis between mental and physical labor, has vanished, after labor has become not merely a means to live but has become itself the primary necessity of life, after the productive forces have also increased with the all-round development of the individual, and all the springs of co-operative wealth flow more abundantly— only then can the narrow horizon of bourgeois right be fully left behind and society inscribe on its banners: from each according to his ability, to each according to his needs. (*Critique of the Gotha Program*)

It should be emphasized that Marx saw this ideal as being realized only after a long process, since the new social order "emerges from capitalist society, which is thus in every respect, economically, morally, and intellectually, still stamped with the birthmarks of the old society from whose womb it emerges." What he did not deal with are the obstacles to achieving the ultimate goal if the "birthmarks of the old society" become encrusted in the new. . . .

But what about the ultimate vision that Marx left to us? Is it within the realm of reason to hold on to such an ideal? There isn't time on this occasion to explore this question in all its ramifications. I would like, however, to point out that behind this vision lie two assumptions, one that is dealt with in the writings of Marx and Engels and another that to the best of my knowledge they ignored.

A basic assumption of the realizability of the communist goal is that human nature is not constant for all time: that acquisitive drives, individualism, and competition are not biological givens. The fact that people do change in their social behavior and attitudes is at the very core of the theory of historical materialism: although "men are products of circumstances and upbringing and therefore changed men are products of other circumstances and changed upbringing" it should not be forgotten "that circumstances are changed precisely by men and that the educator himself must be educated." (Marx, *Theses on Feuerbach*) The support for this proposition comes from a study of history and especially from investigations of anthropologists. "Herr Proudhon does not know," Marx wrote in the *Poverty of Philosophy,* "that all history is but the continuous transformation of human nature."

A frequently met objection to the communist vision is the claim that people will work only if driven by an economic motive. Yet this notion is refuted by many of the primitive societies we know about, where non-economic work incentives predominate: social responsibility, tradition, desire for prestige, and pleasure in craftsmanship. Given the record of past changes in people's attitudes to the community and to their work, it is reasonable to assume that human nature will adapt, and adapt with enthusiasm, to a social order based on cooperation, elimination of a rigid division of labor, and the opportunity for a fuller development of the individual.

But involved here is a second assumption concerning the nature of the needs of the people—a subject to which Marx and Marxists have paid little heed. If the needs of the people are limitless, and especially if they generate a passion for consumption such as that which characterizes the advanced capitalist nations of the West, then it would seem that the prospects for achieving the higher stage of communism are very poor indeed. The problem is not merely the earth's limited resources, though that alone should provide enough reason for skepticism. Limitless expansion in search of an ever higher material standard of living on a world scale could only result in the replication of the worst features of class society. The drive for an incessant increase in production of an ever wider assortment of goods would entail, among other things, continuation of a rigid division of labor, concentration of manufacturing in large enterprises and huge cities. At the same time, equality in distribution would have to go by the board. In the absence of limits on need, there would be no practical way to satisfy every consumer's desire: limited production possibilities would necessarily entail inequality of distribution, along with intensification of conflicts between privileged and deprived sectors.*

What all this adds up to is that a necessary condition for a truly communist society is a *total* departure from the culture of capitalism and consumerism. This would mean a wholly new approach to the design of cities and villages, transportation, location of industry, technology, and much more. Above all, the new culture would have to be grounded in a view of people's needs and a way of life that would be consistent with the maintenance of a cooperative and egalitarian society. . . .

*It should be clear that we are here assuming societies with advanced technology and modern industry. The issue facing underdeveloped countries, whether or not they have gone through a revolution, is the need for a major advancement of their productive resources. However, there too, if the strategy of development is heavily influenced by the standards of the West and its consumerism, the problems of class differentiation and its accompanying evils are bound to persist.

Meaningful Work

IRVING BLUESTONE
WORKER PARTICIPATION IN DECISION MAKING ....

The history of mankind has been marked by struggle between those who govern and those who are governed. In each major conflict, regardless of time, place, and circumstances, the voice of rebellion against authority has manifested itself in the cry for freedom, liberty, human rights, and human dignity. The underlying motivation is the desire for the right to participate in the decisions that affect one's welfare. . . .

The same drive that has moved people and nations toward political freedom exists as well in the workplace—between employer and employee. The owner of capital in the early years of the Industrial Revolution assumed the same mantle in his firm as had monarchs in an earlier day. We are, of course, familiar with

Irving Bluestone, "Worker Participation in Decision Making." This article first appeared in *The Humanist* issue of September–October 1973 and is reprinted by permission.

the oppression and oppressiveness in the factories of the early Industrial Revolution. Control over the employees was almost absolute—short of the worker's right to quit and take a chance of being blackballed from other employment.

Zachary U. Geiger, proprietor of the Mt. Cory Carriage and Wagon Works, listed rules and regulations for his employees in April 1872. Today they appear ludicrous, yet they were the norm in their day.

1. Employes will daily sweep the floors, dust the furniture, shelves, and showcases.
2. Each day fill lamps, clean chimneys and trim wicks; wash the windows once a week.
3. Each clerk will bring in a bucket of water and skuttle of coal for the day's business.
4. Make your own pens carefully. You may whittle nibs to your individual taste.
5. This office will open at 7 a.m. and close at 8 p.m. daily except on the Sabbath, on which day it will remain closed.
6. Men employes will be given an evening off each week for courting purposes, or two evenings if they go regularly to church.
7. Every employe should lay aside from each pay a goodly sum of his earnings for his benefits during his declining years so that he will not become a burden upon the charity of his betters.
8. Any employe who smokes Spanish cigars, uses liquors in any forms, gets shaved at a barber shop, or frequents public halls will give good reason to suspect his worth, intentions, integrity, and honesty.
9. The employe who has performed his labors faithfully and without fault for a period of five years in my service and who has been thrifty and attentive to his religious duties and is looked upon by his fellowmen as a substantial and law-abiding citizen will be given an increase of 5 cents per day in his pay providing that just returns in profits from the business permit it. . . .

AUTHORITARIAN RULE IN THE WORKPLACE

In a society that prides itself on its democratic system of freedom for the individual and rejection of dictatorial rule, the workplace still stands as an island of authoritarianism. The organizational mold of business, especially big business, and the material objective of maximizing profits serve to obstruct, or at least deter, the fulfillment of democracy in the workplace. In fact, the workplace is probably the most authoritarian environment in which the adult finds himself in a free society. Its rigidity leads people to live a kind of double life: at home, they enjoy a reasonable measure of autonomy and self-fulfillment; at work, they are subject to regimentation, supervision, and control by others.

A society anchored in democratic principles should ensure each individual the dignity, respect, and liberty worthy of free people; it should afford opportunity for self-expression and participation in the shaping of one's own life. At work, however, personal freedom is severely curtailed, each worker having to adapt himself to tasks, work speeds, and behavior decided upon by others or by machines.

The American way of life rests on the concept that in public life the "governors" are subject to the will of the "governed." In the private life of business, however, leadership does not stem from the confidence of the "governed" (the workers); rather, it is directed toward protection of the interests of the firm, most often against the "governed," whose activities and patterns of life at work are organized, directed, and dominated by the "governors."

In a democracy, the rules of society are fashioned with the consent of those who must live by them, and the individual is guaranteed a fair trial and is "innocent until proved guilty." In the workplace, management decides the rules to be lived by, then exercises its authority to impose sanctions in cases of individual transgression.

The argument used to support authoritarianism in the workplace is that the organization of production and the goal of maximizing profit make it mandatory. Ownership means control. Ownership means rule by decree. Thus, the pattern of relations between the "governors" and the "governed" in business is contradictory to democracy.

Moreover, the power of ownership is reinforced in society by custom, tradition, and law. The rights of property often supersede the rights of people, and these property rights are buttressed by protective legislation.

This is the heart of the problem that labor-management relations must grapple with. Workers who organize into unions bring an increasing measure of democracy into the workplace. In the broadest possible sense, this is an essential task of unionism and collective bargaining. Moreover, once organized, the workers, as citizens, move to alter the law and to make the rights of people superior to the rights of property and profit. This, too, is an essential task of unionism.

Present-day industrialized society holds to certain economic precepts. Among them are: (1) technological progress is inevitable and desirable; (2) a better living standard for all depends on increased productivity and an expanding gross national product; (3) the purpose of business is to make and maximize profit.

Thus, the underlying thrust of our economic system, anchored in these precepts, has motivated management to develop a production system that is maximally advanced technologically, with maximum production at the lowest possible unit cost, and with maximum profitability.

The pursuit of maximum profit received remarkable stimulus with the advent of industrial organization and its system of production. Very soon, individuals and their needs became extensions of that tool. Skills were broken down to the least common denominator so that humans became as interchangeable as machine parts. Specialization through fractioning the job into the simplest, most repetitive acts of performance reduced skill requirements to the minimum. This production process evolved into scientific management.

The granddaddy of the principles of scientific management, Frederick Taylor, once observed that the average workingman is "so stupid and so phlegmatic that he more resembles the ox in his mental makeup than any other type." Obviously, this is more than mere exaggeration. It is a cynical expression concerning human beings who happen to be workers.

Over the years, scientific management evolved refinements that have robotized workers, removing to the greatest degree possible requirements of education, knowledge, skill, creativity, brain power, and muscle power. The assembly line, with its repetitive, monotonous sameness, developed into the ultimate symbol of scientific management. Taylor's principles have served industry well as a guide toward ever increasing productivity, lower unit costs, and higher profits. They also dovetailed neatly into the concept of "profits before people."

WINDS OF CHANGE IN THE PRODUCTION SYSTEM

Times and circumstances are now beginning to modify the eighty-year-old practices of refined technology—in part because workers' attitudes toward the meaning of work are changing, but also because society as a whole is paying closer attention to the total environment and the quality of life.

About the time that Henry Ford announced the "five-dollar day," he remarked, "The assembly line is a haven for those who haven't got the brains to do anything else." His "enlightened" wage scale was accompanied by rules reminiscent of Geiger's rules of 1872. Mr. Ford's hiring practices were strict and stifling. No women were to work in his factories; they belonged at home in the kitchen and with their children. Men who failed to support their dependents would find no work at Ford, nor would divorced men or others who were "living unworthily"—those who smoked or drank hard liquor. Once hired, the workers were subjected to a spy system. "Social workers" on the Ford payroll visited workers' homes and reported on living habits: Did the man raise his own garden as instructed? Did his family house male boarders (which was taboo)? Did the worker complain to his family about his job and factory conditions? And so forth.

Today, the employer no longer has control of the worker outside the workplace, and unionization has wrested from the employer a measure of the control he exercises at the workplace. The next step is to provide the worker with a more meaningful measure of control over his job through participation in decisions affecting the job.

Contrast Henry Ford's stifling authoritarianism with the words of Richard Gerstenberg, chairman of the board of directors of General Motors Corporation, in 1972: "Productivity is not a matter of making employees work longer or harder. . . . We must improve working conditions and take out the boredom from routine jobs. . . . We must increase an employee's satisfaction with his job, heightening pride of workmanship, and, as far as is feasible, involve the employee personally in decisions that relate directly to his job. . . ."[1]

Within its limited meaning, this statement marked an unfashionable awareness of Robert Heilbroner's thesis that ". . . the ultimate challenge to the institutions, motivations, political structures, lifeways, and ideologies of capitalist nations is whether they can accommodate themselves to the requirements of a society in which an attitude of 'social fatalism' is being replaced by one of social purpose."[2]

Mr. Gerstenberg's statement hopefully represents a conscious departure from the historic trickle-down theory that profits come first, that profits exemplify good in themselves and can only redound to the benefit of all society. Yet, more income and more material wealth, in and of themselves, do not guarantee a life of satisfaction or worth, and certainly cannot compensate for lives converted into deadened extensions of the tools of production. . . .

A study undertaken by HEW, published in 1973 as *Work in America,* leaves no doubt that worker dissatisfaction with jobs, both blue-collar and white-collar, is widespread, is on the rise, and presents an urgent problem for management, union, and government. The report notes: "And significant numbers of American workers are dissatisfied with the quality of their working lives. Dull, repetitive, seemingly meaningless tasks, offering little challenge or autonomy, are causing discontent among workers at all occupational levels."[3]

The report makes a point that the failure to solve this problem will mean increased social costs. It points to the relationship between job dissatisfaction on the one hand and mental health, alcohol and drug abuse, heart disease, early death, and other factors on the other; it concludes that unless the situation is corrected society can expect these costs to impose an increasing tax burden on the total community.

It is important to understand that reasonable satisfaction with meaningless, repetitive work may simply mean that man, highly adaptable creature that he is, has made his peace with an unhappy situation. There is strong evidence that workers write off deadening jobs as "inevitable" and seek their satisfaction in other pursuits. The HEW study makes a point of the relationship between the meaninglessness of the job and the adverse effect on the physical and mental well-being of the worker.

It is also important to note that workers who have been given the opportunity to enlarge their horizons at work, to participate in the decisions affecting their jobs, and to lend their innovative input toward getting the job done have a focal point against which to compare their previous work experience. These workers usually do not want to return to the simple monotonous tasks of little or no responsibility. They have tried a better way and they like it. . . .

It is axiomatic that people respond more affirmatively to their role in society as they share in the opportunity to participate significantly in decisions affecting their welfare. History teaches, moreover, that at some point people who are denied this opportunity will reach out to grasp it.

This is equally true in the workplace. The stirrings of job dissatisfaction, in my judgment, relate in large measure to denial of participation in the decision-making process, denial of the opportunity to be creative and innovative and to control the machine, instead of being controlled by it.

The ferment of union activity in the 1930s and 1940s consolidated the organizing strength of industrial workers. It was the first stage toward accomplishment of a larger goal: industrial democracy. It provided the base on which workers were then able to improve their standard of living, win better working conditions, and achieve a greater measure of dignity and security as important members of society. Every gain constituted an incursion into the traditional authority wielded by management. The vast array of benefits won in collective bargaining over the years relates essentially to protecting the worker and his family against the hazards of economic insecurity. Workers, young and old, continue to aspire toward a better life, to be won at the bargaining table and through legislation. Their unions will, of course, persist in innovative collective-bargaining efforts as well as in improving upon already established benefit programs. They mobilize politically, cognizant of the intimate relationship between the bread box and the ballot box.

There is little need to spell out the enormously important progress workers have made through their unions. In *quantitative* terms, organized workers have won, and continue to win, a larger share of economic well-being. Unorganized workers have, of course, reaped the advantages of the gains made by unionized workers. Working conditions have also been vastly improved under the pressure of collective bargaining. Yet in *qualitative* terms, workers have not made as marked progress and are still struggling to play a more meaningful role in the decisions that affect their welfare in the business enterprise. Emphasis on qualitative improvement of life on the job is, I believe, the next step on the road toward industrial democracy.

WHITHER WORKER PARTICIPATION?

Two distinct, somewhat overlapping directions are indicated. One relates to "managing the enterprise"; the other relates to "managing the job." The latter is part and parcel of the former, but it is of more immediate concern to the worker.

Experiments with worker participation in "managing the enterprise" are under way in Yugoslavia (worker control of management), Germany (*Mitbestimmung*—codetermination established by law), Sweden (voluntary acceptance of worker representation on a company's board of directors), and Israel (union owned and operated cooperative enterprises). But in the United States, labor contracts, with their hundreds of provisions establishing and protecting workers' rights, leave substantially to management the "sole responsibility" to determine the products to be manufactured, the location of plants, production schedules, the methods, processes, and means of manufacture, as well as administrative decisions governing finances, marketing, purchasing, pricing, and the like. Unions traditionally have moved in the direction of improving wages, benefits, and working conditions. Generally, they have left "managing the enterprise" to management, only *reacting* to managerial acts objectionable to the workers.

They have not embraced a political philosophy to motivate their overall policies and programs. This is not to say that American unions have no socioeconomic-political concepts. Quite the contrary; but they are not married to an "ism" governing and directing their behavior.

Rather, American unions move to meet practical problems with practical solutions. It is highly improbable that they will approach the problem of worker participation in decision making via fierce ideological struggle founded in socioeconomic theory. They are not prone to beat their wings in ideological or doctrinaire frustration. Where workers feel victimized, they combine their forces to correct the situation, case by case, problem by problem. Gradual persistent change, not revolutionary upheaval, has marked the progress of the American worker. When explosions occur, as in the 1930s, they are responses to specific problems and are searches for specific solutions. We can anticipate that worker participation in managing the enterprise or job will manifest itself in a similar way. . . .

Increasing attention is currently being devoted to this problem of "managing the job." Rising rates of absenteeism, worker disinterest in the quality and quantity of production, job alienation, and the insistence on unit-cost reduction are motivating some employers to reevaluate current practices and customs governing management-worker relationships. Concurrently, workers rebel against the authoritarian atmosphere of the workplace and the subordination of their personal dignity, desires, and aspirations to the drive for more production at lower cost; they find little challenge, satisfaction, or interest in their work. While the worker's rate of pay may dominate his relationship to the job, he can be responsive to the opportunity for playing an innovative, creative, and imaginative role in the production process.

One of the essential tasks of the union movement is to "humanize the workplace." A pleasant, decent management is desirable but does not alter the basic managerial design. "Human engineering" concepts may make for more comfortable employer-employee relationships, but here, too, managerial administration of the workplace remains fundamentally unchanged. "Humanizing the workplace" not only must include the normally recognized amenities of life in the workplace but it also must move to a higher plateau and relate to job satisfaction—a closing of the widening gap between the mechanization of production by scientific management and the worker's participation in the production and decision-making process. "Humanizing the workplace" in this sense represents one additional step toward the fulfillment of industrial democracy.

But humanizing the workplace must not become simply another gimmick designed essentially to "fool" the worker by having as its primary goal or hidden agenda an increase in worker productivity. Manipulation of the worker will be recognized for what it is—another form of exploitation; it will breed suspicion and distrust.

In this regard, Delmar Landan, an expert in personnel development for General Motors, has said: ". . . where we have to aim is participation—it is the only way to work in this increasingly complex society. The man at the top can't have all the answers. The man doing the job will have some of them."[4]

Worker participation in decision making about his job is one means of achieving democratization of the workplace. It should result in a change from the miniaturization and oversimplification of the job to the evolution of a system embracing broader distribution of authority, increasing rather than diminishing responsibility and accountability. It should combine the imaginative creation of more-interesting jobs with the opportunity to exercise a meaningful measure of autonomy and utilization of more-varied skills. It requires tapping the creative and innovative ingenuity of the worker to the maximum.

Hundreds of experiments have been and are being undertaken in American industry, following the European lead. They are directed toward opening up opportunities for meaningful worker participation. The HEW report describes some of them. In the auto industry, the industry with which I am most closely associated, a myriad of demonstration projects are under way. They cover innumerable facets of the problem and some are a sharp departure from the assembly-line concept.

It is too early to describe precisely what form or forms humanizing the workplace will take. Certain criteria, however, deserve serious consideration.

1. The worker should genuinely feel that he or she is not simply an adjunct to the tool, but that his or her bent toward being creative, innovative, and inventive plays a significant role in the production (or service) process.
2. The worker should be assured that his or her participation in decision making will not erode job security or that of fellow workers.
3. Job functions should be adapted to the worker; the current system is designed to make the worker fit the job, on the theory that this is a more efficient production system and that, in any event, economic gain is the worker's only reason for working. This theory may be proved wrong on both counts.
4. The worker should be assured the widest possible latitude of self-management, responsibility, and opportunity to use her or his brain. Gimmickry and manipulation of the worker must be ruled out.
5. Changes in job content and the added responsibility and involvement in decision making should be accompanied by upgrading pay rates.
6. The worker should be able to foresee opportunities for growth in his or her work and for promotion.
7. The worker's role in the business should enable her or him to relate to the product or services rendered, as well as to their meanings in society; in a broader sense, it should also enable her or him to relate constructively to her or his role in society.

The union, as the workers' representative, will naturally share with management in implementing these and other criteria. But crisis negotiating— setting a wage dispute before a midnight strike deadline—is not the time to seek precise means of humanizing the workplace. This task requires careful experiment and analysis. While issues of economic security (wages, fringe benefits) and continuing encroachment on what management terms its sole prerogatives will remain adversary in nature, there is every reason why humanizing the workplace should be undertaken as a joint, cooperative, constructive, nonadversary effort by management and the union. The initial key to achieving this goal may well be open, frank, and enlightened discussion between the parties, recognizing that democratizing the workplace and humanizing the job need not be matters of confrontation but of mutual concern for the worker, the enterprise, and the welfare of society.

NOTES

[1] Richard C. Gerstenberg, speech to the Annual Meeting of the American Publishers Association, New York, April 26, 1972.

[2] Robert Heilbroner, "The Future of Capitalism," *World Magazine,* Sept. 12, 1972, p. 30.

[3] *Work in America,* Report of a Special Task Force to the Secretary of Health, Education, and Welfare (Cambridge, Mass.: MIT Press, 1973), p. xv.

[4] Delmar Landan in Judson Gooding, *The Job Revolution* (New York: Walker Publishing Co., 1972), p. 111.

ADINA SCHWARTZ
MEANINGFUL WORK* ....

In the opening pages of *The Wealth of Nations,* Adam Smith describes how pins are made in a factory: "One man draws out the wire, another straights it, a third cuts it, a fourth points it,"[1] and so on to eighteen distinct operations. Some workers may perform two or three of these tasks; many repeatedly execute

*Versions of this paper were read at a meeting of the New York Group of the Society for Philosophy and Public Affairs on February 14, 1978, to the philosophy department at Oberlin College on February 15, 1979, and at Douglass College of Rutgers University on February 6, 1979. I would like to thank those present for their comments. I would also like to thank Bruce A. Ackerman, Brian Barry, and Owen M. Fiss for helpful criticism and discussion.

[1] Adam Smith, *An Inquiry into the Nature and Causes of the Wealth of Nations,* ed. Edwin Cannan, 2 vols. in 1 (Chicago: University of Chicago Press, Phoenix Books, 1976), 1:8.

Adina Schwartz, "Meaningful Work," *Ethics* 92, July 1982. Reprinted from *Ethics* 92 (1982) by Adina Schwartz by permission of The University of Chicago Press. ©1982 by The University of Chicago. All rights reserved.

only one operation. In contemporary industrial societies, many people work at analogues of Smith's jobs: jobs in which persons are hired to perform series of set actions such as assembly line work, keypunching, or being a clerk on an automated checkout line.[2] These routine jobs provide people with almost no opportunities for formulating aims, for deciding on means for achieving their ends, or for adjusting their goals and methods in the light of experience. Smith's workers and their modern counterparts do not design the overall goals of the factories, offices, or service operations in which they are employed. More important, individual workers do not decide how to perform their particular jobs. Instead of being hired to achieve certain goals and left to select and pursue adequate means, workers are employed to perform precisely specified actions. Even the order in which they perform those operations, the pace at which they work, and the particular bodily movements they employ are largely determined by others' decisions. When the entire job consists of such mechanical activity, workers are in effect paid for blindly pursuing ends that others have chosen, by means that they judge adequate.

The existence of these jobs is of little concern to contemporary social and political philosophers.[3] This paper will argue, however, that this unconcerned stance is fundamentally at odds with the widely held view that a just society respects all its members as autonomous agents. If we care about the free development of all members of society, I will show, we must demand that no one be employed at the sorts of jobs that have just been described. We must also advocate a certain alternative to the current arrangement of industrial employment and must ask for government measures to effect this rearrangement.

I

My argument for these claims can best begin with a brief account of what I mean by 'autonomy.' I am concerned here with the central notion that is employed when philosophers argue that a society must grant extensive liberties in order to respect its members as autonomous agents. According to this conception, being autonomous is not simply a matter of having a capacity.

---

[2] Harry Braverman, *Labor and Monopoly Capital: The Degradation of Work in the Twentieth Century* (New York: Monthly Review Press, 1974), is the most detailed and illuminating account available of the routinization of work in contemporary industrial societies. Other useful empirical works include Elwood S. Buffa, *Modern Production Management: Managing the Operations Function,* 5th ed. (New York: John Wiley & Sons, 1977), pp. 207–36; Louis E. Davis and James C. Taylor, eds., *Design of Jobs: Selected Readings* (Harmondsworth: Penguin Books, 1972); *Work in America: Report of a Special Task Force to the Secretary of Health, Education, and Welfare* (Cambridge, Mass.: MIT Press, 1973); and Studs Terkel, *Working* (New York: Avon Books, 1975).

[3] Their existence is alluded to only in one vague paragraph of John Rawls, *A Theory of Justice* (Cambridge, Mass.: Harvard University Press, 1971), p. 529. One of the main implications of the brief discussion in Robert Nozick, *Anarchy, State, and Utopia* (New York: Basic Books, 1974), pp. 246–50, is that political philosophers should not care about what persons do at work.

Individuals are only free, or autonomous, persons to the extent that they rationally form and act on some overall conception of what they want in life. They also must adjust those conceptions to allow for changing circumstances and for faults in their original goals. This notion can be more sharply delineated by showing that it rules out certain claims about autonomous persons' behavior. An individual can decide on an overall system of aims without leading an autonomous life. Living autonomously means planning effectively to achieve one's aims instead of simply reacting to the circumstances that face one. Thus, autonomous agents take responsibility for decisions and rationally choose actions to suit their goals. For an autonomous agent, this activity is closely joined to the practice of revising goals and methods in the light of observations of the consequences of choices. These agents are also interested in learning of differences between their and others' decisions and in understanding how these differences result from various factual beliefs and normative commitments. Considering this, they attempt to decide rationally whether to revise or retain their beliefs, methods, and goals.

We can say, then, that people achieve autonomy to the extent that they lead lives of intelligence and initiative. It would be a mistake, however, to posit any straightforward correlation between how nearly autonomous people are and how many decisions they make. An autonomous agent makes certain *types* of decisions: rational choices informed by an awareness of alternatives. In addition, the actions of autonomous agents are not guided by series of unrelated choices, but by choices that are themselves guided by their overall conceptions of their purposes in life.

Proceeding from this brief account, we can show, I believe, that all who hold that a society should respect all its members as autonomous agents must be greatly concerned by the correlation that has so far obtained between industrialization and the existence of increasing numbers of the sorts of jobs described in the first paragraph of this article.[4] As we saw above, when persons are employed at these jobs, they are hired to pursue unquestioningly ends that others have chosen, by means that others judge adequate. The account of autonomy just given entitles us to claim that these jobs are degrading because persons cannot act as autonomous agents while performing them.

This claim might be met by the rejoinder, however, that an individual's work is not his or her whole life. We need not care, it might be argued, whether individuals have opportunities for framing, adjusting, and pursuing their own plans during their working hours or, indeed, at any particular time. What is important is that a society aid all its members to lead autonomous lives on the whole. There need be nothing wrong, then, with a social arrangement in which most adults devote large amounts of time to remunerative employment and in which some persons have jobs that consist mainly in the performance of machine-like tasks. This arrangement would be acceptable, according to this objection, so long as these persons were given opportunities

---

[4] For a detailed argument showing that this correlation has obtained, see Braverman.

in the rest of their lives for formulating goals and for rationally choosing means for effecting their ends.

Analogous arguments are not employed to justify restrictions on legal freedoms. No one claims that it is all right for persons to be legally prevented from framing and pursuing plans during considerable lengths of time so long as they are legally free to devote the rest of their lives to acting as autonomous individuals. It is widely held, instead, that if a society so restricts liberties, it degrades its members by preventing them from acting autonomously. It does not foster their autonomous development on the whole.

Granted that similar justifications are not advanced for curtailing legal freedoms, we do well to ask whether we can accept the above justification of the current arrangement of industrial employment if we respect all persons as autonomous beings. To answer this question, let us note that this justification stands or falls with the following premise: in general, when persons devote significant amounts of time to remunerative employment and when they are prevented from acting autonomously while performing their jobs, they are not caused to lead less autonomous lives on the whole. We can dismiss this premise on both empirical and conceptual grounds.

Taking the empirical grounds first, an opposing claim has been advanced both by contemporary psychologists and sociologists and by such noted social scientists as Adam Smith and Émile Durkheim. When persons work for considerable lengths of time at jobs that involve mainly mechanical activity, they tend to be made less capable of and less interested in rationally framing, pursuing, and adjusting their own plans during the rest of their time. They are thereby caused to lead less autonomous lives on the whole. Durkheim's general enthusiasm for modern industrial developments did not prevent him from scoffing at the view that persons would not be made less autonomous by machine-like work if they were encouraged to devote other time to intellectual and cultural pursuits. "Who cannot see," he exclaimed, "that two such existences are too opposed to be reconciled and cannot be led by the same man!"[5] Similarly, although Smith praised the factory arrangements described in the first pages of The Wealth of Nations, he did not deny their dehumanizing effects. "The understandings of the greater part of men," he claimed, "are necessarily formed by their ordinary employments. The man whose whole life is spent in performing a few simple operations . . . has no occasion to exert his understanding, or to exercise his invention in finding out expedients for removing difficulties which never occur. He naturally loses, therefore, the habit of such exertion. . . . His dexterity at his own particular trade seems . . . to be acquired at the expense of his intellectual virtues."[6]

The claims of Smith and Durkheim are echoed in recent statistical investigations. In a longitudinal study of a group of men representative of all

[5] Émile Durkheim, The Division of Labor in Society (New York: Free Press, 1964), p. 372.

[6] Smith, 2:302–3.

men employed in civilian occupations in the United States, Melvin L. Kohn and Carmi Schooler argue that there is a reciprocal relationship between what they term the substantive complexity of work and intellectual flexibility, or, in other words, between the degree to which work in its very substance demands thought and independent judgment and the degree to which persons are flexible in coping with the intellectual demands of complex situations. To start with, their data indicate that "current job demands affect current thinking processes. . . . If two men of equivalent intellectual flexibility were to start their careers in jobs differing in substantive complexity, the man in the more complex job would be likely to outstrip the other in further intellectual growth."[7] This effect would most likely be compounded, according to the evidence of Kohn and Schooler, because one's current intellectual flexibility significantly affects the future course of one's career. Once differences in the substantive complexity of their first jobs cause individuals to differ in intellectual flexibility, the substantive complexity of their second jobs is likely to vary directly with those created intellectual differences. In turn, this is likely to broaden the gap between these individuals' intellectual capacities, thereby tending to increase the differences between the substantive complexity of their third jobs, and so on.

An implication of Kohn and Schooler's study is that the jobs described in the first paragraph of this article do not prevent persons from acting autonomously only while at work. They also hinder them from developing the intellectual abilities that they must have if they are rationally to frame, adjust, and pursue their own plans during the rest of their time. Other quantitative work argues, in addition, that these routine jobs cause persons to be less inclined, in all aspects of their lives, to engage in the purposeful striving that is characteristic of autonomous individuals. Arthur Kornhauser's classic study of Detroit automobile workers concludes, for example, that "factory employment, especially in routine production tasks, does give evidence of extinguishing workers' ambition, initiative, and purposeful direction toward life goals. . . . The unsatisfactory mental health of working people consists in no small measure of their dwarfed desires and deadened initiative, reduction of their goals and restriction of their efforts to a point where life is relatively empty and only half meaningful."[8] According to Kornhauser, "Mental health is poorer among factory workers as we move from skilled, responsible, varied types of work to jobs lower in those respects."[9] "By far the most influential attribute [of the comparatively high or low average mental health of occupational groups] is

---

[7] Melvin L. Kohn and Carmi Schooler, "The Reciprocal Effects of the Substantive Complexity of Work and Intellectual Flexibility: A Longitudinal Study," *American Journal of Sociology* 84 (1978): 43, 48.

[8] Arthur Kornhauser, *Mental Health of the Industrial Worker: A Detroit Study* (New York: John Wiley & Sons, 1964), pp. 252, 270.

[9] *Ibid.*, pp. 75–76.

the opportunity the work offers—or fails to offer—for use of the worker's abilities."[10]

The empirical literature has thus consistently argued that persons are hindered from leading autonomous lives when their jobs provide them with almost no opportunities for rationally framing, adjusting, and pursuing their own plans. It seems to me, however, that there is an even more convincing a priori argument for that conclusion. Becoming autonomous is not a matter of coming to exercise intelligence and initiative in a number of separate areas of one's life. Rather, it is a process of integrating one's personality: of coming to see all one's pursuits as subject to one's activity of planning and to view all one's experiences as providing a basis for evaluating and adjusting one's beliefs, methods, and aims. This granted, concern for the autonomous development of all members of society commits us to objecting to institutional arrangements that prevent individuals from acting autonomously while at work, even if they encourage them to do so during their leisure time. Such arrangements foster schizophrenia. Given my analysis of autonomy, we must claim, instead, that a society must encourage all its members to pursue unified lives if it is to aid each one of them to achieve autonomy.

II

We can conclude, then, that persons' autonomous developments are stunted when their jobs severely restrict their opportunities for rationally framing, pursuing, and adjusting their own plans. If we care about the free development of all members of society, we thus are committed to considering how industrial employment could be restructured so that all persons' jobs allow them to act as autonomous individuals. To pursue this inquiry, we need to recognize that industrialization has been correlated with the rise of a distinctive type of division of labor. Once we see this, we can proceed to develop an account of how the current arrangement of industrial employment would need to be changed to allow all persons to act autonomously while at work. We can then show that these changes are both possible and desirable.

In all societies where there is production for exchange, there is a social division of labor. In other words, different productive specialties (e.g., hunting, fishing, being a medicine man or a physician) are pursued by various members of society, and the products produced by those specialties are exchanged in society at large. Only in industrial societies, however, has there also been a significant development of what Karl Marx called the detailed division of

---

[10] *Ibid.*, p. 263. For discussion of Kornhauser's work and of other studies that confirm his results and extend them to workers in other industries, see pp. 81–92 of *Work in America*, and Charles Hampden-Turner, "The Factory as an Oppressive and Non-emancipatory Environment," in *Workers' Control: A Reader on Labor and Social Change*, ed. Gerry Hunnius, G. David Garson, and John Case (New York: Random House, 1973), pp. 30–45.

labor, a division that can also appropriately be termed the hierarchical division of labor.[11]

This detailed, or hierarchical, division obtains only when a productive specialty is divided into various tasks and when persons specialize in performing one, or at most a few, of those tasks. Under this division, a number of individuals cooperate to produce products that can be exchanged in society at large. This cooperation is essentially hierarchical. When specialists cooperate, under the detailed division of labor, to produce products that can be exchanged in society at large, some of these specialists are managers. These experts coordinate and schedule others' activities, deciding on what persons will do in their jobs and on the precise manner in which they will execute their tasks. The reverse side of this coin is that the detailed, or hierarchical, division of labor entails the existence of detail workers: persons whose jobs consist almost entirely in performing actions that others precisely specify and whose work thus prevents them from acting autonomously. . . .

It follows from this description that an alternative to the detailed, or hierarchical, division of labor is needed if industrial employment is to be meaningfully structured or, in other words, arranged to allow all persons to act as autonomous agents while performing their jobs. The reason for rejecting the detailed division of labor is not that it involves cooperation among specialists per se. Rather, that division of labor is objectionable because it is a cooperative arrangement in which some persons specialize in framing plans and in deciding how they are best pursued and others specialize in unquestioningly executing those decisions. Applying this criterion, we can now evaluate some contemporary proposals for the redesign of employment. Thereby, we can arrive at a relatively clear picture of what it would mean for industrial employment to be meaningfully structured.

Often, routine clerical or factory jobs are enlarged by a process of horizontal integration: instead of performing one mechanical task, a worker executes a number of routine operations. For example, assembly line workers may rotate jobs so that individuals can follow a product through all the stages in its production.[12] Or, bank tellers may sort returned checks when the loads at their counters are light.[13] Given our discussion, such horizontal restructurings clearly do not constitute a meaningful alternative to the current arrangement of employment. Although persons' tasks are made more various, their jobs consist, exactly as before, in performing actions that are precisely specified by others. Thereby, their work still prevents them from acting autonomously: from rationally framing, pursuing, and adjusting their own plans.

---

[11] Karl Marx establishes and explores the concept of the detailed division of labor in vol. 1, pt. 4 of *Capital,* ed. Frederick Engels (New York: International Publishing Co., 1967), esp. chap. 14, sec. 4, pp. 350–59.

[12] For this example and a general account of horizontal integration, see Buffa, p. 230.

[13] For this example, see Braverman, p. 37.

A similar criticism applies to proposals for employing some persons as detail workers and others as managerial experts but allowing all employees to participate in democratic decision making.[14] Even if all employees vote on administrators, mergers, hiring and financial policies, and so forth, the relations between managers and detail workers are still hierarchical. On the one hand, the managerial experts are employed to decide how to implement policies. On the other hand, the detail workers are hired to effect those decisions by repeatedly performing actions that those experts precisely specify. This daily distinction between those who decide and those who execute others' decisions seems to carry over to the roles that detail workers and managers assume when they both participate in democratic decision making. Under Yugoslav workers' self-management, at least, the managers' control of relevant information and their greater experience in making decisions appear to give them a powerful advantage in having their proposals accepted by others.[15]

If, then, industrial employment is to be restructured so that all persons can act autonomously while at work, detail workers cannot simply be assigned greater numbers of routine operations and formal democracy cannot simply be imposed on workplaces where the division of labor remains hierarchical. Rather, jobs must be democratically redesigned, tasks must be shared out in a way that abolishes the distinction between those who decide and those who execute others' decisions. A significant start in this direction was made in a dog-food plant opened by the General Foods Corporation in Topeka, Kansas, in 1971.[16] There, each worker was hired to be part of a small group of persons, each group was made responsible for intellectually demanding functions (e.g., maintaining and repairing machines, quality control operations), and all groups of workers shared in the routine work that was not eliminated by automation. Within each group, work was also democratically distributed. All workers

---

[14] There are more conservative and more radical versions of this reform. Democracy in the workplace may involve, as in West German codetermination, consulting selected workers about management's policies (see the article collectively written by the executive board of the West German Trade Union Federation [DGB], "Co-Determination in the Federal Republic of Germany," in Hunnius, Garson, and Case, eds., pp. 191–210; and Helmut Schauer, "Critique of Co-Determination," in Hunnius, Garson, and Case, eds., pp. 210–24). Or, it may extend, as in Yugoslav workers' self-management, to allowing all employees to vote on policies (see Gerry Hunnius, "Workers' Self-Management in Yugoslavia," in Hunnius, Garson, and Case, eds., pp. 268–321). Likewise, workplace democracy may amount, as in many American experiments, only to allowing workers to decide relatively trivial matters such as the colors of their offices, the pace of the assembly lines on which they work, and so forth (see Buffa, pp. 232–33; Daniel Zwerdling, "Workplace Democracy: A Strategy for Survival," *Progressive*, August 1978, pp. 16–24, esp. pp. 18–19; and Richard Edwards, *Contested Terrain: The Transformation of the Workplace in the Twentieth Century* (New York: Basic Books, 1979), pp. 155–56. Or it may mean, as in the Yugoslav experience, that all major policy questions are decided by all employees (see Hunnius).

[15] Hunnius, p. 297.

[16] For descriptions of this plant, see *Work in America*, pp. 96–99; Zwerdling, pp. 17–18; and "Stonewalling Plant Democracy," *Business Week*, March 28, 1977, pp. 78–82.

were given opportunities to learn to perform all the tasks assigned to their group, no group member was mainly assigned to routine operations, and all the members of the group shared in supervising its operations, democratically deciding job assignments, pay raises, breaks, and so forth.

As a result of this sharing of supervisory functions and of routine and intellectually demanding production work, no person in this plant was employed mainly to perform actions that others precisely specified. Each person's job gave him or her significant opportunities for rationally framing, adjusting, and pursuing plans. Given, however, that the General Foods management unilaterally decided what should be produced, how fast it should be produced, how profits should be used, what hiring policies should be, and whether its democratic reforms should continue, the workers in this plant could only plan to implement policies that others set. If, then, industrial employment is to be meaningfully restructured to abolish the distinction between those who decide and those who execute others' decisions, labor must be still more democratically divided than it was by General Foods. In addition to functions being shared out so that no person is employed mainly at routine operations, there must be a sharing of information and provision of opportunities such that all persons can participate in shaping their enterprise's policies.

It seems to me that this discussion provides a general picture of what it would mean for industrial employment to be meaningfully structured, or, in other words, arranged so that all persons' jobs allow them to act as autonomous individuals and thus foster instead of stunt their autonomous development. Serious objections can be raised, however, as to the general practicability of such arrangements in a highly industrialized society, regardless of their desirability. These objections can be answered.

It might be argued, in the first place, that it would be impossible for an industrial society to institute a meaningful alternative to the detailed division of labor because the presence of that division is dictated by the presence of a machine technology. This claim is refuted by the facts. On the one hand, the factory arrangements of Adam Smith's time and current drives to routinize office employment show that a detailed division of labor may be imposed where there is little or no machinery.[17] On the other hand, automatic machine systems can be operated without a detailed division of labor. The machinery itself does not dictate that employees be divided into those who perform the routine tasks involved in assisting machine operations and those who decide how the machines are to be used.[18]

It might be objected, nonetheless, that my proposed alternative to the detailed division of labor should not be instituted because all moves away from

---

[17] For a description of the growing routinization or detailed division of office employment, see Braverman, chap. 15, pp. 293–358.

[18] *Ibid.*, chap. 9, esp. pp. 230–31. Also see Nehemiah Jordan, "Allocation of Functions between Man and Machines in Automated Systems," in Davis and Taylor, eds., pp. 91–99; and James G. Scoville, "A Theory of Jobs and Training," in Davis and Taylor, eds., pp. 225–44.

this division would be inefficient. The current arrangement of employment in industrial societies is Pareto-optimal: at least some persons prefer that arrangement to any alternative. If, therefore, an industrial society were to seek to eliminate the detailed, or hierarchical, division of labor, it would pursue a Pareto-inefficient policy: one that violated some persons' preferences.

If we hold, however, that all members of society should be respected as autonomous individuals, our sole criterion for judging proposed reforms cannot be whether they would violate the preferences of some individuals. No one would seriously claim to care about all persons' autonomous development and yet argue that a dictatorship's restrictions on freedom of expression should be maintained because eliminating them would violate the rulers' preferences. All would agree that these preferences should not be respected because they are preferences for depriving others of liberties that they need for leading the rational, choosing lives of autonomous individuals. To generalize, respect for all persons' free development demands that we meet Paretian objections to proposed reforms by asking what preferences a given reform would satisfy or violate and whether, in doing so, it would foster the autonomous development of all members of society. Thus, in the case at hand, we need to consider why my proposed move away from the hierarchical division of labor might be expected to be Pareto-inefficient. *Whose* preferences for *what* would this reform be likely to violate? We can then show that our commitment to autonomy allows us to dismiss these individuals' objections.

It might be argued that owners would prefer that my alternative to the detailed division of labor not be instituted because instituting this reform would cause their profits to fall. If all workers are skilled, as they would be under this meaningful rearrangement of employment, none can be paid as low a wage as the detail worker whose entire job can be learned in a few weeks.[19] If all persons' jobs require significant training, as they would under my proposed alternative, owners will bear the cost of providing that training. These factual claims do not prove that my alternative to the detailed division of labor must decrease profits. Proving this, however, would not provide a reason for maintaining that hierarchical arrangement of employment. If we hold that social institutions should be arranged to respect all persons as autonomous, we cannot believe that individuals should be free to acquire wealth at the cost of others' development as free agents.

It might be urged, nonetheless, that industrial employment should not be meaningfully restructured because doing this would cause a society's level

[19] The nineteenth-century economist Charles Babbage "noted that: (1) wages paid were dictated by the most difficult or rarest skill required by the jobs; (2) the division of labor enabled skills to be made more homogeneous within jobs more easily; and (3) for each job, one could purchase exactly the amount of skill needed. The result would be a lower total labor cost" (Buffa, p. 208). Two of the most important developments contributing to the growth of the detailed division of labor, "scientific management under F. W. Taylor and motion study under Frank Gilbreth, about 1910, can be seen as an extension of the work of Babbage" (Davis and Taylor, eds., p. 16).

of production as a whole to fall. Many persons, whether workers or owners, would thereby suffer a decrease in wealth, presumably in violation of their preferences. We need to recognize, however, that the view that a society should foster all its members' autonomous development is incompatible with an unconditional commitment to economic growth. Certainly, it is desirable that a certain level of economic development be attained. How can persons be expected rationally to frame and evaluate beliefs, methods, and goals when they are starving or when poverty forces them to remain illiterate? Once a society attains a sufficient level of productivity, however, to provide all its members with the leisure time, educational opportunities, and level of health and material comfort that persons need for achieving autonomy, respect for autonomy does not demand further economic growth. To the contrary, increased productivity should not be pursued at the cost of depriving individuals of the liberties and working conditions that humans need for leading autonomous lives. This means, therefore, that the current arrangement of industrial employment could only justifiably be maintained if it were certain that my proposed alternative would so lower productivity that persons could not enjoy the material and educational prerequisites for achieving autonomy. The available evidence argues for the opposite conclusion. A special task force to the Secretary of Health, Education, and Welfare concluded in 1973 that American business enterprises could increase productivity by eliminating the detailed division of labor. "The redesign of work . . . *can* lower such business costs as absenteeism, tardiness, turnover, labor disputes, sabotage and poor quality. . . . The evidence suggests that meeting the higher needs of workers can, perhaps, increase productivity from 5% to 40%, the latter figure including the 'latent' productivity of workers that is currently untapped.[20] Such results have indeed been obtained by the General Foods Corporation plant described above. "Unit costs," *Business Week* reported in 1977, "are 5% less than under a traditional factory system. . . . This . . . should amount to a saving of $1 million a year."[21]

In sum, then, we cannot justify maintaining the detailed, or hierarchical, division of labor by claiming that it is the only technologically possible arrangement of industrial employment or the only one that is sufficiently profitable or productive. If we care about the free development of all members of society, we are therefore committed to demanding that this hierarchical division be replaced by a meaningful, or democratic, division of labor that will ensure that no one is employed mainly at routine operations, that all employees participate in shaping their enterprise's policies, and, consequently, that all persons' jobs allow them to act as autonomous individuals and thus foster instead of stunt their autonomous development. . . .

---

[20] *Work in America*, p. 27.

[21] "Stonewalling Plant Democracy," p. 78.

THEODORE ROSZAK
WORK: THE RIGHT TO RIGHT LIVELIHOOD ....

> Man needs work even more than he needs wage; it imprints the form of man on matter and offers itself to him as a means of expression. Work, bodily work, is for nine-tenths of humanity their only chance to show their worth in this world.
>
> —*Lanzo del Vasta*

> A job is death without the dignity.
>
> —*Brendan Behan*

OUR WORK IS OUR LIFE

The going style of industrial progress calls for the maximum amount of labor-saving technology. Where that progress is left to be made by private capital, the guiding criterion will surely be profit, and the result is apt to be technological unemployment. *But* the justification offered will be that "labor-saving" equals "leisure-making," and leisure is what life is all about.

Here, I adopt a radically different position, arguing that our personhood is realized in responsible work. Therefore, the true direction of progress is not to save labor, but to *preserve* it from indiscriminate technological advance: to preserve it, to make it whole, to make it real. If anything must be saved, it is the very concept that work is a necessity of the human condition—not a mere means of survival, but a paramount means of self-discovery. We have a need to work; we have a right to work; and neither the need nor the right has to be justified by proving its profitability or productivity, any more than our need to love, play, or grow should be made to present its cost-benefit credentials. Our work is our life, and we cannot exercise our right to self-discovery in a world that deprives us of our natural vocation.

Does this face us with a conflict that requires the world to turn away from all industrial technology and to "go primitive"? Not in the least. There is no incompatibility between craftsmen and their tools, and the right machine in the hands of a skilled and autonomous worker can only enhance the joy of the task and the beauty of the work. The inventing of better tools and machines is a natural action of craftsmanship and one of its highest expressions. But an honest concern for vocation is clearly incompatible with big system industrialism and the economic science that undergirds it. Where mechanization moves in massively from outside the working community and its traditions—as it has in Western society over the past two centuries, as it does today everywhere in the third world—the result is bound to be the destruction of craftsmanship, the displacement of responsible work. Then we are thrown into a vocational vacuum. This is "progress" that covets the inert product of labor, but neglects the living means; it wants the wealth of the selling, but forgets the value of the making.

Nor is it any solution to say that an expanding economy makes up for the work it destroys by generating new jobs. That it does, but at a very different economic level. Big systems take us into a new economic universe where work is keyed to another rhythm and character. There, work is fragmented, hierarchical, and minutely specialized; it is dependent on opening up massive new markets by stimulating wants and wasteful appetites; it becomes ever more embedded in promotion and merchandising, administration and co-ordination, paper work and personnel management; it citifies more and more of the population drawing people away from their ecological roots; it drifts steadily away from responsibility and personal engagement. It is altogether a different quality of work.

I cannot say this historical pattern, which has repeated itself in every high industrial economy, capitalist and collectivist alike, is inevitable. But I am sure it is inevitable where new technology is not respectfully grafted on to the pre-existing work tradition with a steady resolve to preserve work that possesses vocational integrity. I cannot say how big or small a factory or an economy must be to stay vocationally healthy; but certainly that vital balance will not be achieved where bigness is not disciplined by a standard outside itself. That standard is responsible work, and the most obvious way for it to be applied is by letting workers themselves assimilate to their craft the tools and machines and systems that facilitate their labor.

No worker is unwilling to see his or her work become useful to more people by being technologically amplified. But workers who love their work will not readily see it destroyed or cheapened by a technique whose only promise is to produce *more*—even before we ask how much *more* might be gained within the traditional pattern.

In recent years, the so-called Green Revolution techniques of high-yield agriculture have encountered such popular resistance in many poor countries. Peasant farmers have correctly sensed that the new approach, which derives from the American agrindustrial system, threatens the survival of small-scale farming. The methods are too technical, too expensive, too capital-intensive for peasant economies to assimilate. But in some quarters where that resistance has held firm, other cheaper and more adaptable ways of increasing production have been found—methods as simple as intercropping, introducing more annual plantings each with a shorter growing season, developing more secure storage facilities or better water collection methods. At least a few agrarian economists are coming to see that the resourcefulness of the world's two billion peasant farmers is one of our most undeveloped assets.

We are talking about a prospect here which, I realize, must sound to some like a prescription for indigence: the project of winning work back from the machines by scaling down the industrial establishment—an item that is nowhere on the agenda of government, business, or organized labor in the developed societies. What would it cost us in material terms to build such an alternative economy of modest means and high fulfillment? The question is impossible to answer because we have no rational idea of how much of anything we really need to be healthy, happy, and secure; there is no such word in our economics as "enough." Certainly poor countries need lots of everything, especially food. But how much of what they need is here and available, being used up by the self-indulgent habits of affluence? How much of the food and land that the poor need is being squandered on the unhealthy tastes of rich societies that must have their coffee, tea, and tobacco, and insist on eating only cattle who have eaten the world's most expensive feed grain?

We have no way whatever of knowing how much productivity the developed nations genuinely require. We are only beginning to come to grips with the colossal waste their affluence includes. When we decide we must keep people at work at mass-production levels to provide us with shoes, how many pairs of shoes per person do we think we have to own, and how long is each pair supposed to last? Certainly we need assembly lines to produce automobiles; but how many cars do we need to a family, how big and classy need they be, and how long can we make them to last, free of planned obsolescence? Ask the same question of everything in sight from where you sit right now. How much of it really needed to be made, by any standard you would be willing to defend on your own moral responsibility?

If we could imagine cutting away the fat on which our middle and upper classes spend so freely (let us start there, but eventually we may include the junk the poor also waste their meager incomes upon), how much heavy production would still have to be done in our society? Of course, it is this fat which now employs most of our work force. But that is precisely the madness of the system, is it not? If we stop buying luxuries off the top, the corporate powers-that-be make sure the system stops producing bread and butter at the bottom, and nobody works. No waste, no essentials: the secret of the expanding economy.

Until we have some idea of what a rational and becoming standard of living demands, we have no way of knowing how much work needs to be done on a mechanized big scale. And we have no such idea. Our supposedly hardheaded economic science is the plaything of wild consumer fantasies and infantile prodigality. No one should be admitted into the profession who has not read Tolstoi's fable *How Much Land Does a Man Need?*

THE COMING LIBERATION OF WORK

Considerations of rational need aside, one may still wonder if it is realistic to make the demands raised here of the world industrial economy. Is this not rather like butterflies making demands of dinosaurs?

I think the question is put wrong way around. We should rather ask: Is it realistic to go on scorning people's need for fulfilling work? Is it realistic to conduct ourselves as if we might continue to intensify the alienation of work life without producing a socially crippling epidemic of demoralization? The fact to hold firmly in mind is that, spiritually and ecologically, urban-industrialism is indeed a dinosaur whose days are numbered—a culture that is flirting with extinction. It is weighing that heavily upon the limits of human and environmental tolerance. Our planet will not much longer endure the spread of an economy that makes so many of us dependent for our life's work on wasteful and irresponsible employment. That is the deep reason why the ideal of vocation has begun to assert itself in our day. Once again, in a crucial area of life, the needs of the person vibrate sympathetically to the needs of the planet, and we see people spontaneously disaffiliating from the big Earth-tormenting systems in search of the human scale.

The disaffiliation begins at the fringes, of course, and it proceeds by fits and starts. But the signs of new growth are as vividly there as the symptoms of discontent. Let me turn some of my own random observations into a few predictions: an impressionistic survey of the future of work life in the industrial societies. In the coming generation, I would expect to see a sequence of reforms and experiments rapidly unfolding as people delve deeper and deeper into the root causes of alienation.

1. There will be more and more demands for job enrichment and restructuring in all areas of the economy, especially in clerical routine and assembly-line work. Experiments in flextime scheduling, mixing skills teams, job sharing, work-gang and "whole-job" assignments, and a growing emphasis on variety and flexibility will become the new frontier of personnel management. Major organizations, both private and public, will proudly advertise their repertory of morale-boosting inducements. They will tell us how they have "personalized" and "custom-tailored" their jobs to the needs of their employees. Concurrently, unions will press for more paid holidays, sabbaticals, a shorter work week, and longer vacations as independently desirable fringe benefits that may come to weigh more heavily in contract negotiations than wage and overtime demands. Soon these reforms will be hailed in the media as a "revolution" in industrial work life, though, in fact, they make no structural changes in the economy and are little more than temporary palliatives.

2. There will be increasing pressure for industrial democracy and self-management in the workplace. In the major industries, an aggressive new breed of union leaders will demand representation in top managerial decisions and more shop-floor democracy, perhaps taking their lead from the "co-determination" arrangements that the Scandinavian and West German trade

unions have enjoyed for a generation or more, and which the French Government is now urgently promoting. The success of their efforts will vary and will probably be effectively stymied in the big corporations. But in smaller firms and newer industries we will hear about a new enlightened style of management which strives to take workers into responsible partnership and even shares the profits. The models for these experiments will be companies like the Scott-Bader Commonwealth in England, International Group Plans of Washington, D.C., Texas Instruments, and Bolivar Rearview Mirrors in Tennessee.

3. We will see more people dropping out of conventional employment to pursue livelihoods in the crafts and trades with a new spirit of self-discovery and ethical commitment. Many will be university-educated, even potential professionals, but they will be looking for a quality of work the professional world rarely offers. Perhaps they will have to rely on public assistance and food stamps to make the transition, and many may have to settle down to a simple, low-consumption living pattern, but that will be part of the autonomy and dignity they seek. We already have a crafts renaissance blossoming in America; its wares are in the streets and in many an urban bazaar. Craftsmanship has become one of the havens for the dropped-out young of the sixties who have rescued countless good old crafts from extinction. I think we will see more people turning to this alternative economy as they discover that they can find better value for their money in these new handicrafts and services than they can find at Sears or Wards. The danger with the new crafts is that they will steadily drift out of the *People's Yellow Pages* into more opulent boutiques to become the next generation of gourmet merchandise.

4. We will see a growing number of work collectives and producer's co-operatives spring up in which people will band together to support one another's vocational needs. These may take the form of crafts co-ops, maintenance and repair collectives, or collectively owned shops and businesses. Some will be Community Development Corporations based in rural slums or urban ghettos modeled after experiments like the OEO-financed FIGHT organization in Rochester, New York, or HELP in New Mexico. Others may be worker-controlled industries reclaimed from the ruined businesses that many failed conglomerates of the sixties are leaving behind, an imaginative salvage operation which the Federation for Economic Democracy in Washington, D.C., is now pursuing. I suspect many of the new collectives will be women's groups organized by resourceful refugees from home and family in need of a liberating security and determined not to fall into conventionally masculine careers. Whatever the form or origin, the spirit of these enterprises will be the same. Because they will be worker-owned and managed, they will offer the most advanced forms of authentic job enrichment; the fulfillment of people in their work, rather than the size of earnings and output, will be part of their basic standard of efficiency and success. Above all, they will want an honest commerce with the daily needs of people: good value at a fair price, with maximum personal attention. That has certainly been my experience in dealing with such collectives. One is confronted with people of competence and conscience who take a simple delight in having at last found a useful purpose in life.

5. There will be an increasing number of dissenting professionals among us—in medicine, law, education, welfare, counseling, city planning, science, and engineering—who will strive to recapture the waning idealism of their callings. Many will assume "advocacy" or ombudsman positions outside their professions; they will become full-time troublemakers and boat-rockers, watchdogging the ethics of their colleagues—on the model of Ralph Nader's "Raiders." They will project a new relaxed professional image that strives to set aside the defensive formalities and to undo the mystifications of their work. Many will finally band together to practice in legal collectives, free clinics, free schools, or radical think-tanks, placing their skills at the service of the vulnerable and the dispossessed. The economists among them will take an especially interesting turn as they become the champions of causes like land reform, community development, environmental defense. They will infuse their profession with a new ethical concern, as passionately principled as Marxism, but less rigidly scientistic, less ethnocentrically hostile to traditional ways and wisdom. Their research will do much to argue the viability of the work reforms listed here. They will set about inventing new criteria of efficiency, practicality, and economic reality that will be grounded in the vocational needs of people.

6. Finally, there will be more family farms and rural communes appearing in the wake of an aggressive national campaign for land reform and rural rehabilitation. These efforts will introduce a variety of organic techniques into the agricultural economy and will achieve astonishingly high levels of productivity with maximum economy. The open secret of their success will be the use of labor-intensive methods and small-scale technology. Unlike the agrindustrial combines that now blanket rural America, these will be people who came to the land to work in partnership with the soil, rather than to poison the land for profit. Perhaps they will begin to make the country look somewhat like a Jeffersonian democracy once again.

If I am right in believing that the central impetus behind contemporary dissent and disaffiliation is the need for self-discovery, then no reform that fails to bring a true spirit of vocation to our work life will prove satisfactory for more than a little while. One by one, we will see the layers of alienation stripped away as people try this reform and that. The real issue will not always be clearly articulated; at times, it will seem that a shorter work week or a little more say-so about working conditions is enough. But I suspect that phony job-enrichment ploys will rapidly prove inadequate; forms of managerial participation that simply implicate workers in the waste or folly of their employers will quickly be discarded. Gradually, it will become clear that what people are really seeking is the chance to create an identity through their work which rises to their highest personal aspiration. They will finally see that the discontentment of their work life can only be remedied by finding the responsibility of a true vocation. With that realization—a truth that validates itself in every working hour—we shall have a new economics which is grounded in the value of labor, not the price of commodities, and which will take its proper place among the moral sciences.

Men and Women on the Job

PATRICIA H. WERHANE
SEXUAL STATIC AND THE IDEAL OF PROFESSIONAL OBJECTIVITY: CONFLICTS IN MANAGEMENT RELATIONSHIPS ....

Recent studies of management relationships have documented a new phenomenon in the workplace, a phenomenon called "sexual static." There is a great deal of evidence to suggest that in situations where there is a mix of male and female managers there is often, too, a sexually charged atmosphere; that is, men and women feel uneasy about their professional interrelationships and how these might be misinterpreted as sexual ones. This atmosphere is engendered at least in part because of the changing roles of women in the workplace. Increasingly, women are occupying important management roles formerly held primarily by males. Yet many men still think of women first in their traditional sex roles as mothers, sisters, lovers, or wives. Most male managers want to treat women as equals and give them the same professional respect and opportunities they give men. But gender differences and cultural and social mores specifying these differences create an uneasiness between male and female managers, an uneasiness that Professor Judith Rosener aptly calls "sexual static."[1] Men often do not know how to treat women as equals and working partners without fearing that their actions might be misconstrued as sexual advances. Women's professional actions too are often wrongly interpreted. Women are often unsure how to act professionally without implying sexual overtones in their behavior. Such uneasiness in management relationships is not merely uncomfortable. It contributes to management dysfunctions as well. A manager simply cannot be effective if there are professional confrontations such as these in the workplace.

Sexual static is sometimes confused with discriminatory hiring or promotion practices, or its existence is sometimes given as an excuse for *not* hiring or promoting more women. It is true that women are not always accepted or accepted equally into the corporate culture. Few women are CEOs of major corporations, and women in higher management are pimarily in public relations and personnel. Moreover, as Professor Rosener states, "[I]n the male-dominated corporate culture, women managers are too often denied the support of a mentor,"[2] that is, an older senior manager who acts both as a role model and as a leader and protector. In studies of recent MBA graduates conducted at

Stanford and Harvard, both universities discovered that while initially MBA women graduates were hired for positions equal to those of their male classmates, five years after graduation, on the average, women graduates with similar performance records in the MBA programs were earning between $5,000 and $10,000 less than their male classmates with similar academic records. In fact, according to a recent article in *Crain's Chicago Business,* the number of women in executive positions in major Chicago corporations has *declined* in the past year.[3] Is this because of sexual static? Or do other factors play a role?

Accepting the fact that sexual static occurs in the workplace and disrupts professional relationships between men and women, I shall seek to clarify this notion, and I will explore some of the kinds of values implicitly and explicitly imbedded in, and contributing to, this phenomenon. I shall suggest that raising the question of sexual static is itself a value-laden issue. I shall argue that it is not merely gender differences but rather friction between a number of sets of values which form the basis for sexual static. Finally, I shall conclude that sexual static is part of a larger problem in contemporary society, the failure of the ideal of professional objectivity in management relationships.

First, let me briefly address a prior question. Why should the issue of sexual static be addressed in the field of work? In studying management, management science, and organizational behavior, one learns the logic of being a good manager and eliciting appropriate behavior from others in the workplace. Sexual static gets in the way of communication in the workplace and restricts the development of good management skills and good managers. Secondly, the problem of sexual static is not an issue exclusively for women. Homosexuals face similar and sometimes more difficult problems. By focusing on this topic as a women's issue one has a means to get at the values underlying the phenomenon—conflicting values, I shall argue, that unduly create interpersonal hostilities. Such analyses and the methodologies that one develops to study and deal with this phenomenon can then serve in other, more sensitive, areas where similar dilemmas occur.

Third, if we lived in a sex-gender-color-ethnic-age neutral environment where people were hired and promoted by merit or other objective criteria set out by color-blind, biracial, handicapped, foreign-born eunuchs of mixed religious background perhaps the phenomenon of sexual static would not be an issue, and questions of management relationships could be discussed more objectively or even scientifically. But we live in a society in which business is conducted in an atmosphere where merit or worthiness is the ideal but not the practice. We do discriminate, we are prejudiced, we are guided by sexual preferences, friendships, first impressions, and tradition or custom even in what are allegedly value-neutral management situations. So the phenomenon of sexual static is only one of the many difficulties facing management in a less than fair business environment. It is an important phenomenon to study, because it vividly illustrates these kinds of problems.

Fourth, sexual static is often attributed to a conflict between stereotypical and managerial expectations. Some of us were raised in a value system that stereotyped male and female roles—the woman as wife, mother, homemaker, and, sometimes, a behind-the-scenes matriarch of power, or preserver of moral values; and the male as patriarch, leader, family supporter, hero. Most women who worked did so out of economic necessity, and working was a job, something to be avoided under more propitious economic circumstances. The effects of these stereotypes on male-female relationships in the workplace are obvious and have been discussed at length in the literature. I shall give one example to remind us of these.

In the early 1900s, long before women were accepted in the workplace except as teachers or secretaries, the American Telephone and Telegraph Company (AT&T) hired women (and minorities too) as telephone operators. Yet in the 1970s the U.S. Government brought suit against AT&T accusing them of discrimination against women! It turned out that although almost all telephone operators were women, until almost the 1970s no women were ever promoted to supervisory positions. No written policy dictating this procedure was ever found at AT&T, nor apparently was the issue discussed by AT&T management. It was just the accepted more—the custom—and managers at AT&T did not consider promoting women or even think this might be an issue. So while AT&T was in the forefront of hiring women, they lagged badly in promoting the women they had hired. And this occurred, I would suggest, not because of a deliberate policy, but because they did not even consider such promotions as part of management policy. Interestingly, too, until the 1970s women telephone operators at AT&T did not protest this treatment. They did not see themselves in the role of supervisor or manager. It was not part of their expectations in the workplace. The operators thought of their work as a job, a way to make a living, not a career; and even while working these women saw their primary role as wives, mothers, or lovers.

The traditional male-female stereotypes have broken down in the last twenty-five years. Women have moved into responsible management positions and many of these women see their work as a career, something to which they will devote much of the most important part of their lives and energies. Sexual static as it occurs in the 1980s, then, cannot be fully attributed to a conflict between stereotypical and managerial expectations. Still, there are residual effects of these older customs. Many younger people entering business come from two-career families where both parents have responsible careers. Yet sexual static occurs nevertheless not only between younger and older managers but also between younger managers. Younger men may feel comfortable with women managers, but women are still valued more as wives, lovers, or mothers than as business equals. Even younger managers remember a mother or an aunt who had to have a *job* in order to support their family, but few knew older career women who worked because they loved it or felt it was their life plan. So few male managers, even today, are familiar with older female role models as exemplars.

That there is sexual static in management relationships and that this phenomenon is described as disruptive to communication and good management relationships raise some ethical questions. Is it sexual static that is the primary issue, or are there other problems for which sexual static is merely the symptom? Professor Rosener is careful not to argue that all male-female management relationships involve sexual static nor that all management miscommunication is due to sexual static. But the question I want to raise is whether one can make too much of sexual static, important as it is, and overlook a more basic difficulty that underlies the existence of sexual static and contributes in a variety of ways to miscommunication and management dysfunctions.

The existence of sexual static, I want to suggest, is part of a larger ethical issue in management which crosses gender lines. That issue involves a conflict between the ideal of management objectivity—an ideal pervasively espoused in our system—and other forces, some of which themselves embody important values that interfere with the realization of this ideal. At the root of the conflict is the notion of what constitutes fairness in management practice. Let me begin with a stipulative definition that, ideally, fairness in management practices and management relationships entails professional objectivity. Professional objectivity is a *very* vague notion. In management personnel relationships and practices, at least, the topic we are focusing on here, the principle of objectivity requires that the most skilled and effective persons (appropriate skill and nature of effectiveness being determined by the context) be hired or promoted to leadership positions. In other organizational relationships between managers professional objectivity requires, in brief, that these relationships not be swayed by personal feelings or biases or influenced by issues not relevant to achieving the needs, goals, and objectives of the organization. Notice I am not describing what is the case in fact. I am saying that professional objectivity is an *ideal*—a standard for what, under the best conditions, should be management practice and for evaluating excellence in management training and practice.

What is the basis for arguing that this is the ideal? All of us, male and female, young and older, have been raised on work ethic values. These values form the basis for what has somewhat parochially been called an ideal of meritocracy, an ideal which according to popular literature is highly esteemed in American business culture.

> Today we have an elite selected according to brains and educated according to desserts, with a grounding in philosophy and administration as well as in the two S's of science and sociology. . . . Today we frankly recognize that democracy can be no more than aspiration, and have rule not so much by the people as by the cleverest people; not an aristocracy of birth, not a plutocracy of wealth but a true meritocracy of talent.[4]

A meritocracy, in brief, is an ideal system in which those who are most deserving, e.g., the most intelligent, the strongest, hardest-working, most able, are, or should be, the intellectual, economic, and political leaders. The ideal of meritocracy or dessert is that those who are most able and diligent should and will succeed.

The roots of meritocracy derive from the philosophical individualism of two seventeenth- and eighteenth-century British philosophers, John Locke and Adam Smith, and are fully developed in the nineteenth-century theory of Social Darwinism. One of the justifications of constitutional rights in this country is John Locke's argument, in brief, that every person, just because she or he is a human being, has a right to life and to freedom, which Locke interprets to mean at a minimum the right to noninterference in the pursuit of one's own ends. Included in these rights are the rights to survive and to pursue economic goals, including working and owning property.

Given these basic rights, Adam Smith goes farther. Smith argues that the free but self-restrained and self-interested pursuit of economic ends in competition with others in a free market (laissez-faire) economy creates optimal conditions for economic growth and a progressively higher standard of living.

In the nineteenth century Locke's and Smith's views on freedom were coupled with a theory of social evolution paralleling that of Darwin's theory of biological evolution. Social Darwinists argued, in brief, that societies follow, or should emulate, evolutionary patterns similar to those exhibited by biological evolution, including the principle of evolution of the species—this time the human species—from simple primitive societies to complex industrial ones. In that process the changing social, cultural, and political environment will reflect the principle of the adaptability of the species. Left alone, individuals freely competing among themselves will develop an advanced culture in which only the strongest will survive and flourish. Adam Smith's ideal society, the unregulated free market system, which champions individualism and competition, reflects the evolutionary advance of the human species. As cultures evolve from simple agrarian communities to complex industrial cultures—a pattern mirroring species evolution—those who are most fit adapt themselves to changing and more complex social and technological conditions. Those who cannot should be allowed to wither away. Indeed, it was Herbert Spencer, the father of Social Darwinism, not Darwin himself, who coined the phrase "survival of the fittest" as the motto for Social Darwinism.

Social Darwinism in its crudest form criticized any sort of welfare or assistance to the poor, believing that poverty was a result of an inability to adapt. But Social Darwinists did not focus merely on the poor. They protested against such activities as preventive health measures—for example, sanitation, sewers, and vaccinations—as interfering with one's development of natural resistance to disease. Social Darwinists did not advocate genocide since those who are able should have the opportunity to rescue themselves from poverty, handicap, or disease, but no one should be helped, either to succeed or to fail. It was contended that every person should begin life from an equally inauspicious position, thereby allowing only the innately strongest of the species to succeed. Nor was Social Darwinism racist or sexist since conceivably the fittest could be minorities or women.

The modern welfare state appears to be in contradiction to Social Darwinism. But what has remained in the minds of some is at least an implicit lingering belief that the poor do not wish to work or are incapable of improvement. Those who can will succeed, and our economic system and its institutions are run by the most qualified people. However, this notion of meritocracy, while not an incorrect description of some of what is espoused in management, is perhaps too simple a concept to describe adequately management standards of excellence. In fact, as those trained and training in management know, there are no universal qualities of management leadership easily quantified into the category of "merit." Nor can one identify talented elite nor even determine what training is most appropriate to create such an elite. Success in management depends on mastering a core of technical skills which are appropriate depending on the situation, and developing an effective management style in that context. Moreover, as Henry Mintzberg has carefully demonstrated, other factors such as authority or personal control, organizational ideology, politics, and bureaucracy also play important roles in determining who will be management leaders.[5] Thus despite the popular view that "the cream rises to the top," one cannot identify who is "The Best" nor who is most likely to succeed. Moreover, since it is difficult to define "dessert," it is not clear whether those who have attained leadership positions truly deserved to do so. Nevertheless, a form of the ideal of merit is at least implicitly assumed in management and management training in various guises. Management is considered a science. One learns how to manage as if there were certain rational and logical skills and rules. Those who are most able at acquiring these skills will, in turn, have at least the necessary qualifications to be top managers. Secondly, it is presumed those who choose managers will themselves disinterestedly seek to select the most skilled and effective leaders. Third, management practice, like management training, is based on a body of technical skills and principles, and excellence in management, at least in theory, should reflect the use of those skills and principles. These assumptions exhibit what I call the ideal of professional objectivity—that there is a body of facts and knowledge that constitute the discipline of management, and that management practices can and should be unbiased and impersonal.

Interestingly, this ideal of objectivity, a positive goal for management that is usually present but seldom stated, sometimes contributes to a conflict of values one of which exhibits itself as sexual static. As we noted earlier, traditionally, most women only worked when they had to—to earn money to support themselves or their families. But women now see working as a career— as something to which they devote their intelligence, their emotions, and the better part of their lives. Working has become a life commitment, not merely a means to survival. Sexual static arises in part because women have changed their own ideas of work and their place in the working world.

It is clear that sexual static eschews objectivity because personal feelings and ungrounded misperceptions get in the way of professional relationships. Notice here the assumption is that professional relationships, at least in management, are or should be objective and separated from subjective feelings and biases. But another force is also at work. Managerial standards of objectivity clash with so-called traditional male-female stereotypes since in principle these standards are sex-blind. So there is no reason—no logical reason—why qualified women should not have equal opportunity on all levels of management. Yet studies demonstrate that they do not. This is often attributed to an inequality of talent in business, or to the fact that women have only recently entered management. Sexual static arises in part, then, not only because of the conflict between stereotypical roles and a new view of women in management, but also because both men and women value objectivity and professionalism, yet sometimes see it not realized. For men the conflict is between women as mothers, wives, or lovers, women as managers, and the ideal of excellence which should allow women (i.e., wives, mothers, and lovers, as well as managers) equal management opportunity. At the same time most top managers in the Fortune 1000 corporations are white males. So if the ideal of objectivity has been realized, men are in positions of leadership and increasingly so because they are the most effective, not because they are white or male. Women also see men as lovers, husbands, or fathers, as managers, *and* in positions of power, positions allegedly "earned" by reason of skill and expertise. Yet at the same time both men and women in management see people in leadership positions who are not as able as themselves. Women often attribute this to discrimination or as a result of sexual static, but it is more complicated than that, because, men, too, suffer from an imperfect realization of professional standards. That the ideal of objectivity is not always realized in management is due, at least in part, to other sets of forces operating in organizations, including those listed by Mintzberg (authority relationships, organizational ideology, and politics). For the sake of brevity I shall focus on one element: what I shall call personal loyalties and friendships. I want to oversimplify and concentrate on personal loyalties and friendships in management relationships because loyalty and friendship are themselves positively valued. They are not ordinarily thought of as divisive although they can be. So they illustrate what will be my general point that even conflicts between positive values can be unethical and unfair in management relationships.*

What I have conveniently named personal loyalty and friendship is sometimes referred to derisively as "ol' boy networks" or office politics. More technically, personal loyalties and friendships are part of the "system of politics" that functions to varying degrees in any organization. Mintzberg defines politics as by and large a negative system of influences in organizations.

> . . . politics refers to individual or group behavior that is informal, ostensibly parochial, typically divisive, and above all, in the technical sense, illegitimate—sanctioned neither by formal authority, accepted ideology, nor certified expertise. . . .[6]

---

*In the literature on management the term "loyalty" is used in at least two senses: (a) to describe commitment to an organization and (b) to describe personal relationships. I shall focus on (b) in this paper.

Management politics used in this technical sense includes a number of elements. One is what I refer to as loyalty and friendship. These involve individual alliances, sponsorships, mentoring, and personal alignments which develop friendships, commitments, and loyalties between managers or between managers and executives.[7] These loyalties are designed or lead to favors, alliances, promotions, etc. within organizations. While Rosabeth Moss Kanter finds such sponsorships and alliances crucial for management success, Mintzberg sees these relationships primarily as "illegitimate," because they arise from a weakness of what he sees as legitimate—or what I would call professional and objective—influences in organizations.

> [In the organizational "System of Politics"] group pressures and direct links to external influences abound; the personal needs of the insiders dominate their behaviors; formal goals and objectives, should they exist at all, get distorted; suboptimization is common; and means are commonly inverted with ends. Privileged information and access to the influential are used to their limits, games are won and lost on the basis of effort expended and the political skills of the players, and the legitimate systems of influence—to the extent that they exist at all—are exploited in illegitimate ways without hesitation.[8]

When the organizational politics of personal loyalties and friendships function extensively within an organization—although professional objectivity may be hailed as the ideal—they play important roles in management decision making and success. Hiring and promotions, for example, are usually rationalized on the basis of qualifications and skills, but in fact they are sometimes due to loyalty, friendship, sponsorship, and even mentorship. It is not that poorly qualified people always become top managers. Rather, it is that in the pool of qualified capable people success can be attributable to loyalty, to whom one knows, and the alliances one makes, as well as to managerial effectiveness. This is evidenced, for example, when CEOs who change companies take valued managers with them or replace managers in acquired companies with their own "people." These particular managers are "known quantities," skilled effective persons who are also trustworthy, compatible, and committed to that CEO.

On the face of it, there appears to be nothing wrong with taking into account loyalty and friendship as well as skills in management personnel practices. Indeed, some philosophers argue that loyalty and friendship often do, and should, take precedence. The example is often given that if two children are drowning, one of which is your severely handicapped child and the other is, say, Mozart (a recognized child prodigy), saving your child is the right thing to do on the basis of loyalty even though from the point of view of disinterested fairness, both drowning persons should be treated equally, and on crude utilitarian standards Mozart obviously should be saved first.[9]

There is a problem, however, in transferring the value of loyalty to management relationships. There we espouse the principle that Mozart should be saved first, not merely because of the utility of this act, but because the notion of fairness in management practice is based on the view that the most able and effective management persons should be placed in leadership positions. Familial relationships and personal loyalties, important in other contexts, are ordinarily supposed not to enter into management choices even if they are developed in a professional context. In choosing between objectivity and loyalty we are usually choosing between two *goods*. That is not the difficulty. The difficulty is that in management it is said that one functions on the basis of excellence in management skills. So when we do not practice this principle or practice it consistently, or when we give management skills and loyalties equal consideration, we are acting unfairly in this context. To put it more bluntly, if objectivity is the ideal in management theory and practice, then in management personnel relationships, for example, criteria of professionalism, skills, and effective management must preempt personal loyalties, friendships, and commitments. It is inconsistent and unethical to do otherwise. Of course, because objectivity does not in fact exist perfectly, it could be the case that it is not the ideal or standard to which we aspire. But if that is the case, management relationships are reduced to a most subjective level.

But what about our CEO who takes managers with whom he has confidence and allegiances into executive positions in a new or acquired company? It is not that this is a bad management practice per se. But it is unfair to those in management positions in the new company not to give them equal opportunity.

That we do not put into practice the principle of professional objectivity creates problems that cross gender differences and are unfair to men as well as to women. At the same time these problems complicate male-female relationships in organizations and cause sexual static. This is because both men and women expect equal opportunity and success based on professional objectivity. Yet other less explicit values often dominate, values which by the fact of traditional male prominence in management jobs often precludes equal opportunity for women. To put it more simply, women are new in management. Loyalties have been built up between male managers, loyalties that perpetuate themselves in a male-dominant organizational culture. Women sometimes feel left out and they sometimes are left out. Women then blame this on sexual static, and managers sometimes use the possibility of the disruptive quality of sexual static as a rationalization for not promoting women to sensitive positions. Notice in these cases that sexual static sometimes becomes a scapegoat or excuse—a negative value to which to appeal to account for unfair management practices. In fact, however, often these practices are the result of a conflict between two positive values: professional objectivity and personal loyalties, which cannot always coexist in a management culture.

Finally, loyalties, mentoring, networking, and politicking can and do involve men *and* women, and male-female loyalties do develop in organizations. Unfortunately these are often interpreted to have sexual overtones. But this is in part because these friendships and loyalties, even between men and women, are not themselves professional practices. So it is not strange that they create or are attributed to sexual static since sexual static, as a negative manifestation of personal loyalties or friendships, is as unprofessional as personal politics.

Sexual static in management relationships, then, is a complex phenomenon and part of a larger issue involving a number of conflicting values. I have presented only some aspects of what is at issue. Traditional, culturally defined sex roles, women's changing concept of work as a career, the ideal of professional objectivity, loyalties and friendships, all contribute to this phenomenon. What is to be done about it? First, clarifying values entailed in sexual static does not solve the problem, but it may clear the air for further analysis of the issue. Workshops, discussions, and conferences on this topic do help in this matter. An analysis of the failed ideal of professional objectivity in management relationships helps to get at the issue in a less sensitive manner, because this failed ideal is destructive to the morale of men *and* women. Moreover, as more women become managers and even CEOs of major corporations the problem of sexual static should diminish, but unfortunately this in itself does not guarantee that objectivity in management practices will improve. An analysis of the ideal of professional objectivity helps to get at the issue in a less sensitive manner, because when one neglects this ideal for other interests this is destructive to men and women managers. Management literature is replete with ways to create, institute, and carry out objective standards for management excellence. It is now imperative in modern management practice to realize that goal, and in so doing we will help to clear up at least part of the problem of sexual static.

NOTES

[1] Judith Rosener, "Coping with Sexual Static," *New York Times Magazine: The Business World,* December 7, 1986, pp. 89ff.

[2] Rosener, p. 12.

[3] Joe Cappo, "Women Execs: After 11 Polls, No Gains," *Crain's Chicago Business,* July 6, 1987, p. 6.

[4] M. Young, *The Rise of Meritocracy: 1870–1933* (New York: Random House, 1959), pp. 18–19.

[5] Henry Mintzberg, *Power in and Around Organizations* (Englewood Cliffs, N.J.: Prentice-Hall, 1983), p. 128.

[6] Mintzberg, p. 172.

[7] Rosabeth M. Kanter, *Men and Women of the Corporation* (New York: Basic Books, 1977).

[8] Mintzberg, p. 424. Mintzberg, however, also notes that sometimes organizational politics can play a positive role in forcing organizational changes in a static bureaucratic situation (p. 447).

[9] See Thomas Donaldson, "Duties to Strangers," in *Ethics in the Global Market,* forthcoming; and Andrew Oldenquist, "Loyalties," *Journal of Philosophy,* LXXIX (1982): 173–192.

HELENA ZNANIECKA LOPATA
TRENDS IN WOMEN'S PAID EMPLOYMENT AND OCCUPATIONS IN AMERICA[1] ....

One of the main problems of tracing trends in the employment and occupational involvement of American women, or anyone else for that matter in any country, lies in the methods by which such data are obtained. Generally speaking, we must depend upon the census of populations for such information. Unfortunately, every method of trying to reach and record each person in a large and complex society has its drawbacks, and an additional problem for social scientists lies in the attempts by governments to offset these difficulties by changing procedures or instructions given to enumerators. This is particularly true of census data on the occupations of women. Hill (1929), who summarized information on *Women in Gainful Occupations 1870–1920* for the United States Department of Commerce's Bureau of the Census, pointed to examples of such changes:

> While an attempt was made in 1820 and again in 1840 to classify the population by main divisions of industry, distinguishing agriculture, manufactures, and commerce, the first complete census of occupations was taken in 1850, when for the first time the name of each person enumerated was recorded on the census schedule, together with sex, age, and other personal data including occupation. . . . The 1850 occupation inquiry was restricted to adult males . . . in 1870 it applied to each person, male or female, without limitation as to age.
>
> Regarding homemakers and housekeepers, in 1870 and again in 1880 the enumerators were instructed that "women keeping house for their own families or for themselves without any other gainful occupation" were to be entered on the schedules as "keeping house," and grown daughters assisting them were to be reported as without occupation, the term "housekeeper" being reserved for such persons as received wages or salaries for their services (Hill, 1929: 3).

The fact that married American women refrained from working in jobs outside of the home until rather recently can be documented statistically as illustrated by Table 1. In 1890, only 4.6 percent of married women were officially listed as in the civilian labor force. The percentage of married women in paid employment, or at least in jobs, remained low until the last few

[1] I wish to thank Debra Barnewolt and Cheryl Allyn Miller for their encouragement during the writing of *City Women: Work, Jobs, Occupations, Careers*, vol. 1 *America* (Praeger, 1984). This chapter is a modified version of Chapter 2 in that volume.

TABLE 1 Marital Status of Women in the Civilian Labor Force: 1940–1986

(As of March, except as indicated. Persons 14 years old and over through 1965; 16 years old and over thereafter. Prior to 1960, excludes Alaska and Hawaii. Figures for 1940 based on complete census revised for comparability with intercensal series. Later data based on Current Population Survey; see text, section 1 and Appendix III. See also Historical Statistics, Colonial Times to 1970, series D 49–62)

| | | PERCENT DISTRIBUTION, FEMALE LABOR FORCE | | | FEMALE LABOR FORCE AS PERCENT OF FEMALE POPULATION | | | MARRIED | |
| | | | | | | | | | |
Year	Total (1000)	Single	Married[1]	Widowed or divorced	Total	Single	Total[1]	Husband present	Widowed or divorced
1940	13,840	48.5	36.4	15.1	27.4	48.1	16.7	14.7	32.0
1944[2]	18,449	40.9	45.7	13.4	35.0	58.6	25.6	21.7	35.7
1947[2]	16,323	37.9	46.2	15.9	29.8	51.2	21.4	20.0	34.6
1950	17,795	31.6	52.1	16.3	31.4	50.5	24.8	23.8	36.0
1955[2]	20,154	25.2	58.7	16.0	33.5	46.4	29.4	27.7	36.0
1960	22,516	24.0	59.9	16.1	34.8	44.1	31.7	30.5	37.1
1965	25,952	22.8	62.2	15.0	36.7	40.5	35.7	34.7	35.7
1970	31,233	22.3	63.4	14.3	42.6	53.0	41.4	40.8	36.2
1975	36,981	23.2	62.3	14.5	46.0	57.0	45.1	44.4	37.7
1980	44,934	25.0	59.7	15.3	51.1	61.5	50.7	50.1	41.0
1985	50,891	25.4	58.5	16.1	54.5	65.2	54.7	54.2	42.8
1986	51,732	25.4	58.5	16.1	54.7	65.3	55.0	54.6	43.1

[1] Includes married, spouse absent.
[2] As of April.

Source: U.S. Bureau of the Census, Statistical Abstracts of the United States, 1987, 107th Edition, Table 653, p. 382.

decades, although it moved up gradually until it hit the 40 percent level in 1970. Interestingly enough, it did not drop during the "great depression," for several reasons (Milkman, 1979). In the first place, the sex segregation of jobs had solidified by the 1930s and the labor market continued to expand in the female dominated sector even during the depression years (Bell, 1973; Oppenheimer, 1970). In addition, women cost employers less than men did, so they were less apt to be fired "during a period of worsening business conditions" (Milkman, 1979: 511). Women were already underemployed, so that the figures for that period were not very different from those of the preceding or following times. Finally, many women were pushed into the labor force by the unemployment of their husbands. Milkman (1979) noted, however, that it was the work of women in the home which altered most during the depression, since they had fewer resources for the purchase of commodities produced outside of the home.

World War II involved women in paid employment even more than before because men were drafted into the armed services, leaving their jobs behind. Women were thus employed in jobs previously identified as male, but always with an understanding that such employment would last "for the duration" only and that the return of the men from the war would require the firing of the women.

> Sixty percent of the women who entered the labor market between 1940 and 1944 were 35 years old or more, and more than half of them were or had been married (Milkman, 1979: 529).

The society made every effort to accommodate the needs of working mothers—factories even set up nurseries nearby, all of which closed with the end of the war. The percentage of married women in the labor force increased from 16.7 to 25.6 between the years of 1940 and 1944, but it dropped to 21.4 in 1947 (see Table 1).

The post–World War II years were accompanied by an extensive campaign to get the women back into full-time homemaking, a campaign based on what Betty Friedan (1963) labeled "the feminine mystique." Reminiscent of the "true womanhood" ideology,[2] the mystique identified all women with homemaking, wifehood, and motherhood and discouraged any thoughts of, or commitment to, occupations and careers outside of these roles. The strength of the campaign, which capitalized on work of such psychiatrists as Freud (see Friedan, 1963; La Pierre, 1959), Helene Deutsch (1944), or Lundberg and Farnham *Modern Woman: The Lost Sex* (1947), and utilized print as well as film (see *Lady in the Dark*), is documented elsewhere and appears to have been effective (Lopata, 1971). Even when marriage became less of a stumbling block to women seeking paid employment, motherhood did not. The percentage of women in the labor force with at least one child under six remained very low—that is, below 20—until the 1960s, and it has increased dramatically only recently (see Table 2).

However, there as been little agreement among social scientists as to the nature of the ebb and flow of women in the world of work. Friedan (1963)

[2]"The attributes of True Womanhood, by which a woman judged herself and was judged by her husband, her neighbors, and society, could be divided into four cardinal virtues—piety, purity, submissiveness, and domesticity. Put them all together and they spelled mother, daughter, sister, wife—woman. Without them, no matter whether there was fame, achievement, or wealth, all was ashes. With them she was promised happiness and power" (Welter, 1966: 151).

TABLE 2 Married Women (with husband present) in the Labor Force, by Age and Presence of Children: 1948 to 1970 (as of March, except as noted)

		LABOR FORCE PARTICIPATION RATE[1]					
					WITH CHILDREN UNDER 6 YEARS		
Year	*Total (1000)*	*Total*	*With no children under 18 years*	*With children 6 to 17 years only*	*Total*	*No children 6 to 17 years*	*Also children 6 to 17 years*
1986*	—	54.8	48.2	68.7	53.9	—	—
1980*	—	50.2	46.0	61.5	45.3	—	—
1975*	—	44.5	44.0	52.8	38.6	—	—
1970	18,377	40.8	42.2	49.2	30.3	30.2	30.5
1965	14,708	34.7	38.3	42.7	23.3	23.8	22.8
1960†	12,253	30.5	34.7	39.0	18.6	18.2	18.9
1955[2]	10,423	27.7	32.7	34.7	16.2	15.1	17.3
1950	8,550	23.8	30.3	28.3	11.9	11.2	12.6
1949	7,959	22.5	28.7	27.3	11.0	10.0	12.2
1948	7,553	22.0	28.4	26.0	10.8	9.2	12.7

* U.S. Bureau of the Census. *Statistical Abstracts of the United States*, 1987, 107th Edition, Table 655, p. 383.

† Denotes first year for which figures include Alaska and Hawaii.

[1] Married women in the labor force as percent of married women in the population.

[2] As of April.

Source: U.S. Bureau of the Census, *Historical Statistics of the United States: Colonial Times to 1970*, Bicentennial Edition, Part II (Washington, D.C.: U.S. Government Printing Office, 1975), p. 134.

claimed that movement away from commitment to the public, especially the occupational, world occurred in the late 1940s and 1950s, after a peak in the 1920s. Bernard (1964) dated the redirection of attention by women who had taken up the feminist banner away from higher education and professions after a period of disillusionment in the 1920s. Stricker (1979), on the other hand, claimed that there never was a decrease in the total number of women so oriented, only a relative decrease in the proportion of women among all those achieving higher degrees and involvement in professions due to the upsurge in the number of men so involved.

Whichever argument is accepted, the fact remains that the numbers and proportions of women oriented toward careers, rather than just jobs, outside of the home have been very small until recent years. Many of those so committed had to renounce marriage and motherhood because American society was unwilling to provide public resources that made dual or triple role commitment possible, and because men were generally unwilling to marry highly educated career women (Komarovsky, 1953).

The increase of female labor force participation may have been partly due to the expansion of jobs in service and clerical sectors (see Table 3).

A service economy is largely a female-dominant economy—if one considers clerical, sales, teaching, health technicians and similar occupations. In 1960, 80 percent of all workers in the goods-producing area were men, and 20 percent women; conversely, in the service sectors only 54 percent of all workers were men and 46 percent women. Looked at along a different axis, 27 percent of all employed females worked in the goods-producing sector, while 73 percent of all women worked in the service sector (Bell, 1972: 179).

These trends, both in the expansion of these sectors and in the concentration of women in them, continue.

The large increase in the number of women professional workers may be attributed to a variety of social and economic developments. The school-age population expanded greatly, resulting in the employment of a rising number of women as teachers, other educational personnel, and librarians. The concern for the health of the American population, and especially of older persons, resulted in enlarged medical facilities and expanded health programs which provided increasing numbers of jobs for women as nurses, therapists, dieticians, pharmacists, clinical laboratory technologists and technicians, and other professional and technical health workers. The growth of business and industry and of governmental operations provided opportunities for many more women as accountants and computer specialists. The sharp growth in social welfare and recreation programs contributed to an increase in the number of women as professional, social and recreation workers (U.S. Department of Labor, 1975: 95).

Other theories as to the increase of women in the labor force abound. Smith (1979a) summarized a few explanations. One is given by economists who posit that the ratio of costs and benefits associated with employment outside the home has changed. If real wages increase and the returns from housework do not, then the net benefits for working outside of the home grow and more women decide to look for employment. This model assumes that the "income effect" (a decrease in the "push" into the labor force for women as family income from husband's earnings increases) will be outweighed by the "pull" of growing real wages for wives. A second explanation is in terms of the expansion of the gender-specific jobs. Demographic explanations focus on the effect of later marriages, rising divorce rates, and falling birth rates. Lastly, Smith (1979b), as well as Oppenheimer (1970) and Gordon (1978),

TABLE 3   Occupational Distribution of Employed Women, Annual
Averages, Selected Years 1900–1979

OCCUPATION	PERCENTAGE OF EMPLOYED WOMEN									PERCENTAGE OF ALL WORKERS
	1900[1]	1910[2]	1920[2]	1930[2]	1940[1]	1950[3]	1960[3]	1970[3]	1979[3]	1979[3]
Professional-technical	8.2	9.8	11.7	13.8	13.6	12.5	12.4	14.5	16.1	43.3
Managerial-ad-ministrative, of-ficials, proprie-tors (nonfarm)	1.4	2.0	2.2	2.7	3.6	4.4	5.0	4.5	6.4	24.6
Sales	4.3	5.1	6.3	6.8	7.3	8.7	7.7	7.0	6.9	45.1
Clerical	4.0	9.2	18.7	20.9	21.6	27.8	30.3	34.5	35.0	80.3
Craft, foremen	1.4	1.4	1.2	1.0	1.0	1.5	1.0	1.1	1.8	5.7
Operatives (in-cluding trans-portation)	23.7	22.9	20.2	17.4	18.5	19.6	15.2	14.5	11.3	32.0
Nonfarm laborers	2.6	1.4	2.3	1.5	0.9	0.8	0.4	0.5	1.3	11.3
Service, private	28.7	24.0	15.7	17.8	18.0	12.4	14.8	16.5	17.2	97.6
Service, nonpri-vate	6.7	8.4	8.1	9.7	11.2	8.7	8.9	5.1	2.6	59.1
Farm workers	19.0	15.7	13.5	8.4	4.3	3.6	4.4	1.8	1.2	18.0

Sources: [1] Gordon, Margaret. "Women and Work: Priorities for the Future." In C. Kerr and J. M. Rosow (eds.) *Work in America: The Decade Ahead.* New York: D. Van Nostrand, 1979: p. 117.

[2] U.S. Bureau of the Census. *Historical Statistics of the United States: Colonial Times to 1970, Bicentenial Edition, Part II.* Washington, D.C.: U.S. Government Printing Office, 1975: Table D182–232, p. 140.

[3] U.S. Department of Labor. *Perspectives on Working Women: A Databook, Bulletin 2080.* Washington, D.C.: U.S. Government Printing Office, 1980: Table 10, p. 9 (includes 14- and 15-year-olds).

saw changes in the attitudes toward women and their "proper" place as contributing to the increasing female labor force participation rates.

In sum, during most of the period since World War II, all the factors discussed here—improvement in job opportunities, demographic change, and the liberal-ization in attitudes—have contributed to the expansion of the female labor force (Smith, 1979b: 7).

Not only are more women now in paid employment, but the profile of the female labor force has also changed. The greatest increase has been in the number and percentage of married women and mothers who are employed outside the home (Smith, 1979b). As Gordon (1978) asserted, if this trend continues, and it is expected to do so (Smith, 1979a, 1979b), there are widespread implications for both family and market structures in the future. As more married women of childbearing age and more mothers of preschool children work outside of the home, the age, marital, and mothering characteristics of the female labor force more closely approximate the profile of the total female population (Blau, 1978). This means that the female labor force is increasingly diversified as to its personal characteristics so that assumptions as to the "type" of woman who is employed are no longer valid.

At the same time as women of all marital and socioeconomic backgrounds have expanded their labor force participation, the feminist movement has been working for equality in career opportunities and job compensation. In spite of these changes, the earnings gap between men and women is only now beginning to narrow. In 1955, the average female employee earned 64 percent of the wages paid to a similarly employed man. This dropped to 59 percent by 1970 (Special Task Force to the Secretary of HEW, 1973), and by 1974 the median earnings of women was only 57 percent of the median for men (Howe, 1977). By 1982, it increased to 63 percent (Blau and Ferber, 1985: 42). The legislation against wage discrimination (The Equal Pay Act of 1963) does little to alleviate this problem since discrimination against women most often takes the form of job segregation rather than unequal pay for the same job. Recently, the call for equal pay for work of comparable value has proven to be a rallying cry for organized employed women.

OCCUPATIONAL SEGREGATION AND SCHEDULE INFLEXIBILITY IN AMERICA

Although Bird (1979) called the influx of married women into the labor force a "revolution," there are two aspects of the change which have not been fully developed as of yet. In the first place, women are still segregated in relatively few female dominated occupations with easy entrance and exit boundaries, but low pay and restricted mobility opportunities (Blau and Ferber, 1985; Lopata and Norr, 1979, 1980; Oppenheimer, 1970). This gender segregation has only recently begun to decline.

The second lag in the American working situation is the failure of the system to make adjustments in the rhythm of work, in terms of time and career lines, to accommodate women, or men for that matter, who face role conflict arising from needs of children or other persons in their lives. The economic institution is still focused on itself, demanding that people adjust their lives to its schedule without flexibility.

There are many explanations for the concentration of women in female dominated occupations. Blau (1978) pointed to a historical explanation in that the influx and absorption of women into the labor force has occurred in three ways: the expansion of the traditional female occupations, the rise of new occupations which are defined as female, and a shift in the sexual composition of some occupations from male to female. However, we still do not know why occupations become so labeled, and the changes in composition are often historically idiosyncratic. An examination of both occupations and industries shows women drawn to jobs in the fastest growing industries, but they are concentrated at the lower levels and seldom move into supervisory, managerial, or technical positions.

Baker (1964) explained the distribution of women in occupations in terms of technology. The technological structure of the work in many jobs has helped move women in or out of particular occupations, as in the case of the textile mills when looms were introduced. However, the social role characteristics of jobs have also influenced whether women are allowed entrance into them or consider them a viable alternative. Early textile mills were specifically organized to attract the unmarried daughters of farmers, and they changed when the influx of immigrants and the increased willingness of native men to enter factory doors made other ways of organizing the job possible. One of the reasons American business and industry have failed to provide, or to encourage the government to provide, adequate arrangements for maternity leaves or day-care centers is that this society still does not really approve of paid employment outside of the home for mothers. At the time when America was pushing women back home, countries such as Poland, which lost a high proportion of men during World War II (one-sixth of the total population), went out of their way to attract, train, and retain women not only in female dominated occupations, but also in previous masculine occupations (Lobodzinska, 1970, 1974; Lopata, 1976; Piotrowski, 1963; Roby, 1973; Szczepanski, 1970). The majority of doctors, dentists, lawyers, and engineers in Poland, as well as in the Soviet Union, are women, which is still not true of the United States (Sokolowska, 1965). Creches and free nursery schools exist in countries wanting women in the labor force; maternity and paternity leaves, as well as time off to care for an ill child, are instituted in several countries (Kahn and Kamerman, 1975; Kamerman and Kahn, 1978; Lipman-Blumen and Bernard, 1979).

One of the theories attempting to explain the occupational segregation of women refers to them as a "reserve army," pulled into the labor force as needs arise. Milkman (1979) documented the weakness of this theory by showing that women were less affected by the great depression than men were. Hartmann (1976) argued that the transition to capitalism did not start the sexual segregation of jobs, but simply expanded the already established patriarchal system, one which Lipman-Blumen (1976) called the "homosocial" control of public life. It is Hartmann's thesis that the better organized male workers maintained their domination through sex-ordered job segregation; "capitalism grew on top of patriarchy" (Hartmann, 1976: 168). With the separation of work from the home during the industrial revolution, women grew more dependent on men economically as they became increasingly excluded from industry and job training. And, as capitalism developed to its more advanced stages, men enforced the segregation in the labor market *and* strengthened the domestic division of labor.

A combination of historical and sociological approaches to the analysis of occupational segregation by sex in the United States was undertaken by Gross (1968). Using an index of segregation (the percentage of females who would have to change their occupation in order that the distribution of sexes in occupations be the same) for each census year from 1900 to 1960, he found no significant difference in sexual segregation over the years. There has been some "reduction in segregation, which seems to be accomplished by men entering female occupations, rather than the reverse" (1968: 208), but this is masked by the fact that the occupations that are more segregated have been growing faster than those which are less segregated. Oppenheimer (1970) cautioned the social scientist against conceiving of *the* labor market and *the* demand for labor, rather than positing a multiplicity of labor markets, some of which are competitive with each other, while others are not competitive at all. She discussed six factors keeping certain jobs female dominated. First, the past availability of segments of the potential labor force permitted certain new occupations to be monopolized by women. Second, they are a source of cheap but educated—especially recently—labor leading to reliance on them by certain types of employers. Third, beliefs in gender-linked personality characteristics held by employers, union leaders, and job training personnel influence their behavior toward women. Fourth, the power of tradition which labels job as appropriate to one gender leads to an unwillingness of people of the other gender to even try entry. Fifth, strain in work relationships, assumed or real, in mixed groups or ones in which women supervise or are on a higher level than men, lead employers to gender discrimination. Sixth, and finally, other problems of past or current work limitations of women, such as lack of geographical mobility, career interruptions, educational specialization, and so forth, contribute to images of women and men workers that lead to occupational segregation (Laws, 1976; Suelzle, 1973).

Economists also offer numerous explanations of the gender segregation of occupations, focused mainly on the characteristics of the labor force. The overcrowding, employer "tastes," and "human capital" approaches fall outside of the province of this paper, and are only mentioned in case the reader wishes a deeper analysis of the situation (see Blau and Jusenius, 1976; Sokoloff, 1980; Stevenson, 1978). Among others, Doeringer and Piore (1971) have evolved a "primary" and "secondary" labor market dichotomy, explaining that most women work in the secondary market, which is less structured, has multiple channels of entry with short promotion ladders (or nonexistent ones), low wages, and less worker and job stability. The primary market, on the other hand, is highly developed, entry is restricted to high-level jobs with long promotion ladders, and work stability is encouraged through high wages and provisions for job security. (For more information on dual labor market theory see Bibb and Form, 1977; Edwards, 1980; Edwards, Gordon, and Reich,

1975; Kalleberg and Soreson, 1979; Piore, 1975; Stevenson, 1975.) Blau and Jusenius (1976) are critical of the dual labor market analysis because it does not explain the further sex segregation within each sector, the differentiation within the female sector, or the differential treatment accorded to women and men within the primary sector.

All in all, there are numerous theories attempting to explain the very striking sex segregation of occupations and industrial sectors in the United States, though none do so too successfully. The most segregated occupation, of course, is that of homemaking—very few men enter this occupation at the present time, although there is much media coverage of the few couples who are involved in "role reversal." Another obvious characteristic of this type of job is that it does not draw direct pay. Glazer (1976), in reviewing the literature on housework, pointed out that its monetary value to the family and to the economy of the nation (often referred to as the market-cost approach) has never been determined (see also Barker and Allen, 1976; and Malos, 1980 for mainly Marxist explanations of the politics of housework). Time allocation studies of housework have documented that there has been no drop in the average work week of the full-time housewife over the past 50 years (Vanek, 1974, 1978) and that employed married women still continue to perform the bulk of domestic work (Berk and Berk, 1979; Epstein, 1970; Lopata, Barnewolt, and Norr, 1980; Oakley, 1974a, 1974b; Walker, 1969, 1970). Glazer (1980) identified four characteristics of domestic work which she feels impinge on women's paid work: governmental trivialization of domestic work, the fact that domestic work has undergone more apparent than real changes, the additional fact that household laborsaving technology has not reduced the work of full-time homemakers, and finally that mothering has become more time consuming than ever before. Glazer's (1980) argument is founded on the thesis that housewifery is ascribed on the basis of gender, and other social relations in society assume that women are responsible for housework and child care. Thus, the paid work that women are channeled into is limited by "occupational compatibility"—work that is compatible with their domestic responsibilities. The sex-labeling of jobs and women's discontinuous involvement in the labor force are tied to women's domestic labor. The history of women's work as wage laborers first in the textile industry and later on in other factory systems was defined by their domestic labor. Glazer shows how women's domestic responsibilities in the family have affected women's activities outside the family; how women's paid labor force participation is organized around the assumption that domestic labor is their primary concern. (For another discussion of the link between female work and family roles and how that can be conceptualized as a gender segregated, dual market mechanism see Pleck, 1977.)

We can expect the strain between paid work and family roles to continue as the proportion of women in the labor force grows. In addition, as women become increasingly aware of the double burden they have to carry and if the division of labor within the home is broken down, it will become a problem for more and more men as well. One way of dealing with this has been to restructure the work schedules of women and men who are employed outside the home. It is probable that the number of alternatives to full-time work as now organized will increase in the future as it has in the recent past. The temporary employment industry, for instance, has grown faster than any other segment of the work force (Tepperman, 1976). This type of employment offers flexibility in both scheduling of hours and number of hours worked per week. Several experiments concerning flexible work hours and shortened work weeks have been conducted in the United States and Europe. These experiments began in 1967 in the research and development of a German aerospace company, Messerschmitt-Bolkow-Blohm. Flex-time was adopted at that plant to deal with problems of traffic jams and tardiness, but it proved to have other positive effects on the work force. The use of flexible schedules proliferated in Europe during the 1970s, and by 1975 about 6,000 European firms had adopted such schedules. The use of such alternative work schedules has been much slower in the United States, although it seems to be accelerating in the last half of the decade (Polit, 1979).

In the past 20 years, the incidence of part-time employment, involving mainly women (80 percent), has increased at a remarkable rate, nearly twice that of the increase in female employment. In 1974, 31 percent of the working wives in the United States were employed part-time (Hayghe, 1976; Polit, 1979). Among the 30.2 million women working in nonagricultural occupations in 1974, 21.7 million (almost 72 percent) were on full-time schedules and 8.5 million worked part-time. Of those women who worked part-time, 7.4 million do so for voluntary reasons and 1.1 million worked part-time due to economic slowdown (U.S. Department of Labor, 1975). Part-time work is particularly common in occupations in the education and service industries. In 1973 approximately 60 percent of the women who worked in sales, transport operation, and farm labor did so on a part-time basis. In addition, two out of three private household workers did not hold full-time jobs (U.S. Department of Labor, 1975).

Women are most affected by the growth of alternatives in work scheduling. Traditionally they, the elderly, young people, and the disabled have been the workers who have been concentrated in "marginal" work force participation.

> Those who are represented by the part-time work movement include women who are reentering the work place but do not wish to work full-time, dual career couples who are faced with an increasingly difficult time finding two full-time jobs (that is, in the same university or even in the same town); persons with cardiac and other medical problems who are instructed to return to work but on a part-time basis; and persons ideologically committed to maximizing time for private non-work-related interests (Arkin and Dobrofsky, 1979: 161–162).

Not all part-time work is undertaken voluntarily, however. "Involuntary part-time work, including short work weeks, layoffs for a day or two, and the like, greatly exceeds 20 percent; like recent rates for employment, these figures run considerably higher among women workers than men" (Bell, 1973: 80).

"Worksharing" is also on the rise. Under such arrangements weekly hours, as well as pay, are reduced so that all workers may retain their jobs, even at a lower salary. Advocates of such plans argue that their implementation spreads the impact of a recession and fosters a higher degree of job attachment, keeps employment skills fresh, and allows workers to retain fringe benefits. Critics maintain, however, that such plans interfere with seniority privileges and, when subsidized by the government, may discourage firms from adapting to technological and organizational changes (Bednarzik, 1980; Best and Mattesich, 1980). Demographically, blacks and women were disproportionately more likely to be on involuntarily shortened schedules because of decreased demand for their labor.

When female part-time workers are compared to male part-time workers it becomes apparent that many of the inequities faced by female full-time workers are also faced by the part-timers. Especially telling is the continuation of sexual segregation in part-time jobs. Seventy percent of all female part-time workers were in sales, clerical, and nondomestic service occupations as compared to 45 percent of the men who were employed part-time. It is interesting to note that part-time pay rates for men are about on a par with rates for women. This probably reflects the fact that male part-time workers are minorities and are either younger or older than average (68 percent of male part-timers are either less than 22 years old or over 55, compared to 42 percent of the women; Barrett, 1979).

Part-time jobs usually pay lower rates than comparable full-time work, and fringe benefits are scanty if they are included at all. Representative of this, Smith (1979c) found part-time employment to be heavily concentrated in low-wage occupations. In addition, the wage rates of women part-timers are usually lower than those of women full-time workers in the same occupation. Tuckman and Vogler (1979) state that there was a substantial gap in basic insurance coverage for those with part-time academic jobs. Less than half of the part-timers surveyed were covered by social security at their academic job, less than 20 percent had an institutional retirement plan, only 6 percent received life insurance coverage, and about 11 percent were eligible for workers' compensation. As reported by Polit (1979), the 1972 Wage Survey in four urban areas found part-time employees receiving a prorated portion of the paid holidays and vacations in only about half the cases. Less than one-fourth of the part-time workers were able to participate in pension plans, and life and health insurance were "generally not provided." In addition to these drawbacks, part-time jobs are frequently "dead-end" positions with few career opportunities. Polit (1979: 202) found that "most women working part-time in well-paying, challenging jobs appear to have obtained their positions by first demonstrating their competency as full-time employees." However, in spite of the low pay, lack of fringe benefits, and general lack of promotional opportunity, the demand for part-time work may outstrip the supply of part-time jobs. Such scheduling is particularly appealing to mothers of pre-adult children.

SUMMARY

The organization of work and its allocation to different kinds of societal members provide a fascinating subject for sociological and historical analysis. So does the connection between the work as a set of tasks and various social roles, such as those of employee, wife, or mother. A third subject of interest to social scientists is the social status of people, which is reflected in the complex of rights surrounding a person and derived from identities, social roles, and positions vis-à-vis others in the family, community, and society. These topics are complex, and the examination of changes in the work, social rules, and status of women over time provides alternate evaluations and explanations. The safe generalization is that there has always been a division of labor, although the distribution of tasks beyond the bearing and nursing of children has varied enormously. Taking just the last three centuries of Western European history (English and French for the most part) and variations on the themes which developed in America as *The First New Nation* (Lipset, 1979), we find that an important change in the work of women has been the removal and modification of much of their traditional work and its structuring into jobs in organizations outside of the home. A similar process occurred to much of the work of men but with higher status and greater innovation, as agriculture became so dramatically changed during the modernization as to make large numbers of dependent helpers superfluous.

The organization of traditional work into jobs and the introduction of new jobs within broad occupational categories accompanied the introduction of personal property as a means of exchanging work and products for money. The transformation of only part of women's work into jobs affected their lives and made them economically dependent upon men whenever the social system or cultural ideologies prevented their self-support. Men were freed of their dependence upon clans, families, and communities when their work became "public" or evaluated as contributing to the gross national product (Eichler, 1973; Engels, 1884/1972; Hartmann, 1976; Hill, 1929).

Ideologies that affect the work women do, as well as its organization and position in the prestige hierarchy, include not only the hierarchical evaluation of work roles but also definitions of "women," "men," and "children." A major change in such definitions occurred in the English-French form of Western European history and in America with the introduction of "true womanhood," public and private "domains" or "spheres," "childhood," etc. The ideologies, forcefully elaborated upon in America, discouraged women from becoming involved in the public sphere of life if they could afford to do so. However, the process of keeping women at home resulted in a backlash as the more educated middle-class woman combined with the male Protestant clergy to feminize and "moralize" the society. The welfare and protective activities had their own backlash in turn—they restricted the earning power of those women who wanted to be employed outside of the home and increased male hostility to women's employment activity. Although this argument sounds very much like the tendency to "blame the victim" of discrimination in the job market, it has been argued that this movement contributed to continued and even increased occupational sex segregation.

What ever the historical, structural, and psychological reasons for the distribution of women in paid and unpaid work, the recent "revolution" so touted in mass media and social science has changed the female world of work only partially. The contribution of traditional and modern trends has created dissonance in the lives of many American women. Women, particularly married ones, and more surprisingly in view of the ideological history of the United States, mothers of young children, are now working for pay, in addition to their work as homemakers, wives, and mothers. However, they are still working mainly in female dominated jobs, at 60 percent of what men earn in their jobs, and with short promotional ladders. Gross's (1968) analysis indicated that many women and men would have to change occupation and work locus before the second stage of the "revolution" in women's employment were to take place. In addition, the presence of women in the labor force has not yet affected the organization of work in occupational and career terms. According to Kahn and Kamerman (1975) and numerous others involved in comparative research (Roby, 1973), the political and economic sectors in America are not willing to modify work scheduling in recognition of the fact that a job is not the only role in which women and men are involved. Few attempts are made to facilitate their lives over the life course.

This chapter has mainly documented some of the trends which have led American society to its current division of labor and the policies affecting the work that women do.

REFERENCES

Arkin, William and Lynne R. Dobrofsky
    1979 "Job Sharing Couples." Pp. 159–176 in K. W. Feinstein (ed.) *Working Women and Families.* Beverly Hills, Calif.: Sage Publications.
Baker, Elizabeth Fulkner
    1964 *Technology and Woman's Work.* New York: Columbia University Press.
Barker, Diana Leonard and Sheila Allen (eds.)
    1976 *Dependence and Exploitation in Work and Marriage.* New York: Longman.
Barrett, Nancy
    1979 "Women in the Job Market: On Employment and Work Schedules." Pp. 63–98 in R. E. Smith (ed.) *The Subtle Revolution: Women at Work.* Washington, D.C.: The Urban Institute.
Bednarzik, Robert W.
    1980 "Worksharing in the U.S.: Its Prevalence and Duration." *Monthly Labor Review* 103 (July): 3–12.
Bell, Carolyn Shaw
    1973 "Age, Sex, Marriage and Jobs." *The Public Interest* (Winter): 75–89.
Bell, Daniel
    1972 "Labor in the Post-Industrial Society." Pp. 159–197 in I. Howe (ed.) *The World of the Blue-Collar Worker.* New York: Quadrangle Books.

Berk, Richard and Sarah Fenstermaker Berk
   1979 *Labor and Leisure at Home: Content and Organization of the Household Day.*
      Beverly Hills, Calif.: Sage Publications.
Bernard, Jessie
   1964 *Academic Women.* University Park, Pa.: Pennsylvania State University Press.
Best, Fred and James Mattesich
   1980 "Short-time Compensation Systems in California and Europe." *Monthly
      Labor Review* 103 (July): 13–22.
Bibb, Robert and William H. Form
   1977 "The Effects of Industrial, Occupational, and Sex Stratification on Wages
      in Blue-Collar Markets." *Social Forces* 55 (4): 974–996.
Bird, Caroline
   1979 *The Two-Paycheck Marriage: How Women at Work Are Changing Life in
      America.* New York: Rawson, Wade Publishers.
Blau, Francine D.
   1978 "The Data on Women Workers, Past, Present and Future." Pp. 29–62
      in A. H. Stromberg and S. Harkess (eds.) *Women Working.* Palo Alto,
      Calif.: Mayfield Publishing Co.
Blau, Francine D. and Marianne A. Ferber
   1985 "Women in the Labor Market: The Last Twenty Years." Pp. 19–49 in
      Laurie Larwood, Ann H. Stromberg, and Barbara A. Gutek (eds.) *Women
      and Work,* vol. 1.
Blau, Francine D. and Carol L. Jusenius
   1976 "Economists' Approaches to Sex Segregation in the Labor Market: An
      Appraisal." Pp. 181–200 in M. Blaxall and B. Reagan (eds.) *Women and
      the Workplace.* Chicago: University of Chicago Press.
Deutsch, Helene
   1944 *The Psychology of Women.* New York: Grune and Stratton.
Edwards, Richard C.
   1980 *Contested Terrain.* New York: Basic Books.
Edwards, Richard C., David M. Gordon, and Michael Reich (eds.)
   1975 *Labor Market Segmentation.* Lexington, Mass.: D.C. Heath and Company.
Eichler, Margrit
   1973 "Women as Personal Dependents." Pp. 36–55 in M. Stephenson (ed.)
      Women in Canada. Toronto: New Press.
Engels, Frederick
   1884/1972 *The Origin of the Family, Private Property and the State.* New York:
      International Publishers.
Epstein, Cynthia F.
   1970 *Woman's Place: Options and Limits on Professional Careers.* Berkeley, Calif.:
      University of California Press.
Friedan, Betty
   1963 *The Feminine Mystique.* New York: Norton.
Glazer, Nona
   1976 "Housework." *Signs* (Summer): 905–922.
   1980 "Everyone Needs Three Hands: Doing Unpaid and Paid Work." Pp. 249–
      273 in S. F. Berk (ed.) *Women and Household Labor.* Beverly Hills, Calif.:
      Sage Publications.
Gordon, Michael
   1978 *The American Family: Past, Present and Future.* New York: Random House.

Gross, Edward
  1968 "Plus Ca Change: The Sexual Structure of Occupations Over Time." *Social Problems* 16: 198–208.
Hartmann, Heidi
  1976 "Capitalism, Patriarchy and Job Segregation by Sex." *Signs* 18 (Spring special supplement): 137–169.
Hayghe, H.
  1976 "Families and the Rise of Work Wives—An Overview." *Monthly Labor Review* 99 (May): 3–17.
Hill, Joseph A.
  1929 *Women in Gainful Occupations 1870–1920*. Washington, D.C.: U.S. Government Printing Office.
Howe, Louise Kapp
  1977 *Pink Collar Workers: Inside the World of Women's Work*. New York: G. P. Putnam's Sons.
Kahn, Alfred J. and Sheila B. Kamerman
  1975 *Not for the Poor Alone: European Social Services*. New York: Harper Colophon Books.
Kalleberg, Arne L. and Aage B. Soreson
  1979 "The Sociology of Labor Markets." *Annual Review of Sociology* 5: 351–379.
Kamerman, Sheila B. and Alfred J. Kahn
  1978 *Family Policy: Government and Families in Fourteen Countries*. New York: Columbia University Press.
Komarovsky, Mirra
  1953 *Women in the Modern World: Their Education and Their Dilemmas*. Boston: Little, Brown and Company.
La Pierre, Richard
  1959 *The Freudian Ethic*. New York: Duell, Sloan, and Pearce.
Lipman-Blumen, Jean
  1976 "Toward a Homosocial Theory of Sex Roles: An Explanation of the Sex-Segregation of Social Institutions." Pp. 15–31 in M. Blaxall and B. Reagan (eds.) *Women and the Workplace*. Chicago: University of Chicago Press.
Lipman-Blumen, Jean and Jessie Bernard (eds.)
  1979 *Sex Roles and Social Policy*. Beverly Hills, Calif.: Sage Studies in International Sociology.
Lipset, Seymour Martin
  1979 *The First New Nation: The United States in Historical and Comparative Perspective*. New York: W. W. Norton.
Lobodzinska, Barbara
  1970 *Malzenstwo w Miescie*. Warszawa: Panstwowe Wydawnictow Naukowe.
  1974 *Rodzina w Polsce*. Warszawa: Widawnictow Interpress.
Lopata, Helena Z.
  1971 *Occupation: Housewife*. New York: Oxford University Press.
  1976 *Polish Americans: Status Competition in an Ethnic Community*. Englewood Cliffs, N.J.: Prentice-Hall.
Lopata, Helena Z., Debra Barnewolt, and Kathleen Norr
  1980 "Spouses' Contributions to Each Other's Roles." Pp. 111–141 in F. Pepitone-Rockwell (ed.) *Dual Career Couples*. Beverly Hills, Calif.: Sage Publications.

Lopata, Helena Z. and Henry Brehm
 1987 *Widows and Dependent Wives: From Social Problem to Federal Policy.* New York: Praeger.
Lopata, Helena Z. and Kathleen Norr
 1979 "Changing Commitments of American Women to Work and Family Roles and Their Future Consequences for Social Security." Final report to the Social Security Administration.
 1980 "Changing Commitments of American Women to Work and Family Roles." *Social Security Bulletin* 43 (June): 3–14.
Lundberg, Ferdinand and Marynia F. Farnham
 1947 *Modern Woman: The Lost Sex.* New York: Harper and Brothers.
Malos, Ellen (ed.)
 1980 *The Politics of Housework.* London: Allison and Busby.
Milkman, Ruth
 1979 "Women's Work and the Economic Crisis: Some Lessons from the Great Depression." In N. F. Cott and E. H. Pleck (eds.) *A Heritage of Her Own: Toward a New Social History of American Women.* New York: Simon and Schuster.
Oakley, Ann
 1974a *Women's Work: A History of the Housewife.* New York: Pantheon Books.
 1974b *The Sociology of Housework.* Bath, England: Pitman Press.
Oppenheimer, Valerie K.
 1970 *The Female Labor Force in the United States.* Westport, Conn.: Greenwood.
Piore, Michael J.
 1975 "Notes for a Theory of Labor Market Stratification." Pp. 125–150 in R. C. Edwards, M. Reich, and D. M. Gordon (eds.) *Labor Market Segmentation.* Lexington, Mass.: D.C. Heath and Company.
Piotrowski, Jerzy
 1963 *Praca Zadowowa Kobiety a Rodzina.* Warszawa: Ksiazka i Wiedza.
Pleck, Joseph
 1977 "The Work-Family Role System." *Social Problems* 23 (April): 417–427.
Polit, Denise F.
 1979 "Nontraditional Work Schedules for Women." Pp. 195–210 in K. W. Feinstein (ed.) *Working Women and Families.* Beverly Hills, Calif.: Sage Publications.
Roby, Pamela (ed.)
 1973 *Child Care—Who Cares? Foreign and Domestic Infant and Early Childhood Development Policies.* New York: Basic Books.
Smith, Ralph E.
 1979a "The Movement of Women into the Labor Force." Pp. 1–29 in R. E. Smith (ed.) *The Subtle Revolution: Women at Work.* Washington, D.C.: The Urban Institute.
 1979b *Women in the Labor Force in 1990.* Washington, D.C.: The Urban Institute.
 1979c "Hours Rigidity: Effects on the Labor-Market Status of Women." Pp. 211–222 in K. W. Feinstein (ed.) *Working Women and Families.* Beverly Hills, Calif.: Sage Publications.
Sokoloff, Natalie
 1980 *Between Money and Love: The Dialectics of Women's Home and Market Work.* New York: Praeger.

Sokolowska, Magdalena
1965 "Some Reflections on the Different Attitudes of Men and Women Towards Work." *International Labor Review* 92 (July).
Special Task Force to the Secretary of HEW
1973 *Work in America: Report of a Special Task Force to the Secretary of Health, Education and Welfare.* Cambridge, Mass.: MIT Press.
Stevenson, Mary Huff
1975 "Women's Wages and Job Segregation." Pp. 243–256 in R. C. Gordon (ed.) *Labor Market Segmentation.* Lexington, Mass.: D. C. Heath and Company.
1978 "Wage Differences Between Men and Women: Economic Theories." Pp. 89–107 in A. H. Stromberg and S. Harkess (eds.) *Women Working.* Palo Alto, Calif.: Mayfield Publishing Company.
Stricker, Frank
1979 "Cookbooks and Law Books: The Hidden History of Career Women in Twentieth Century America." Pp. 476–498 in N. F. Cott and E. H. Pleck (eds.) *A Heritage of Her Own: Toward a New Social History of American Women.* New York: Simon and Schuster.
Szczepanski, Jan
1970 *Polish Society.* New York: Random House.
Tepperman, Jean
1976 *Not Servants, Not Machines: Office Workers Speak Out.* Boston: Beacon Press.
Tuckman, Howard P. and William D. Vogler
1979 "The Fringes of a Fringe Group: Part-Timers in Academe." *Monthly Labor Review* 102 (November): 46–49.
U.S. Department of Labor
1975 *Handbook on Women Workers.* Washington, D.C.: U.S. Government Printing Office.
Vanek, Joann
1974 "Time Spent in Housework." *Scientific American* 231 (November): 116–120.
1978 "Housewives as Workers." Pp. 492–516 in A. H. Stromberg and S. Harkess (eds.) *Women Working.* Palo Alto, Calif.: Mayfield Publishing Company.
Walker, Kathryn E.
1969 "Time Spent in Household Work by Homemakers." *Family Economic Review* 3 (July): 5–6.
1970 "Time Spent by Husbands in Household Work." *Family Economic Review* 4 (December): 8–11.
Welter, Barbara
1966 "The Cult of True Womanhood: 1820–1869." *American Quarterly* 18 (Summer): 151–160.

DONNA H. GREEN AND THOMAS J. ZENISEK
DUEL CAREER COUPLES: INDIVIDUAL AND ORGANIZATIONAL IMPLICATIONS ....

Families where both spouses are actively pursuing a career are observed to be moving away from the traditional household division of labor toward a more "equitable" division of household tasks. Most two-career families today are in transition, somewhere between the traditional structure and the dual-career structure; few truly egalitarian couples are functioning in today's society (Haas, 1980). This paper reviews current research on dual-career couples. It focuses upon marital satisfaction levels within this structure and upon current findings in relation to the obtainment of egalitarian relationships. . . .

The term dual-career families was first introduced by Rapoport and Rapoport (1969, 1971, 1977) in what have become foundation studies of two career families. These authors report case studies of 17 couples (5 of which are published in detail) involved in this "new deviant" lifestyle. In the years since these early studies it has become acceptable to discuss, research, and live the life of a dual-career family. . . .

ADVANTAGES AND DISADVANTAGES

As with most lifestyles the choice of a dual-career structure possesses positive and negative dimensions. A major advantage of the dual-career structure is financial gain, which is important for several reasons. First, the increased standard of living possible with the increased income is often sufficient to induce both members of the couple to be gainfully employed. Also, as money is very important in our society, an individual's worth to society is often measured by the size of their pay check. In addition, when both members of the couple work they are both recognized as contributing to society, which often leads to increased self esteem for the previously unemployed spouse.

Two pay checks are also beneficial because job flexibility is increased. That is, if one spouse is locked into an unrewarding occupation the security of a second income allows greater opportunity for seeking additional education and/or a career change. Neither partner must endure a distasteful career merely to insure that the family is able to eat.

A second advantage of the dual-career structure is that both members may operate outside of the activity restrictions that exist within the traditional family structure. For example, men are not automatically closed out of child

D. H. Green and T. J. Zenisek, "Dual Career Couples: Individual and Organizational Implications," *Journal of Business Ethics*, Vol. 2, No. 3, August 1983, pp. 171–184. Copyright ©1983 by D. Reidel Publishing Company. Reprinted by permission.

care and domestic activities and women may participate in activities formerly considered to be within the male's domain (e.g., auto maintenance and woodworking). Thus household tasks may be redivided in such a manner that both spouses have the opportunity to shed traditional duties that may be disliked and to take up other activities.

A third asset is the increased level of social interaction the wife receives at work (as compared with full-time home-makers). She no longer needs to rely on her husband for the majority of her social interactions and intellectual stimulation (Hall and Hall, 1979, pp. 116–117). As both members have similar pressures and demands placed upon them at work, they are more easily able to understand each other's positions and therefore able to provide mutual support when needed. This mutual sharing of problems also leads to increased respect as the other's accomplishments can be viewed more realistically and with greater mutual admiration and pride in accomplishments.

Dual-career couples also learn about other fields of study or specialties to which they otherwise would not be exposed. A study by Heckman *et al.* (1977, p. 329) reveals that husbands often state that their ". . . wife's professional interests give them knowledge of related fields and techniques." Spouses in similar careers also gain in this manner. Evidence indicates that when both members of the couple work in similar fields and at the same institutions, the female half of the couple is proportionately more successful than her female colleagues. There is no evidence of a disruptive effect on the marriage due to these ties (Martin *et al.*, 1975; Butler and Paisley, 1980). Hall and Hall (1979, p. 52) state:

> . . .we have found that being in the same area or related areas increases each partner's understanding of the pressures and responsibilities the other is feeling. By knowing the partner's work it is easy to provide support and show commitment to the other's career.

Other studies however (Berger *et al.*, 1978; Matthews and Matthews, 1980) point out some of the problems similar careers cause when one or both members of the couple are engaged in a job search. It is difficult, if not impossible for the careerists to both find their optimal job opportunities in the same geographical location. This leads to conflict, compromise and/or separation.

There are other costs associated with the dual-career structure. Because neither spouse possesses a "full-time wife" to take care of the household and provide support services, both must take on more domestic responsibilities than the "bread-winner" of the traditional family. This situation creates time pressures for both spouses that do not exist in the traditional structure because energy must now be divided between career and home and not solely devoted to only one area; which, in turn, creates conflict and stress. Compromises must therefore be made, usually in all areas, as it is difficult to combine several roles (e.g., spouse, occupation, homemaking and sometimes parental) outside the traditional family structure. When both spouses engage in all the roles, new rules must be developed to handle the situation because the traditional division of labor no longer works. Floors may be dusted and cleaned once a week instead of once a day (Hall and Hall, 1979; Ehrenreich, 1979). Prepared foods, instead of "made from scratch" meals may be necessary. The number of desired children (and their additional demands) may be reduced or eliminated. Career advancement may be moderated. All of these are important choices a family pursuing a dual-career lifestyle must face. These couples usually "can't have their cake and eat it too"—something must give.

Career aspirations are affected by both the restricted mobility and the additional time constraints the dual-career family structure imposes. For example, one spouse's career goals may be lowered if relocation would damage the partner's career or if a promotion would require additional time away from the family. Also

> . . . in pursuing careers with traditional auxiliary partners, both spouses in the dual-career family share some of the problems of a single male (who may be handicapped by the absence of a wife as a symbolic and social asset) plus the problem of childcare and domestic work overload, which the single male without children does not incur. This can place the dual-careerists in a double jeopardy relative to their traditional counterparts—married males with conventional wives (Hunt and Hunt, 1977, p. 410).

On a macro level,

> . . . the progressive participation of women will mean a larger throng pursuing a stable or declining number of jobs under increasingly competitive conditions. This heightened competitiveness will accentuate the disadvantage of the dual-careerists, and may generate pressures to alleviate strain by getting women to withdraw from the job market (Hunt and Hunt, 1977, p. 410).

This job scarcity affects dual-careerists in two ways. First without a full-time homeworker they are less competitive as more energies are devoted to the family. Secondly it accentuates the problem of coordinating the career paths of spouses (e.g., job training, the pursuit of new jobs and job moves). Career moves for either spouse are much more difficult when jobs are scarce because it is difficult to combine the advancement of one career without inducing regression in the other career.

MARITAL SATISFACTION

Those with doubts about the desirability of wives' employment have suggested that the normative deviance involved might strain the quality of the marital relationship, and undermine the case of companionability between the marital partners. In contrast, proponents of wives' employment have drawn attention to frustration arising in the normative nuclear family arrangement and have argued that wives' employment provides a solution to some of the features of a single-worker marriage especially oppressive to women (Locksley, 1980, p. 344).

The body of research comparing marital satisfaction levels of dual-worker and traditional couples indicates that what might be termed "an evolution of adjustment" has taken place. The results of early studies indicated a negative impact, while later results indicated no impact, while the most recent results indicate either neutral or positive effects. . . .

Locksley (1980), in a cross-sectional study of 2300 persons 21 years or older living in private households in the United States, conducted ninety minute interviews with 72% of the sample. The results indicate that a wife's employment has no effect on marital adjustment and companionship.

More recently, a study of 106 faculty women at Northwestern University showed that "an overwhelming majority of the women surveyed believed their marriages to be happy and that their career improved rather than harmed the marriages. In fact 73 women, 70.5 percent of the sample saw their careers as improving the marriage" (Yogev, 1981, p. 867). It should be noted that Yogev's study examines dual-career couples while the Locksley study does not differentiate between dual-career and dual-worker families.

Another body of literature investigates the level of a woman's work commitment and its relationship to marital satisfaction. These studies distinguish between dual-worker and dual-career families, an aspect which was overlooked by earlier studies. Safilios-Rothschild (1970) examines this issue in a study of 896 women from the Greater Athens metropolitan area. For analytical purposes the sample was classified into high work commitment (HWC) and low work commitment (LWC) groups. The results indicate that ". . . there is no difference in the degree of marital satisfaction reported by all working and non-working women, or by women with LWC and non-working women, women with HWC report a significantly higher marital satisfaction than non-working women" (Safilios-Rothschild, 1979, p. 689).

The impacts of other moderating variables have also been investigated. For example, Ridley (1973) studied job involvement, job satisfaction and marital adjustment in a sample of married female teachers. The results indicated a significant positive relationship between job satisfaction and marital adjustment for males but only a positive nonsignificant relationship for females. However, the results also indicate that women who view their work as important also demonstrate a positive relationship. Higher combined levels of marital adjustment result when wives exhibit low job satisfaction and husbands exhibit high job satisfaction, or when both members of the couple exhibit high job satisfaction. In relation to the impact of job involvement, the findings indicate that "Marital adjustment was highest when: (1) husband and wife were low on job involvement, and (2) the husband was medium on job involvement and the wife was low on job involvement. When either spouse became highly involved in his job marital adjustment tended to suffer" (Ridley, 1973, p. 236). Based upon these results, marital adjustment is highest if HWC women and men are high in job satisfaction and low in job involvement. One could therefore infer that these types of individuals are content at work, still have time to devote to their spouses and families, and therefore able to make their marriage work.

Houseknecht and Macke (1981) extended Ridley's (1973) work by studying highly educated females, who are typically high in job satisfaction and high in work involvement. After reviewing their data, these authors reported

> that it is *not* employment per se that is important in determining marital adjustment but rather the extent to which family experiences accommodate the wife's employment. Having a supportive husband seems to be a major factor. . . . Freedom from child-bearing responsibilities is also important. All of these variables represent possible sources of conflict between the wife's family role and her career role and, for this reason, are significant in determining the level of adjustment she perceives in her marriage (Houseknecht and Macke, 1981, p. 660). . . .

EGALITARIAN RELATIONSHIPS

Many proponents of the dual-career family structure assume that this lifestyle will automatically bring with it a more equitable division of household duties. There are a number of studies which examine this question. This section outlines the problems dual-career couples must overcome to achieve an egalitarian relationship and examines the actual practices of dual-career couples. It appears that an egalitarian relationship is an ideal type that is rarely achieved in extant society.

Haas (1980) contacted 154 dual-career couples in Madison, Wisconsin that had been referred to her as representing egalitarian couples. Of these 31 were deemed to be truly egalitarian and were interviewed. These couples cited four major problems that had to be overcome in order to achieve an "equitable" division of household labor. First each member of the couple found it difficult to do non-traditional tasks for their gender. Part of this may be due to the second problem area cited: the lack of non-traditional skills. Most of today's adults were raised in traditional families where they were taught traditional skills for their gender. A fact that leaves many unequipped, at least initially, to share in all types of domestic tasks.

The third problem results from the discrepancy between the generally high housekeeping standards of the wife, as instilled by a traditional mother, and the lower expectations of the husbands which often leads to conflict. Haas (1980) contends that most couples eventually arrive at a compromise standard. Hall and Hall (1979) also discuss housekeeping standards and conclude that couples must adjust their overall housekeeping standards downwards because there is not enough time for two working individuals to maintain the same level of standards that a couple with a full-time homemaker can maintain.

The fourth and final problem ". . . mentioned by half the couples was the wife's reluctance to give up her traditional authority over many domestic chores" (Haas, 1980, p. 294). The women often expressed guilt in giving up some of their traditional roles and found it very difficult to break the traditional pattern they had observed in their parents' households. Ehrenreich (1979) discusses this problem in greater detail and arrive at much the same conclusion.

A review of the literature concerning the division of household tasks since the early 1960s shows a progressive development. The early studies make no attempt to quantify the relative contributions of each spouse, they merely examine general trends, and report that husbands do help employed wives with traditionally female duties (Hoffman, 1960; Safilios-Rothschild, 1970). Later studies attempt to quantify how much time each spouse spends doing both "male and female" duties in an effort to determine if there is an equitable division of household tasks. A review of only the most recent studies (i.e., the last 5 years) follows.

Stafford (1977) compared cohabitating married and unmarried college students. This study is included because both members of all of these couples possessed achievement oriented commitments, in a university rather than employment setting, outside of their relationships. The findings indicate that if the women are working or going to school the married women do less housekeeping than the unmarried women.

> Although ultimate responsibility for many tasks is shared, generally wives and the female partners do the women's work and husbands and males do the men's work. This division leaves the women most of the household duties whether or not they are also employed in the labor force (Stafford et al., 1977, p. 54).

Bryson and Bryson (1980) report similar divisions of labor in dual-career couples where both partners are professionals (either as professors or practicing psychologists). They summarize their results by stating:

> In sum, the professional pair is not egalitarian. Instead, like other dual-career couples, they tend to divide household responsibilities along sex-stereotypic lines and to place differential values on their career. It also seems clear that the pressures for such differentiation fall disproportionately upon the wife (Bryson and Bryson, 1980, p. 256).

This finding is substantiated in another study by Keith and Schafer (1980, p. 486) who state that, "Women were much more worried than men about the quality of the others' performance of household tasks. Only 16% of the women compared with 43% of the men never worried about how well the other person would complete household tasks."

Lopata et al. (1980) relate the husband's educational background to his degree of participation in household duties. According to the wives only 7% of the men do 50% or more of the household duties; in 93% of the families the women do over one-half the household duties. The lower the husband's education level the more apt he is to not help at all. "More than four times as many of the most educated husbands than the least educated do at least some work around the house if the wife is employed" (Lopata *et al.,* 1980, p. 133). . . .

[Nevertheless] Haas (1980) located 31 ideal type egalitarian couples in Madison, Wisconsin, which would indicate that egalitarian marriages are possible in today's world. These couples contend that they adopted their way of life, not out of an ideological commitment to sexual equality but as a practical way of achieving benefits for both individuals that they couldn't achieve in a traditional family. "Over four-fifths of the sample adopted role-sharing so the wife could satisfy her desire to work outside the home for personal fulfillment. Almost three-fourths of the couples wanted to eliminate the overload dilemmas faced by working women who remain primarily responsible for household and childcare" (Haas, 1980, pp. 291–292). These couples have arrived at an egalitarian relationship as is indicated by the following data:

Task	Hours per week spent by husband	Hours per week spent by wife
Housework	16.2	16.0
Childcare	10.4	12.2
Leisure	26.2	26.8

These studies indicate a general evolution over time toward an egalitarian dual-career family structure. First, beliefs changed regarding the acceptability of female employment; more women began to work and pursue careers. Next beliefs changed regarding the acceptability of males participating in household tasks; husbands of working wives began "helping out." Finally, the belief that men and women are equals both at work and at home, and should therefore share the responsibilities of both, began growing in acceptance. With this evolutionary change one might hypothesize a concomitant growth in the number of egalitarian couples. . . .

EMPLOYER'S STAKE IN DUAL-CAREER COUPLES

With a growing number of dual-worker and especially dual-career families, organizations are becoming more involved in the family's dilemmas. Sick children or babysitters mean one employee must cope somehow. Career plans for individual employees, especially if they involve a great deal of travel or a large number of relocations may involve more sacrifices to the family than the employee is willing or is able to make. With these and other problems that arise in this type of family structure employers are now being challenged to modify their policies and to become more flexible.

Before discussing some possible employer adaptations it is important to determine what employers' present attitudes are in relation to dual-career families. Rosen *et al.* (1975) sampled 5,000 managers and executives via a sample survey, drawn from the list of subscribers to a well known business publication. The questionnaire consisted of inbasket incidents where male and female roles are reversed in one half the questionnaires. Two themes were apparent throughout the responses. First there

> . . . is a degree of managerial skepticism about women's abilities to balance work and family demands. . . . Secondly there is somewhat less organizational concern or interest in the careers of women compared to men. . . . The end result of current managerial sex-role stereotypes appears to be heightened conflict and stress for both parties in a dual-career marriage who attempt to pursue professional careers but are unwilling to downgrade the importance of family life and child care responsibilities (Rosen *et al.*, 1975, pp. 571–572).

In light of these findings any changes in employer practices may be very gradual.

Flexible working schedules is the most frequently advocated organizational adaptation to dual-career families (Bryson and Bryson, 1980; Hall and Hall, 1979; Holmstrom, 1973; Rosow, 1982). "Generally new work schedules fall into three categories: part-time employment, flexitime and compressed work weeks of less than 5 days" (Rosow, 1982, p. 49). There are many variations on each of these major types of schedules but all are designed to allow greater flexibility to the employee in meeting the demands of dual-career life.

Flexible work hours, however are not a cureall for the problems faced by a dual-career family. This fact is highlighted by an extensive study by Bohen and Viveros-Long (1982) of a flexitime program for U.S. federal employees. This study which analyzes two matched work places, one with a traditional 40 hour work week, the other with a modest flexitime program (i.e., employees work 8 hours a day, 5 days a week, but are free to choose the hours of their employment). The results indicated that this version of flexitime had little impact on work-family conflicts. These authors state that:

> The complexities of the social, economic, and demographic changes that now encourage men and women to have comparable work roles throughout their child-rearing years require policy responses beyond flexitime—if the goals for families with children are, in part, those held out for flexitime, namely to reduce parental job-family stress, to enable parents to spend more time with their children, and to increase equity between males and females in paid work and family work (Bohen and Viveros-Long, 1982, p. 199).

These authors also go on to suggest the implementation of more far reaching programs such as: Parental work leave policies where either parent may stay home with a new born. More flexible work schedules. For example, choice of hours for a two week period, no restriction on number per day and flexiplace (e.g., allowing work at home when practical).

Another frequently mentioned adaptation is additional support services such as day-care centers. Although not as popular a solution as it was once seen to be, day-care can help employees meet the demands of both home and family. A further reaching employer policy is job sharing or work sharing where each member of the couple works part-time, shares a full-time job (with the spouse or someone else), and also shares all household activities. This is an especially good arrangement if children are involved as each parent can participate more fully in parenting and each have the opportunity to derive satisfaction outside the home (Arkin and Dobrofsky, 1978; Gronseth, 1978). . . .

It is thus apparent that there are many options available to employers who wish to adapt to the dual-career couple. Given present management attitudes toward dual-career couples and the additional expense of many of the proffered programs it is doubtful that such policies will be adopted in the near future. As the numbers of dual-career couples increase employers will need to make reforms if they are to recruit and retain the best employees.

CONCLUSION

Dual-career couples are here to stay and their numbers are growing. The labor participation rate for married women living with their spouses has increased from 23.8% to 43% (Locksley, 1980, p. 337). Both male and female adolescents expect to work for pay after completing school and a majority (94%) state that their spouses would work. "Only 1.7% said their spouses would not work and only 4% stated their spouse would be a homemaker" (Tittle, 1981, pp. 39 and 117).

Change is taking place both within and outside families. Dual-career couples are striving for, and some are now achieving, true egalitarian marriages (Haas, 1980). As this type of a relationship makes it easier for the wife to be committed to a career the spouse's marital satisfaction and adjustment also increases. This prediction is based upon the finding by Houseknecht and Mache (1981) that the extent to which family experiences accommodate the wife's employment affects the family's marital adjustment. The increase in the number of dual-career couples not only provides the youth of today with role models to emulate but also increases the social acceptability of this family structure.

Dual-career couples today are facing the challenges of relocations and long-distance marriages. As couples gain more experience in this area and disseminate the information other couples faced with these types of choices will be better able to anticipate the problems and rewards of this lifestyle.

External from the couple itself society is recognizing the existence of and some of the special needs of the dual-career couple. This is illustrated by the information presented in the *AMBA's MBA Employment Guide 1981* (Association of MBAs Executives, Inc., 1981). This book is published to provide guidance to new Master of Business Administration graduates seeking employment. To help graduates decide on a specific geographic location they provide a multidimensional quality of life rating on the major U.S. urban centers. One of the dimensions measured is "dual-careers potential."

Organizations are beginning to recognize that an employee who is a partner in a dual-career couple is a different category of worker, and that old policies, that worked well with traditional families and single employees, bring about unexpected reactions from members of dual-career families. Dual-career employees are not as willing to uproot themselves to climb higher up the success ladder unless the impact on the spouse is minimal or nonexistent. After hours time is spent keeping the home running smoothly leaving companies with fewer 50 to 60 hour a week executives, and emergencies on the home-front make the standard 9:00–5:00 day difficult. To help employers cope with these changing employee needs, organizational adaptations are being suggested (e.g., Rosow, 1982; Gilmore and Fannin, 1982).

As organizations and dual-career couples gain more experience with this type of family structure it will be easier for couples to establish successful, more equitable dual-career relationships. Today's dual-career couples are becoming the role models for today's youth. As they prove it is possible to possess both a successful career and a satisfying marriage the youth of today appear to have a choice: try to emulate these couples and strive for egalitarian relationships or accept the traditional familial structure.

BIBLIOGRAPHY

Arkin, William and Lynne R. Dobrofsky: "Job Sharing," in Rhona and Robert N. Rapoport (eds.), *Working Couples* (Harper Colophon Books, New York, 1978), pp. 122–137.

Association of MBA Executives Inc.: *AMBA's MBA Employment Guide 1981* (Alberta P. Hegyi, New York, N.Y., 1981).

Axelson, Leland J.: "The Marital Adjustment and Marital Role Definitions of Husbands of Working and Non-working Wives," *Marriage and Family Living* 25 (1963), 189–195.

Berger, Michael, Martha Foster, and Barbara Struder Wallston: "Finding Two Jobs," in Rhona and Robert N. Rapoport (eds.), *Working Couples* (Harper Colophon Books, New York, 1978), pp. 23–35.

Bohen, Halcyone H. and Anamaria Viveros-Long: *Balancing Jobs and Family Life: Do Flexible Work Schedules Help?* (Temple University Press, Philadelphia, Pa., 1982).

Booth, Alan: "Wife's Employment and Husband's Stress: A Replication and Refutation," *Journal of Marriage and the Family* 39 (1977), 645–650.

Broschart, Kay Richards: "Family Status and Professional Achievement: A Study of Women Doctorates," *Journal of Marriage and the Family* 40 (1978), 71–76.

Bryson, Jeff B. and Rebecca Bryson: "Salary Performance Differentials in Dual-Career Couples," in Fran Pepitone-Rockwell (eds.), *Dual Career Couples* (Sage Publications, Beverly Hills, Calif., 1980), pp. 241–259.

Burke, Ronald J. and Tamara Weir: "Relationship of Wive's Employment Status to Husband and Pair Satisfaction and Performance," *Journal of Marriage and the Family* 38 (1976), 279–287.

Burke, Ronald J. and Tamara Weir: "Some Personality Differences Between Members of One-Career and Two-Career Families," *Journal of Marriage and the Family* 38 (1976), 453–459.

Butler, Matilda and William Paisley: "Coordinated-Career Couples: Covergence and Divergence," in Fran Pepitone-Rockwell (ed.), *Dual Career Couples* (Sage Publications, Ltd., Beverly Hills, Calif., 1980), pp. 207–228.

Douvan, Elizabeth and Joseph Pleck: "Separation as Support," in Rhona and Robert N. Rapoport (eds.), *Working Couples* (Harper Colophon Books, New York, 1978), pp. 138–146.

Ehrenreich, Barbara: "How to Get Housework Out of Your System," *Ms* 8 (1979), 47.

Farris, Agnes: "Commuting," in Rhona and Robert N. Rapoport (eds.), *Working Couples* (Harper Colophon Books, New York, 1978), pp. 100–107.

Frank, Robert H.: "Why Women Earn Less: The Theory and Estimation of Differential Overqualification," *American Economic Review* 68 (1978), 360–373.

Gilmore, Carol B. and William R. Fannin: "The Dual Career Couple: A Challenge to Personnel in the Eighties," *Business Horizons* 25 (1982), 36–41.

Gronseth, Erik: "Work Sharing: A Norwegian Example," in Rhona and Robert N. Rapoport (eds.), *Working Couples* (Harper Colophon Books, New York, 1978), pp. 108–121.

Gross, Harriet Engel: "Dual-Career Couples Who Live Apart: Two Types," *Journal of Marriage and the Family* 42 (1980), 567–576.

Haas, Linda: "Role-Sharing Couples: A Study of Egalitarian Marriages," *Family Relations* 29 (1980), 289–296.

Hall, Francine S. and Douglas, T.: *The Two-Career Couple* (Addison-Wesley Pub. Co., Don Mills, Ontario, 1979).

Heckman, Norma A., Rebecca Bryson, and Jeff Bryson: "Problems of Professional Couples: A Content Analysis," *Journal of Marriage and the Family* 39 (1977), 323–330.

Hiller, Dana V. and William W. Philliber: "The Derivation of Status Benefits from Occupational Attainments of Working Wives," *Journal of Marriage and the Family* 40 (1978), 63–69.

Hiller, Dana V. and William W. Philliber: "Necessity, Compatibility and Status Attainment as Factors in the Labor-Force Participation of Married Women," *Journal of Marriage and the Family* 42 (1980), 347–354.

Hiller, Dana V. and William W. Philliber: "Predicting Marital and Career Success Among Dual-Worker Couples," *Journal of Marriage and the Family* 44 (1982), 53–62.

Hoffman, Lois Wladis: "Effects of Employment of Mothers on Parental Power Relations and the Division of Household Tasks," *Marriage and Family Living* 22 (1960), 27–35.

Holmstrom, Lynda Lytle: *The Two-Career Family* (Schenkman Pub. Co., Cambridge, Mass., 1973).

Houseknecht, Sharon K. and Anne S. Macke: "Combining Marriage and Career: The Marital Adjustment of Professional Women," *Journal of Marriage and the Family* 43 (1981), 651–661.

Hunt, Janet G. and Larry L. Hunt: "Dilemmas and Contradictions of Status: The Case of the Dual-Career Family," *Social Problems* 24 (1977), 407–416.

Keith, Pat M. and Robert B. Schafer: "Role Strain and Depression in Two-Job Families," *Family Relations* 29 (1980), 483–488.

Knox, David: "Trends in Marriage and the Family—The 1980s," *Family Relations* 29 (1980), 145–150.

Leo, John: "Marital Tales of Two Cities: The Ways and Means of Long-Distance Marriages," *Time,* January 25, 1982, pp. 60–62.

Locksley, Anne: "On the Effects of Wives' Employment on Marital Adjustment and Companionship," *Journal of Marriage and the Family* 42 (1980), 337–346.

Lopata, Helena Z., Debra Barnwolt, and Kathleen Norr: "Spouse's Contributions to Each Other's Roles," in Fran Pepitone-Rockwell (ed.), *Dual Career Couples* (Sage Publications, Beverly Hills, Calif., 1980), pp. 111–141.

Martin, Thomas W., Kenneth J. Berry, and R. Brooke Jacobsen: "The Impact of Dual Career Marriages on Female Professional Careers: An Empirical Test of a Parsonian Hypothesis," *Journal of Marriage and the Family* 37 (1975), 734–742.

Matthews, Janet R. and Lee A. Matthews: "Going Shopping: The Professional Couple in the Job Market," in Fran Pepitone-Rockwell (ed.), *Dual Career Couples* (Sage Publications, Ltd., Beverly Hills, Calif., 1980), pp. 261–282.

Pepitone-Rockwell, Fran (ed.), *Dual Career Couples* (Sage Publications Ltd., Beverly Hills, Calif., 1980).

Pleck, Joseph H.: "The Work-Family Role Systems," *Social Problems* 24 (1977), 417–427.

Rapoport, Rhona and Robert N. Rapoport: "The Dual Career Family: A Variant Pattern and Social Change," *Human Relations* 22 (1969), 3–30.

Rapoport, Rhona and Robert N.: "Further Considerations on the Dual Career Family," *Human Relations* 24 (1971), 519–533.

Rapoport, Rhona and Robert N.: *Dual-Career Families* (The Chaucer Press, Suffolk, G. B., 1971).

Rapoport, Rhona and Robert N.: *Dual-Career Families Re-examined* (Harper Colophon Books, London, 1977).

Rapoport, Rhona and Robert Rapoport with Janice M. Bumstend (eds.), *Working Couples* (Harper Colophon Books, New York, 1978).

Ridley, Carl A.: "Exploring the Impact of Work Satisfaction and Involvement on Marital Interaction When Both Partners Are Employed," *Journal of Marriage and the Family* 25 (1973), 229–237.

Rosen, Benson, Thomas H. Jerdee, and Thomas L. Prestwich: "Dual-Career Marital Adjustment: Potential Effects of Discriminatory Managerial Attitudes," *Journal of Marriage and the Family* 37 (1975), 565–572.

Rosow, Jerome M.: "New Work Schedules for a Changing Office," *Administrative Management* 43 (1982), 48–65.

Rule, Sheila: "Long Distance Marriage on Rise," *New York Times* Oct. 31, 1977, pp. 33 and 60.

Safilios-Rothschild, Constantina: "The Influence of the Wife's Degree of Work Commitment upon Some Aspects of Family Organization and Dynamics," *Journal of Marriage and the Family* 32 (1970), 681–691.

Safilios-Rothschild, Constantina: *Toward a Sociology of Women* (Xerox College Publishing, Toronto, 1972).

Skinner, Denise A.: "Dual-Career Family Stress and Coping: A Literature Review," *Family Relations* 29 (1980), 473–482.

Stafford, Rebecca, Elaine Backman, and Pamela Dibona: "The Division of Labor Among Cohabiting and Married Couples," *Journal of Marriage and the Family* 39 (1977), 43–57.

Tyree, Andrea and Judith Treas: "The Occupational and Marital Mobility of Women," *American Sociological Review* 39 (1974), 293–302.

Wright, James D.: "Are Working Women Really More Satisfied? Evidence from Several National Surveys," *Journal of Marriage and the Family* 40 (1978), 301–313.

Yogev, Sara: "Do Professional Women Have Egalitarian Marital Relationships?" *Journal of Marriage and the Family* 43 (1981), 865–871.

5

....

Work and the Self

INTRODUCTION

This chapter represents a look at the relationships between self, work, and identity.

Lee Braude's analysis of "Work and the Self" argues a relationship between work and identity that goes beyond that of nearly all the other authors quoted. While this piece refers nearly exclusively to men, and may appear somewhat dated in this respect, it is nonetheless important. He argues that, because of the investment of time and attention, the adjustment between personality and job requirements, and, most of all, the learning of work concepts and symbols, the self is necessarily changed. Who we are, he argues, is inextricably linked to what we do.

John Shack, whose article follows, is a former student of F. B. Herzberg's and has developed Herzberg's model. Shack begins by examining a wide range of cognitive, personality, and attitude differences and their effect on worker behavior and choice. He offers a taxonomy that serves as a useful guide to understanding the mystery of why some work is seen as both satisfying and stultifying by different individuals.

The Herzberg article is a *Harvard Business Review* piece—working advice for managers based on his "motivator-hygiene" model of job satisfaction. The model divides incentives into two classes: those which reduce anxiety versus those which enhance personal growth. The article deals with job enrichment as a motivator and is included less for the model itself than as an example of concrete advice about management style.

Abraham Maslow's article comes out of his model of self-actualization and analysis of human needs. While based on what can be called grand theory, the language is both colloquial and cuts to basic issues of work and self. He begins ". . . the only happy people I know are the ones who are working well at something they consider important. . . ." He compels belief in the general truth of that very specific statement.

The final article of the first section is Melvin Kohn's "Job Complexity and Adult Personality"—a study of the relationship between intellectual flexibility and job complexity and, by extension, between psychological processes

211

and work. The piece is a careful, detailed analysis returning to the position that we are indeed what we do.

The second section looks at two sides of work and well-being. The first is a summary of a fifteen-year HEW task force on health and work. Perhaps the most startling conclusion is that work satisfaction ranks first as a predictor of longevity. The other side, by Marilyn Machlowitz, is less scholarship than a popularized look at "workaholism" as a phenomenon. While it reaches no real conclusions, its subject, if only as an anecdotal footnote, is of interest.

The final section opens with an article by Moncrieff Cochran and Urie Bronfenbrenner which addresses child-rearing as it is affected by working patterns. While some conclusions may seem obvious, it is one of the few examples of a call for corporate America to recognize that two-career families require alterations in the workplace.

The second piece is a study by Jeylan Mortimer and Glorian Sorensen of the effect on families of women's increased participation in the workplace. The article is careful and comprehensive, with implications for future public policy decisions. Among the conclusions, the authors point out that traditional patterns of sex-role behavior have changed less than popular impressions would imply, and that women are "frequently overloaded by excessive role demands."

Finally, the Keating article is a popular magazine survey of little research value but, like the Machlowitz article, of interest as a wide-ranging look at what 32,000 respondents report about their work and its effect on their families.

Work and Self-Definition

LEE BRAUDE
WORK AND THE SELF ....

"[A] man's work is one of the more important parts of his social identity, of his self; indeed, of his fate in the one life he has to live, for there is something almost as irrevocable about choice of occupation as there is about choice of a mate."

The title of this chapter, as well as the lines above, is taken from a classic paper by Everett C. Hughes.[1] His argument there is simple but enormous in

[1]Everett C. Hughes, "Work and the Self," in John H. Rohrer and Muzafer Sherif, eds., *Social Psychology at the Crossroads* (New York: Harper, 1951), pp. 313–23.

Lee Braude, *Work and Workers: A Sociological Analysis* (Malabar, Fla.: Robert E. Krieger Publishing Co., Inc., 1983). Reprinted by permission of the author.

its implications. Work is so fundamental to the life of man, says Hughes, that we cannot understand the human condition unless we can make some sense of the ways in which man comes to terms with his work; these terms provide clues to the ways in which men live out their lives and see their destinies. Indeed, for many, work becomes a "central life interest" in which the concerns of the work place intrude on and inform nonwork relationships. . . .

RECRUITMENT TO WORK

Since the founding of America, a basic premise of the American dream has been the idea that no man in this country need be fettered by caste or class, that achievement in the occupation of one's choice is dependent solely upon initiative and ability. Therefore, perhaps the most heinous sin that could be committed by an American (and the least forgivable) is the admission of failure to achieve, with the concomitant renunciation of the success orientation altogether. Nevertheless, fulfillment of the dream is still elusive for many. Rapid technological growth, the explosion of knowledge, and changes in social needs and goals have changed the occupational options open to individuals from generation to generation. Ethnicity, income level, intellectual ability, availability of training, or cultural impoverishment may serve as a bar to achievement despite the apparent societal commitment to that idea. Finally, because occupational choice often must be made early in the life of the individual, persons may not have the knowledge necessary to choose wisely, may not be aware of the opportunities open to them—or may have the choices made for them. . . .

THE MEANING OF WORK

Although man and occupation are eventually brought together, it does not follow that the meeting is necessarily a happy one or that the relationship that ensues will result in anything more than a marriage of convenience. One man's "chore" or "daily grind" or, simply, "job" may be another's sport or consuming passion or "calling," with all the religious conviction and dedication implied by the term.

. . . [w]ork today receives a "bad press." The economic historian John U. Nef has suggested that the conquest of the material world, which brought the comfort and luxury of an expanded standard of living, substituted quantity and utility for beauty and the conscious cultivation of morality.[2] Work was dehumanized.

Putting it somewhat differently, Adriano Tilgher, author of the classic book on the subject, noted that when work lost its religious imperative, as

[2]John U. Nef, *Cultural Foundations of Industrial Civilization* (Cambridge, England: Cambridge University Press, 1958).

the Renaissance merged into modern times, work also lost its power to ennoble. He said that men no longer seek work done well for the sheer satisfaction it affords. Western man is no longer interested in the beautiful but expends his energies in sport and play and ostentation in order to find the refreshment of spirit that work once provided. People who work mindlessly have their lives created for them from the opinions of others and become as automatic in response as the machines they tend.

Harvey Swados argues that, for all the money it may bring to a man, work is slavery. A person who curls up after dinner with a full attaché case and a pad of yellow paper or who sits at his typewriter pecking insights at 1:45 in the morning is chained to his work as surely as is a man at a Hamtramck assembly line. The industrial worker is not being absorbed by the "middle class," according to Swados; rather, the white collar is slowly assuming a bluish tint. The slavery of work plays no favorites; the agony is intense whether it is felt in the ghetto of Detroit or the suburbanized "ghetto" of Glen Cove, New York, or Marin County, California.[3] And when even sexual activity is represented in marriage manuals to be work, to be doggedly pursued *on schedule,* how little valued has work become then?[4]

The meanings that work—a specific occupational task or work "in general"—assume for the individual derive from two sources. Early socialization experiences provide the origins of reactions toward work. As a person is prepared for appropriate adult role performance through interaction in his family of orientation, with peers and adults in his community and his school, he learns to place a value on work behavior as others approach him in situations demanding increasing responsibility for productivity. The praise or blame, affection or anger, leveled at the growing child in such transactions as "picking up the toys," "setting the table," "going to the store for mother," and later part-time jobs enables him to assess his performance from the perspective of others, particularly those others, like parents, whom he regards as significant for conduct. As the person matures, these perspectives are internalized, and he takes upon himself the direction and evaluation of his own behavior, rather than requiring direction by others. In work as in all other aspects of human life, the sociologist claims, the child grows socially by approaching himself as others approach him. The consistency of others toward him makes for consistency in his own behavior, particularly as he develops an identity and concept of self. . . .

The second source of work meanings is related to the work drama. But here, too, socialization is involved, for socialization does not cease with entry

---

[3]Harvey Swados, "The Myth of the Happy Worker," *The Nation* 185 (August 17, 1957): 65–68

[4]Lionel S. Lewis and Dennis Brisset, "Sex as Work: A Study of Avocational Counseling," *Social Problems* 15 (Summer, 1967): 8–18. See also Horace Miner, "Body Ritual Among the Nacirema," *American Anthropologist* 58 (June, 1956): 503–8, in which the author speaks of intercourse being "taboo as a topic and scheduled as an act."

into adulthood; whenever a person tries out new interpersonal situations with new demands and obligations on the part of the several participants, he is being socialized. People "on the job" in both the intensive and the extensive work drama (insofar as the latter may involve the specific individual) provide cues to their responses to the work situation in both its technical and its affective components. Few individuals can for long remain oblivious to the perceptions of others. To the degree that these others are accepted as legitimate communicators, their views are assimilated by the individual.

The culture of an occupation is validated "on the job." The culture, too, embodies an attitude toward the work, but the attitude may approach idealization as it seeks to give the work a prestige it might not have "out there" in the real world. But at work, "out there," the worker develops his own perceptions of his work, whether he be an apprentice or a member of the "inner fraternity" of colleagues. However valid these perceptions may be, he does in fact act as a result of them, and his responses to the work will be colored accordingly. . . .

To sum up to this point, then, the meaning of work for an individual results from his childhood and adult socialization experiences *and* the perceptions of the work world he has formed in the course of work, of being exposed to particular occupational cultures.

The meaning of work for the individual can be as varied as the gamut of human emotional responses. Factors that appear to structure work meanings, particularly as they are expressed in attitudes of satisfaction or dissatisfaction with the work, include absenteeism, achievement, advancement and promotion, a sense of alienation, job and career aspirations, degree of autonomy in work, automation, a sense of challenge, clarity of goals, education, job involvement, intellectual stimulation, social and occupational mobility opportunities provided by the job, personal and social motivations of the job, morale, needs, interpersonal relationships, organizational structure, salary, race, sex, ethnicity, job skills, status and prestige of the work, supervision, tenure, training, recognition provided by peers and superiors, conditions and hours of work, and performance and productivity.

Further, the meaning work has for the worker depends on his location within the functional division of labor. In 1952–53, Robert Dubin studied the extent to which work was viewed as more than a mandatory involvement in some enterprise and was in fact a "central life interest" among 1,200 workers in three plants in three Midwestern communities.[5] The plants, all in urban areas, were a manufacturer of industrial equipment, a maker of industrial, dress, and novelty gloves, and a producer of advertising items. Forty questions constituted a "central life-interest questionnaire" and were addressed to the respondent's preference for a particular locus in the community—work,

[5]Robert Dubin, "Industrial Workers' Worlds: A Study of the 'Central Life Interests' of Industrial Workers," *Social Problems* 3 (January, 1956): 131–42.

nonwork, or indifferent (i.e., neutral)—for the conduct of some activity. A typical question was:

I would most hate
———— missing a day's work
———— missing a meeting of an organization I belong to
———— missing almost anything I usually do

Analysis of 491 completed questionnaires led Dubin to conclude that the primacy of work in the American experience appears to have receded, at least for industrial workers. Perhaps work may still be a means to an end, but work as an arena for satisfying social relationships is clearly outdistanced by relationships not involving the work place. However—and this is an important proviso—when these workers were asked about the centrality of organizational affiliation in their lives, 61 per cent chose the work organization as the most meaningful formal organizational structure in their lives. When satisfactions involved in technical operations were considered, 63 per cent were job-oriented; they found greatest satisfaction in performing technical operations on the job as against a home shop in the basement or the like. In other words, although work is no longer a central concern for industrial workers, although they do not find it a focus for meaningful interpersonal relations, nevertheless the formal requirements of organizational life in industry—both interpersonally and technologically—do provide a source of identification as the most appropriate context in which organizational experience and technical involvement can be realized. A man need not love what he does, but the factory becomes the best place to do it. He certainly does not organize his life out of an infatuation with work. He does not value it; work is simply necessary.

Orzack attempted to apply Dubin's findings to professionals.[6] He administered Dubin's central life-interest schedule to 150 registered professional nurses employed in public and private hospitals and in a state mental hospital in a Midwestern city. Scoring procedures were identical to Dubin's. His findings using Dubin's analytical categories are presented in Table 1. They indicate, according to Orzack, that work does in fact loom as a dominant interest of professional nurses. It serves as a focus for personal satisfactions as well as for most meaningful relations within a formal organizational context. That nurses do not find informal relations in work to the same extent as industrial workers may indicate that the professions in general strongly lack collegial relations, or this lack may be endemic to occupations composed largely of females, who, despite training, are socialized to finding interpersonal satisfactions in nonwork situations. In any case, the saliency of work for the professional in contrast to the industrial worker suggests that more aspects of a professional's life are structured by his training, his ideological commitments,

[6]Louis H. Orzack, "Work as a 'Central Life Interest' of Professionals," *Social Problems* 7 (Fall, 1959): 125–32.

TABLE 1 Total "Central Life Interests" and Subordinate Experience Patterns for Professional Nurses and Industrial Workers

PATTERN	PROFESSIONAL NURSES (ORZACK) %	INDUSTRIAL WORKERS (DUBIN) %
Total "central life interest"		
Work	79	24
Nonwork	21	76
Informal relations		
Work	45	9
Nonwork	55	91
General relations (personal satisfactions)		
Work	67	15
Nonwork	33	85
Formal-organization relations		
Work	91	61
Nonwork	9	39
Technological relations		
Work	87	63
Nonwork	13	37
N	150	491

Source: Louis H. Orzack, "Work as a 'Central Life Interest' of Professionals," Social Problems 7 (Fall, 1959): 127.

and his service orientation, thus rendering his life course more "vulnerable" to the demands of work. Work thus tends to have greater meaning or "centrality" for the professional. Consequently, to reiterate, the meaning of work varies with its place on the functional division of labor—i.e., with increments of indispensability (stemming, of course, from differences in skill and training).

But, however "central" or peripheral work may be to various groups, both studies point to the fact that in our society work is at least valued as something necessary. The unemployed or "unemployables"—derelicts, individuals with checkered work histories—frequently feel isolated from their fellows until they can get work, for some work is better than no work at all. Friedman and Havighurst indicate that all work provides common threads of meaning even though a particular occupation may stress one or more strands at the expense of others.[7] All work seems to provide income, to regulate life

[7]Eugene A. Friedman and Robert J. Havighurst, The Meaning of Work and Retirement (Chicago: University of Chicago Press, 1954).

activity, and to provide a source of identity, association, and meaningful experiences. Their study of five occupations that vary in skill, prestige, and commitment—steel workers, coal miners, skilled craftsmen, retail salespeople, and physicians—attests to these commonalities. Thus, the centrality of the meaning of work in an occupation should not obscure the fact that all work does possess meaning. As we remarked very early in this book, work is that activity which permits a person to survive socially as well as physically. . . .

THE DEVELOPMENT OF A WORK IDENTITY

Ultimately, any consideration of work must focus on the relation between work and the individual. To be sure, this discussion has not been absent in previous pages, but now we must focus explicitly on that very intimate relation between performance in an occupation and the person who performs, between work and the self.

Until recently, it was characteristic of sociologists to restrict their treatment of socialization to the years of childhood. Thus, socialization was viewed solely as the process by which the growing child developed a sense of self—i.e., the process by which the maturing individual achieved the ability to look objectively at himself and to regulate his responses to the world in terms of others' perceptions of him. Increasingly, sociologists are examining any situation in which an individual is prepared for a new status and learns the role performance appropriate to that status as an instance of socialization. Consequently, it becomes possible to conceive of life itself as one long (and perhaps often agonizing) socialization experience. . . .

We tend to think of ourselves in many ways: I am fat, I am thin, I am handsome, I am ugly, I am intelligent, I am a nincompoop. We have names that evoke responses in us. In addition to the family name by which we are called, which in itself ties us to an entire social heritage and a set of expectations and obligations implicit in that history, we are of one sex or the other, we bask in the pride of particular accomplishments—which can be named—and we work at particular tasks. Whatever the criteria may be, we tend to name ourselves in particular ways. And this act of naming—the acquisition of identity—results in the classification through symbols of ourselves, of the world and the ways in which we come to terms with the world. All one need do is ask the question: Who am I? Answer the question, and the idea of identity should become clear. Anselm Strauss points out that, however elusive an identity may be, a central aspect is the individual's response to the appraisals he and others make of his conduct. From what he observes of himself in the mirror of others (including those situations in which he stands back and observes himself from their perspective), he fashions a kind of interpersonal mask through which he presents himself, as Goffman has put it, to others and in terms of which he attempts to anticipate how others will respond to him in the future (which may be only seconds away). . . .

In the development of an identity, the part of the self that emerges when we name ourselves, work looms large. One of the most important names we provide for ourselves in North American society derives from the work we do. Indeed, Strauss has suggested that the shaping of one's work identity is the prototype of identity formation.

Central to the development of the work identity are those critical junctures or contingencies that not only serve to redirect ongoing activity but also force the person to realize that he is not the same person he was, that a redefinition of his situation is very much in order. He must question the nature of the change both interpersonally and against the backdrop of the standardized, or traditional, patterns of movement through the occupation. This means that, like the traveler who periodically compares his map with road signs and landmarks in order to note his progress, the worker must compare his progress with the progress of others *and* against the benchmarks or indicators of progress within the occupation. . . .

JOHN R. SHACK
TOWARD A DYNAMIC-INTERACTIONALIST TAXONOMY OF WORK STYLE ....

"No man is born into the world whose work is not born with him."

—*James Russell Lowell*

In 1979, when executives at Transamerica created the company's management development program using ideas on motivation developed by David Mc-Clelland, a Harvard psychologist, they found that by adding a measure of personality typology, as described by Carl Jung, they could improve their personnel problem solutions (Moore, 1987). The Myers-Briggs Type Indicator, and other measures of Jung's type dimensions of personality, have become the hottest thing going since the T-Group in many business organizations. In some ways like astrology in that the origins of the type descriptions are unclear, this approach to sorting out personalities has the virtue of making it easy to accept others for their "trait fate." Instead of saying "The reason Bill is so expansive is because he is a gemini," the new language is ". . . because he is an ENFP," a Myers-Briggs configuration predicting a similar characteristic.

The assumption inherent in the trait approach is that trait characteristics are probably inherited temperamental tendencies that cannot be blamed on anyone. Such a perspective takes the wrath out of interpersonal conflict. If we can understand that someone makes decisions slowly because of a processing style that requires more data, that person may not be looked upon as oppositional or dumb. If someone is forgetful and disorganized as part of an introverted-thinking style, we understand and accept the trait trade-off. When work behavior is explained in terms of a person's enduring trait structure, greater work-style tolerance and predictability seem to prevail. While there is some overlap, different approaches to personality classification emphasize different traits. How are we to know what classification structure really taps the most basic and enduring underlying traits? How do we organize all these traits into a system that will serve as a framework for including all that we know about individual differences?

Trait theory and measurement is back in business and is quickly becoming a central theme in understanding how individuals relate to all aspects of the work scene. This article will look at the major influences behind this trend and try to see in the trend an emerging biological perspective. This will in turn serve to route the trait approaches and will allow for the use of a contemporary view of human development to address the problems of people at work.

Psychology has contributed to issues of man-in-work in numerous ways: designing environments to facilitate human adaptation and productivity, developing psychometric devices to assist in fitting personal qualities to optimal work environments, and speculating on the origin of career choices and the factors influencing job satisfaction, among others. All of these efforts ultimately relate to a theory of personal work style. Personal work style is that subset of a more general personality style that addresses those enduring patterns of needs, experiences, and behaviors that characterize how an individual relates to work functions and environments. Most theories of personal work style have taken their lead from constructs and methods derived in academic personality theory and research.

Osipow (1983), in his review of the theories and methods of career choice and satisfaction, concludes that the field is made up of a collection of miniature and circumscribed theories. Most efforts in the areas of work psychology borrow from the miniature conceptual systems that come from measurement devices or novel new constructs out of general personality theory. No new major perspective has emerged from general personality theory in several years. Instead a new sophisticated twist of statistical method will launch a generation of personality research where design form becomes more important than the relevance of the questions to which the method is put. Osipow calls for a larger conceptual system to account for personality functions and development as they relate to work.

Kuhn (1962) suggests that scientific fields emerge in this random and somewhat fortuitous manner until a particular set of ideas assumes the status of a *paradigm*. Paradigms serve to define and organize problem sets and methods of research for succeeding generations of practitioners and, as suggested by Kuhn, often take the form of a classic text reviewing and integrating the field.

The primary value of a paradigm is that it establishes a "bigger picture" framework that both organizes existing information and identifies subsequent questions in light of a more comprehensive perspective.

Before a paradigm or any organizing framework that will serve to organize this field can be considered, a system of classification or taxonomy of relevant personality traits is a prerequisite. First, though, we must look at the current thinking regarding the nature of personality structure.

WHAT'S IN A TAXONOMY?

We begin with the assumption that there is a basic underlying consistency in how any one person behaves, feels, and thinks that we call *personality*. The next assumption is that this consistency is not merely in the eye of the beholder, as Walter Mischel contends (Mischel, 1968), but rather exists in some structural reality of a person's make-up. Clearly, behavioral consistency is affected by the demand of transient factors. However, there is evidence from multiple research sources that strongly suggests a link between dimensions of personality and biological realities. The next basic question is concerned with which traits to address in explaining this cross-situational stability. The dictionary lists 18,000 trait names (Allport and Odbert, 1936). There is a need for a taxonomy that tells us which personality distinctions are more important than others in classifying people.

Taxonomies should best be anchored in the holding ground of replicated empirical findings and connect with psychological and biological fact. While most personality theorists do not make it a key concept in their perspectives, there is general agreement that personality emerges from a biological base of temperamental differences which provides the fundamental "stuff" for subsequent development through dynamic interaction with the environment. Typically, temperament is dealt with in many larger personality perspectives as a necessary evil to be mentioned but not expanded upon. It is simply viewed as a "given." It is not without reason that the bulk of the systematic work in the area of temperament and the biological basis of aspects of personality comes from outside of the United States. Old views of temperament, such as Sheldon's body-type work, were largely static and descriptive and threatened the important American perspective of freedom to be anything we aspire to be. The same viewpoint overinterpreted Skinner's concept of stimulus or environmental control as a threat to human dignity and freedom. Both biological and environmental controls are realities that require understanding to foster personal control over one's life. Abraham Maslow (1970), the champion of the positive self-expression perspective in personality psychology, states

> I believe that helping a person toward a full humanness proceeds inevitably via awareness of one's identity (among other things). A very important part of this task is to become aware of what one *is*, biologically, temperamentally, consti-

tutionally, as a member of a species, of one's capacities, desires, needs, and also one's vocation, what one is fitted for, what one's destiny is (p. 32).

The reality is that factors in our biology, as well as factors in our environments, place limits on our global potential. We can choose to deny or ignore them or we can confront them directly in a creative manner. By explicating and then harnessing them for our personal purposes, we achieve a real freedom.

THE HISTORY AND THEMES OF THE BIOLOGICAL PERSPECTIVE

The history of the biological perspective, as it is emerging in its present form, can be traced to several major independent influences. The first is the vast influence that Ivan Pavlov's views on temperament and character have had on Soviet and Eastern European psychology. When J. A. Gray published *Pavlov's Typology* in 1964, Western psychologists were first introduced to the important implications of Pavlov's work on nervous system traits for personality style development. While most Western psychologists were familiar with Pavlov's theory of cortical excitation, few were familiar with the modifications of B. M. Teplov and V. D. Nebylitsyn who, through their work with human subjects, creatively extended Pavlov's concepts into the realm of human personality types. Subsequently, the work coming out of the Department of Psychophysiology and Individual Differences at the University of Warsaw, since its 1966 inception, has been building on the Pavlovian paradigm (a paradigm at least among Soviet and Eastern European researchers). This group organized two international conferences (*Temperament and Personality, 1974; Temperament, Need for Stimulation and Activity, 1979*) that began to draw like-minded workers from many different countries. In 1985, Jan Strelau, of the University of Warsaw, Frank Farley, of the University of Wisconsin, Madison, and Anthony Gale, of the University of Southampton, England, coedited the two-volume *The Biological Basis of Personality and Behavior* (1985), drawing from a host of international contributors sharing the same temperamental perspective.

A second major influence on the biological perspective is the extensive work of Hans Eysenck (1967, 1981, among many others). Born in Germany and migrating to England at the start of World War II, he received his Ph.D. in psychology from the University of London where he was subsequently named professor of psychology in 1954. His scientific interests range over such diverse territories as humor, aesthetics, psychotherapy, intelligence, criminal behavior, parapsychology and, of course, the structure of personality. His work on extraversion-introversion (his atypical spelling of the word extraversion became the accepted spelling in the subject index of the *Psychological Abstracts* in 1974) spans over 30 years and has stimulated a vast amount of research. He views these biologically determined and factor analytically derived dimensions of personality, along with neuroticism-stability, and psychoticism, to explain most of what constitutes differences among individuals. When he addressed the International Congress of Psychology in Moscow in 1966, the Eastern European researchers in this area recognized the similarities of his conception of the biological basis of extraversion-introversion and their views of nervous system strength. The key construct is that of differences in arousal capacities of the higher brain centers in response to stimulation. A massive array of research has related Eysenck's model to nearly all areas of human function.

Another important influence on the current emerging American view of the importance of temperament in human development comes from the work of Alexander Thomas and Stella Chess (1968, 1977). For over 25 years these researchers examined the temperamental basis of personality through longitudinal investigation of the effects of relatively stable patterns of behavior in young children on subsequent outcomes. They have been especially attentive to the temperament-environment interaction and found the concept of *goodness of fit*. Goodness of fit results when the properties of the environment and its expectations and demands are consonant with the organism's own capacities and characteristics. They espouse an *interactionalist* concept of human development in which temperament is never considered by itself but rather in interaction with a person's abilities, motives, and external environmental stresses and opportunities in a constantly spiraling and evolving process. What a person "picks" to interact with in the environment at any time in development is a function of his previous interactive history. Presently the *dynamic-interactionalist* view of development is finding both empirical and philosophical support in mainstream psychological theory. Thomas and Chess (in Strelau, *et al.*, 1985) clearly define temperament to refer to the "how" of behavior. They discriminate temperament from ability in that the latter is concerned with the "what" and the "how well" of behavior. Motivation, in turn, accounts for the "why" a person behaves in a particular way.

There have been many others who have contributed to this perspective. However, for the sake of a general survey of the different major theory and research directions that have influenced the biological perspective, the preceding will suffice.

Strelau, Farley, and Gale (in Strelau, Farley, and Gale, 1985) list a set of recurrent themes that unify the theoretical and empirical studies in this area.

1. Individual variation is, in part, attributable to *biological factors*.
2. Such factors are transmitted through *genetic mechanisms*.
3. There is a constant *interplay* between biologically determined dispositions and their interaction with the external world.
4. The individual is seen as *regulating* crucial aspects of this interplay.
5. The principles of regulation are themselves derivable from the biological dispositions and their interaction with the external world.
6. Factors that play an important role in the regulation of behavior are *arousal level, optimal levels of arousal, optimal levels of stimulation, changes in stimulation,* and *activity*.

7. The dispositional variables may be tapped by use of *psychometric instruments*.

8. Because of the range of identified dispositional variables and because each person evolves within a constantly emerging *feedback system*, it is not expected that there will be a simple one-to-one relation between trait variables and behavior, even where the number of traits specified by the theory is limited.

9. The appropriate description of the individual will encompass *behavioral, psychophysiological,* and *experiential* domains of description.

10. The understanding of personality structure is impossible without consideration of dynamics; therefore experimental studies are obliged to focus on *process* as well as *outcome*.

11. There are no grounds for sustaining the historical division between the *psychology of individual differences* and *general experimental psychology,* nor between physiological, cognitive, and social psychological approaches. Indeed, the psychophysiology of individual differences has the power to integrate these various fields. Data derived from studies of individual differences may provide a base for describing general processes.

12. The examination of individual differences and the *patterning of behavior* is therefore of heuristic value in all branches of psychology.

13. In examining data derived from experiments, the investigator must be aware that individual differences will determine not only the patterning of response, but the *individual's response to the experimental situation per se*.

14. It is the recognition of the biological nature of temperamental characteristics that enables a cross mapping of constructs devised in both Western and Eastern laboratories, and thus provides for the evolution of a common language for the description of crucial aspects of human behavior (pp. 18–19).

The authors caution that there is much work to be done to clarify the way various researchers relate to the construct of optimal arousal and to the need for a standard set of procedures that will not stifle creative approaches. There has not been a coordinated direction for looking at work behavior. These operating themes offer a framework for approaching the various problems of man-in-work. Next we can take a look at how a biologically rooted, dynamic-interactionist perspective can be related to work style and, eventually, work satisfaction.

A DYNAMIC-INTERACTIONALIST VIEW OF PERSONAL WORK STYLE

The foundation qualities of an individual's work style are present at birth. One very important quality that seems to appear in the center of this foundation is the individual's capacity to manage stimulation. This difference presumably can range from no capacity (in which case we may have the basis for autism and schizophrenia) to a strong capacity. The general attributes associated with lesser capacities for managing stimulation involve behaviors aimed at reducing stimulation. Conversely, those with greater capacities for consuming stimulus input are more prone to behave in ways that will produce greater amounts of stimulation. Clearly a significant difference in this capacity at birth will account for a vast array of significant differences among individuals in how engagement with environment will occur.

Another way of stating this is that individuals differ in their fundamental ability to screen and select, from the vast array of stimulus input, only that which is meaningful or relevant to current needs. Those who work with autistic children recognize their general inability to carry out this function. Those who work with highly hysterical individuals recognize their tendencies to overly restrict conscious awareness of very much input at all. These two forms of clinical pathology represent extremes in the taxonomy of psychological disorders. In the case of the hysteric we have a strong tendency for repression to play a role. If repression can be viewed as nothing more than the storing of memories that have not yet passed through cortical consciousness, we have a further explanation for the great need for stimulus input that typifies the hysterical personality. The more input that doesn't pass cortical awareness, the greater the amount that must be mustered to keep the cortex awake and to avoid boredom.

We can imagine this stimulus management mechanism as a type of squelch function similar to that found on emergency radios to spare the listener from having to hear all the background noise while waiting for important signal transmissions. Of course, the higher the squelch is set, the more information (less-discernible signals) is ignored. Individuals differ in the level at which the squelch is set. Those with a greater capacity for stimulation management set the squelch control higher and thus screen out more unimportant input. Those with a lesser stimulus management capacity will tend to take in more "noise" in order to get the more relevant information. They will also, therefore, be witness to more information. To have to consciously sort out meaningful from less meaningful information, however, is a more bothersome task.

Another analogy that includes the construct of repression and unconscious storage of information is that of the relationship between the executive officer and executive secretary. The executive officer, like cortical conscious control, makes decisions based upon information input. The executive secretary, on the other hand, screens information for the officer (holds calls, diverts unwanted intrusions, sorts mail). Information that is not relevant for the executive at the moment is put on hold. File cabinets become the reservoir for information for further reference. Presumably secretaries will differ in the amount of preselection of information that will be made accessible to the executive. We all know that a "good" secretary reads the boss's mind and anticipates what and how much information to let through based on current issues and needs. Some secretaries will under- and some will overanticipate this need, however, and cause the boss to be either overstimulated or bored. In the former case the boss may become anxious or tired and in extreme cases need to go home early or retire to a quiet place for rest. If the latter occurs, the boss becomes bored and looks for diversions—perhaps precipitating a stimulating crisis or looking for a more challenging job. In the meantime the secretary, who is filing information away to spare the boss, may go to lunch or become ill and leave. Suddenly the boss, who thought everything was under control, is inundated with previously filed (without awareness) information that is overwhelming and, perhaps, frightening. Now anxiety, fatigue, and depression set in. Eventually, however, the secretary returns and the boss is again protected from unwanted input until the next time the secretary is absent or less diligent. We can expect this executive to be more variable with regard to negative emotions and to be much more selectively aware of the surrounding realities. At the same time, this executive will be better able to sort through priorities and see the bigger picture, as an executive should.

If we view stimulus management capacity and repressive capacity as somehow interrelated on a normally distributed continuum anchored by the above pathological styles, we have a foundation trait basis for understanding a considerable amount of human behavior. Let's take this trait factor and walk it through a dynamic interaction with developmental experiences for individuals with relatively high and low stimulus management capacities, to illustrate the role of foundation traits on the development of secondary and higher-level derived trait patterns. For the sake of discussion, we will refer to *normal* individuals who can handle and require larger amounts of stimulation as *reactive,* and those who cannot handle and so avoid larger amounts of stimulation as *reflective.* The choice of these terms will begin to make sense as the differences in developmental style emerge.

Given a reactive individual's greater foundation capacity for managing (sorting, screening, prioritizing) stimulation, this individual requires more stimulation and therefore seeks it. Greater amounts of input are kept from awareness and possibly stored for future assimilation. We might assume that, as a neonate, the reactive child will take positively to the relatively higher amounts of stimulation involved in engaging the environment with all senses. Engagement with a primary caregiver is a source of incredible stimulation and, because the reactive child handles and needs more input, the positive and optimistic roots of social interest needs and social skill development are established. This requires, of course, that early social experiences are both present and positive. Subsequently what is "picked" from the environment for engagement will be weighted on the side of social stimulation. Subsequent exposure to the values and expectations of the family and local culture will be attended to with a greater need to maintain social connection and stimulation. Power, status, achievement, and affiliation needs, among others, will develop from this foundation need for stimulation and derived need for social stimulation.

Subsequently, this greater social dependence may be the basis for developing a need to please everyone. This in turn may lead to a developmental configuration that is rich in the ability to check out social expectations and alter behavior in accordance. The outcome of this overreaching pattern is a trade-off of a sense that a deeper core of personal identity resides inside the person. The reactive individual may tend to be all things for all persons at the cost of feeling there is someone home inside.

This same relative strength in stimulus management will be the basis for the capacity to handle and seek out such stimulus-rich experiences as change, risk, adventure, cultural contrast, and, of course, an audience. All of these possibilities are mitigated by the stimulus opportunities available in the environment, the quality of reinforcement resources, and the influence of other basic traits in interaction, such as global intelligence and special sensory processing strengths (such as differences in auditory and visual discrimination preferences that lead to greater musical or visual art abilities, to touch on the vast array of possible individual differences in heritable sensory discrimination differences).

The reactive individual brings to the world of work a greater capacity, and therefore need, for variety, challenge, and change. If the derived social side of this foundation trait has developed, as it most often but not necessarily does, then the reactive individual will be drawn to people for stimulation at the minimum and, usually, for all the other derived social needs. Given a developmental history that included reinforcement for particular attention-getting behaviors, these derived patterns will also achieve salience in the individual's style as a social performance need and ability. Since social stimulation is usually important for the reactive worker, this along with more challenge, variety, and risk will be important work environment requirements. Their sense of optimism, which can also sometimes be a naïve awareness of reality, allows reactive individuals to dwell on future possibilities. The unknown future is a rich source of stimulation to confront.

A reflective-style individual, with a lower theoretical squelch setting, will begin life with a greater tendency to be overwhelmed by stimulation. Early maternal engagements may not be so pleasant as they were for the more reactive individual because of the amount of stimulation involved. As a consequence, this individual works to reduce or avoid this form of social stimulation. Social interest and, subsequently, social skills are traded for interest in environmental experiences, over which more predictability and control can be exerted. Technical competencies develop around less social issues. Mechanical, numerical, logical, or data-base development become the primary focus of interest. Details rather than impressions are plucked from the environment. Stimulus-rich experiences such as change, adventure, and social attention are avoided. Interaction with family and local culture will shade this tendency, even to the point of creating a good capacity for relating to social circumstances or easier tolerance for change. Still, the underlying basis for behavior will be different from that of the more reactive individual. Rather than feeling the reactive person's experience of lacking a center, the reflective individuals will more likely feel that no one knows them, or cares to know them. They will trust others only after long data collection. Once the decision to trust has been made, however, they will usually dig deeper into themselves to give to the relationship. Because they may tend to feel different from others due to their more meager social involvements, they will be inclined to assume there is something basically wrong with them. This in turn can lead to a greater tendency to assume responsibility and guilt when things go wrong.

Due, perhaps, to the greater tendency of the reflective individual to withdraw rather than reach out in the face of stimulation, the tendency to think, collect, and weigh data more, leads to a work style that requires more structure, fewer people, fewer decisions, and less extraneous noise. Since stimulus overload can produce anxiety, fatigue, irritability, and depression, noise-reduced environments are important considerations in developing working conditions for the reflective worker. Reflective individuals should be better able to deal with the controllable facts of the past than the ambiguous and unknown future. Staying with what is known is consciously managing stimulation.

In short, the flavor of a person's adult style will result from a continual interaction between the foundation trait of stimulus management style and more fortuitous environmental opportunities, in a manner that can be visually represented by the well-worn tree analogy. With a tree we have a well-rooted trunk that serves to support the various branches that emerge through the interaction with the forces of the environment. The tree trunk varies much less than the branches as a result of this encounter and continues to service the branches, which in turn provide modifying information to the trunk.

A reasonable question at this point is how the process of deduction that produced the above descriptions differs from any other system of traits or types. The major difference is that we are able to see the relative strength and implied origins of traits to better predict their endurance and primacy. While there are many trait descriptive systems currently being used with success in industry, most of them generate their descriptive typologies from clinical observation or statistical method. None as yet has developed a comprehensive taxonomy that links the biological framework with the developmental process to better understand the origins and primacy of traits and needs as they relate to work choices and satisfaction. Much has happened in recent years in better understanding the biological basis of personality and the complex interactional phenomenon of development. Both of these sources need to become integrated into the framework from which we study man-in-work. With such a dynamic-interactional taxonomy we can then begin to examine the "goodness of fit" between the nature of the person and the demands of the workplace that leads to work satisfaction. As implied when discussing the Myers-Briggs approach to typology, the ability to sort out people's traits in terms of degree of biological rootedness allows us to assign culpability more reasonably. Behaviors and motives based on the foundation traits are those we accept and perhaps even embrace in ourselves and others since they will not be easily altered. Derived trait patterns, however, are another story. The more a trait is a result of learning, presumably the greater the chance it will be alterable. We can prune and rearrange the tree's branches but we cannot do much for the trunk but love it for what it is, and make the world understand and work with it.

This perspective obviously has important implications for theories and methods of psychological intervention. Work, for example, with troubled marriages (or partnerships) can be approached with a view to knowing and learning to work with durable style differences. When someone does something we dislike, it is usually easier to handle it when we realize the behavior comes from a foundation difference that is unlike our own. For example, if I work fast and make quick decisions and recognize that when I don't operate this way it is because I have lost interest in the subject, I may judge the slowness of another as loss of interest when it may simply relate to a different rate of processing. Response to the former assumption may be anger while the latter will elicit more acceptance. This same possibility can be used for understanding larger social systems. For example, for those of European origin to relate to Asians requires a larger-scale version of the above.

Many years ago, Fred Herzberg postulated that Maslow's hierarchy of needs did not perhaps operate the same for everyone. Instead he suggested that individuals differed in the degree to which they needed growth or adjustment needs met; different work-demand strokes for different work-style folks. This individual difference aspect of his perspective was less attended to than was the importance of meeting self-actualization needs in the workplace. His suggestion that the need hierarchy was not bipolar but rather two parallel and independent dimensions has implications for looking at stimulus approach and avoidance. Certainly his suggestion that true work (or life) satisfaction is only achieved through the meeting of growth needs may be applied to optimal stimulus absorption.

So many exciting relationships exist already in psychology that relate to the man-in-work set of problems. We need a larger framework into which to draw these diverse efforts and perspectives. Hopefully the dynamic-interactional perspective can provide this framework.

REFERENCES

Allport, G. W., and Odbert, H. S. (1936). Trait-names: a psychological study. *Psychological Monographs 47 (Whole No. 211)*.

Eysenck, H. J. (1967). *The biological basis of personality*. Springfield, Ill.: Charles C. Thomas.

Eysenck, H. J. (1981). *A model for personality*. Berlin, Heidelberg, New York: Springer-Verlag.

Gray, J. A. (1964). *Pavlov's typology*. Oxford: Pergamon Press.

Herzberg, F. (1966). *Work and the nature of man*. Cleveland: World.

Kuhn, T. S. (1962). *The structure of scientific revolutions*. Chicago: Univ. of Chicago Press.

Maslow, A. H. (1954, 2nd ed., 1970). *Motivation and personality*. New York: Harper.

Mischel, W. (1968). *Personality and assessment*. New York: Wiley.

Moore, T. (1987). Personality tests are back. *Fortune*, 115, 74–84.

Myers, Isabel B. (1962). *The Myers-Briggs Type Indicator*. Princeton: Educational Testing Service.

Osipow, S. H. (1983). *Theories of career development*. Englewood Cliffs, N.J.: Prentice-Hall.

Strelau, J., Farley, F., and Gale, A. (1985). *The biological basis of personality and behavior*. Vol I & II, Washington, D.C.: McGraw-Hill.

Thomas, A., Chess, S., and Birch, H. C. (1968). *Temperament and behavior disorders in children*. New York: New York University Press.

Thomas, A., and Chess, S. (1977). *Temperament and development*. New York: Brunner/Mazel.

FREDERICK HERZBERG
ONE MORE TIME: HOW DO YOU MOTIVATE EMPLOYEES? ....

Frederick Herzberg, a clinical psychologist by training, has devoted many years to the study of motivational factors as they relate to work satisfaction. His motivator-hygiene model of job satisfaction divides work motivators into those that serve to reduce anxiety and maintain adjustment (*hygiene*) versus those that foster personal growth (*motivator*). The theory proposes that, while both sets of needs must be addressed, satisfying the hygiene needs results only in the reduction of job dissatisfaction. "Real" job satisfaction can only be met through meeting the motivator needs. The theory further suggests that both individuals and particular jobs can be assessed for their intrinsic balance of these two sets of needs in order to foster a more satisfactory match. These ideas are best explained in Dr. Herzberg's *Work and the Nature of Man* (World Publishing Company, 1966).

The present material is a further application of the motivator-hygiene model to the issues of management style. The "kick-in-the-pants" management technique for enhancing work motivation, delivered negatively or positively, has been demonstrated to be cost ineffective in producing self-generated work interest leading to satisfaction and optimal productivity. Such incentives as reducing the time spent at work, spiraling wages, human relations and sensitivity training, improved job participation, and communication and counseling result in only short-term movement rather than internalized work motive.

Herzberg points out that industry strives to enlarge rather than enrich work experience in its attempt to bring about effective utilization of

Frederick Herzberg, "One More Time: How Do You Motivate Employees?" *Harvard Business Review*, January-February, 1968. Reprinted by permission of the *Harvard Business Review*, Copyright © 1968 by the President and Fellows of Harvard College; all rights reserved.

personnel. Job enrichment (motivator need applications) provides the opportunity for the employee's psychological growth, while job enlargement (hygiene need applications) simply creates more work demand.

—J. Shack

. . . How do you install a generator in an employee? A brief review of my motivation-hygiene theory of job attitudes is required before theoretical and practical suggestions can be offered. The theory was first drawn from an examination of events in the lives of engineers and accountants. At least sixteen other investigations, using a wide variety of populations (including some in the communist countries), have since been completed, making the original research one of the most replicated studies in the field of job attitudes.

The findings of these studies, along with corroboration from many other investigations using different procedures, suggest that the factors involved in producing job satisfaction (and motivation) are separate and distinct from the factors that lead to job dissatisfaction. Since separate factors need to be considered, depending on whether job satisfaction or job dissatisfaction is being examined, it follows that these two feelings are not opposites of each other. The opposite of job satisfaction is not job dissatisfaction but, rather, *no* job dissatisfaction.

Stating the concept presents a problem in semantics, for we normally think of satisfaction and dissatisfaction as opposites—i.e., what is not satisfying must be dissatisfying, and vice versa. But when it comes to understanding the behavior of people in their jobs, more than a play on words is involved.

Two different needs of man are involved here. One set of needs can be thought of as stemming from his animal nature—the built-in drive to avoid pain from the environment, plus all the learned drives which become conditioned to the basic biological needs. For example, hunger, a basic biological drive, makes it necessary to earn money, and then money becomes a specific drive. The other set of needs relates that unique human characteristic, the ability to achieve and, through achievement, to experience psychological growth. The stimuli for the growth needs are tasks that induce growth; in the industrial setting, they are the *job content*. Contrariwise, the stimuli inducing pain-avoidance behavior are found in the *job environment*.

The growth or *motivator* factors that are intrinsic to the job are: achievement, recognition for achievement, the work itself, responsibility, and growth or advancement. The dissatisfaction-avoidance or *hygiene* factors that are extrinsic to the job include: company policy and administration, supervision, interpersonal relationships, working conditions, salary, status, and security.

A composite of the factors that are involved in causing job dissatisfaction and job satisfaction, drawn from samples of 1,685 employees, is shown in Exhibit I. The results indicate that motivators were the primary cause of satisfaction and hygiene factors the primary cause of unhappiness, on the job. The employees, studied in twelve different investigations, included lower-level supervisors, professional women, agricultural administrators, men about to

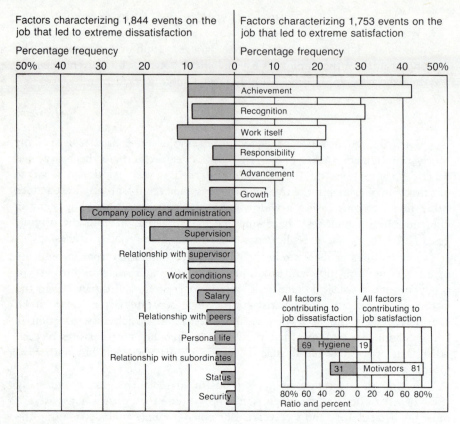

Factors characterizing 1,844 events on the job that led to extreme dissatisfaction

Percentage frequency

50% 40 30 20 10 0

Factors characterizing 1,753 events on the job that led to extreme satisfaction

Percentage frequency

0 10 20 30 40 50%

Achievement
Recognition
Work itself
Responsibility
Advancement
Growth
Company policy and administration
Supervision
Relationship with supervisor
Work conditions
Salary
Relationship with peers
Personal life
Relationship with subordinates
Status
Security

All factors contributing to job dissatisfaction

All factors contributing to job satisfaction

69 Hygiene 19
31 Motivators 81

80% 60 40 20 0 20 40 60 80%
Ratio and percent

EXHIBIT I. Factors Affecting Job Attitudes, as Reported in Twelve Investigations

retire from management positions, hospital maintenance personnel, manufacturing supervisors, nurses, food handlers, military officers, engineers, scientists, housekeepers, teachers, technicians, female assemblers, accountants, Finnish foremen, and Hungarian engineers.

They were asked what job events had occurred in their work that had led to extreme satisfaction or extreme dissatisfaction on their part. Their responses are broken down in the exhibit into percentages of total "positive" job events or total "negative" job events. (The figures total more than 100 percent on both the "hygiene" and "motivators" sides because often at least two factors can be attributed to a single event. Advancement, for instance, often accompanies assumption of responsibility.)

To illustrate, a typical response involving achievement that had a negative effect for the employee was, "I was unhappy because I didn't do the job successfully." A typical response in the small number of positive job events in the company policy and administration grouping was, "I was happy because the company reorganized the section so that I didn't report any longer to the guy I didn't get along with."

As the lower right-hand part of the exhibit shows, of all the factors contributing to job satisfaction, 81 percent were motivators. And of all the factors contributing to the employees' dissatisfaction over their work, 69 percent involved hygiene elements.

ETERNAL TRIANGLE

There are three general philosophies of personnel management. The first is based on organizational theory, the second on industrial engineering, and the third on behavioral science.

The organizational theorist believes that human needs are either so irrational or so varied and adjustable to specific situations that the major function of personnel management is to be as pragmatic as the occasion demands. If jobs are organized in a proper manner, he reasons, the result will be the most efficient job structure, and the most favorable job attitudes will follow as a matter of course.

The industrial engineer holds that man is mechanistically oriented and economically motivated, and his needs are best met by attuning the individual to the most efficient work process. The goal of personnel management therefore should be to concoct the most appropriate incentive system and to design the specific working conditions in a way that facilitates the most efficient use of the human machine. By structuring jobs in a manner that leads to the most efficient operation, the engineer believes that he can obtain the optimal organization of work and the proper work attitudes.

The behavioral scientist focuses on group sentiments, attitudes of individual employees, and the organization's social and psychological climate. According to his persuasion, he emphasizes one or more of the various hygiene and motivator needs. His approach to personnel management generally emphasizes some form of human relations education, in the hope of instilling healthy employee attitudes and an organizational climate which he considers to be felicitous to human values. He believes that proper attitudes will lead to efficient job and organizational structure.

There is always a lively debate as to the overall effectiveness of the approaches of the organizational theorist and the industrial engineer. Manifestly they have achieved much. But the nagging question for the behavioral scientist has been: What is the cost in human problems that eventually cause more expense to the organization—for instance, turnover, absenteeism, errors, violation of safety rules, strikes, restriction of output, higher wages, and greater fringe benefits? On the other hand, the behavioral scientist is hard put to document much manifest improvement in personnel management, using his approach.

The three philosophies can be depicted as a triangle, as is done in Exhibit II, with each persuasion claiming the apex angle. The motivation-hygiene theory claimed the same angle as industrial engineering, but for opposite goals. Rather than rationalizing the work to increase efficiency, the theory suggests that work be *enriched* to bring about effective utilization of personnel. Such a systematic attempt to motivate employees by manipulating the motivator factors is just beginning.

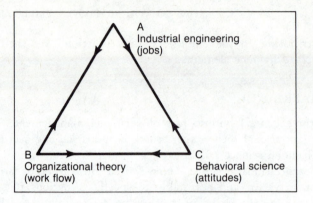

EXHIBIT II. "Triangle" of Philosophies of Personnel Management

The term *job enrichment* describes this embryonic movement. An older term, job enlargement, should be avoided because it is associated with past failure stemming from a misunderstanding of the problem. Job enrichment provides the opportunity for the employee's psychological growth, while job enlargement merely makes a job structurally bigger. Since scientific job enrichment is very new, this article only suggests the principles and practical steps that have recently emerged from several successful experiments in industry.

JOB LOADING

In attempting to enrich an employee's job, management often succeeds in reducing the man's personal contribution, rather than giving him an opportunity for growth in his accustomed job. Such an endeavor, which I shall call horizontal job loading (as opposed to vertical loading, or providing motivator factors), has been the problem of earlier job enlargement programs. This activity merely enlarges the meaninglessness of the job. Some examples of this approach, and their effect, are:

- Challenging the employee by increasing the amount of production expected of him. If he tightens 10,000 bolts a day, see if he can tighten 20,000 bolts a day. The arithmetic involved shows that multiplying zero by zero still equals zero.
- Adding another meaningless task to the existing one, usually some routine clerical activity. The arithmetic here is adding zero to zero.
- Rotating the assignments of a number of jobs that need to be enriched. This means washing dishes for a while, then washing silverware. The arithmetic is substituting one zero for another zero.
- Removing the most difficult parts of the assignment in order to free the worker to accomplish more of the less challenging assignments. This traditional industrial engineering approach amounts to subtraction in the hope of accomplishing addition. . . .

STEPS TO JOB ENRICHMENT

Now that the motivator idea has been described in practice, here are the steps that managers should take in instituting the principle with their employees:

1. Select those jobs in which (a) the investment in industrial engineering does not make changes too costly, (b) attitudes are poor, (c) hygiene is becoming very costly, and (d) motivation will make a difference in performance.
2. Approach these jobs with the conviction that they can be changed. Years of tradition have led managers to believe that the content of the jobs is sacrosanct and the only scope of action that they have is in ways of stimulating people.
3. Brainstorm a list of changes that may enrich the jobs, without concern for their practicality.
4. Screen the list to eliminate suggestions that involve hygiene, rather than actual motivation.
5. Screen the list for generalities, such as "give them more responsibility," that are rarely followed in practice. This might seem obvious, but the motivator words have never left industry, the substance has just been rationalized and organized out. Words like "responsibility," "growth," "achievement," and "challenge," for example, have been elevated to the lyrics of the patriotic anthem for all organizations. It is the old problem typified by the pledge of allegiance to the flag being more important than contributing to the country—of following the form, rather than the substance.
6. Screen the list to eliminate any *horizontal* loading suggestions.
7. Avoid direct participation by the employees whose jobs are to be enriched. Ideas they have expressed previously certainly constitute a valuable source for recommended changes, but their direct involvement contaminates the process with human relations hygiene and, more specifically, gives them only a sense of making a contribution. The job is to be changed, and it is the content that will produce the motivation, not attitudes about being involved or the challenge inherent in setting up a job. That process will be over shortly, and it is what the employees will be doing from then on that will determine their motivation. A sense of participation will result only in short-term movement.
8. In the initial attempts at job enrichment, set up a controlled experiment. At least two equivalent groups should be chosen, one an experimental unit in which the motivators are systematically introduced over a period of time, and the other one a control group in which no changes are made. For both groups, hygiene should be allowed to follow its natural course for the duration of the experiment. Pre- and post-installation tests of performance and job attitudes are

necessary to evaluate the effectiveness of the job enrichment program. The attitude test must be limited to motivator items in order to divorce the employee's view of the job he is given from all the surrounding hygiene feelings that he might have.

9. Be prepared for a drop in performance in the experimental group the first few weeks. The changeover to a new job may lead to a temporary reduction in efficiency.

10. Expect your first-line supervisors to experience some anxiety and hostility over the changes you are making. The anxiety comes from their fear that changes will result in poorer performance for their unit. Hostility will arise when the employees start assuming what the supervisors regard as their own responsibility for performance. The supervisor without checking duties to perform may then be left with little to do.

   After a successful experiment, however, the supervisor usually discovers the supervisory and managerial functions he has neglected, or which were never his because all his time was given over to checking the work of his subordinates. For example, in the R & D division of one large chemical company I know of, the supervisors of the laboratory assistants were theoretically responsible for their training and evaluation. These functions, however, had come to be performed in a routine, unsubstantial fashion. After the job enrichment program, during which the supervisors were not merely passive observers of the assistants' performance, the supervisors actually were devoting their time to reviewing performance and administering thorough training.

What has been called an employee-centered style of supervision will come about not through education of supervisors, but by changing the jobs that they do.

CONCLUDING NOTE

Job enrichment will not be a one-time proposition, but a continuous management function. The initial changes, however, should last for a very long period of time. There are a number of reasons for this:

- The changes would bring the job up to the level of challenge commensurate with the skill that was hired.
- Those who have still more ability eventually will be able to demonstrate it better and win promotion to higher-level jobs.
- The very nature of motivators, as opposed to hygiene factors, is that they have a much longer-term effect on employees' attitudes. Perhaps the job will have to be enriched again, but this will not occur as frequently as the need for hygiene.

Not all jobs can be enriched, nor do all jobs need to be enriched. If only a small percentage of the time and money that is now devoted to hygiene, however, were given to job enrichment efforts, the return in human satisfaction and economic gain would be one of the largest dividends that industry and society have ever reaped through their efforts at better personnel management.

The argument for job enrichment can be summed up quite simply: If you have someone on a job, use him. If you can't use him on the job, get rid of him, either via automation or by selecting someone with lesser ability. If you can't use him and you can't get rid of him, you will have a motivation problem.

ABRAHAM MASLOW
HUMAN NEEDS AND WORK ....

. . . The only happy people I know are the ones who are working well at something they consider important. . . . this [is] universal truth for all my self-actualizing subjects. They [are] metamotivated by meta-needs . . . expressed in their devotion to, dedication to, and identification with some great and important job. This was true for every single case. . . .

. . . S-A [self-actualizing] work transcends the self without trying to, and achieves the kind of loss of self-awareness and self-consciousness that the easterners, the Japanese and Chinese and so on, keep on trying to attain. S-A work is simultaneously a seeking and fulfilling of the self *and* also an achieving of the selflessness which is the ultimate expression of *real* self. It resolves the dichotomy between selfish and unselfish. Also between inner and outer—because the cause for which one works in S-A work is introjected and becomes part of the self so that the world and the self are no longer different. The inner and the outer world fuse and become one and the same. The same is true for the subject-object dichotomy. . . .

If you take into yourself something important from the world, then you yourself become important thereby. You have made yourself important thereby, as important as that which you have introjected and assimilated to yourself. At once, it matters if you die, or if you are sick, or if you can't work, etc. Then you must take care of yourself, you must respect yourself, you have to get plenty of rest, not smoke or drink too much, etc. You can no longer commit suicide—that would be too selfish. It would be a loss for the world. You are needed, useful. This is the easiest way to feel needed. Mothers with babies do not commit suicide as easily as nonmothers. People in the concentration camps who had some important mission in life, some duty to live for or some other people to live for tended to stay alive. It was the other ones who gave up and sank into apathy and died without resistance. . . .

. . . If work is introjected into the self (I guess it always is, more or less, even when one tries to prevent it), then the relationship between self-esteem and work is closer than I had thought. Especially healthy and stable self-esteem (the feeling of worth, pride, influence, importance, etc.) rests on good, worthy work to be introjected, thereby becoming part of the self. Maybe more of our contemporary malaise is due to introjection of nonprideful, robotized, broken-down-into-easy-bits kind of work than I had thought. The more I think about it, the more difficult I find it to *conceive* of feeling proud of myself, self-loving and self-respecting, if I were working, for example, in some chewing gum factory, or a phony advertising agency, or in some factory that turned out shoddy furniture. I've written so far of "real achievement" as a basis for solid self-esteem, but I guess this is too general and needs more spelling out. Real achievement means inevitably a worthy and virtuous task. To do some idiotic job very well is certainly *not* real achievement. I like my phrasing, "What is not worth doing is not worth doing well." . . .

NOTES ON SYNERGY

Social synergy as used first by Ruth Benedict to apply to the degree of health of the primitive culture she was studying meant essentially that a synergic institution was one that arranged it so that a person pursuing his selfish ends was automatically helping other people thereby, and that a person trying to be altruistic and helping other people and being unselfish, was also automatically and willy-nilly helping along his own selfish advantages. That is to say, it was a resolution of the dichotomy between selfishness and unselfishness, showing very clearly that the opposition of selfishness and unselfishness or their mutual exclusiveness was a function of a poorly developed culture. I have shown this to be true within the individual in about the same way, winding up with the statement that where selfishness and unselfishness are mutually exclusive, this is a sign of mild psychopathology within the individual.

Self-actualizing people rise above the dichotomy between selfishness and unselfishness, and this can be shown in various ways. One is that they get pleasure from the pleasures of other people. That is, they get selfish pleasures from the pleasures of other people, which is a way of saying unselfish. The example that I used a long time ago can serve here—if I get more pleasure out of feeding my strawberries into the mouth of my little beloved child, who loves strawberries, and who smacks her lips over them, and if I thereby have a wonderful time and enjoy myself watching her eat the strawberries, which would certainly give me pleasure if I myself ate them, then what shall I say about the selfishness or the unselfishness of this act? Am I sacrificing something? Am I being altruistic? Am I being selfish, because after all I'm enjoying myself? Obviously, the best way to say this is that the words "selfish" and "unselfish" as opposites, as mutually exclusive, have become meaningless. The two words have fused together. My action is neither selfish exclusively nor unselfish exclusively, or it can be said to be both selfish and unselfish simultaneously. Or, as I prefer the more sophisticated way of saying it, the action is synergic. That is, what is good for my child is good for me, what is good for me is good for the child, what gives the child pleasure gives me pleasure, what gives me pleasure gives the child pleasure, and all the lines of difference fall and we can say now that these two persons are identified and in certain functional theoretical ways have become a single unit. Very often this is so. We learn to treat a loving wife and husband as a single unit; an insult to the one is an insult to the other, shoes on the feet of one make the other's feet feel good, etc., etc.

This happens to be also a pretty decent definition of love, namely, that the two separate sets of needs become fused into a single set of needs for the new unit. Or love exists when the happiness of the other makes me happy, or when I enjoy the self-actualization of the other as much as I do my own, or when the differentiation between the word "other" and the words "my own" has disappeared. Where there is mutual property, where the words change into "we," "us," "ours." Another definition of love is that happiness of the other is the condition of my own happiness. Synergy is the same kind of thing, and it involves a kind of love-identification. One might say it means in certain respects different people can be treated as if they were not different, as if they were one, as if they were pooled, or lumped, or fused into a new kind of unit which was superordinate and included them both, fusing their separateness. . . .

ON LOW GRUMBLES, HIGH GRUMBLES, AND METAGRUMBLES

. . . People can live at various levels in the motivation hierarchy, that is, they can live a high life or a low life, they can live barely at the level of survival in the jungle, or they can live in an eupsychian society* with good fortune and with all the basic needs taken care of so that they can live at a higher level and think about the nature of poetry or mathematics or that kind of thing.

There are various ways of judging the motivational level of life. For instance, one can judge the level at which people live by the kind of humor that they laugh at. The person living at the lowest need levels is apt to find hostile and cruel humor very amusing, e.g., the old lady who is getting bitten by a dog or the town moron who is being plagued by the other children, etc. The Abraham Lincoln type of humor—the philosophical, educational type of humor—brings a smile rather than a belly laugh; it has little to do with hostility or conquest. This higher type of humor cannot be understood at all by the person living at the lower need levels. . . .

*[Ed. note: An "eupsychian society" (pronounced *yew-'sig-key-an*) is Maslow's speculative description of a Utopia in which all people are psychologically well-balanced and healthy.]

In the same way it was my thought that the level of complaints—which is to say, the level of what one needs and craves and wishes for—can be an indicator of the motivational level at which the person is living; and if the level of complaints is studied in the industrial situation, it can be used also as a measure of the level of health of the whole organization, especially if one has a large enough sampling.

For instance, take the workers living in the authoritarian jungle industrial situation in which fear and want and even simple starvation are a real possibility, and determine the choice of job and the way in which bosses will behave and the submissiveness with which workers will accept cruelty, etc., etc. Such workers who have complaints or grumbles are apt to be falling short of basic needs which are low in the hierarchy. At this lowest level this means complaints about cold and wet and danger to life and fatigue and poor shelter and all of these basic biological necessities.

Certainly, in the modern industrial situation, if one runs across complaints of this sort, then this is an indication of extremely poor management and an extremely low level of living in the organization. In even average industrial situations, this kind of complaint, this sort of low grumble hardly ever comes up. On the positive side, that is, those complaints which represent a wish or craving out ahead of what is now available—these are at this same low level approximately. That is, the worker in Mexico might be making positive grumbles at the security and safety level, at such things as being fired arbitrarily, of not being able to plan his family budget because he does not know how long the job will last. He may complain about a total lack of job security, about the arbitrariness of the foreman, about the kinds of indignities that he has to take in order to keep his job, etc. I think we can call low grumbles those grumbles which come at the biological and at the safety level, perhaps, also, at the level of gregariousness and belonging to the informal, sociable group.

The higher-need levels would be mostly at the level of esteem and self-esteem, where questions would be involved of dignity, of autonomy, of self-respect, of respect from the other; feelings of worth, of getting praise and rewards and credit for one's accomplishments and the like. Grumbles at this level would probably be mostly about something that involved loss of dignity or the threat to self-esteem or to prestige. Now, so far as the metagrumbles are concerned, what I have in mind here are the metamotivations which hold in the self-actualizing life. . . . These metaneeds for perfection, for justice, for beauty, for truth, and the like also show themselves in the industrial situation where there might very well be complaints about inefficiency (even when this does not affect the pocket of the complainer). In effect, then, he is making a statement about the imperfection of the world in which he lives (again not a selfish complaint but an impersonal and altruistic philosopher's complaint, one might almost call it). Or he might complain about not being given the full truth, all the facts, or about other blocks in the free flow of communications.

This preference for truth and honesty and all the facts again is one of the metaneeds rather than one of the "basic" needs, and people who have the luxury of complaining at this level are strictly living a very high-level life. In the society which is cynical, which is run by thieves or by tyrants or by nasty people, one would get no such complaints as this—the complaints would be at a lower level. Complaints about justice are also metagrumbles, and I see plenty of them in the protocols from the workers in a well-managed place. They are apt to complain about an injustice even where it is to their personal financial advantage. Another kind of metagrumble is the complaint about a virtue not being rewarded, and about villainy getting these rewards, i.e., a failure of justice.

In other words, everything above implies very strongly that human beings will always complain. There is no Garden of Eden, there is no paradise, there is no heaven except for a passing moment or two. Whatever satisfactions are given to human beings, it is inconceivable that they should be perfectly content with these. This in itself would be a negation of the highest reaches of human nature because it would imply that no improvements could be made after this point—and this, of course, is nonsense. We cannot conceive of a million years of further development bringing such a perfection to pass. Human beings will always be able to tuck in under their belts whatever gratifications, whatever blessings, whatever good fortune are available. They'll be absolutely delighted with these blessings for a little while. And then, as soon as they get used to them, they'll forget about them and start reaching out into the future for still higher blessings, as they restlessly perceive how things could be even more perfect than they are at this moment. This looks to me like an eternal process going on into the future forever. . . .

MELVIN L. KOHN
JOB COMPLEXITY AND ADULT PERSONALITY ....

There have been several distinct approaches to the study of work, each of them emphasizing some aspect that bears on a particular theoretical concern of the investigator. Rarely, though, has that concern been the effect of work on personality. Sociologists have learned much about social stratification and mobility, for example, by focusing on the dimension of work most pertinent to the stratificational system, the status of the job (Blau and Duncan, 1967; Duncan, Featherman, and Duncan, 1972; Sewell, Hauser, and Featherman, 1976). But however important status may be for studies of mobility, it would

Melvin L. Kohn, "Job Complexity and Adult Personality," in N. J. Smelzer and E. H. Erickson (eds.), *Themes of Work and Love in Adulthood* (Cambridge, Mass.: Harvard University Press, 1980). Reprinted by permission of the publisher.

be unwise to assume—as is often done—that the status of a job is equally pertinent for personality. In terms of impact on personality, job status serves mainly as a gross indicator of the job's location in the hierarchical organization of the economic and social system. The status of the job is closely linked to such structural conditions of work as how complex it is, how closely it is supervised, and what sorts of pressures it entails. It is these structural realities, not status as such, that affect personality (Kohn and Schooler, 1973).

It is also indisputable that economists have learned much about the functioning of the economic system by focusing on the extrinsic rewards the job confers—in particular, income. Just as with occupational status, though, it would be incorrect to assume that because income is important for an understanding of the economic system qua system, income is also the most significant aspect of the job in terms of the meaning of work to the worker or the impact on work of his sense of self and orientation to the rest of the world (Whyte, 1955; Kohn and Schooler, 1973).

Organizational theorists, both the Weberian sociologists and those more applied scholars who call themselves administrative scientists, have, by studying formal organizational structure, undoubtedly contributed much to our understanding of how organizations function (Blau and Schoenherr, 1971). But the very strength of their approach—its systematic attention to how formal organizations function as systems, regardless of the personalities of those who play the various organizational roles—means that they largely ignore the effect of organizational structure on the individual worker and his work. When they do pay attention to the individual worker, their interest rarely goes beyond his role as worker.

The human-relations-in-industry approach, in deliberate juxtaposition to the formal organizational approach, focuses on informal, interpersonal relationships and the symbolic systems that emerge out of such relationships (Whyte, 1961; 1969). Scholars using this approach supply a needed corrective to the formal organizational perspective. But they sometimes seem unaware that people not only relate to one another on the job; they also work. Moreover, this perspective has been concerned almost exclusively with the implications of work for on-the-job behavior, paying little attention to the effects of the job on other realms of life.

Occupational psychologists come close to understanding the relationship between work and personality, but there are two major limitations to their studies. First, many of them misinterpret Kurt Lewin (and, I would add, W. I. Thomas) by dealing exclusively with how people perceive their work while neglecting the actual conditions under which that work is performed. (This criticism applies as well to most sociological studies of alienation in work.) Thus, they measure boredom rather than routinization, interest in the work rather than its substantive complexity, and "alienation in work" rather than actual working conditions. Such an approach ignores the possibilities that there can be a gap between the conditions to which a person is subjected and his awareness of those conditions; that the existence or nonexistence of such a gap is itself problematic and may be structurally determined; and that conditions felt by the worker to be benign can have deleterious consequences, while conditions felt to be onerous can have beneficial consequences. The second limitation is the preoccupation of most occupational psychologists with job satisfaction, as if this were the only psychological consequence of work. I am less disturbed by the technical difficulties in measuring job satisfaction—a notoriously slippery concept—than I am by the assumption that work has no psychological ramifications beyond the time and place during and within which it occurs. Work affects people's values, self-conceptions, orientation to social reality, even their intellectual functioning. Job satisfaction is only one, and far from the most important, psychological consequence of work.

The research that comes closest of all to dealing straightforwardly with work and its consequences for personality employs an old tradition of sociological study—case studies of occupations. Practitioners of this art have sometimes done a magnificent job of depicting the reality of work as it impinges on the worker. Unfortunately, though, their studies cannot determine which aspects of work are most pertinent for which aspects of psychological functioning. W. Fred Cottrell's (1940) classic study of railroaders, for example, pointed out a multitude of ways that the job conditions of men who operate trains differ from those of men in many other occupations—including the unpredictability of working hours, geographical mobility, precision of timing, outsider status in the home community, and unusual recruitment and promotion practices. Since all these conditions are tied together in one occupational package, it is not possible to disentangle the psychological concomitants of each. . . .

DISENTANGLING OCCUPATIONAL CONDITIONS

Disentangling occupational conditions to assess their psychological impact requires a mode of research different from that employed in studies of particular occupations and particular industries. Carmi Schooler and I have dealt with the problem of shifting the focus from named occupations—carpenter, surgeon, or flight engineer—to dimensions of occupation (Kohn, 1969; Kohn and Schooler, 1969; 1973). Our strategy has been to secure a large and representative sample of employed men, who necessarily work in many occupations and many industries. [1] We have inventoried the men's job conditions and then differentiated the psychological concomitants of each facet of occupation by statistical analysis. In our most recent research, my colleagues and I have done comparable analyses for employed women (Miller et al., 1979).

Even though occupational conditions are intercorrelated, they are not perfectly intercorrelated. Thus, substantively complex jobs are likely also to be time-pressured; but there are enough jobs that are substantively complex yet not time-pressured, and enough that are substantively simple yet time-pressured, for us to examine the relationship between substantive complexity and, say, receptiveness or resistance to change, while statistically controlling time pressure. We can also look for statistical interaction between the two, asking whether the impact of substantive complexity on, let us say, stance toward change is different for men who are more time-pressured and for men who are less time-pressured. And, at the same time, we can statistically control many other occupational conditions, as well as important nonoccupational variables, for example, education, which usually precedes and is often a prerequisite for the job.

In all, we have indexed more than fifty separable dimensions of occupation, including such diverse aspects of work experience as the substantive complexity of work, the routinization or diversity of the flow of work, relationships with co-workers and with supervisors, pace of work and control thereof, physical and environmental conditions, job pressures and uncertainties, union membership and participation, bureaucratization, job protections, and fringe benefits. (For complete information, see Kohn, 1969, pp. 236, 244–253.) These indices provide the basis for a broad descriptive picture of the principal facets of occupations, as experienced by men in all types of industries and at all levels of the civilian economy. . . .

We found that nearly all of the more than fifty occupational conditions that we had inventoried are correlated with at least some of the several aspects of values, self-conception, social orientation, and intellectual functioning that we had measured (Kohn and Schooler, 1973).[2] But most of these statistical relationships reflect the interrelatedness of occupational conditions with one another and with education. Only twelve of the occupational conditions we studied appear to have any substantial relationship to men's psychological functioning when education and all other pertinent occupational conditions are statistically controlled. Few though they are, these twelve occupational conditions are sufficient to define the "structural imperatives of the job," in that they identify a man's position in the organizational structure, his opportunities for occupational self-direction, the principal job pressures to which he is subject, and the principal uncertainties built into his job.[3] These job conditions are "structural" in two senses: they are built into the structure of the job and they are largely determined by the job's location in the structures of the economy and the society.

SUBSTANTIVE COMPLEXITY

Because of its theoretical and empirical importance, I devote the remainder of this essay to one of the twelve structural imperatives of the job, the substantive complexity of work.[4] By the substantive complexity of work, I mean the degree to which the work, in its very substance, requires thought and independent judgment. Substantively complex work by its very nature requires making many decisions that must take into account ill-defined or apparently conflicting contingencies. Although, in general, work with data or with people is likely to be more complex than work with things, this is not always the case, and an index of the overall complexity of work should reflect its degree of complexity in each of these three types of activity. Work with things can vary in complexity from ditch digging to sculpting; similarly, work with people can vary in complexity from receiving simple directions or orders to giving legal advice; and work with data can vary from reading instructions to synthesizing abstract conceptual systems. Thus, the index of substantive complexity that we have generally employed is based on the degree of complexity of the person's work with things, with data, and with people; our appraisal of the overall complexity of his work, regardless of whether he works primarily with things, with data, or with people; and estimates of the amount of time he spends working at each type of activity (Kohn and Schooler, 1973; Kohn, 1976). The several components receive weightings based on a factor analysis.[5]

I focus on substantive complexity for two reasons. The first is that I conceive substantive complexity to be central to the experience of work. The other structural imperatives of the job—even closeness of supervision and routinization—set the conditions under which work is done but they do not characterize the work itself. The substantive complexity of work, by contrast, is at the heart of the experience of work. More than any other occupational condition, it gives meaning to this experience.

The second reason for my preoccupation with substantive complexity is empirical. Our analyses show that substantive complexity of work is strongly related to a wide range of psychological variables. The substantive complexity of work is of course correlated with job satisfaction and with occupational commitment. It also bears on many facets of off-the-job psychological functioning, ranging from valuation of self-direction to self-esteem to authoritarian conservatism to intellectual flexibility. It is even related to the intellectual demands of men's leisure-time pursuits. Moreover, these correlations remain statistically significant and large enough to be meaningful even when education and all other pertinent dimensions of occupation are statistically controlled. Thus, the substantive complexity of work has a strong, independent relationship to many facets of psychological functioning, a relationship stronger than that of any other dimension of occupation we have studied. This is true for men, and our most recent analyses show it to be equally true for employed women (Miller et al., 1979).

THE DIRECTION OF CAUSAL EFFECTS

There is evidence that the substantive complexity of work is not only correlated with, but has a causal impact on, psychological functioning. The evidence of causal directionality is of two types. The more extensive but less definitive evidence comes from our analyses of cross-sectional data, derived from a large sample of men employed in civilian occupations. Social scientists have long recognized that one cannot make inferences about the direction of causal effects from cross-sectional data unless some of the described phenomena clearly preceded others in their time of occurrence. But where one can realistically assume reciprocity—that *a* affects *b* and *b* also affects *a*—it is possible to assess the magnitude of these reciprocal effects, using econometric techniques for solving simultaneous equations. The simplest of these, which we used, is called two-stage least squares.[6] With this technique, we have assessed the relationships between the substantive complexity of work and many facets of psychological functioning: occupational commitment, job satisfaction, valuation of self-direction or of conformity to external authority, anxiety, self-esteem, receptiveness or resistance to change, standards of morality, authoritarian conservatism, intellectual flexibility, the intellectuality of leisure-time activities, and three types of alienation—powerlessness, self-estrangement, and normlessness.

Our findings indicate that the substantive complexity of men's work affects all these facets of psychological functioning, independent of the selection processes that draw men into particular fields of work and independent of their efforts to mold their jobs to fit their needs, values, and capacities. Moreover, the substantive complexity of work in every instance affects psychological functioning more—often, much more—than the particular facet of psychological functioning affects the substantive complexity of work. This evidence is not definitive—only longitudinal studies can provide definitive evidence—but it does establish a strong prima facie case that the substantive complexity of work has a real and meaningful effect on a wide range of psychological phenomena.

More definitive, albeit less extensive, evidence comes from a follow-up study we conducted with a representative subsample of men in the original study ten years after the initial survey (Kohn and Schooler, 1978). Analyses of longitudinal data require the development of "measurement models". . . . These models permit us to take into account that errors in the measurement of any indicator at the time of the initial survey may well be correlated with errors in the measurement of that same indicator at the time of the follow-up survey. Disregarding such correlated errors in the indicators might make the underlying concept seem more stable or less stable than it really is—thereby distorting any causal analysis in which the index is employed.

We have thus far constructed measurement models for the substantive complexity of work and for one facet of psychological functioning—intellectual flexibility. We choose intellectual flexibility as the first aspect of psychological functioning to be assessed because it offers us the greatest challenge—intellectual flexibility obviously affects recruitment into substantively complex jobs, and there is every reason to expect it to be resistant to change. Still, intellectual flexibility—though not much studied by sociologists—is so important a part of psychological functioning that we must not unthinkingly assume it to be entirely the product of genetics and early life experience. Rather, we should empirically test the possibility that intellectual flexibility may be responsive to adult occupational experience.

Our index of intellectual flexibility is meant to reflect men's actual intellectual performance in the interview situation. We used a variety of indicators—including the men's answers to seemingly simple but highly revealing cognitive problems, their handling of perceptual and projective tests, their propensity to agree when asked "agree-disagree" questions, and the impression they made on the interviewer during a long session that required a great deal of thought and reflection. None of these indicators is believed to be completely valid; but we do believe that all the indicators reflect, to some substantial degree, men's flexibility in coping with an intellectually demanding situation.

The stability of intellectual flexibility, thus measured, is remarkably high over time: The correlation between men's intellectual flexibility at the time of the original study and their intellectual flexibility ten years later, shorn of measurement error, is 0.93. It would be erroneous to assume, though, that the high over-time stability of intellectual flexibility means that it is unaffected by adult experience; it might even be that this stability reflects unchanging life circumstances. In fact, we find that the effect of the substantive complexity of work on intellectual flexibility is striking—on the order of one-fourth as great as that of the men's ten-year-earlier levels of intellectual flexibility. This effect is essentially contemporaneous: The path from the substantive complexity of the job held at the time of the initial survey to intellectual flexibility at the time of the follow-up survey ten years later is small and statistically nonsignificant, while the path from the substantive complexity of the current job to current intellectual flexibility is much more substantial and is statistically significant.[7]

The reciprocal effect of intellectual flexibility on substantive complexity is still more impressive than the effect of substantive complexity on intellectual flexibility. This effect is entirely lagged, that is, it is the men's intellectual flexibility at the time of the initial survey that significantly affects the substantive complexity of their current jobs, and not their current intellectual flexibility. The longitudinal analysis thus demonstrates something that no cross-sectional analysis could show—that, over time, the relationship between substantive complexity and intellectual flexibility is truly reciprocal. The effect of substantive complexity on intellectual flexibility is more immediate: current job demands affect current thinking processes. Intellectual flexibility, by contrast, has a time-lagged effect on substantive complexity: current intellectual flexibility has scant effect on current job demands, but considerable effect on the future course of one's career. Cross-sectional analyses portray only part of this process, making it seem that the relationship between the substantive complexity of work and intellectual functioning were mainly unidirectional, with work affecting intellectual functioning but not the reverse. Longitudinal analysis portrays a more intricate and more interesting, truly reciprocal process.

The data thus demonstrate, beyond reasonable doubt, what heretofore could be stated only as a plausible thesis buttressed by presumptive evidence—

that the substantive complexity of work both considerably affects, and is considerably affected by, intellectual flexibility.

My colleagues and I have recently completed two further analyses that extend these conclusions. A much more extensive longitudinal analysis of job conditions and intellectual flexibility (Kohn and Schooler, in press) confirms that the substantive complexity of work affects intellectual flexibility not only when prior levels of intellectual flexibility and pertinent aspects of social background are taken into account but also when all other structural imperatives of the job are taken into account as well. We further find that substantive complexity is not the only job condition that affects intellectual flexibility; several other job conditions that stimulate and challenge the individual are conducive to intellectual flexibility. But, clearly, substantive complexity plays a key role, not only because it has such a great effect on intellectual flexibility, but also because it provides the principal mechanism through which other job conditions affect intellectual functioning.

In another analysis (Miller et al., 1979), we found that the substantive complexity of work is as important for women's psychological functioning as it is for men's. In particular, a causal analysis using measurement models similar to those described above, but limited to cross-sectional data, shows the contemporaneous effect of substantive complexity on intellectual flexibility to be at least as great for employed women as for employed men.

These findings come down solidly in support of those who hold that occupational conditions affect personality and in opposition to those who believe that the relationship between occupational conditions and personality results solely from selective recruitment and job molding. Admittedly, personality has great importance in determining who go into what types of jobs and how they perform those jobs; in fact, our analyses underline the importance of these processes. But that has never been seriously at issue. What has been disputed is whether the reverse phenomenon—of job conditions molding personality—also occurs. The evidence of our longitudinal analysis supports the position that it does occur.

In particular, this analysis adds to and helps specify the growing evidence that the structure of the environment has an important effect on cognitive development (Rosenbaum, 1976) and that cognitive processes do not become impervious to environmental influence after adolescence or early adulthood but continue to show "plasticity" throughout the life span (Baltes, 1968; Horn and Donaldson, 1976; Baltes and Schaie, 1976). Our findings reinforce this conclusion by showing that intellectual flexibility continues to be responsive to experience well into midcareer. In fact, it appears that the remarkable stability of intellectual flexibility reflects, at least in part, stability in people's life circumstances. Intellectual flexibility is ever responsive to changes in the substantive complexity of people's work; for most people, though, the substantive complexity of work does not fluctuate markedly.

This analysis demonstrates as well the importance of intellectual flexibility for substantive complexity. I think it noteworthy that this effect appears to be lagged rather than contemporaneous. The implication is that the structure of most jobs does not permit any considerable variation in the substantive complexity of the work: job conditions are not readily modified to suit the needs or capacities of the individual worker. But over a long enough time—certainly over a period as long as ten years—many men either modify their jobs or move on to other jobs more consonant with their intellectual functioning. Thus, the long-term effects of intellectual flexibility on substantive complexity are considerable, even though the contemporaneous effects appear to be negligible.

Our models, of course, deal mainly with the events of midcareer or later. I think it reasonable to assume that men's intellectual flexibility in childhood, adolescence, and early adulthood have had a considerable effect on their educational attainments, and our data show that educational attainment is very important for the substantive complexity of the early jobs in men's careers. Since the substantive complexity of early jobs is a primary determinant of the substantive complexity of later jobs, it seems safe to infer that intellectual flexibility's long-term, indirect effects on the substantive complexity of later jobs has been even greater than our analysis depicts.

The reciprocal relationship between substantive complexity and intellectual flexibility implies an internal dynamic by which relatively small differences in substantive complexity at early stages of a career may become magnified into larger differences in both substantive complexity and intellectual flexibility later in the career. If two men of equivalent intellectual flexibility were to start their careers in jobs differing in substantive complexity, the man in the more complex job would be likely to outstrip the other in further intellectual growth. This, in time, might lead to his attaining jobs of greater complexity, further affecting his intellectual growth. Meantime, the man in the less complex job would develop intellectually at a slower pace, perhaps not at all, and in the extreme case might even decline in his intellectual functioning. As a result, small differences in the substantive complexity of early jobs might lead to increasing differences in intellectual development. . . .[8]

Our studies have led me to conclude that the intrinsic meaning and psychological impact of a job result not just from the status or income or interpersonal relationships that the job provides but also—and especially—from the meaningful challenges the work itself poses (or fails to pose). The most important challenge is that of mastering complex tasks, that is, the substantive complexity of the work. Our data indicate that substantive complexity affects people's psychological functioning regardless of their needs, values, and personal capacities and regardless of their social class (but, of course, the type of work one does is intimately related to one's social class; so, too, are one's values). What matters most about work, in short, is not any of its attendant rewards or social experiences, but the work itself.

Moreover, the relationship between work and psychological functioning is quintessentially reciprocal. There is an ongoing process, throughout all of adult life, whereby the occupational conditions encountered by the individual both mold his psychological processes and in turn are molded by his personality and behavior. No theory of adult personality development that fails to take account of the ongoing effects of occupational (and, presumably, other social) conditions can be regarded as realistic. By the same token, no social psychology of occupations that fails to take account of the ongoing effects of individual psychological functioning can be regarded as realistic.

NOTES

[1] Our primary source of data is a sample survey of 3,101 men, representative of all men employed in civilian occupations in the United States. These men were interviewed for us by the National Opinion Research Center (NORC) in the spring and summer of 1964. For more detailed information on sample and research design, see Kohn, 1969, pp. 235–264. In 1974 NORC reinterviewed a representative subsample of these men for us; this time, the wives (and, where applicable, one of the children) were interviewed, too. For detailed information on the follow-up study, see Kohn and Schooler (1978) and Kohn (1977).

[2] Our principal indices of psychological functioning measure subjective reactions to the job itself (that is, job satisfaction and occupational commitment), valuation of self-direction or of conformity to external authority (both for oneself and for one's children), self-conception (self-confidence, self-deprecation, fatalism, anxiety, and idea conformity), social orientation (authoritarian conservatism, criteria of morality, trustfulness, and receptiveness or resistance to change), alienation (powerlessness, self-estrangement, and normlessness), and intellectual functioning (intellectual flexibility, intellectuality of leisure-time activities). For detailed information about our definitions of these concepts and our methods of indexing them, see Kohn, 1969, pp. 47–58, 73–84, 265–269; Kohn and Schooler, 1973, pp. 99–101; Kohn, 1976, pp. 114–118.

[3] Specifically, these twelve crucial occupational conditions are: (1) ownership/nonownership; (2) bureaucratization; (3) position in the supervisory hierarchy; (4) closeness of supervision; (5) routinization of the work; (6) substantive complexity of the work; (7) frequency of time-pressure; (8) heaviness of work; (9) dirtiness of work; (10) the likelihood, in this field, of there occurring a sudden and dramatic change in a person's income, reputation, or position; (11) the probability, in this line of work, of being held responsible for things outside one's control; and (12) the risk of loss of one's job or business.

[4] The concept "substantive complexity" has been the subject of much research that goes considerably beyond the issues addressed in this essay. Many writers have adopted the concept and used it for such diverse purposes as reinterpreting the status-attainment model (Spaeth, 1976), proposing a new method of classifying the occupational structure of the U.S. economy (Temme, 1975), reassessing the psychological effects of complex role sets (Coser, 1975), interpreting the effects of fathers' occupational experiences on their sons' occupational choices (Mortimer, 1974; 1976), and searching out the sources of powerlessness (Tudor, 1972).

[5] To validate this index, which is specifically tailored to each respondent's description of his own job, we have compared it to assessments of the average level of complexity of work with things, with data, and with people for the entire occupation,

made by trained occupational analysts for the *Dictionary of Occupational Titles* (United States Department of Labor, 1965). The multiple correlation between our index of substantive complexity and the independently coded *Dictionary* ratings is 0.78 sufficiently high to assure us that our appraisals of substantive complexity accurately reflect the reality of people's work.

[6] The two-stage least squares technique is described in detail by Kohn and Schooler (1973) and the references cited therein. This method attempts to "purge" each variable of the effects of all others with which it is reciprocally related by estimating from other pertinent data what each individual's score on that variable would have been if the other variables had not had an opportunity to affect it. These estimated scores are then used as independent variables in the (second stage) multiple-regression equations.

[7] Concretely, the time-lagged path (that is, from substantive complexity in 1964 to intellectual flexibility in 1974) is 0.05 and the contemporaneous path is 0.18. A path of 0.18 might not under ordinary circumstances be considered striking; but a continuing effect of this magnitude on so stable a phenomenon as intellectual flexibility is impressive, because the cumulative impact will be much greater than the immediate effect at any one time. Continuing effects, even small-to-moderate continuing effects, on highly stable phenomena become magnified in importance. The effect of the substantive complexity of work on intellectual flexibility is especially noteworthy when we take into account that we are dealing with men who are at least ten years into their occupational careers.

[8] Such evidence as we have from other countries is based on only approximate indices of substantive complexity. This evidence suggests that substantive complexity has psychological effects similar to those we have found in the United States, in West Germany (Hoff and Grueneisen, 1977a), in Italy (Pearlin, 1971; Kohn, 1969), in Ireland (Hynes, 1977), and in Peru (Scurrah and Montalvo, 1975), but probably not in Taiwan (Olsen, 1971). For a detailed discussion of these findings, see Kohn (1977). More definitive information may come from studies now being undertaken in Poland by Kazimierz Slomczynski, Jadwiga Koralewicz-Zebik, and Krystyna Janicka, and in West Berlin by Wolfgang Lempert, which use more precise indices of substantive complexity.

REFERENCES

Baltes, Paul B. 1968. Longitudinal and cross-sectional sequences in the study of age and generation effects. *Human Development*, 11:145–171.

Baltes, Paul B., and K. Warner Schaie. 1976. On the plasticity of intelligence in adulthood and old age. *American Psychologist*, 31:720–725.

Blau, Peter M., and Otis Duncan. 1967. *The American occupational structure*. New York: Wiley.

Blau, Peter M., and Richard A. Schoenherr. 1971. *The structure of organizations*. New York: Basic Books.

Blauner, Robert. 1964. *Alienation and freedom: the factory worker and his industry*. Chicago: University of Chicago Press.

Breer, Paul E., and Edwin A. Locke. 1965. *Task experience as a source of attitudes*. Homewood, Ill.: Dorsey.

Coser, Rose Laub. 1975. The complexity of roles as a seedbed of individual autonomy. In *The idea of social structure: papers in honor of Robert K. Merton,* ed. L. A. Coser. New York: Harcourt Brace Jovanovich.

Cottrell, W. Fred. 1940. *The railroader.* Stanford: Stanford University Press.

Duncan, Otis D., David L. Featherman, and Beverly Duncan. 1972. *Socioeconomic background and achievement.* New York: Seminar Press.

Hoff, Ernst-Hartmut, and Veronika Grueneisen. 1977a. Arbeitserfahrungen, Erziehungseinstellungen und Erziehungsverhalten von Eltern. In *Familiare Sozialisation: Probleme, Ergebnisse, Perspektiven,* ed. H. Lukesch and K. Schneewind. Stuttgart: Klett.

―――. 1977b. Personal communication (unpublished data).

Horn, John L., and Gary Donaldson. 1976. On the myth of intellectual decline in adulthood. *American Psychologist,* 31:701–719.

Hynes, Eugene. 1977. Personal communication (unpublished data).

Jöreskog, Karl G. 1969. A general approach to confirmatory maximum likelihood factor analysis. *Psychometrika,* 34:183–202.

Kohn, Melvin L. 1977. Reassessment, 1977. In *Class and conformity: a study in values.* 2nd ed. Chicago: University of Chicago Press.

―――. 1976. Occupational structure and alienation. *American Journal of Sociology* 82:111–130.

―――. 1969. *Class and conformity: a study in values.* Homewood, Ill.: Dorsey. (2nd ed., Chicago: University of Chicago Press, 1977.)

Kohn, Melvin L., and Carmi Schooler. In press. Job conditions and intellectual flexibility: a longitudinal assessment of their reciprocal effects. In *Factor analysis and measurement in sociological research: a multi-dimensional perspective,* ed. E. F. Borgatta and D. J. Jackson. Beverly Hills: Sage Publications.

―――. 1978. The reciprocal effects of the substantive complexity of work and intellectual flexibility: a longitudinal assessment. *American Journal of Sociology,* 84:24–52.

―――. 1973. Occupational experience and psychological functioning: an assessment of reciprocal effects. *American Sociological Review,* 38:97–118.

―――. 1969. Class, occupation, and orientation. *American Sociological Review,* 34:659–678.

Miller, Joanne, Carmi Schooler, Melvin L. Kohn, and Karen A. Miller. 1979. Women and work: the psychological effects of occupational conditions. *American Journal of Sociology,* 85:66–94.

Mortimer, Jeylan T. 1976. Social class, work, and the family: some implications of the father's occupation for familial relationships and sons' career decisions. *Journal of Marriage and the Family,* 38:241–256.

―――. 1974. Patterns of intergenerational occupational movements: a smallest-space analysis. *American Journal of Sociology,* 79:1278–1299.

Olsen, Stephen. 1971. Family, occupation, and values in a Chinese urban community. Ph.D. diss., Cornell University.

Pearlin, Leonard I. 1971. *Class context and family relations: a cross-national study.* Boston: Little, Brown.

Rosenbaum, James E. 1976. *Making inequality: the hidden curriculum of high school tracking.* New York: Wiley.

Scurrah, Martin J., and Abner Montalvo. 1975. *Clase social y valores en Peru.* Lima, Peru: Escuela de Administracion de Negocios Para Graduados.

Sewell, William H., Robert M. Hauser, and David L. Featherman, eds. 1976. *Schooling and achievement in American society*. New York: Academic Press.

Spaeth, Joe L. 1976. Cognitive complexity: a dimension underlying the socioeconomic achievement process. In *Schooling and achievement in American society*, ed. William H. Sewell, Robert M. Hauser, and David L. Featherman. New York: Academic Press.

Temme, Lloyd V. 1975. *Occupation: meanings and measures*. Washington, D.C.: Bureau of Social Science Research.

Tudor, Bill. 1972. A specification of relationships between job complexity and powerlessness. *American Sociological Review*, 37:596–604.

United States Department of Labor. 1965. *Dictionary of occupational titles*. Washington, D.C.: United States Government Printing Office. 3rd ed.

Whyte, William F. 1969. *Organizational behavior: theory and application*. Homewood, Ill.: Richard D. Irwin.

———. 1961. *Men at work*. Homewood, Ill.: Dorsey.

———. 1955. *Money and motivation: an analysis of incentives in industry*. New York: Harper.

Work and Well-Being

TASK FORCE TO THE SECRETARY OF H.E.W.

WORK AND HEALTH ....

WORK AND LONGEVITY

In an impressive 15-year study of aging, the strongest predictor of longevity was work satisfaction.[1] The second best predictor was overall "happiness." These two socio-psychological measures predicted longevity better than a rating by an examining physician of physical functioning, or a measure of the use of tobacco, or genetic inheritance. Controlling these other variables statistically did not alter the dominant role of work satisfaction.

Another link between work and longevity is provided by an examination of the Abkhasian people of the Soviet Union that was undertaken by anthropologist Sula Benet. In 1954, the last year for which figures are available, 2.5% of the Abkhasians were 90 years of age or older, compared with 0.1% of all Russians, and 0.4% of Americans. This society displays, along with other traditional societies, a close social system and the increasing prestige of Abkhasians with age. They also have, as some other societies do, healthy diets.

Work In America: Report of a Special Task Force to The Secretary of Health, Education and Welfare (Cambridge, Mass.: MIT Press, 1980). Reprinted by permission of the publisher.

But a major distinguishing characteristic is lifelong work. Abkhasians at the age of 100 or more still put in as much as 4 hours a day on their farms. Benet writes:

> Both the Soviet medical profession and the Abkhasians agree that their work habits have a great deal to do with their longevity. The doctors say that the way Abkhasians work helps the vital organs function optimally. The Abkhasians say, "without rest, a man cannot work; without work, the rest does not give you any benefit. . . ."

Why is job satisfaction perhaps one of the best ways of extending the length of life? Other factors are undoubtedly important—diet, exercise, medical care, and genetic inheritance. But research findings suggest that these factors may account for only about 25% of the risk factors in heart disease, the major cause of death. That is, if cholesterol, blood pressure, smoking, glucose level, serum uric acid, and so forth, were perfectly controlled, only about one-fourth of coronary heart disease could be controlled.[2] Although research on this problem has not led to conclusive answers, it appears that work role, work conditions, and other social factors may contribute heavily to this "unexplained" 75% of risk factors. As Harry Levinson writes, such a finding may be difficult to accept:

> Despite having learned the power of that which is not readily visible, physicians as a profession have not caught up altogether with other powerful non-visible, toxic agents, namely, feelings. It seems extremely difficult to grasp the idea that feelings are the primary participants of behavior and a major influence in health and sickness.[3]

HEART DISEASE

Given the fact that heart disease accounts for about half of all deaths, and that socio-psychological factors may account for much of the risk, the question has arisen—and has been treated at length: What factors in work are associated with a high risk of heart disease? Risk refers to above-average mortality and abnormal blood pressure, cholesterol, blood sugar, body weight, and the like.[4] The high risk factors that have been identified are as follows:

Job dissatisfaction, represented by tedious work, lack of recognition, poor relations with co-workers, and poor working conditions.[5]

Low self-esteem, in both white-collar and blue-collar workers, and particularly observed when jobs were lost by the closing of factories.[6]

Occupational stress, components of which include extraordinary work overloads, responsibility, and conflict or ambiguity in occupational roles. The effects of stress in relation to heart disease have been uncovered among professors,[7] among tax accountants as income tax deadlines approached,[8] and among medical students on the day before examinations.[9] The stress of work overload appears to result from the feeling that one does not have enough resources, time, or ability and, hence, may fail.[10] Responsibility, especially for other people rather than for things, has been pinpointed as a risk factor among managers, scientists, and engineers in NASA, as well as among executives.[11] Retrospective studies of heart disease patients also found this factor to be highly significant.[12] Certain occupations, such as air traffic control and railroad train dispatching, share the extraordinary stress of having to make life-and-death decisions minute after minute, with considerable tolls in heart mortality.[13] Stress was indicated in a variety of blue-collar and white-collar jobs,[14] as well as among several categories of practice in fields of medicine, dentistry, and law.[15]

Excessively rapid and continuous change in employment.[16]

Incongruity between job status and other aspects of life, such as having high educational attainment but low job status.[17]

Certain personality characteristics, in particular, excessive drive, aggressiveness, ambitiousness, competitiveness, and a sense of urgency about time.[18] This factor has been found to increase risk among blue-collar workers and NASA professionals.[19] Personality traits *alone* do not account for increased risk of heart disease, but the important point is that jobs affect personality, and certain kinds of jobs affect certain kinds of personalities differently. Moreover, there is no conclusive evidence that people with these personality characteristics select themselves into stressful positions and that, therefore, nothing can be done about their stress and its consequences.[20]

Lack of stability, security, and support in the job environment has been documented in several recent studies.[21] It has also been found that a low risk of heart disease occurs in situations where stability, security, and support were present among NASA professionals,[22] industrial workers,[23] and Japanese workers.[24]

WORK AND OTHER PHYSICAL ILLNESS

In addition to heart disease, several other illnesses have been found to be highly associated with occupational stress. The most convincing evidence pertains to peptic ulcers[25] and both arthritis[26] and rheumatoid arthritis.[27] Links also have been suggested for stroke and gout (a form of arthritis).

In uncovering the relationships between physical illness and work problems, investigators also note psychological effects as well. For example, in the study of individuals with high educational achievement but low job status, anger, irritation, anxiety, tiredness, depression, and low self-esteem were also found.[28] We turn now to a somewhat more detailed examination of the relationship between work and mental health. . . .

WORK AND MENTAL HEALTH

. . . "Mental health" is a broad concept. It can be narrowed if we say an individual is mentally healthy if he has a variety of sources of gratification; he is not self-centered, yet he understands and accepts his assets and limitations; he sets realistic goals; and he is a productive member of society and participates in the world around him.[29] In short, the mentally healthy person feels he is leading a rewarding life and esteems himself.

In studies such as those conducted by the University of Michigan's Institute for Social Research, a variety of mental health problems have been related to the absence of job satisfaction. These include: psychosomatic illnesses, low self-esteem, anxiety, worry, tension, and impaired interpersonal relations. The factors correlating with these problems seem to be: low status, little autonomy, rapid technological change, isolation on the job, role conflict, role ambiguity, responsibility for managing people, shift work, and threats to self-esteem inherent in the appraisal system.[30]

Other correlations, which have been established in numerous studies, are: low socio-economic status with high rates of psychiatric hospitalization and symptomatology; lengthy unemployment periods with high rates of suicide and psychiatric hospitalization; and a positive association between job satisfaction and mental health. These correlations, it should be noted, do not yield to unambiguous interpretation; occupation frequently cannot be isolated from such other variables as education and income. One exception appears to be the conclusive evidence of a causal link between physically hazardous conditions of work, as encountered by soldiers and mine workers, and symptoms of mental illness.[31]

It has also been found that workers in low-skilled and unskilled jobs have poorer mental health than do workers in skilled jobs. This is particularly true with respect to such indices of poor mental health as little satisfaction with life and job, but less so in relation to psychiatric signs and symptoms. The findings also show that workers in these low-level jobs adapt by limiting their aspirations and their expectations and that, in effect, the greatest mental health deficit suffered by these workers is lack of involvement in the job and, consequently, lack of self-fulfillment. . . .

Coping, or Adjustment Downward

Failure to adjust to other personalities and to one's environment as a definition of mental illness is to be rejected out of hand. An apathetic worker, for example, is not necessarily mentally ill. Where mobility is blocked, where jobs are dehumanized, where rewards are slight, failing to strive hard at the job can hardly be a criterion of mental illness. Madness may lie in adjusting to the pathologies of organizations.[32] A person who becomes an automaton in an automated factory or office may have adjusted perfectly, but he hardly enjoys good mental health.

The best description of coping through limiting one's aspirations comes from Eli Chinoy's classic study of automobile workers.[33] Many of these workers were found to have very few ambitions, even regarding the rather realistic goal of becoming a foreman. Their idea of a better job was merely one that was off the assembly-line but still in a low, blue-collar level in the same plant. Some may have fantasized about leaving the factory and opening their own gas stations, but they never took any realistic steps in this direction. Only in their hopes that their children would get white-collar jobs could one measure any strong expression of their aspirations. . . .

Special Means of Coping: Alcoholism, Drug Abuse, and Suicide

Alan McLean writes that "workers with personality disorders, including alcoholism and drug abuse, may find that their psychiatric disorders stem partially from job insecurity, unpleasant working conditions or hazardous work."[34] Although little quantitative research has been done to support this statement, many doctors and social scientists corroborate it from their own clinical observations. For example, stress has long been linked to alcoholism among executives. Our interviews with blue-collar workers in heavy industry revealed a number who found it necessary to drink large quantities of alcohol during their lunch to enable them to withstand the pressure or overwhelming boredom of their tasks.

Our interviews with younger workers on similar jobs uncovered a surprising amount of drug use on the job, particularly among assembly-line workers and long-haul truck drivers. A recent study by the New York Narcotics Addiction Control Commission showed that drug use varied significantly by type of occupation.[35] In another study, of a UAW local affiliated with a plant employing 3,400 people, 15% of the workers were estimated to be addicted to heroin.[36]

Like drug abuse, alcoholism probably has no single cause. However, several occupational risk factors appear to lead to excessive drinking.[37] Non-supportive jobs in which the worker gets little feedback on his performance appear to cause the kind of anxiety that may lead to or aggravate alcoholism. Work "addiction," occupational obsolescence, role stress, and unstructured environments (for certain personality types) appear to be other important risk factors for both alcoholism and drug addiction.

While the Federal Government fails to gather suicide statistics by occupation of the victim, we do know that the suicide rate is higher among white men than among black men and higher among men than women. If the tendency to commit suicide is not a race-linked or sex-linked genetic factor (as it most probably is not), then it is possible that the differences in suicide rates are a function of the roles played by people in society.

Tentative support for this hypothesis is provided by a study which found that women doctors and chemists had extremely high suicide rates: for women chemists, the rate was nearly five times higher than the rate among white women in general.[38] One might attempt to account for these rates through the chemists' and doctors' access to and knowledge of lethal chemicals, but other studies indicate that professionals who are competitive, compulsive, individualistic, and ambitious tend to have a high risk of suicide. In this respect one might note the rising rate of suicide among blacks at the same time that many are moving into occupational roles similar to those held by whites. And finally, other evidence links cyclical fluctuations in the unemployment rate of suicide rates and psychiatric hospitalization.

Although *causal links* between alcoholism, drug abuse, or suicide and working conditions have not been firmly established (and, because of inadequate measuring devices, may never be established), there is considerable evidence concerning the *therapeutic value* of meaningful work for these and other mental health problems.

For example, several experiments designed to rehabilitate drug addicts are underway in New York. Most important for all concerned will be the attitude of businessmen toward drug abusers. Especially, they must recognize both the value of work as therapy and their responsibility for reducing the social costs of drug abuse. In a recent newspaper article, Howard Samuels, a member of New York City's Narcotics Control Commission, is quoted as saying:

> Most drug-treatment programs lack what many addicts need most—sufficient vocational training, job development and placement, rehabilitative support when they get jobs. Almost no existing drug treatment programs are able to cope adequately with the job needs of addicts.[39]

In the same account, W. Wayne Stewart, medical director of the Sun Oil Company, said:

> Industry increasingly has become aware that firing drug addicts isn't the long-run answer because firing them simply shifts the burden to some other company or to the nation's welfare rolls. . . . Because half of all addicts are so hooked they can't quit, it would be better if industry and government would try to give them jobs to improve their economic stability and social adjustment. . . .[40]

It is probably fair to say that all the evidence available to date is *suggestive* rather than conclusive; yet the recalcitrance of alcoholism, drug abuse, and suicide to abate when treated with non-work alternatives indicates that if changes in work were only a remotely possible solution they should be pursued vigorously. For while it is patently difficult to change habits and attitudes directly, work can be altered relatively easily. . . .

CONCLUSION

Throughout this chapter we have assumed that workers are sufficiently healthy in the first instance to show a decline in health as a result of their jobs. We have ignored, mainly because of the lack of data, the level of health a person must have in order to work at all, or to work as much as he would like to, or in jobs which he may only secretly aspire to. Quite rightly, these matters cannot be ignored. They deal with nutrition and caloric intake, with one or another debilitating conditions, chronic and acute, and with physical imperfections correctible by so-called cosmetic surgery. Certainly, in this latter instance, the person whose mirror daily assails his self-esteem will be hard put to derive self-esteem from a job he really does not want, while he is denied the job he wants because he lacks the requisite physical attributes.

If we look upon work as a means of avoiding certain mental and physical health problems, we must also look upon our health specialists and others in our society as a means of enabling people to work. All parts of society are, after all, mutually interactive—a central point of this report.

NOTES

[1] Sula Benet, "Why They Live to Be 100, or Even Older, in Abkhasia," *New York Times Magazine,* December 26, 1972.

[2] J. R. P. French, R. D. Caplan, "Organizational Stress and Individual Strain," in *The Failure of Success,* ed. A. Marrow (forthcoming).

[3] Harry Levinson, "Emotional Toxicity of the Work Environment," *Archives of Environmental Health,* V. 19, August 1969.

[4] French, Caplan, *op. cit.*

[5] C. D. Jenkins, "Psychologic and Social Precursors of Coronary Disease," *New England Journal of Medicine,* V. 284, 1971.

[6] S. Cobb, C. V. Kasl, "Blood Pressure Changes in Men Undergoing Job Loss: A Preliminary Report," *Psychosomatic Medicine,* January/February, 1970.

[7] J. R. P. French, J. Tupper, E. Mueller, "Work Load of University Professors," Cooperative Research Project No. 2171, U.S. Office of Education, University of Michigan, Ann Arbor, 1965.

[8] M. Friedman, R. H. Rosenman, V. Carroll, "Changes in the Serum Cholesterol and Blood Clotting Time of Men Subject to Cyclic Variation of Occupational Stress," *Circulation,* V. 17, 1957.

[9] S. M. Sales, "Organizational Roles as a Risk Factor in Coronary Heart Disease," *Administrative Science Quarterly,* V. 14, No. 3, 1969.

[10] A. Pepitone, "Self, Social Environment and Stress," in *Psychological Stress,* ed. M. H. Appley, D. Trumbell (New York: Appleton-Century-Crofts, 1967).

[11] H. J. Montoye, et al., "Serum Uric Acid Concentration Among Business Executives with Observation on Other Coronary Disease Risk Factors," *Annals of Internal Medicine,* V. 66, 1967.

[12] H. H. W. Miles, et al., "Psychosomatic Study of 46 Young Men with Coronary Artery Disease," *Psychosomatic Medicine,* V. 16, 1954.

[13] Cary, P. McCord, "Life and Death by the Minute," *Industrial Medicine,* V. 17, No. 10, October, 1948.

[14] J. S. House, *The Relationship of Intrinsic and Extrinsic Work Motivations to Occupational Stress and Coronary Heart Disease Risk,* Unpublished Ph.D. Thesis, University of Michigan, 1972.

[15] H. I. Russek, "Emotional Stress and Coronary Disease in American Physicians, Dentists, and Lawyers," *American Journal of Medical Science,* V. 243, 1962.

[16] R. Caplan, *Organizational Stress and Individual Strain: A Social-Psychological Study of Risk Factors in Coronary Heart Disease Among Administrators, Engineers, and Scientists,* Unpublished Ph.D. Thesis, University of Michigan, 1971.

[17] S. Kasl, S. Cobb, "Physical and Mental Health Correlates of Status Incongruence," *Social Psychiatry,* V. 6, No. 1, 1971.

[18] C. D. Jenkins, R. H. Rosenman, M. Friedman, "Development of an Objective Psychological Test for Determination of Coronary-Prone Behavior Pattern," *Journal of Chronic Diseases,* V. 20, 1967.

[19] Caplan, *op. cit.*

[20] M. Kohn, C. Schooler, "Occupational Experience and Psychological Functioning: An Assessment of Reciprocal Effects," N.I.M.H., 1972.

[21] Caplan, *op. cit.*

[22] *Ibid.*

[23] S. Seashore, *Group Cohesiveness in the Industrial Work Group* (Ann Arbor: Institute for Social Research, 1954).

[24] Y. S. Matsumoto, "Social Stress and Coronary Heart Disease in Japan: A Hypothesis," *Milbank Memorial Fund Quarterly,* V. 48, 1970.

[25] M. Susser, "Causes of Peptic Ulcer: A Selective Epidemiologic Review," *Journal of Chronic Diseases,* V. 20, 1967.

[26] S. H. King, S. Cobb, "Psycho-social Factors in the Epidemiology of Rheumatoid Arthritis," *Journal of Chronic Diseases,* V. 7, 1958.

[27] S. Cobb, *The Frequency of the Rheumatic Diseases* (Cambridge: Harvard University Press, 1971).

[28] S. Cobb, S. V. Kasl, "Some Medical Aspects of Unemployment," Institute for Social Research, University of Michigan, 1971.

[29] C. M. Sulley, K. J. Munden, "Behavior of the Mentally Healthy," *Bulletin of the Menninger Clinic,* V. 26, 1962.

[30] Studies undertaken at the Survey Research Center, University of Michigan, over the last twenty years.

[31] A. Zaleznik, J. Ondrack, A. Silver, "Social Class, Occupation, and Mental Illness," in *Mental Health and Work Organizations,* ed. A. McLean (Chicago: Rand McNally, 1970).

[32] C. R. DeCarlo, "Technological Change and Mental Health," in *Mental Health and Work Organizations,* 1970.

[33] E. Chinoy, *Automobile Workers and the American Dream* (Garden City: Doubleday, 1955).

[34] A. McLean, ed., *Mental Health and Work Organizations* (Chicago: Rand McNally, 1970).

[35] New York Narcotics Addiction Control Commission, "Differential Drug Use Within the New York State Labor Force," July 1971.

[36] Special Action Office for Drug Abuse Prevention, Executive Office of the President, 1972.

[37] P. M. Roman, H. M. Trice, "The Development of Deviant Drinking Behavior," *Archives of Environmental Health,* V. 20, March 1970.

[38] F. P. Li, "Suicide Among Chemists," *Archives of Environmental Health,* V. 20, March 1970.

[39] *The Washington Evening Star* and *Daily News,* July 20, 1972.

[40] *Ibid.*

MARILYN MACHLOWITZ
WORKAHOLISM: WHAT IT IS...........................

No ethic is as ethical as the work ethic.

—John Kenneth Galbraith

All around us, signs, symptoms, and signals seem to suggest that the almighty, all-American work ethic is eroding. Factory workers opt for time off instead of overtime. Students seem to favor self-worth over net worth; they aim, they say, for fun, family life, and $30,000 a year. They won't slave away for $60,000, as dear old dad may have done. Upwardly mobile executives are refusing to move when their companies ask them to relocate. And social scientists persistently portray a workforce that suffers from the white collar woes as well as the blue collar blues.

Employers have adjusted. Mandatory transfers have been removed from many career paths. Menial jobs have been enriched and enlarged almost beyond recognition. Experiments with time—from four-day workweeks to "flextime"— have rearranged and, in some cases, reduced the total time spent working. Even President Carter, in an impassioned speech to his staff soon after taking office, expressed opposition to the overwork characteristics of earlier administrations. He said, in part, "All of you will be more valuable to me and the country with rest and a stable home life."

In spite of President Carter's well-publicized wishes to the contrary, his aides and associates still work well into the night. One White House cleaning woman apparently complained that David Rubinstein, a deputy to presidential advisor Stuart Eizenstat, doesn't leave his office long enough for her to dust it. Former H.E.W. secretary Joseph Califano's appetite for work cost taxpayers plenty: He reportedly had to hire a second shift of secretaries and installed a separate air-conditioning system for those times when the main unit is shut off. And the president himself isn't practicing what he once preached: His eighteen-hour day led one wag to christen him "The Bionic Grind."

Elsewhere in Washington the story is the same. In *The Powers That Be,* David Halberstam described Robert Woodward, *The Washington Post* reporter of Watergate fame, as

> a totally compulsive person, a classic workaholic, wildly ambitious, utterly obsessed by his work and his career. . . . His work habits were terrifying. Even before Watergate the regular work hours of the *Post* were not enough for him. . . .

Although Washington seems to attract an unusually large number of workaholics, New York City also fosters them. *New York Times* music critic Harold C. Schonberg feels that "New York really is faster than the rest of the

Marilyn Machlowitz, *Workaholics: Living with Them, Working with Them* (Addison-Wesley Publishing Co., 1980). Reprinted by permission of the author.

world. If you live in New York and expect to get anywhere, you have to hop to it. You move faster, talk faster, work faster. . . ."

Workaholism isn't just peculiar to the East Coast. At the other side of the country, even seemingly laid-back Californians may be closet workaholics. As a West Coast woman reported, "In California we try to act casual as if we've been playing tennis all day, but in reality, I work as hard here as I did in New York—but pretend not to."

Who are all of these people and why are they working so hard? They're work junkies—workaholics—and they are addicted to their jobs. They love their work. They *live* their work. . . . And most of them find it very difficult to ever leave their work, even in extreme circumstances. One elderly attorney toiled away while his office building burned down around him. He ignored the warnings, sirens, and screams until he was finally forcibly ejected by firefighters. A pregnant publicist I know was enjoying the rare luxury of a leisurely lunch when she felt her first labor pains. She rushed from the restaurant to her obstetrician's office. When he assured her that delivery was still hours away, she went back to work.

So, despite the dire warnings that opened this chapter, the work ethic is not only alive and well, but in certain circles it is flourishing. As psychologist Robert L. Kahn suggests, "There's no viable alternative to work, no other activity that uses energy, demands attention, provides regular social interaction around some visible outcome, and does so in a socially approved way."

As retirees rapidly come to realize, a job provides a lot more than just a paycheck. Jobs structure people's time. They permit regular interpersonal interaction and provide a sense of identity, self-esteem, and self-respect. But for all these positive effects attributed to working, alienated workers have received far more of scholars' attention than have their highly absorbed counterparts, the workaholics.

The popular press has paid some attention to work addicts. It's an unusual business magazine that doesn't mention the word at least once per issue. One career guide advises job applicants to answer the inevitable question "What are your weaknesses?" with a quality that is apt to be attractive to a prospective employer. It tells readers to say, "I'm such a workaholic that I tend to get completely caught up in my work." And a woman's magazine told its readers to end a summer or vacation romance by warning men about being a workaholic back at home.

But there is scant scientific research on workaholics. My own master's thesis and doctoral dissertation were the first systematic studies of the phenomenon. My best estimate suggests that workaholics comprise no more than 5 percent of the adult population. They probably make up a slightly higher percentage of the workforce, since workaholics are the least likely to be unemployed. Somehow, it seems, workaholics have overcome or averted the difficulties and dissatisfactions that plague today's workers. Perhaps, once workaholism is better understood, it will be possible to use the experience of the work addict to enrich and enhance the working lives of others. But first we need to dispel some of the negative attitudes we have about workaholics.

Most descriptions of the phenomenon do not define workaholism as much as they denigrate and deride workaholics. Lotte Bailyn of M.I.T. described the workaholic as the "victim of a newly recognized social disease presumably responsible for the disintegration of the family, [and] for severe distortion of full personal development. Likewise, a respected *New York Times* writer, Charlotte Curtis, portrayed the workaholic as someone who was "anxious, guilt-ridden, insecure, or self righteous about . . . work. . . . a slave to a set schedule, merciless in his demands upon himself for peak performance . . . compulsively overcommitted."

The word "workaholism" owes its origin, as well as its negative overtones, to "alcoholism." What distinguishes workaholism from other addictions is that workaholism is sometimes considered a virtue, while others, such as alcoholism, or drug addiction, are invariably considered vices.

Yet workaholics are usually portrayed as a miserable lot. This bias stems from the ways we learn about them. The clergy hears their confessions; physicians and therapists, their complaints; and judges, their divorces. The few articles about workaholics that have appeared in scientific journals typically emphasize the psychosocial problems of specific patients. The workaholics that I interviewed had few such problems.

Another major bias against workaholics are the beliefs of nonworkaholics. People who work to live cannot understand those who live to work and love it. They watch in amazement and wonder about those who delight in what they do. Workaholics' unorthodox attitude—that their work is so much fun they'd probably do it for free—causes nonworkaholics to question their own situation. The latter group begins to worry "What's wrong with my job?" or, worse, "What's wrong with me?" To resolve these feelings, nonworkaholics resort to denouncing workaholics rather than running down themselves. They say, "Sure, workaholics are successful at work, but aren't they really ruining the rest of their lives?" This logic is akin to that of "Lucky in cards, unlucky in love" and equally untrue. Satisfaction with work and with life are more apt to be intertwined than mutually exclusive.

Workaholism is almost exclusively American, but it is also un-American. You are *supposed* to lead lives that are well-rounded, balanced, and more "normal" than those of workaholics. Sure, you should go to work weekdays, but you better not spend evenings and weekends at work, as well. Those times should be spent with the family or playing ball or seeing friends or gardening. Have you ever heard of a beauty pageant contestant who couldn't list at least half a dozen hobbies, from basket weaving to opera singing? In contrast, when faced with an employment application, a workaholic might have to leave that item blank. Workaholics are more willing to settle for excellence in one endeavor and to admit that they are inept and uninterested in anything else. As playwright Neil Simon said (italics mine), "I wish I *could* do other things well besides write, . . . play an instrument, learn other languages, cook, ski. My greatest sense of accomplishment is that I didn't waste time *trying* to learn those things."

Nor is it American to like your job that much, and those who do are suspect. To look forward to Monday instead of Friday is regarded as strange and even abnormal. Production workers attach posters to their machines that say "Hang in there; Friday's coming." In the executive suites such signs are understandably absent, but sentiments like "Thank God it's Friday" are frequently heard.

As a result, workaholics are often openly maligned. A top health insurance organization placed a full-page magazine ad warning of the alleged health hazards and related costs of working too hard. The photo featured an angry-looking man with a cigarette dangling from his lips and butts spilling out of an overflowing ashtray; his tie loosened, his collar undone, his shirt straining at his paunch, a styrofoam coffee cup in one hand and several others strewn about an incredibly cluttered desk. The headline read, "He's working twelve hours a day to increase the cost of health care." The copy continued, "In the Horatio Alger story the hero works day and night to get ahead and everybody looks up to him with admiration. Now, millions of Americans are following this example. . . . we're not asking you to stop working. Just try not to overdo it. And when you see someone who thinks he's Horatio Alger, don't think of him as a hero. Think of him as a villain."

Most workaholics won't admit that's what they are because the word has such negative connotations. In fact, so many of the people I interviewed objected to the word that I frequently substituted other phrases ("the role of work in the lives of successful hard workers") when talking to them. Everyone I interviewed acknowledged that they had been accused of being a workaholic. And almost all admitted that my characteristics of workaholism came a little too close for comfort. As television anchorwoman Jessica Savitch wrote me, "I do not like the label since it conjures up a negative addiction such as alcoholic. But the qualities you ascribe to a workaholic are qualities I seek and admire in others."

Not everyone, however, dismisses workaholics as dismal or dangerous. When a young mathematician heard I was writing a book about workaholics, he eagerly asked me, "Does your book tell how to become one?" And, indeed, in certain governmental, professional, and academic circles, workaholism has managed to develop considerable cachet. In, say, Washington, D.C., New York City, or Cambridge, Massachusetts, you can hear quite a few people claim to be workaholics. I, for one, doubt that too many of them really are simply because they brag about it. Real workaholics will doubt, demur, or deny outright that that's what they are.

Then, too, workaholics do not necessarily recognize or realize just how hard they do work. But they don't mind working hard. While the masses may moan and grumble about having to work hard, workaholics enjoy and exult in it. In fact, Dr. John Rhoads, a psychiatrist on the faculty of Duke University, maintains that it is almost axiomatic that those who complain of being overworked are not. For example, Dick Vermeil, head coach of Philadelphia's pro football team, the Eagles, and a man who is invariably called a workaholic, told me, "I don't actually know what the word means, but I am tired of its being used in describing my personality. I do what I'm doing because I enjoy it very much and really don't consider it hard work."

While workaholics do work hard, not all hard workers are workaholics. I will use the word workaholic to describe those whose desire to work long and hard is intrinsic and whose work habits almost always exceed the prescriptions of the job they do and the expectations of the people with whom or for whom they work. But the first characteristic is the real determinant. What truly distinguishes workaholics from other hard workers is that the others work only to please a boss, earn a promotion, or meet a deadline. Moonlighters, for example, may work sixteen hours a day merely to make ends meet, but most of them stop working multiple shifts as soon as their financial circumstances permit. Accountants, too, may sometimes seem to work non-stop, but most slow down markedly after April 15th. For workaholics, on the other hand, the workload seldom lightens, for they don't *want* to work less. As Senator William Proxmire has found, "The less I work, the less I enjoy it."

Time spent working would be an appealing index of workaholism, but it would also be a misleading measure. Although workaholics may work from 5 A.M. to 9 P.M. instead of the more usual 9 A.M. to 5 P.M., the hours they work are not the *sine qua non* of workaholism. It is in fact preferable to view workaholism as an approach or an attitude toward working than as an amount of time at work. Workaholics will continue to think about work when they're not working—even at moments that are, well, inappropriate. One energy specialist recalls dreaming about Con Ed and seeing barrels of oil in her sleep. One research and development director mentally designs new studies while making love to his wife.

But numbers and totals do count: Workaholics are given to counting their work hours and especially their achievements. Dr. Denton Cooley, the founder and chief surgeon of the Texas Heart Institute of Houston, enclosed a six-page vitae and a two-page biography with his finished questionnaire, which was handwritten in the illegible scrawl for which physicians are famous. The vitae listed a string of international honors; the biography, his achievements: By 1978, Cooley had performed over 30,000 open heart operations, more than any other surgeon in the world. He and his staff perform 25 to 30 such operations a day. An aide explains:

> I don't think you'll talk to anyone who likes to operate more than Cooley. People like him don't go into medicine for mankind. They do it because they like it. I mean he could relax, he doesn't need the money. His dad was a successful dentist who invested very wisely in Houston real estate. And Denton's surgical fees are more than one million dollars a year. But he just wouldn't be happy if he couldn't operate every day. Hell, I've seen him call in from a morning meeting in New York to set up an afternoon surgey schedule. The guy is hooked.

Dr. Cooley defended his dedication far more simply. He works as he does, he said, "because I enjoy it."

Workaholism is not restricted to hospital corridors, Congressional offices, or elegant executive suites. While we sneer at it in corporate executives, workaholism is something we've come to accept—and even admire—in artists, and it is what we expect of our personal physicians. It is also part and parcel of our image of most scientists, such as Edison and Einstein. As Wilfred J. Corrigan, former chairman of Fairchild Camera and Instrument Corporation told *Business Week*, "A lot of people in this industry are totally involved with their work. Everyone sees this as appropriate for an artist painting the Sistine chapel or an author writing a novel. But in science and technology, there are times when you just don't want to go home."

Although I interviewed far more white collar than blue collar workers, I found that workaholics exist in every occupation, from managers and doctors to secretaries and assembly line workers. One man had a combined M.D.– Ph.D.; another had only a high school diploma. A friend once described her apartment building's janitor as a workaholic. "I feel very fortunate," she said, "to have a super who's a compulsive worker. He won't even stop and talk. Occasionally, he'll have a conversation with someone while he's sweeping the sidewalk."

Nor is workaholism restricted to just one sex. While women have been almost completely overlooked in the little that has been written about workaholism, there have always been women workaholics. If housework, for instance, were rightfully regarded as work, generations of compulsive cleaners could be considered workaholics. And so would the tireless organizers of charity events. Today, women's workaholism is merely more apparent, since more and more women work outside their homes.

Dr. Helen De Rosis, associate clinical professor of psychiatry at New York University School of Medicine and the author of several books about women, cautions against confusing women workaholics with the so-called Superwomen. A Superwoman tries to be Supermom and Superwife as well as Superworker. Superwoman, according to syndicated columnist Ellen Goodman, is not only a Wonder Woman at work but an elegant dresser and an excellent cook as well. Her kids do not subsist on cold cereal: Superwoman gets up at the crack of dawn to make them a hot, nutritious, and nitrite-free breakfast. Her husband has a delicious dinner every night: She not only has time to get the groceries, but to whip up gourmet delights, courtesy of Julia Child and Cuisinart. Her relationship with her children is characterized, of course, by the *quality*—not by the quantity—of the time she spends with them. Similarly, her marriage can only be called a meaningful relationship. She and her husband are not only each other's best friend but also ecstatic lovers, because Superwoman is never too tired at night. Instead, she is, in the words of Ellen Goodman, "multiorgasmic until midnight."

According to Dr. De Rosis, whose books include *Women and Anxiety*, Superwomen and workaholics share a basic similarity: Both use their work as a defense against anxiety. While workaholics appear to enjoy their work, Dr. De Rosis explains that the enjoyment they experience is distinct from the pleasure felt by women who are able to shift their priorities for different occasions. "The workaholic can't do this. She can't say, 'Today I'll stay home because my child is sick.' She can't make that decision."

Nor should women workaholics be mistaken for women who must do double time to make up for sex-related obstacles in their careers. When Monica Bauer joined Xerox in 1966, she found that she "really did have to put in more time than my male associates just to get the information." Back then, Bauer was excluded from the "old boy network" and other informal channels of communication and had no "new girl network" to turn to. The times have changed, but Bauer's drive shows no decline. She continues to put in long days at Xerox, where she is now manager of low volume products and pricing, and recently completed an M.B.A. at the University of Rochester while working full-time.

So, despite the fact that workaholics come from all classes, sexes, and occupations, they all share one over-riding passion: work. After interviewing more than one hundred work addicts over several years, I have some good news and some bad news. The good news is that as a group, workaholics are surprisingly happy. They are doing exactly what they love—work—and they can't seem to get enough of it. If the circumstances are right—that is, if their jobs fit and their families are accommodating—then workaholics can be astonishingly productive. But here's the bad news: The people who work with and live with workaholics often suffer. Adjusting to the frenetic schedule of a workaholic is not easy and only rarely rewarding. At work these addicts are often demanding and sometimes not very effective. At home, well, you'll seldom find a workaholic at home. The tensions implicit in this rather unbalanced life-style cause very real dilemmas for those involved. . . .

Balancing Love, Children, Work, and Self

MONCRIEFF M. COCHRAN AND URIE BRONFENBRENNER
CHILD REARING, PARENTHOOD, AND THE WORLD OF WORK ....

Who cares whether parents are good workers, or workers good parents? Is anyone interested in where all those fathers and mothers go when they leave

Moncrieff M. Cochran and Urie Bronfenbrenner, "Child Rearing, Parenthood, and the World of Work," in Clark Kerr and Jerome M. Rosow. eds., *Work in America: The Decade Ahead* (New York: Van Nostrand Reinhold, 1979). Reprinted by permission of the publisher.

home at 8 A.M. every weekday morning, or where all those workers go when they leave work at 5 P.M.? Most people will reply in the affirmative, for these questions relate to a sizable portion of the population. This polite show of interest, however, is nothing more than that.

Let us look at the record. The American employer apparently does not care about parents, for only in rare instances are maternity leaves, flexible working hours, and day care considered as practical options.

The disinterest shown by employers is, perhaps, exceeded only by that manifested in the university setting, where those who seek an understanding of family life have virtually ignored the interface between the workplace and the rearing of the young. On the one hand, changes in the American family are being documented and analyzed by increasing numbers of social scientists. They point to the fact that divorces are taking place at an unprecedented rate and that family violence is surfacing as a major American epidemic. They remind us that women are entering the work force in growing numbers and that fatherhood increasingly involves more than just bringing home the monthly paycheck. Each of these changes might both affect and be affected by the world of work, but their relationship to jobs and conditions on the job is rarely recognized by family researchers.

On the other hand, industrial sociologists have been studying worker performance for decades with virtually no mention of workers as parents. They look at how business and factories are organized, and how jobs are defined and structured, but, from most accounts, one could as easily assume that the workers live in barracks attached to the plant. Families simply are not mentioned.

The thesis of this chapter is that the institution with the greatest influence over the future of the American family in its child-rearing role is the word of work. Underlying this thesis is the contention that employers have great influence upon workers *as parents*, for better or for worse. If true, then social policies that strengthen families must include, and even begin with, changes in the world of work. This does not imply that employers alone can create conditions of work that are ideal for family life. On the contrary, to achieve the objective of strengthening families, social policy will also have to provide supports and incentives for employers to effect the needed changes in conditions of employment. As the foregoing statement indicates, neither the issues nor the solutions are simple ones. To deal with them effectively, we must first learn why, in today's society, increasing numbers of parents work outside the home and are even more likely to do so in the future. Next we explore the effects of unemployment upon the care provided children by their parents and review what is known about the effects of parental employment and day care on the development of children. The chapter culminates with the presentation of six policy-related issues that employers and the society at large must address if they are to improve the fit between the roles of parent and worker, and so contribute to the strengthening of the family and to the quality of succeeding generations of Americans.

WHY PARENTS WORK

In order to understand the impact of the workplace upon child rearing, it is necessary, first, to understand why parents go to work. Before answering that question, let us consider the numbers of workers shown in Table 1.

Over 38 million workers, more than 40 percent of our entire work force, have at least one dependent child. If we are to understand the motives driving this vast number of parents into the work force, the various types of working families represented in this table must be distinguished.

The single parent is almost always a woman and poor. Women are the sole wage earners in at least 3 million American families with children under the age of 18. They constitute 62 percent of all single-parent famlies. These women work outside the home because they must take a job to earn a living and "keep off welfare." Some argue that such women would be better parents if they remained at home with the children, on public assistance, instead of working outside the home. Such persons do not understand either the American work ethic or the American tradition of "rugged individualism." These values are reflected in such common expressions as "You can't get something for nothing," and "Dependence is degrading." Income supports from the public coffers, disbursed as they now are by departments of social welfare, implement this orientation by requiring that clients constantly reiterate their helplessness and worthlessness in order to qualify for aid. Such degradation is, of course, felt by parents, who can neither put up with it themselves nor keep it from infecting their children. Thus the "stay at home" alternative becomes unacceptable for most single parents, some of whom keep jobs otherwise intolerable in order to remain independent of a repressive and family-weakening system of public assistance.

In families in which there are two wage earners (a category that constitutes 45 percent of all intact families with children), it might at first appear that a

TABLE 1 Workers with Children, by Family Type*

| | TWO PARENTS | | | |
	ONE PARENT WORKING	BOTH WORKING	ONE PARENT† WORKING	TOTAL
Number of workers	12,613,000	22,714,000	3,352,000	38,678,000
Percentage of total work force	13	24	4	41

*Includes at least one child under age 18, and excludes military families.

†Excludes one-parent families headed by men.

Source: H. Hayghe, 'Special Labor Force Reports—Summaries: Marital and Family Characteristics of Workers, March 1977," *Monthly Labor Review* (February 1978): 51–54.

shift back to one parent at home might be a viable alternative. But consider the economic realities of child rearing. Conservative estimates put a $40,000 price tag on the support of a child through high school.[1] This financial burden is difficult to bear on a single salary; it should, therefore, come as no surprise that the number of families with two working parents is on the rise. Total family income increases at least 25 percent when both parents work outside the home.[2] This increase is so important that the wife will work for pay outside the home despite the fact that her husband almost never makes an equal commitment to household tasks.

Some observers note that where two-earner families are in the higher income brackets, they have a choice as to whether one of them will stay home with the children. "One of them" generally means the mother, of course. It is important to point out, in this connection, that two relatively recent demographic changes in the American family are related to the changing attitudes of women toward work. First, parents are having fewer children, and thus full-time child rearing is increasingly seen as a short-term occupation rather than as a lifetime career. Thus, increasing numbers of women are preparing themselves for work roles outside the home, and attitudes are changing accordingly. The second demographic change is in the frequency of divorce. Faced with the possibility of having to support themselves and their children someday, more and more women are acquiring skills and experience to ensure their employability before they venture into parenthood. As a matter of fact, salaried work for both partners, which leads to the development and maintenance of an equalitarian spouse relationship, may actually prevent divorce. Thus, American values of work and independence, previously limited in practice only to men, are now being responded to by women who can "afford" to make the choice of staying at home or entering the job market.

The "traditional" family, in which one parent (usually the man) works while the other (usually the woman) takes care of the children, is no longer the major family-work arrangement in American society (see Table 1). Its relative decline as an economic and social response to child rearing may indicate that it has now become an all too vulnerable alternative. That vulnerability stems from a combination of the pressures already described: (1) the high cost of rearing children, and (2) the movement to equality of opportunity for *both* sexes. For a working man, the press is increasingly likely to come from two directions within the family—costly children and a wife convinced that there is more to life than "raising the kids."

The preceding analysis leads to the conclusion that the overriding reason that parents work is to provide, through earned income, some degree of independence for themselves and their families. Several other reasons for working require mention. Parents work outside the home because such work often brings with it regular and frequent social contact. Workmates sometimes become friends and, even as acquaintances, are resources to whom one can turn for information and advice. Studies of work inside the home (housework), on the other hand, indicate that adults doing such work (overwhelmingly women) often feel isolated and lonely.[3]

Finally, there are parents who work because they receive a good deal of intrinsic satisfaction from the job. Whether the work is with hands or head, with people or things, there are those who find pleasure in their work that is provided by the nature of the tasks themselves. Although there is great fulfillment to be found in child-rearing activities, and in some aspects of housework, such as cooking, much of the variety and complexity that contribute to the intrinsic pleasures of work are to be found outside one's own home.

UNEMPLOYMENT AND CHILD CARE

Income, however, remains the overriding factor leading parents to enter the job market. Supporting a family is expensive, and American families are "on their own" in their search for the means to provide such support. What happens when support is not found? How does unemployment affect child care?

The inability to find a paying job has two kinds of impact upon children. One impact is that of poverty. Very little money is available for the needs of children in families with no wage-earning member. The second and less visible effect of unemployment is related to the behavior of the unemployed adults, whether or not the family is destitute.

JOBLESSNESS AND POVERTY

Most estimates indicate that "between a quarter and a third of all American children are born into families with financial strains so great that the children will suffer basic deprivation."[4] The Carnegie Council on Children reported in 1977 that these children are two thirds more likely than nonpoor children to die in the first year of life, four times more likely to have "fair to poor" health, and one fifth as likely to attend college, regardless of intellectual ability. Although seemingly self-evident, the statistics remind us that child care is basic to the survival of the species. Poverty inhibits the care of children to the point at which that very survival is threatened. The Carnegie report goes on to state:

> Parenthood is deeply rewarding, but it is not easy and it is not cheap. We believe that those who choose to bear children must be expected to support and care for them, barring unexpected catastrophes. Today, far too many parents are unable to accept the full responsibilities of parenthood because there are no jobs or support for them, or jobs they can find do not pay a living wage.[5]

Unemployment is, perhaps, most devastating when it involves young people. Finding and holding a job is a fundamental prerequisite for entrance into the adult world. Yet over 20 percent of the young people between the ages of 16 and 20 who are looking for work cannot find it. Among blacks 16 to 20 years old that unemployment rate is almost one in two. A recent article in the *New York Times* magazine section refers to "a fundamental and systematic failure to bring the new generation of inner-city youth into the adult world of jobs and families."[6] Pointing to the fact that such young people are ten times as likely to have criminal records as youth with jobs, the writers go on to state that

> if lawlessness is a symptom of the state of emergency of inner-city youth, the emergency itself is joblessness. . . . For minority youth, these are the years of the great depression, far worse in its impact on them than any depression the country as a whole has ever encountered.[7]

Within the context of the present welfare system, joblessness has a direct and devastating impact upon the young parent, because he or she cannot marry, especially if there is a child in the picture. As the *Times* points out, the father

> . . . cannot marry because he cannot earn nearly as much as the amount that the welfare system and associated poverty benefits grants to a woman and child, and most of those benefits are lost if he is reported as a working spouse. If he doesn't marry, on the other hand, his woman can keep all her benefits and he can retain his earnings.[8]

The emerging picture is one in which joblessness, psychologically and economically debilitating in its own right, pushes young parents into a welfare system that operates to separate them even farther from the adult world by penalizing those spouses who acknowledge their responsibilities to each other and their child by sharing the same household.

Young people denied access to the job market are likely to become involved in criminal activities, and, as parents, to become dependent on a welfare system that encourages them to avoid acceptance of responsibility for the needs of their spouses and children. This is the danger for one group of jobless families, the "never-employed parents." What about the more visible victims of the unemployment picture, those parents who had a job, but were laid off when work became scarce? How does that kind of unemployment affect child care?

Unemployment and Violence

In a study of families in the process of divorce, O'Brien (1971) found that when violent behavior by a parent was reported, either toward a spouse or a child, that behavior was strongly related to work and earning capacity. In O'Brien's words, "The men in the violent subgroup of families apparently were not fulfilling the obligations connected with the work/earner role."[9] O'Brien found a high incidence of family violence in what was essentially a middle-class sample; none of the families was from the "lower-lower" class, and none lived in an urban ghetto. He proposes dissatisfaction with the work situation as the "trigger" for the violence that occurred. Gelles (1974) cites O'Brien's work as lending support for the proposition that unemployment of the husband is a contributing factor in intrafamily violence.[10] As additional corroboration, he points to the finding of Gill (1971) that nearly half of the fathers of abused children were not employed during the year preceding the abusive act and 12 percent were jobless at the time of the incident.[11] Galston (1964) also found that in abusive families the father was more often unemployed or worked part time.[12]

None of the foregoing researchers meant to focus on conditions of unemployment as a potential influence on family interaction. In each case, the investigator initiated research in a different problem area (divorce, violence, child abuse) and then stumbled across the link to unemployment. One research study carried out by the United Auto Workers in Flint, Michigan, did begin with an examination of unemployment. In 1975, 20 percent of the labor force in that city was out of work. The investigators found that, during that year, alcoholism increased 150 percent and the incidence of verified child abuse doubled.[13] At a more general level, Dr. Harvey Brenner at Johns Hopkins University conducted an analysis of economic trends between 1940 and 1974 and found that periods of depressed economy and high unemployment were accompanied by significant increases in infant mortality, mental disorders, homicide, heart disease, and alcoholism.[14]

It is obvious that intrafamily violence and alcoholism are related to child rearing and that alcoholics and the beaters of spouses and children are not healthy, productive parents. To the extent that unemployment contributes to such circumstances, and our economic system contributes to unemployment, this pattern constitutes a causal chain for producing family instability and unhealthy child-rearing practices in American society.

WORKING PARENTS AND CHILD CARE

When the subject of the working parent is associated with child care, the typical American reflex is to think "mothers." We shall shortly adduce evidence that the relation of the father to the world of work may be even more critical for family life and the process of child rearing than the mother's job situation. First, however, the few available studies on the effect of a mother's working on the development of her child are reviewed here. Hoffman and Nye (1974) summarize the results of their study by stating that the mother's working outside the home appears to have no negative impact on the child, and, in the case in which the mother is sole support for the family, appears to be beneficial.[15] Evidence gathered in an interview study by Colletta (1977) indicates that economic stability and increased self-esteem, which often accompany successful job performance, strengthen mothers in their parental roles and outweigh the difficulties of finding reliable day-care services and providing time each day for activities with the children.[16] Viewed within the context of the status given work by society and the economic necessity of income for family survival and stability, these findings are hardly surprising.

The other body of data related to the effects of working parents on child care has emerged from research on day care. Many investigations of alternative care arrangements turn out to be work-related, because the parent would be providing that care personally were he or she not employed outside the home. Once again, reviews of this research (Ricciuti 1976; Bronfenbrenner et al. 1976) indicate that reliance upon nonparental child care while the mother is employed outside the home is not harmful to the children involved.[17] It is clear from the evidence that parents remain the most important adults in the lives of their children regardless of the child-care arrangements used by a family. It is also apparent that children develop normally within any day-care arrangement utilizing a stable, stimulating environment provided by warm, loving adults.

EFFECTS OF THE FATHER'S WORK ON FAMILIES AND CHILDREN

In sum, maternal employment appears to have little enduring impact upon the child, except when the mother is the only wage earner in the family, and then the effects are positive. But what about paternal employment? How does it influence family life and the development of the child? The evidence we have reviewed on the consequences of the father's inability to find work suggests that not only the fact but also the conditions of employment might turn out to be significant in affecting the course of family life. In modern industrialized societies, work requirements have moved primary wage earners farther and farther from their families, both physically and psychologically; and in the United States, these wage earners have most often been men. The impact on children of the increased alienation of fathers from family activities has gone unexamined, perhaps because the appropriateness of full-time and even overtime employment has never been questioned in our society, regardless of the demands of the job vis-a-vis family life. But the growing movement of mothers into jobs outside the home has provoked a new look at the role of fathers in family life. We propose that this reexamination must include attention to the interface between the father's workplace and the home.

A search of the published literature revealed no systematic investigations in this area, but results from a recently completed pilot study of our own raise some provocative questions. The study was carried out in connection with a five-nation project on the impact of formal and informal support systems on family functioning and the development of the child. The data emerged from the pretest of an interview designed to identify and assess aspects of the environment experienced by parents as assisting or impairing their child-rearing efforts. The pretest was conducted with a sample of seventy families with young children, stratified by social class (three levels), family structure (one versus two parents), and mother's job status (not working, working part time, working full time).[18]

The results of the pilot study revealed that, along with financial worries, the conditions of the husband's work constituted the principal source of stress for two-parent families with young children. The problems in the father's job situation obtained whether or not the mother was also employed. Indeed, even in the families with working mothers (comprising 56 percent of the two-parent households in our sample), both mothers and fathers saw more difficulties from a parent's viewpoint in the husband's job than in the wife's.

Mentioned most frequently as sources of strain were the father's working hours, averaging forty-nine hours per week for the group studied. As might be expected under these circumstances, both parents viewed as a particular source of strain the husband's working overtime and on weekends, or having to make trips out of town.

Parents also described work features that made child rearing easier, such as flexible schedules, convenient job location, and an opportunity to have the child visit at work. In the case of the father, however, the job stresses tended to outweigh the supports. Understandably, aspects of the work situation viewed as beneficial to family life were more likely to be recognized by the jobholder than by the spouse, who tended to be more sensitive to the problems of the job. On balance, however, the husband's work situation was described as much more stressful and offering somewhat fewer supports to family life than the wife's.

Some indication of the impact on the family of the varying conditions of work as experienced by husbands and wives is provided by the reports of parents in the study sample. These parents saw their jobs as affecting both their sense of personal well-being and their capacity to function as parents. In general, the mother's employment was perceived as having more positive than negative effects, whereas for fathers the impact of the job situation was reversed—the effects were slightly more negative than positive. Mothers were also more likely to see these negative consequences of the father's job situation than were the husbands themselves.

To what extent are the stresses of the job situation relieved when the mother stays home instead of working, or works part time rather than full time? A mother's not working was indeed seen as an advantage for parenthood by those mothers who stayed home, but this view was not shared by the fathers.

Context and perspective become even more salient for understanding the differences in perceived stress associated with the mother's working part time rather than full time. Upon first glance, it would appear that part-time as against full-time employment for the mothers resulted in greater stress both at work and in family life. Paradoxically, however, these marked negative consequences were associated not with the mother's own job, but with the father's. When the mother worked part time rather than full time, both parents, and especially the mother, described the father's job as not paying well, affording fewer opportunities for advancement, demanding longer hours, and resulting in problems within the family for both parents and children. In contrast, the mother's own part-time job was viewed by both parents as considerably less stressful and disruptive to family life than the father's. It appears likely that mothers who take part-time jobs often do so because the husband's job does not provide sufficiently for the family's needs. But when this occurs, the task of parenthood is not made any easier.

Because of the small size and the ad hoc character of our sample, the foregoing results must be viewed with caution. Even if reliable, they may be valid only for situations found in predominantly professional communities. Nevertheless, the data point to one consistent trend: In the experience of the parents in our sample, it was the conditions of work for the husband, rather than for the wife, that were mainly seen as frustrating the parents' ability to care for and bring up their young children in the way they thought best.

This finding is consistent with the line of evidence and argument adduced in this chapter. In terms of social policy, it argues for adaptations in the world of work to enable and assist families, and especially fathers, to function effectively, not only as workers on the job, but also as family members engaged in a task that is equally critical for any society—the process of making human beings human.

HOW EMPLOYERS CAN HELP FAMILIES

Most businessmen will agree that the family is the backbone of American society, and that as our society goes, so goes American business. Families are changing in both structural and functional terms. Whether they continue to be able to fulfill one of their most fundamental responsibilities, the rearing of the young, depends in good measure on the nature and availability of work for pay. Because most salaried work is no longer family-based, the availability and characteristics of jobs are increasingly beyond the control of individual parents. So the survival of American families is dependent in good measure on the farsightedness of employers. To be sure, as we have already emphasized, employers have limited power to provide job opportunities. But our analysis points clearly to the need for incentives for the creation of additional jobs, whether in the public or private sector. In our view, the prime source of expert advice about the kinds of incentives that might work best for employers should be the employers themselves. Yet little attempt has been made, to our knowledge, to gather ideas and proposals from that group of experts. This use of employers as a reservoir of talent and energy committed to the maintenance of family life would provide the resources needed for a major initiative on behalf of the working parent. This initiative could be carried out by major employers themselves and should be encouraged and appropriately supported by the federal government. The goals of the undertaking would be educational, with a format to consist of regional conferences followed by action workshops of two different kinds and subsequent follow-up activities. The process is presented in the accompanying outline.

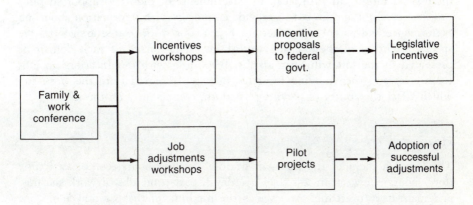

The overall process should be overseen by an advisory group made up of major private- and public-sector employers from across a given state or region. The kickoff conference would focus on the interface between the roles of parent and worker, using information gathered from employees who are parents, at all occupational levels, as a data base for the thoughtful presentation of the challenges faced by parents who are working or looking for work.

As shown in the diagram, the initial conference would be followed by two courses of action, each aimed at the development of family-strengthening public policies. Let us examine each course of action separately.

Workshops would be designed to make maximum use of employers as expert informants on the subject of how to develop the incentives needed to create the additional jobs that mean so much for families with children. Underlying the search for such incentives would be the mounting evidence that unemployment debilitates families by undermining the self-confidence and social attitudes of parents who are seeking work. Resultant anger and frustration are, in turn, related to alcoholism, child abuse, and spouse battering. Included in these workshop discussions might be a reexamination of the relationships between work and welfare and ideas for ensuring continuity in the establishment of new jobs. Particular attention should be focused on incentives for the hiring of young people, who must develop the work habits which will sustain them for a lifetime.

Out of these workshops would come job-creation-incentive proposals for federal and state governments, and other workshops designed to stimulate policy-oriented discussions between employers and public officials. The employer advisory groups could oversee these subsequent discussions and then monitor the progress of any legislative initiatives growing out of them.

The second and simultaneous course of action would begin with workshops designed to examine and discuss innovative work practices already in existence in the world of work that have potential for improving the fit between the roles of parent and worker. Emphasis would be on presentations given by employers and candid discussions of the pros and cons in each approach. These discussions might, in turn, lead to government- or industry-supported pilot projects, carefully monitored to provide employers with information about job performance and parental satisfaction. Five major work-related arenas deserve special attention in these action workshops. A rationale for each domain is presented in the following paragraphs, beginning with modifications in jobs themselves and then moving to arenas one step removed from the work site which affect the ability of parents to perform competently on the job.

Hours of Work

This domain includes the issues of flexible working hours, comprsssed time (forty hours per week in less than five days), part-time jobs or work sharing, and mandatory overtime. At issue is the meshing of the parental and work roles, with our data indicating that fathers deserve special attention in this regard. A flexible work schedule, for instance, permits variation in work start-up and completion times from day to day. This flexibility makes it possible for a parent to fit in a morning visit to the nursery school, or leave early on Wednesday to do the weekly food shopping. Splitting jobs (two people for one job) can free parents in similar fashion. Mandatory overtime, on the other hand, may place a tremendous burden on the scheduling of a parent's life, leaving virtually no time for the children after working, eating, and sleeping.

Benefits

Serious consideration of part-time jobs as a means of supporting families requires careful examination of the benefits question. Health insurance, retirement and pension plans, and vacation time need to be geared to the part-time employee in an equitable fashion. A national health insurance program should be examined by employers as one way to equitably distribute that benefit to part-time workers.

Maternity/paternity leaves permit workers to be full-time parents during the early months of a child's life and to make long-term child-care arrangements carefully. Fathers deserve as much opportunity as mothers to play a central role in the care of the child during infancy.

Transfer Policies

The movement of workers from one area of the country to another for reasons of employment is a widespread phenomenon in American family life. A substantial amount of this movement is involuntary, including workers in the private sector who are moved from one part of a large corporation to another and those in the military or foreign-service segments of the public sector who are shifted from one duty station to another. The social and psychological uprooting associated with such moves is common knowledge, although not well documented in the research literature. Children give up their friends and their familiarity with the neighborhood, and those of school age must readjust to school expectations that often deviate markedly from one locale to the next. The educational and employment opportunities of spouses are often sacrificed to the moves, creating resentment and disillusionment within the family. These family-weakening forces, associated with repeated transfers, combine to produce a family unit at high risk of dissolution. Existing transfer policies should be reassessed in light of the effects of these policies upon workers' families, with particular attention to the possibility that long-term rootedness in neighborhood and community strengthens family life, and with it commitment to the job and job performance.

Day Care

Thirty-four percent of mothers with children under the age of 6 were in the work force in 1977. That percentage will increase over the next five to ten years. There are more and more two-parent families in which both parents work, as noted earlier, and the costs of rearing children continue to rise. Fathers are increasingly expected to become more involved in child-care activities as their wives enter or reenter the job market.

Second only to the availability of the job itself for relieving the pressure on the family, is access to high-quality day-care options for working parents. American parents recognize and accept the fact that they have the primary responsibility for rearing their children. They will, therefore, make every effort to retain that responsibility as they select people to assist them with child care while they work. A pilot study recently conducted at Cornell University documents the critical role played by child-care arrangements in regard to the stresses and supports experienced by working parents. The study found that a mother's satisfaction with her child's care, whether it is performed by herself or someone else, at home or by a substitute in another home or center, determines in large measure how satisfied she is with her work, with herself as a parent, and with her child. Dissatisfaction with the child-care arrangement brought unhappiness with the work situation, disappointment with the parental role, and an increased feeling that the child was difficult to bring up.

Employers can be reassured by the fact that they need not, in most instances, provide child care at the work site. The majority of parents prefer care arrangements close to home and neighborhood rather than on the job. Workshops should be designed to explore ways that employers could best endorse and encourage publicly supported day-care programs that are of high quality and that provide several options to working parents. Contributions to the public coffers, which help finance such family supports, will pay large dividends to employers in the form of worker satisfaction and productivity.

Transportation

Especially in rural America, total reliance on the automobile for transportation has prevented a significant number of job seekers from taking advantage of available employment opportunities. Even when a family can afford a car, use of it by one wage earner completely immobilizes the rest of the family, isolating them from social contact and community services. The escalating costs of automobile purchase and maintenance have made public transportation attractive to an increasing number of Americans, and especially to families with children. Employers might wish to examine the benefits associated with more actively supporting the development and expansion of such transportation options. . . .

Since families are the reservoir from which workers draw the energies needed for good performance on the job, work performance cannot be separated from the rest of family life. It is time now for employers to take a leadership role in the development of work-related social policies that strengthen families. That investment is in their long-term interest, because a commitment to jobs that strengthens the capacity of parents to rear their children as responsible citizens is an investment in the next generation of American workers.

NOTES

[1] Personal communication to authors from Department of Consumer Economics and Housing, Cornell University.

[2] L. Hoffman and F. Nye, *Working Mothers* (San Francisco: Jossey-Bass, 1974), p. 28.

[3] A. Oakley, *The Sociology of Housework* (New York: Pantheon Press, 1974), p. 182.

[4] K. Kenniston and the Carnegie Council on Children, *All Our Children: The American Family under Pressure* (New York: Harcourt, 1977).

[5] *Ibid.,* p. 77.

[6] "To Be Young, Black, and Out of Work," *New York Times Magazine*, October 23, 1977, pp. 38–61.

[7] *Ibid.*

[8] *Ibid.*

[9] J. O'Brien, "Violence in Divorce-Prone Families," *Journal of Marriage and the Family* 33 (November 1971): 692–8.

[10] R. Gelles, "Child Abuse as Psychopathology: A Sociological Critique and Reformulation," in *Violence in the Family*, ed. S. Steinmetz and M. Strauss (New York: Dodd Mead, 1974), pp. 190–204.

[11] D. Gill, "Violence against Children," *Journal of Marriage and the Family* 33 (November 1971): 637–57.

[12] R. Galston, "Observations of Children Who Have Been Physically Abused by Their Parents," *American Journal of Psychiatry* 122 (April 1964): 440–3.

[13] N. Raussell, unpublished report, The Mott Foundation, Flint, Michigan, 1976.

[14] M. H. Brenner, "Estimating the Social Cost of National Economic Policy: Implications for Mental and Physical Health and Criminal Aggression," paper No. 5,

Joint Economic Committee, Congress of the United States, October 26, 1976 (Washington, D.C.: U.S. Government Printing Office, 1976).

[15] Hoffman and Nye, *op. cit.*, pp. 126–66.

[16] N. Colletta, "Divorced Mothers at Two Income Levels: Stress, Support, and Childrearing Practices," unpublished dissertation, Department of Human Development and Family Studies, Cornell University, 1977.

[17] H. Ricciuti, "Effects of Infant Day-Care Experience on Behavior and Development: Research and Implications for Social Policy," and U. Bronfenbrenner, J. Belsky, and L. Steinberg, "Day Care in Context: An Ecological Perspective on Research and Public Policy." Both reviews prepared for the Office of Assistant Secretary for Planning and Evaluation, U.S. Department of Health, Education and Welfare, Fall 1976 (Washington, D.C.: Department of Health, Education and Welfare, 1976).

[18] Because the sample was small (seventy families) and selection of families was not random, caution should be used when generalizing these results to other populations of families. The interviews were carried out in or close to a small city without an urban slum and dominated by a large university. Day-care and public-health services are widely available in this community, and the sample was heavily weighted with families having access to such facilities.

JEYLAN T. MORTIMER AND GLORIAN SORENSEN
MEN, WOMEN, WORK, AND FAMILY* ....

During the past several decades, there have been major structural changes in the family. Declining fertility, rising divorce rates, and the increasing prevalence of the single-parent family have accompanied the rapid influx of married women into the labor force. These concurrent changes have focused public attention on the interrelations of work and the family. . . . It is now well recognized that work and the family are linked together and dependent upon one another in numerous ways, despite their institutional separation. Moreover, there is substantial evidence that their relationship is highly reciprocal; work not only influences family life, but the family also influences behavior in the work place. . . .

*Findings from a recent panel study, conducted by Mortimer and her colleagues, are used in this chapter to illustrate the linkages of work and family for professional and managerial men. They followed up, ten years after graduation, men who had previously participated in an extensive University of Michigan study of the influences of college life. Eighty-eight percent of the seniors in the original study were successfully located, and 84% of these were persuaded to return a mailed questionnaire, yielding a panel of 512 men. The questionnaire assessed their education and work histories, current work experiences, the psychological attributes that had been measured earlier, and information about their family lives. This study will henceforth be referred to as the "Michigan Panel Study." (For further information about the design and findings of this research, see Mortimer and Lorence, 1979a, 1979b; Mortimer, 1980; Mortimer and Kumka, 1982.)

Jeylan T. Mortimer and Glorian Sorensen, "Men, Women, Work, and Family," in K. M. Borman, D. Quarm, and S. Gideonse (eds.), *Women in the Workplace: Effects on Families* (Norwood, N.J.: Ablex Publishing Corp., 1984). Reprinted by permission of the publisher.

In this review, we attempt to apply the same conceptual framework to an examination of the linkages of work and family for men as well as for women. Whether the special circumstances of men or of women are the subject of attention, the impacts of work on family life can be divided into three general categories: work provides socioeconomic resources for the family; it sets time and spatial constraints on family members' activities, particularly the time in which they can be together; and finally, it influences the family through its effects on the attitudes, values, and personality of the working member. The impacts of the family on work can be subsumed in two categories: occupational socialization—the family prepares each new generation of workers; and implications for attainment—it can support or obstruct the occupational achievement of its members. . . . We will first briefly review the nature of these mutual influences. We will then consider some of the literature on work and family, reviewing the findings of research on men and women. We will see that these studies, though differing in their particular concerns and frames of reference, converge in several respects and point to similar policy recommendations. . . .

EFFECTS OF WORK ON THE FAMILY

The Provision of Socioeconomic Resources

Much of the research focused on the work and family linkages of men has been developed in the context of the traditional, single-provider family. Though single-provider families are a diminishing minority, constituting approximately one third of husband–wife families (Aldous, 1981), it is important to understand the linkages of work and family in this context. Because in previous generations single-provider families were the majority, work often continues to be structured as if this traditional family type were the most prevalent. Requirements of work, particularly at high socioeconomic levels, seem most compatible with the single provider structure. The study of single-provider families illuminates the stresses of the homemaker role, and shows that the husband's occupational role can structure the wife's family role as well.

According to the exchange model of family dynamics (Scanzoni, 1970, 1972), the husband in the traditional single-provider family provides economic support to the wife in exchange for her household duties, child care, companionship, and support. In general, as the husband's occupational prestige and income increase, marital satisfaction and stability likewise increase, as does the husband's power and legitimacy as the family head (Scanzoni, 1970). But at the highest status levels, demands on the family may to a large extent offset high occupational rewards (Aldous, Osmond, & Hicks, 1979; Dizard, 1968; Young & Willmott, 1973). Professional and managerial families often face the unique pressures of the career, a vertically structured sequence of positions through which individuals expect to move (Wilensky, 1960). The Michigan

Panel Study supports Aldous's "success constraint theory" (see Aldous et al., 1979) that the husband's occupational attainment may have costs as well as benefits for the family. The more successful of the married men reported greater strains in their families caused by work, strains caused by long working hours, fatigue, preoccupation with problems at the office, extensive travel, and residential moves (Mortimer, 1980).

At the other end of the socioeconomic spectrum, in blue-collar jobs, rarely is there a vertical career line. Young blue-collar men have rather unstable work histories. They move from job to job in search of higher wages and better working conditions (Rubin, 1976). But by midlife, most blue-collar men become "locked in" to their jobs, unable to improve their working conditions and rewards by changing employers. Such mobility may threaten seniority, retirement, and other benefits, constituting a substantial risk to the family. As a result, blue-collar men (and their families) are often stuck in dead-end jobs. Unlike men of professional or managerial status, their incomes do not grow at a pace commensurate with increasing family economic needs. Their "life cycle squeeze" (Oppenheimer, 1974) at midlife is a factor which may propel their wives into the labor force. . . .

The growing prevalence of women's employment outside the home has increased family resources and reduced the costs for families when unemployment strikes the male breadwinner. Indeed, the dual-work family is becoming the dominant pattern of family life. In 1900, only 18% of all women over 14 years of age were employed, most of whom were unmarried (Smith, 1979). By 1980, the labor force included 51% of married women with husbands present (U.S. Dept. of Labor, 1980a). In March of that year, 57% of mothers of children under 18 were in the labor force, and almost half of mothers of children under 6.

However, despite this influx of women into the work force, the jobs women occupy and the salaries they earn have not radically changed. Overall, the income of women is about 59% that of men, a situation which has persisted over the past several decades. Over the course of their work careers, men more often move to positions of higher prestige, whereas women tend to remain at the same prestige level or decline (Rosenfeld, 1979; Sewell et al., 1980). Men's earnings also rise substantially more during their careers than do the earnings of women (Barrett, 1979). Moreover, in terms of their incomes, men benefit far more from their education and occupational prestige than do women (Featherman & Hauser, 1976).

. . . The large difference in the incomes of men and women cannot be attributed to socialization and human capital investments alone. Rather, much of the income differential is linked to occupational segregation. In a segmented labor market, particular occupations are earmarked for women, generally positions offering little opportunity for advancement. Despite their high educational requirements, sex-typed female positions pay relatively little (Oppenheimer, 1975). This segmenting of the labor market that crowds women into relatively few positions has shown little change despite the influx of women into the labor force. According to Oppenheimer (1975), 14 out of 17 jobs that were 70% or more female in 1900 continued to be occupied predominantly by women in 1960. Unfortunately, the number of jobs in this female sector has not kept pace with the rising number of women seeking work (Barrett, 1979). The occupational crowding of women tends to reduce their wages and increase their unemployment. . . .

This segregation of the labor market is perpetuated by "statistical discrimination": employers assess individual job applicants on the basis of their categorical membership (Stevenson, 1978). The assumption that women are unstable workers thus becomes a self-fulfilling prophecy. Due to employers' expectations, women are placed in dead-end positions offering little opportunity for training and advancement. However, both men and women workers in such low level jobs have relatively low commitment to the employing organization and manifest high rates of absenteeism and turnover (Kanter, 1977b). The concentration of women in these kinds of positions thus reinforces their image as unstable workers.

Women's relatively low earning power has important implications for their families. Employed married women do enhance their families' economic resources, contributing, on the average, about one fourth of family income, and 40%, if employed full time (Hayghe, 1979). But according to the resource theory of family dynamics, power in the family increases directly with economic contributions (Scanzoni, 1972, 1979). Women's relatively low economic contributions and their consequent dependence on their husbands decreases their power, and may put them in a relatively poor bargaining position with regard to negotiations over household work, child care, family geographic moves in response to employment opportunities, working hours, and so forth. Hence, women are caught in a vicious circle. Their economic contributions to the family do not provide them with a sufficient resource base to alter their traditional responsibilities, and this very subordination to the demands of their families and their husbands' careers perpetuates their economic disadvantage. Furthermore, as long as women are restricted to low paying jobs in the segmented labor market, the restriction of their occupational careers is the most economically rational course for their families to pursue.

The External Constraints Which Work Poses for the Family

The demands of work certainly limit the time workers can spend with their families. In professional and managerial occupations, there are often heavy time commitments which draw the husband away from the family, placing the major burden of family responsibility upon the wife (Bailyn, 1971; Pahl & Pahl, 1971; Young & Willmott, 1973). Since careers are generally quite demanding and open-ended in their requirements, particularly in the early phases, the career aspirant may feel that work is never finished. It is not uncommon for young professionals and managers to have 60-hour-or-longer work weeks, with little time for the family even in the evenings and on weekends. In such circumstances, the wife becomes, in effect, a single parent. In the Michigan Panel Study, work time emerged as a major constraint on family life. When the men were asked, "Have any of the following requirements of your work caused disruption or strain in your family life?", 59% reported "long hours, the need to work at night or on weekends." Increasing hours at work and time pressure on the job were associated with greater perception of family strain. Kanter (1977b) and Machlowitz (1980) have also described strains in the family surrounding the long working hours of highly successful men.

A common solution to the economic problems of blue-collar families is for the husband to work overtime or to take a second job, either of which results in the husband–father being less physically and emotionally available to other family members (Piotrkowski, 1978; Sennett & Cobb, 1972). Another possible solution is for the wife–mother to enter the labor market. But this increasingly prevalent mode of coping violates traditional sex-role expectations—the husband as economic provider and the wife as mother–homemaker—which are central to conceptions of the "good life" in the working class (Komarovsky, 1972; Rainwater, 1971; Rubin, 1976). . . .

. . . Husbands' long work hours generally place major responsibility for household and child care upon the wife. Because of the asymmetrical sex-role norms applying to men and women (Pleck, 1977), men are permitted to disrupt their families as they pursue their occupational goals. However, women receive relatively little help from their families in accommodating to the time demands and pressures of work. When a wife becomes gainfully employed, she generally maintains the role expectations incumbent upon her as housewife, mother, and contributor to her husband's career. Moreover, it is normatively approved that the woman's family role, if necessary, will lessen or curtail her work activity. Thus, women have a dual work load, in both work and family, even when employed full time.

Pleck and Rustad's (1980) study of time use indicates that although employed women spend about 28 hours on family work each week, their husbands contribute only about 13 hours. Furthermore, the amount of time husbands spend on household tasks does not vary significantly according to the employment status of their wives. When the husband does contribute, he is more likely to care for children than to do routine household tasks (Pleck, 1977). Though employed married women spend less time on housework than do full-time homemakers, their total work time, including both employment and housework, is considerably greater than that of housewives (Pleck & Rustad, 1980). . . .

For couples in which the wife pursues a professional or managerial career with high time demands, the implications for the family are quite pronounced. In these "dual career families" (see Mortimer, 1978, for a review of the literature) both spouses lack the support the wife provides for the single-provider "two-person career" family (Papanek, 1973). They may also feel extreme pressure of time, trying to meet all the demands of two careers plus household and child care duties. Consequently, both spouses may feel that their productivity and occupational achievement is constrained by home responsibilities (Holmstrom, 1972; Hunt & Hunt, 1981). Career demands, including overnight travel and the need to bring work home in the evenings and on weekends, may pose particular problems for mothers, who feel the opposing demands of their children's needs (Poloma, Pendleton, & Garland, 1981). These diverse pressures and strains have led some sociologists to question the viability of the dual career family (Benenson, 1981; Hunt & Hunt, 1981).

The Psychological Impacts of Work Experience

There is considerable evidence, mainly derived from research on men, that work experiences induce psychological change, with important implications for family life. Kohn and Schooler's (1982) ten-year longitudinal study of a nationwide representative panel of male workers demonstrates that experiences in the workplace, especially relating to self-direction, influence parental values, self-confidence and self-deprecation, intellectual flexibility, and authoritarian conservatism. Thus, work generalizes or "spills over" to nonwork areas of life. . . .

Such shifts in the psychological attributes of male workers, shown by the Michigan Panel of college graduates and Kohn's more representative panel, demonstrate the pervasive changes in personality that are linked to work experiences, changes which other family members must come to terms with in their daily interactions with those who are employed. For example, at professional and managerial levels, wives often complain that their husbands are so highly involved or "absorbed" (Kanter, 1977b) in their careers, that they are psychologically unavailable—inaccessible to family members even when they are at home (Fowlkes, 1980; Machlowitz, 1980; Maccoby, 1976). In the Michigan Panel Study (Mortimer, 1980), husbands' high occupational involvement had a direct negative effect on their marital satisfaction. The evidence suggests that men's excessive involvement in work can limit their ability to derive satisfaction from their families. Furthermore, changes in attitudes and orientation toward self and others, found to be linked to work, would likely have pervasive effects on patterns of relationships with family members.

Another body of literature focuses on job stress and its popularized cousin, "burnout." Job stress refers to the subjective experience of workers when they are confronted with a situation on the job (the job stressor) with potentially serious consequences for which their usual modes of behavior are inadequate (House & Wells, 1978; Lazarus & Launier, 1978; McGrath, 1976). New modes of behavior, coping, and adaptation are necessary. Job stressors may take the form of pressures or deprivations. Pressures are produced by a discrepancy between the demands of the job and the worker's abilities. Although pressures are usually the result of excessive demands, or role overload, stress is also produced by the boredom and monotony characterizing work underload (Ferguson, 1973). Deprivations are produced when job rewards do not meet the worker's needs or expectations (French, Rodgers, & Cobb, 1974; House, 1980). Job stress may have substantial importance for the life satisfaction and health of workers and for their behavior when they return home.

Research on blue-collar men shows how their problems on the job influence family interaction (Farrell & Rosenberg, 1981). Piotrkowski (1978) reports that when workers were stressed and upset at work, due to role conflict and overload, boredom, and the underutilization of skills, they came home fatigued, irritable, and worried. They also attempted to create "personal space" between themselves and other family members, blocking out their wives and children. The wives tried to help their husbands by keeping the children "out of their hair," allowing time for rest and recuperation. The children, too, learned to distance themselves from the working parent. When they did not, the fathers became angry and irritable. Piotrkowski called this pattern of linkage between work and family life "negative carryover." A second pattern was called "energy depletion"—there was simply little energy left to become involved with wives and children, and the workers withdrew from their families. But when fathers felt satisfied and challenged by their jobs a very different pattern emerged— one of "positive carryover." The worker, upon returning home, actively initiated contact with family members. The ensuing interactions were characterized by interest, concern, closeness, and warmth. . . .

It is widely assumed that women are less affected than men by the work they do, because of their primary involvement in the home. But research has demonstrated that women and men respond very similarly to their job environments. Although the majority of women enter the labor force in response to economic incentives, they receive more than just financial rewards from their jobs (Komarovsky, 1972; Lein, 1979; Rubin, 1979). Indeed, as in the case of men, the work role can offer women a sense of usefulness and self-esteem (Rubin, 1979; Feree, 1976; Walshok, 1979). . . .

EFFECTS OF THE FAMILY ON WORK

Socialization of Children

A major theme in research on fathering is that men try to inculcate attitudes and values in their children, especially in their sons, which are useful in their own occupations. Kohn's (1969) findings relating social class and parental values are highly consistent with this proposition. According to Kohn, when work is routine and closely supervised and lacks substantive complexity, men will place a high value on children's conformity and obedience to authority, behaviors that are necessary in their work environments. Alternatively, when their work requires independent and complex thought, they will value self-direction for their children as well as for themselves. These class differences in childrearing values have been replicated in many studies in several different national contexts (Kohn, 1977). . . .

Study of the status attainment process has emphasized the implications of parental socioeconomic level for parental encouragement and for children's educational and occupational aspirations. However, research has also identified other, nonvertical dimensions of the father's occupation as sources of variation in socialization (Aberle & Naegele, 1952; Benson, 1968; McKinley, 1964; Steinmetz, 1972). Fathers' occupational functions and attributes have consistently been found to be related to sons' vocational orientations (Turner, 1970). Mortimer's research (1975, 1976) provides evidence that the particular character of the father's occupation, that is, its professional or business orientation, is an important determinant of sons' occupational values. She found that as closeness and communication with the father increased, the intrinsic and people-oriented values of professionals' sons were enhanced. In contrast, in business families, paternal support seemed to strengthen extrinsic occupational values. These differences in socialization, by the father's occupational sector, are consistent with survey data that show that businessmen do, in fact, give more extrinsically oriented responses when asked to evaluate the importance of different occupational rewards, emphasizing high income and advancement, while professionals are likely to indicate concern with the more intrinsic satisfactions of work (Gurin, Veroff, & Feld, 1960; Kilpatrick, Cummings, & Jennings, 1964; Robinson, Athanasiou, & Head, 1969; see also Parsons, 1939, and Goode, 1957). Moreover, these differences in value socialization were found to have implications for sons' later occupational destinations (Mortimer & Kumka, 1982; Mortimer & Lorence, 1979b). Intrinsic and people-oriented values furthered the acquisition of autonomous jobs and work with high social content; extrinsic values predicted high adult income levels. This research supports the conclusion that the father's position in the occupational structure and his particular work experiences have important implications for sons' vocational development and career attainment. . . .

The implications of maternal employment certainly vary with the age of the child. . . . From cross-sectional studies, it is apparent that the major effect of the mother's employment on adolescent girls is to enlarge their conceptions of their future roles, raising their aspirations and encouraging them to consider a wider range of vocational possibilities (Hoffman, 1974; Hartley, 1961). Daughters of employed women have been found to be more likely than those with nonemployed mothers to plan to work in adulthood, and, at the college level, to aspire to nontraditional occupational roles (Tangri, 1972). This relationship between maternal employment and daughter's occupational aspirations may be mediated by the mother's attitudes toward her work.

Working mothers, especially those who are well educated and who enjoy their jobs, may be more likely than nonworking mothers to encourage independence in their children, particularly during adolescence (Hoffman, 1974, 1980). This independence training, coupled with the role model working mothers present, would heighten the aspirations and long-term achievements of daughters (Hoffman, 1974, 1980; Tangri, 1972).

While most attention has been focused on the impacts of maternal employment on girls' vocational attitudes and choices, there is evidence that maternal employment also strengthens the career interests of boys (Hoffman, 1974). Both sons and daughters of employed women have been found to have more flexible sex-role conceptions, perceiving male and female roles as more similar to one another, to hold less rigid conceptions of the appropriate activity spheres of men and women, to approve of female employment, to favor social equality for women, and to evaluate female competence highly. Furthermore, maternal employment appears to reduce the tendency to sex-type the personalities of each sex. That is, daughters of working mothers see women as more competent and effective. Sons of working mothers view men as warmer, perhaps due to an increased tendency on the part of their fathers to participate in childrearing (Vogel, Broverman, Broverman, & Clarkson, 1970). . . .

The Effects of the Family on Occupational Attainment

As noted earlier, several studies have documented the socioeconomic advantages of married men in comparison to the unmarried. But because of the persistence of traditional sex-role norms and task assignments, the effects of marriage appear to be just the opposite for women. While married men have significant advantages over single men, women who restrict their family life have higher socioeconomic attainment than those who do not. Thus, women who never marry have higher attainment than those who marry; women with no children have higher attainment than women with children; and women with few children have higher attainment than those with many children (Card, Steel, & Abeles, 1980; Havens, 1973; Sewell, Hauser, & Wolf, 1980; Sorensen, 1983). Marriage and especially the presence of children clearly have a depressing effect on the continuity of women's labor force participation (Moen, forthcoming) and occupational achievement (Poloma et al., 1981).

Pleck has observed that the boundaries between work and home are more permeable for women than for men. The family role is allowed to intrude into her work role (Pleck, 1977). The demands of marriage and of motherhood may force a woman to work part time, to interrupt her career, or to otherwise limit her occupational options. The discontinuous labor force histories and part-time employment patterns of married women account for a substantial portion of the income differential between married and never married women (Treiman & Terrell, 1975). . . .

It is also apparent that the traditional exchange between husband and wife, in the professional and managerial single-provider family, often extends to the wife's support of the husband's career. The prospects of increasing income and economic security, through advancement in the career, provide incentives for the wife to accommodate to the excessive requirements of the husband's work (Greiff & Munter, 1980). Despite the cultural myth that individuals achieve on their own merits (Kanter, 1977b), the role of wife frequently includes the expectation that she lend active support to her husband's career. The wife's role in the "two person career" has been studied most extensively in large organizations such as corporations (Whyte, 1956; Helfrich, 1965; Handy, 1978; Kanter, 1977b; Greiff & Munter, 1980). But it has also been described in other settings, including politics (MacPherson, 1975), diplomacy (Hochschild, 1969), academe (Hochschild, 1975; Fowlkes, 1980), and the ministry (Douglas, 1965; Scanzoni, 1965; Taylor & Hartley, 1975). The Michigan Panel study (Mortimer, 1980) documents this pattern in a wide range of professional and managerial occupations.

Women often provide necessary services to their husbands, enhancing their productivity, and benefiting the organizations that employ them. For example, wives provide services such as editing, clerical assistance, writing, and attending meetings, thus directly substituting for the work of paid employees. Their entertaining and socializing enhances the husband's position in the organization (Kanter, 1977b). Wives may participate in community and volunteer activities which enlarge their husbands' business contacts or clientele (Fowlkes, 1980), as well as the company's public image (Kanter, 1977b). Many wives provide emotional support and consultation, acting as "sounding boards" for their husbands' ideas. Given the wide range of tasks they perform in fulfilling the obligations of the "two person career," it is no wonder that wives' own careers tend to be restricted. Mortimer, Hall, and Hill (1978) have concluded on the basis of an extensive review of the literature that husbands' occupational attributes act to constrain wives' employment and occupational attainment.

It might appear that married men would be advantaged over their single counterparts, particularly in professional and managerial occupations where the two-person career pattern is most strongly institutionalized. But there has been little systematic research on the causal processes underlying the relationship between marital status and men's attainment. Specifically, it is not known to what extent the higher attainment of married men is attributable to the effects of marriage and wives' contributions to advancement, or to processes of selection to marriage, that is, on the basis of prior attributes that would promote attainment or on the basis of earlier educational and occupational achievement. . . .

IMPLICATIONS FOR SOCIAL POLICY

The research findings that have been discussed in this chapter point to several areas of recommendation for social policy. It is evident that most families are dependent on the workplace to provide them with a continuing flow of income, and therefore, economic security. Many studies have revealed the disruptive impacts of marginal and unstable employment for the family. To promote the welfare of families, surely full employment should be an overriding national goal. Second, the fact that work time impinges on family time, often excessively, is apparent throughout the literature. The number of hours spent at work and their scheduling remain problematic for all workers, men and women, particularly when they have young children. More flexible working hours and greater discretion in overtime work would help workers who are juggling the demands of jobs, maintaining households, and rearing children. Third, we have seen that work experiences have important effects on psychological functioning and also influence health status. To enhance the psychological and physcial well-being of workers, efforts should be made to widen their opportunities for self-direction and work autonomy, increase the level of interest and challenge in their jobs, and reduce work pressure and overload.

Each of these directions of change could be elaborated in great detail. However, given our space limitations, we have chosen to concentrate on one very general and intractable problem: the inequality of men and women in the labor force and in the family. It is clear from our review that inequality in each of these spheres serves to reinforce that in the other.

The growing number of women workers may give the impression that traditional patterns of sex-role behavior have been markedly altered (Young & Willmott, 1973). However, examination of the types of work women perform and the range of home responsibilities they continue to fulfill demonstrates that considerable change is still necessary, if parity with men is to be achieved. As a result of the sex-typed division of labor, both in the home and in the workplace, women are frequently overloaded by excessive role demands. Changes are needed in the workplace, and ultimately in the home, if women are to fully actualize their potential.

Clearly, both traditional social norms and women's relatively low economic contributions contribute to inequality in the distribution of family work. The asymmetrical pattern of spouse support enhances the husband's occupational attainment, but depresses that of the wife. It is interesting to note that these normative and resource-based forces often act counter to one another. That is, in families of higher education and social status, there is stronger ideological support for sexual equality (Farkas, 1976; Scanzoni, 1979; Tallman, 1983). But, as Benenson (1981) has observed, it is in this stratum that husbands' earnings are likely to be far greater than those of their wives. Benenson shows that it is at lower socioeconomic levels, in the lower-middle and working classes, that wives' incomes more closely approximate the earnings of their husbands. But here, as we have seen, there are strong normative supports for the traditional, sex-typed family structure.

This situation argues for a multifaceted policy approach. Traditional sex-role norms will be eroded by the elimination of sex typing in textbooks, in school curricula, and in the more subtle interactions with teachers and counselors. Girls must be socialized to plan for their futures as workers as well as mothers and wives. Boys require experiences that will reinforce their willingness and ability to be active participants in managing home and family responsibilities. For their generation, mutually strong involvement in the family and equal participation and attainment in the labor force remain a possibility. Continuing pressure from the women's movement, media attention, and legal intervention are also necessary to change norms, generating increasing acceptance of the goal of gender equality.

But equalization of the income contributions which men and women bring to their families is also necessary to enhance the resource base for women's equality in the family sphere. For women to increase their incomes, they must break out of their sex-segregated sector of the labor market, gaining access to jobs that have been defined as male positions. Strong enforcement of laws supporting equal opportunity in hiring and promotion and prohibiting discrimination and harassment in the workplace is necessary. A policy of equal pay for comparable worth will not only enhance women's positions vis-à-vis their husbands'; it also will promote their economic self-sufficiency in any circumstance in which they are dependent on their own earnings—if they choose to remain single, in the event of separation, in divorce, or in widowhood.

Moreover, the present structuring of work is designed to enhance the productivity and convenience of the work organization and not to suit the needs of the family. Providing more flexible time arrangements and leave policies would allow families to meet their home obligations, with less need for the subordination of one partner to the other. Some firms are providing more opportunities for part-time work, while maintaining acceptable benefit levels, providing options to job share, or to bring work home during normal work hours (Polit, 1979). Lessening requirements for travel and geographic mobility and the provision of more liberal maternity and paternity leaves, including parental leaves for lengthy childhood illnesses, would do much to assist families. Alteration of the pressure to achieve in careers at predetermined, fixed rates would offer both men and women greater opportunity to balance their interests in, and desire for, both a career and a family.

Of great concern to mothers, fathers, and society at large, is the care of the children of employed parents while they meet their work responsibilities (Bronfenbrenner, 1979). Many families rely on diverse modes of child care and juggle a complex set of supports to assure continuous care (Kamerman, 1980). To promote the equality of women and men in the labor market, the availability of high quality day care facilities must be increased. To help parents obtain child care, some companies are providing referral information regarding day care facilities, giving child care vouchers, subsidizing community day care centers, reserving places in centers or in licensed family day care homes, or offering on-site child care. (Kamerman, 1980, documents the modes of caring for the children of working parents in European countries, which could serve as models for the United States.) There is increasing concern among employers with job dissatisfaction, turnover, and declining productivity. Changes, designed to ameliorate the conflicts of work and family, may lessen these problems in the future.

If present trends in women's employment continue, young men and women face futures in which the roles of the sexes will be less segregated than they are today. If men's rates of participation in the labor force continue to decline as they have in recent decades (Kreps & Clark, 1975; U.S. Dept. of Labor, 1980b, Table 2), and women's continue to increase, they may reach a state of parity in the future. And if attempts to break down the sex-segregated character of the labor force are successful, women's occupational attainment will increasingly become comparable to that of men. But all of this requires change in traditional family roles which subordinate women's achievement to the needs of their husbands and children. The growing literature on work and family linkages converges on the conclusion that inequality in each sphere feeds into, and perpetuates, inequality in the other. To break out of this vicious circle substantial structural change, in both the labor market and in the family, is necessary.

REFERENCES

Aberle, D. F., & Naegele, K. D. Middle class fathers' occupational role and attitudes toward children. *American Journal of Orthopsychiatry*, 1952 (April), *22*, 366–378.

Aldous, J. From dual-earner to dual-career families and back again. *Journal of Family Issues*, 1981 (June), *2*, 115–125.

Aldous, J., Osmond, M. W., & Hicks, M. W. Men's work and men's families. Pp. 227–256 in W. R. Burr, R. Hill, R. I. Nye, & I. L. Reiss, *Contemporary theories about the family* (Vol. 1). New York: The Free Press, 1979.

Bailyn, L. Career and family orientations of husbands and wives in relation to marital happiness. Pp. 545–567 in A. Theodore (ed.), *The professional woman*. Cambridge, MA: Schenkman, 1971.

Barrett, N. S. Women in the job market: Occupations, earnings, and career opportunities. Pp. 31–61 in R. E. Smith (ed.), *The subtle revolution: Women at work*. Washington, DC: Urban Institute, 1979.

Benenson, H. Family success and sexual equality: The limits of the dual-career family model. Paper presented at the American Sociological Association Meeting, August, 1981.

Benson, L. *Fatherhood: A sociological perspective*. New York: Random House, 1968.

Bronfenbrenner, U. *The ecology of human development*. Cambridge, MA: Harvard University Press, 1979.

Bronfenbrenner, U., & Crouter, A. C. Work and family through time and space. Pp. 39–83 in S. B. Kamerman and Cheryl D. Hayes (eds.), *Families that work: Children in a changing world*. Washington, DC: National Academy Press, 1982.

Card, J. J., Steel, L., & Abeles, R. P. Sex differences in realization of individual potential for achievement. *Journal of Vocational Behavior*, 1980 (August), *17*, 1–21.

Dizard, J. *Social change in the family*. Chicago, IL: University of Chicago, Community and Family Study Center, 1968.

Douglas, W. *Ministers' wives*. New York: Harper & Row, 1965.

Farkas, G. Education, wage rates, and the division of labor between husband and wife. *Journal of Marriage and the Family*, 1976 (August), *38*, 473–483.

Farrell, M. P., & Rosenberg, S. *Men at midlife*. Boston, MA: Auburn House, 1981.

Featherman, D. L., & Hauser, R. M. Sexual inequalities and socioeconomic achievement in the U.S., 1962–1973. *American Sociological Review*, 1976 (June), *41*, 462–483.

Feree, M. M. Working-class jobs. *Social Problems*, 1976 (April), *23*, 431–441.

Ferguson, D. A study of occupational stress and health. *Ergonomics*, 1973, *16*(5), 649–663.

Finlayson, E. M. A study of the wife of the army officer: Her academic and career preparations, her current employment and volunteer services. In H. I. McCubbin, B. B. Dahl, & E. J. Hunter (eds.), *Families in the military system*. Beverly Hills, CA: Sage, 1976.

Fowlkes, M. R. *Behind every successful man: Wives of medicine and academe*. New York: Columbia University Press, 1980.

French, J. R. P., Rodgers, W., & Cobb, S. Adjustment as person-environment fit. Pp. 316–333 in G. V. Coelho, D. A. Hamburg, & J. E. Adams (eds.), *Coping and adaptation*. New York: Basic Books, 1974.

Goldman, N. Women in the Armed Forces. *American Journal of Sociology*, 1973 (January), *78*, 892–911.

Goode, W. Community within a community: The professions. *American Sociological Review*, 1957 (April), *22*, 194–200.

Greiff, B. S., & Munter, P. K. *Tradeoffs: Executive, family, and organizational life*. New York: Mentor, 1980.

Gurin, G., Veroff, J., & Feld, S. *Americans view their mental health*. New York: Basic Books, 1960.

Handy, C. The family: Help or hindrance? Pp. 107–123 in C. L. Cooper & R. Payne (eds.), *Stress at work*. New York: Wiley, 1978.

Hartley, R. E. What aspects of child behavior should be studied in relation to maternal employment? In A. E. Siegel (ed.), *Research issues related to the effects of maternal employment on children*. University Park, PA: Social Science Research Center, 1961.

Hayghe, H. Working wives' contributions to family income in 1977. *Monthly Labor Review*, U.S. Dept. of Labor, 1979 (October), *102*, 62–64.

Helfrich, M. L. *The social role of the executive's wife*. Columbus, OH: Ohio State University, Bureau of Business Research, 1965.

Hochschild, A. R. The role of the ambassador's wife: An exploratory study. *Journal of Marriage and the Family*, 1969 (February), *31*, 73–87.

Hochschild, A. R. Inside the clockwork of the male career. Pp. 47–80 in F. Howe (ed.), *Women and the power to change*. New York: McGraw-Hill, 1975.

Hoffman, L. W. Effects on child. Pp. 126–166 in L. W. Hoffman and F. I. Nye (eds.), *Working mothers*. San Francisco, CA: Jossey-Bass, 1974.

Hoffman, L. W. Effects of maternal employment on children. Pp. 47–54 in C. D. Hayes (ed.), *Work, family, and community: Summary proceedings of an ad hoc meeting*. Washington, DC: National Academy of Sciences, 1980.

Holmstrom, L. L. *The two-career family*. Boston, MA: Schenkman Publishing, 1972.

House, J. *Occupational stress and the mental and physical health of factory workers*. Research Report Series, Institute for Social Research, University of Michigan, 1980.

House, J., & Wells, J. Occupational stress, social support, and health. Pp. 8–29 in A. McLean (ed.), *Reducing occupational stress*. Washington, DC: U.S. Dept. of Health, Education and Welfare, Public Health Service, 1978.

Hunt, J. G., & Hunt, L. L. Dual career families: Vanguard of the future or residue of the past? Paper presented at the 1981 meeting of the American Sociological Association, 1981.

Kamerman, S. B. *Parenting in an unresponsive society*. New York: Free Press, 1980.

Kanter, R. M. *Work and family in the United States: A critical review and agenda for research and policy*. New York: Russell Sage Foundation, 1977. (a)

Kanter, R. M. *Men and women of the corporation*. New York: Basic Books, 1977. (b)

Kasl, S., Gore, S., & Cobb, S. The experience of losing a job: Reported changes in health, symptoms, and illness behavior. *Psychosomatic Medicine*, 1975 (March/April), *37*, 106–121.

Kilpatrick, F. P., Cummings, M. C., & Jennings, M. K. *The image of the federal service*. Washington, DC: Brookings, 1964.

Kohn, M. L. *Class and conformity: A study in values*. Homewood, IL: Dorsey, 1969.

Kohn, M. L. *Class and conformity: A study in values*, second edition. Chicago, IL: University of Chicago Press, 1977.

Kohn, M. L., & Schooler, C. Job conditions and personality: A longitudinal assessment of their reciprocal effects. *American Journal of Sociology*, 1982 (May), *87*, 1257–1286.

Komarovsky, M. *Blue-collar marriage*. New York: Random House, 1972.

Kreps, J., & Clark, R. *Sex, age, and work: The changing composition of the labor force*. Studies in Employment and Welfare, Number 23, Johns Hopkins University Press, Baltimore, MD, 1975.

Lazarus, R. S., & Launier, R. *Stress-related transactions between person and environment*. In L. A. Pervin & M. Lewis (eds.), *Perspectives in interactional psychology*. New York: Plenum Press, 1978.

Lein, L. Working couples as parents. Pp. 299–321 in E. Corfman (ed.), *Families today*, Volume 1. Rockville, MD: National Institute of Mental Health, 1979.

Maccoby, M. *The gamesman*. New York: Simon & Schuster, 1976.

McGrath, J. Stress and behavior in organizations. Pp. 1351–1395 in M. Dunnette (ed.), *Handbook of industrial and organizational psychology*. Chicago, IL: Rand McNally, 1976.

Machlowitz, M. *Workaholics. Living with them, working with them*. New York: Mentor, 1980.

McKinley, D. G. *Social class and family life*. New York: The Free Press, 1964.

Mortimer, J. T. Occupational value socialization in business and professional families. *Sociology of Work and Occupations*, 1975 (February), *2*, 29–53.

Mortimer, J. T. Social class, work and the family: Some implications of the father's occupation for familial relations and sons' career decisions. *Journal of Marriage and the Family*, 1976 (May), *38*, 241–256.

Mortimer, J. T. Dual career families—A sociological perspective. Pp. 1–29 in S. S. Peterson, J. M. Richardson, & G. V. Kreuter (eds.), *The two-career family: Issues and alternatives*. Washington, DC: University Press of America, 1978.

Mortimer, J. T. Occupation-family linkages as perceived by men in the early stages of professional and managerial careers. Pp. 99–117 in Helena Z. Lopata (ed.), *Research in the interweave of social roles: Women and men, volume 1*. Greenwich, CT: JAI Press, 1980.

Mortimer, J. T., Hall, R., & Hill, R. Husbands' occupational attributes as constraints on wives' employment. *Sociology of Work and Occupations*, 1978 (August), *7*, 285–313.

Mortimer, J. T., & Kumka, D. A further examination of the 'occupational linkage hypothesis.' *Sociological Quarterly*, 1982 (Winter), *23*, 3–16.

Mortimer, J. T., & London, J. The varying linkages of work and family. Pp. 20–35 in P. Voydanoff (ed.), *Work and the family: Changing roles of men and women*. Palo Alto., CA: Mayfield, 1984.

Mortimer, J. T., & Lorence, J. Occupational experience and the self-concept: A longitudinal study. *Social Psychology Quarterly*, 1979 (December), *42*, 307–323 (a).

Mortimer, J. T., & Lorence, J. Work experience and occupational value socialization: A longitudinal study. *American Journal of Sociology*, 1979 (May), *84*, 1361–1385. (b)

Mortimer, J. T., & Lorence, J. Self-concept stability and change from late adolescence to early adulthood. Pp. 5–42 in R. G. Simmons (ed.), *Research in community and mental health*, Volume 2. Greenwich, CT: JAI Press, 1981.

Mortimer, J. T., Lorence, J., & Kumka, D. Work and family linkages in the transition to adulthood: A panel study of highly educated men. Special issue on "The Sociology of the Life Course." *Western Sociological Review*, 1982 (1), *13*, 50–68.

Mortimer, J. T., Lorence, J., & Kumka, D. *Work, family, and personality: Transition to adulthood*. Norwood, NJ: Ablex Publishing Corporation, 1986.

Oppenheimer, V. K. The life cycle squeeze. *Demography*, 1974 (May), *11*, 227–246.

Oppenheimer, V. K. The sex-labeling of jobs. Pp. 307–325 in M. T. S. Mednick, S. S. Tangri, & L. W. Hoffman (eds.), *Women and achievement*. Washington, DC: Hemisphere Publishing, 1975.

Pahl, J. M., & Pahl, R. E. *Managers and their wives*. London, England: Allen Lane, 1971.

Papanek, H. Men, women and work: Reflections on the two-person career. *American Journal of Sociology*, 1973 (January), *78*, 852–872.

Parsons, T. The professions and social structure. *Social Forces*, 1939 (May), *17*, 457–467.

Piotrkowski, C. S. *Work and the family system*. New York: Free Press, 1978.

Pleck, J. H. The work-family role system. *Social Problems*, 1977 (April), *24*, 417–427.

Pleck, J. H., & Rustad, M. Husbands' and wives' time in family work and paid work in 1975–76 study of time use. Unpublished paper. Wellesley College for Research on Women, 1980.

Polit, Denise F. Nontraditional work schedules for women. Pp. 195–210 in K. W. Feinstein (ed.), *Working women and families*. Beverly Hills, CA: Sage, 1979.

Poloma, M. M., Pendleton, B. F., & Garland, T. N. Reconsidering the dual career marriage. *Journal of Family Issues*, 1981 (June), *2*, 205–224.

Quinn, R., & Staines, G. *Quality of employment survey: 1977*. Ann Arbor, MI: Survey Research Center, Institute for Social Research, University of Michigan, 1979.

Rainwater, L. Making the good life: Working-class family and life-styles. Pp. 204–299 in S. A. Levitan (ed.), *Blue collar workers: A symposium on Middle America*. New York: McGraw-Hill, 1971.

Robinson, J. P., Athanasiou, R., & Head, K. B. *Measures of occupational attitudes and occupational characteristics*. Ann Arbor, MI: Survey Research Center, 1969.

Rosenfeld, R. Women's occupational careers: Individual and structural explanations. *Sociology of Work and Occupations*, 1979 (August), *6*, 283–311.

Rubin, L. B. *Worlds of pain: Life in the working-class family*. New York: Basic Books, 1976.

Rubin, L. B. *Women of a certain age: The midlife search for self*. New York: Harper Colophon Books, 1979.

Scanzoni, J. Resolution of occupational-conjugal role conflict in clergy marriages. *Journal of Marriage and the Family*, 1965 (August), *27*, 396–402.

Scanzoni, J. *Opportunity and the family*. New York: Free Press, 1970.

Scanzoni, J. *Sexual bargaining*. Englewood Cliffs, NJ: Prentice-Hall, 1972.

Scanzoni, J. Social processes and power in families. Pp. 295–316 in W. R. Burr, R. Hill, F. I. Nye, & I. L. Reiss (eds.), *Contemporary theories about the family*, volume 1. New York: Free Press, 1979.

Sennett, R., & Cobb, J. *The hidden injuries of class*. New York: Vintage Books, 1972.

Sewell, W. H., Hauser, R. M., & Wolf, W. C. Sex, schooling and occupational status. *American Journal of Sociology*, 1980 (November), *86*, 551–583.

Smith, R. The movement of women into the labor force. Pp. 1–29 in R. Smith (ed.), *The subtle revolution: Women at work*. Washington, DC: Urban Institute, 1979.

Sorensen, G. Gender differences in the effects of employment on health. Unpublished Ph.D. dissertation. University of Minnesota: Minneapolis, August, 1983.

Steinmetz, S. K. Occupational environment, child rearing, and dogmatism: Test of a linkage hypothesis. Presented at the American Sociological Association Annual Meeting, August 1972.

Steinmetz, S. K., & Straus, M. A. *Violence in the family*. New York: Harper and Row, 1974.

Stevenson, M. H. Wage differences between men and women: Economic theories. Pp. 89–107 in A. H. Stromberg & S. Harkness (eds.), *Women working: Theories and facts in perspective*. Palo Alto, CA: Mayfield Publishing, 1978.

Tallman, I. *Socialization for social change: A comparative study of parent-adolescent relations in Mexico and the United States*. New York: Academic Press, 1983.

Tangri, S. S. Determinants of occupational role-innovation among college women. *Journal of Social Issues*, 1972, *28*(2), 177–200.

Taylor, M. G., & Hartley, S. F. The two-person career: A classic example. *Sociology of Work and Occupations*, 1975 (November), *2*, 354–372.

Treiman, D., & Terrell, K. Sex and the process of status attainment: A comparison of working women and men. *American Sociological Review*, 1975 (April), *40*, 174–200.

Turner, J. H. Entrepreneurial environments and the emergence of achievement motivation in adolescent males. *Sociometry*, 1970 (June), *33*, 147–165.

U.S. Census Bureau. Child support and alimony: 1978, Series P-23, No. 112. Washington, DC: U.S. Govt. Printing Office, 1981.

U.S. Commission on Civil Rights. *Unemployment and underemployment among blacks, Hispanics, and women*. Clearinghouse Publication 74. Washington, DC. November 1982.

U.S. Department of Labor. Bureau of Labor Statistics. Report 631. Employment in perspective: Working women. Washington, DC, 1980. (a)

U.S. Department of Labor. Perspectives on working women: A databook. Bureau of Labor Statistics, Bulletin 2080. Washington, DC: U.S. Government Printing Office, 1980. (b)

Vogel, S. R., Broverman, I. K., Broverman, D. M., Clarkson, F. E., & Rosenkrantz, P. S. Maternal employment and perception of sex roles among college students. *Developmental Psychology*, 1970 (November), *3*, 384–391.

Walshok, M. L. Occupational values and family roles: Women in blue-collar and service occupations. Pp. 63–83 in K. W. Feinstein (ed.), *Working women and families*. Beverly Hills, CA: Sage, 1979.

Whyte, W. H. *The organization man*. New York: Doubleday, 1956.

Wilensky, H. L. Work, careers, and social integration. *International Social Science Journal*, 1960 (Fall), *12*, 543–560.

Young, M., & Willmott, P. *The symmetrical family*. New York: Pantheon, 1973.

KATE KEATING
HOW IS WORK AFFECTING AMERICAN FAMILIES? ....

A REPORT FROM 32,500 READERS

Last June [1981] we published a questionnaire in this magazine to find out how our readers feel about work, and how their jobs are affecting their family living. In the past decade, we have witnessed a dramatic increase in two-job middle-income households in general, and in households with children under 18 in particular. Hand in glove with this trend are often drastic changes in expectations and life-styles for members of such families; men, women, and children are all profoundly affected.

In what ways is the workplace supporting or undermining contemporary American families? And how can society, employers, and workers improve the relationship and strike a better balance between job demands and family needs?

FOCUS ON MIDDLE-CLASS FAMILIES

BH&G readers are largely middle-class, married homeowners with a primary interest in home and family. One expects them to be conscientious, and comfortable with the work ethic. Therefore, this report, rather than being a study of how work is affecting *all* American families, specifically reflects the thinking of concerned, middle-income, American families.

Besides taking the time to respond to our questionnaire, more than 4,000 of the 32,500-plus respondents attached letters, many of which are personal case histories rather than comments on questions. In this report, we give you a representative sampling of excerpts from those letters. Intriguingly, the letters add resonance to the results of the questionnaire, but also sometimes contradict them. It's much as if your neighbor tells you, "Oh, we're getting along just fine, but there's this one problem that's tearing my life apart."

WHO ANSWERED THE QUESTIONNAIRE

Of the 32,500 respondents, 80% are women, the remaining 20% are men, or men and women answering as couples. The great majority of respondents—87%—are married, and 79% have children. Their income and education levels and home-ownership rates are all considerably higher than national medians: Their median household income is $31,250, and 84% are homeowners. Of

Kate Keating, "How Is Work Affecting American Families?" Reprinted from *Better Homes and Gardens* magazine, February 1982. Copyright Meredith Corporation 1982. All rights reserved.

the women, 75% have attended or graduated from college, including 20% who have done postgraduate work. Of the men, 71% have attended or graduated from college, including 27% who have done postgraduate work.

Of the women respondents, 25% are full-time homemakers, 52% are employed outside the home in full-time jobs, 16% in part-time jobs, and 9% are self-employed and/or work in a family-owned business. Female median age is 33.7 years.

Of the men, 76% are employed outside the home in full-time jobs and 17% are either self-employed or work in a family-owned business. (We did hear from a few men who are full-time homemakers, but their number is too small to compute as a percentage.) Male median age is 37 years. Only 1% of the respondents, male and female, are unemployed and looking for work.

THE WORK ETHIC RESTATED

The vast majority of respondents like their jobs, or at least say their jobs are OK. At the same time, many think that *other* people do *not* like their jobs.*

How Do You Feel About Your Job?
(employed respondents)

Like it very much	54%
It's OK	37%
Don't care for it	5%
Hate it	2%

Do You Think That Most People Like Their Jobs?

No	45%
Yes	42%
Don't know	13%

As a nurse-wife-mother from Missouri comments: "In our home, work is not considered a curse but rather something to give life meaning and a way to contribute to society. Our girls would like to go into social work and teaching. That makes my husband and me proud as we feel life is worth most when you are helping and/or serving others."

*Note: We divided our questionnaire into four categories: Questions to be answered by everyone regardless of employment; questions to be answered by employed men and women; questions for full-time homemakers; and questions for dual-job couples or employed single parents with children. For some questions, we requested "check all answers that apply" or "check the three or four that most apply," which is why percentage totals often exceed 100%.

Do You Believe that Hard Work and Self-Sacrifice Lead to Success?

Sometimes	62%
Most times	34%
Seldom	4%

What Do You Like Most About Your Job?
(employed)

Good income/benefits/financial security	53%
Creative satisfaction/fulfillment	36%
Job requirements match your abilities and interests	36%
Employment security	32%
Having adequate time and energy left for family and leisure	31%
Good communication with co-workers	30%

What Do You Dislike Most About Your Job?

Little opportunity for recognition	28%
Low pay	25%
Feeling that your work isn't really appreciated	25%
Repetitious, boring, and/or exhausting work	21%
Little opportunity for professional growth	20%

STICKING WITH WORK

Our readers, like most other Americans, are working for the traditional economic reasons—salary, benefits, and security—but creative satisfaction is another strong factor. The reason most respondents give for sticking with their jobs is that they like what they're doing better than anything else they can think of (39%). The next most popular reason is practical: they need the money and think they couldn't do as well elsewhere (33%). And the reason given by 27% of the respondents is that their jobs allow adequate free time.

Do they enjoy work so much that they would continue to work if the proverbial ship came in and they suddenly became financially secure for life? Yes, say 66% (although half of these would look for different jobs). In general are they happier at home or at work? Well, 61% say they're happy at both places, 29% report they're happier at home, 6% are happier at work, and mercifully, only 2% are happy at neither.

HAPPINESS IS A *GOOD* JOB?

With the evidence indicating so much job contentment, it is important to note that most of the respondents and their spouses have pretty good jobs. For instance, half of the women respondents' jobs fall into our category of *professional/ executive*, which includes jobs requiring extensive, specialized education—anything from architect and auditor to physician, lawyer, teacher, and nurse. The next largest category of women is *homemaker* (the aforementioned 25%) and then *secretarial/clerical* with 16%. For men, 64% fall into the *professional/ executive* grouping, 10% in *semiskilled worker* (anything from factory worker to bus driver) and then 9% *skilled worker* (carpenter, electrician, surveyor, etc.).

Expressing her enthusiasm for her profession, one young single parent from the state of Washington wrote: "I love my three children, my home, and my work. But accounting is my Rock of Gibraltar. When everyone lets me down, the ledgers, etc., always balance!"

However, other letter writers stress that while they enjoy their work, family has first priority. A young father from Florida explains, "Although my wife and I have full-time jobs, our family remains the number one priority. If there is a conflict between job and family, our family automatically comes first. Nevertheless, we are constantly balancing our careers and family." A legal secretary from Ohio writes about the enormous personal and professional satisfaction she gets from her job, but then goes on to say, "I still believe that if success on the job is at the cost of family life success, the price is too high."

SELF-EMPLOYMENT—THE BEST JOB OF ALL?

Content as they are with their work, 59% of our readers think that self-employed people are happier in their work than are people who are employed by someone else. In addition, 75% think that self-employed people work harder. Those who are self-employed emphatically confirm these views: 78% think the self-employed are happier than those employed by others, and 86% believe that the self-employed work harder.

How about youngsters? Are finding and holding a job important factors in developing a teen-ager's sense of responsibility? A resounding majority of respondents (92%) say yes.

TROUBLE ON THE HOME FRONT: WHO OR WHAT IS TO BLAME?

Despite seemingly positive attitudes toward work, all is not entirely well with our readers' lives. Consider that 70% of our respondents say that work pressures frequently or occasionally create a serious strain on their marriage.

How Often Do Work or Career Pressures (Yours or Spouse's) Create a Serious Strain on Your Marriage?

Occasionally	59%
Frequently	11%
Never	30%

Why the marital strain? A spouse too involved with work? Job problems that come home with a worker and sour home life? Guilt about not giving children enough attention? No time for fun? None of those explanations is consistently supported by questionnaire responses. For instance, 63% of respondents do not feel that their spouse often is too involved with work at the expense of family time; only 29% feel they are. Do employed readers frequently bring work home to do on evenings and weekends? No say 64%; 32% say yes. When respondents are upset by a work situation, does that become a problem at home? Well, 58% say they discuss the problem with their spouse, 36% discuss it with a co-worker or friend, and only 13% admit that they brood and become moody at home. Are employed parents satisfied that their children are getting enough parental attention even though the parents are working outside the home? "Yes," claim 73%; only 16% say "No."

Well then, are employers the problem? Generally speaking, our readers give employers a good or at least neutral rating.

Overall, How Would You Assess Your Employer's Attitude Toward and/or Effect on Family Life?

Doesn't have much effect one way or the other	40%
Is sensitive to and supportive of employee's family life	35%
Contributes to tension and difficulty in family life	12%

BIG GRIPES—GOVERNMENT AND THE ECONOMY

We did hear from some readers who complained about chauvinistic and oppressive bosses, of dead-end jobs, low pay, high pressure, and boring routines. But far more often than they criticized employer policies, letter writers took government to task for its perceived failure to control inflation, which they say forces many wives and mothers to seek employment. Typical is this comment from an employed mother: "I blame government and the economic mess for two-income families. One paycheck is just not sufficient anymore. We have reached the point where I have to continue working full time, and when I do we are put in a higher tax bracket so it almost isn't worth it." A couple from Maine echo the sentiment: "The economy has made it so difficult for families to even survive, let alone get ahead, that the job has become the most important aspect of all life, including family life. We have a 16-month-old daughter and another baby on the way, and because of the economy, we cannot live on one salary. How can you be there when your children need you when you spend most of their waking hours on the job?"

THE HANDWRITING IS ON THE WALL

Letter writers helped enormously in identifying stress factors and areas of conflict. Most of these are home rather than job centered—family expectations, child care concerns, parental responsibilities, household responsibilities, financial pressures, and too little time to do all that must be done.

Other Than Preparing or Eating a Meal, What Do You Usually Do at the End of the Day?

	WOMEN EMPLOYED FULL TIME	WOMEN EMPLOYED PART TIME	WOMEN FULL-TIME HOMEMAKERS	MEN
Clean house/do household chores	68%	51%	28%	32%
Watch television	66%	68%	78%	68%
Spend time with family	59%	76%	84%	64%
Do house and/or yard maintenance	41%	43%	44%	61%
Pursue hobbies and other interests[a]	36%	46%	44%	25%
Exercise/participate in sports	23%	16%	13%	23%
Just too tired to do anything	21%	14%	13%	16%

[a]Respondents often indicated such activities as church or community efforts, reading, crafts, music, etc.

In Your Household, Who is Primarily Responsible for the Following:

	WOMAN OF HOUSE	MAN OF HOUSE	OLDER CHILDREN	OTHER PERSON
Child care	60%	11%	2%	5%
Attending school meetings, etc.	54%	13%	0%	0%
Getting children to doctors', dentists', etc., appointments	64%	13%	1%	1%

GUESS WHO STILL DOES THE HOUSEWORK

Clearly, employed or not, women are still primarily responsible for child care and are getting little help from husbands with household chores. Even when we did a cross-tabulation of the above responses to isolate households with employed mothers, we found no measurable increase in the percentage of men doing household chores or taking responsibility for child care.

Indeed, husbands who don't help with domestic chores and child care are high on the gripe list of employed women. And in their letters, some of these women express disturbing bitterness about bearing an unfair burden. Of course, we also heard from women who attribute the success of both their work and family life to their husbands' sharing of responsibilities. Letters also reveal an alarming dichotomy: Women who are forced to work because of financial pressures seem to get the least support from their husbands, while those who freely choose to work (and therefore presumably experience less stress) seem to get the most support.

One member of the former group spells out her all-too-familiar complaint: "My husband (a high school principal) comes home from work tired and exhausted, and lies down and takes a nap or sits and reads the paper. I'm tired, too. [She runs a home-based child-care center.] But I cook supper, wash clothes, run errands, go to the grocery store, take care of our two children. He refuses to help in the house. We cannot make it on his paycheck so I have to work to help pay our bills. I feel he should help in the house as well." Another woman says: "I sure would like it if my husband shared household chores. He says, 'Quit if you can't handle it,' but oh, how he likes my paycheck!"

A letter writer from Wisconsin has a more positive view: "For me, the greatest difficulty in working full-time and still trying to be a 'good' wife and mother was to try to do all of the things I had done before I started working. Finally I just had to face up to the fact that I must lower my standards around the house. But now, my husband and I equally share all household goals and tasks and the children also help, of course. When the dust gets too thick, someone invariably picks up a dust cloth and has at it."

THE SUPERWOMAN SYNDROME

The glamour that once was attached to the super-achieving working woman has significantly eroded now that so many women are confronting the realities of simultaneously earning a living, rearing children, and maintaining a home. Consistently, letter writers attacked the "media-created" image of the superwoman who "does it all"—singlehandedly juggling home, child care, work, and personal time without missing a beat. A few women wrote that they, too, "would like to have a wife."

TEMPUS FUGIT

Indeed, in the real world, time is an elusive commodity for these women. Echoing the sentiments of many, a woman from Illinois mused: "*Time*—I guess that's the biggest problem. Time to do everything, to be alone, to be alone with my husband, time for the children, for the grandparents, for entertaining. It seems to be a 'beat-the-clock' routine." And a teacher from Alabama writes: "With a spouse, child, home, and job all demanding 100% of me, my hardest decision each day is how I will delegate my time among my responsibilities. I feel hopelessly torn."

Another young mother observes: "After I answered your questionnaire, I stopped to take a closer look at our family life. I suddenly realized that I have *no* time to play with and just enjoy my chidlren."

A BRIGHTER FUTURE FOR DUAL-JOB COUPLES?

No doubt about it, many couples must scramble to work out new priorities, responsibilities, and expectations that can accommodate two jobs and family. Some families say it's mighty discouraging, yet many are adapting. A reader in New York observes: "Families with children in which both parents work are like pioneers moving into a new frontier. We have no immediate role models from whom we can get information, ideas, and guidance."

A reader from Florida shares her views: "I believe the impact of work on the family unit is in great part dependent upon the attitudes of the parent(s). My son, age 11, sees working as normal for adults. He is able to divide his day into school/home and to divide *my* day into work/home equally well."

CAN AND SHOULD EMPLOYERS TAKE STEPS TO EASE THE WAY FOR FAMILIES?

In our questionnaire, we asked if readers think that single employees are more productive workers because no demands are made on them by spouse or children. Soundly refuting such a theory, 76% of respondents say no. In fact, letter writers consistently suggest the opposite—that a conscientious family person is a more conscientious worker than his or her single counterpart. We also heard from business owners who confirmed the advantages of having family-involved employees.

A few letter writers are averse to any family-supportive employer benefits because they see no reason for underwriting the raising of children. On the other hand, many more respondents often were eloquent in advocating supportive employer policies.

Which Two or Three of the Following Family-Supportive Benefits Would You Most Like to See Employers Offer Employees?

Flexible hours	66%
Equivalent family leave instead of sick leave	43%
Day care for children	39%
Four-day work week	39%
The opportunity for two people to share a single job	29%
Paternity leave as well as maternity leave	20%
Counseling for personal/family problems	12%

SHARED AND PART-TIME JOBS—A HIGH PRIORITY

Scores of letter writers—men and women—focused on the need for good part-time jobs and job sharing to meet the needs of parents who want to devote large amounts of time to family life, but also need an opportunity to use their professional skills. "A friend with a very demanding career admitted to me that she doesn't remember any of her three children as babies," wrote a woman who has forsaken her own career to stay at home rearing their three children. "The housekeeper saw their first smiles and heard their first words. I think that is unspeakably sad. Can't our society find a solution to this dilemma? Sharing jobs could be an answer to the conflict between home and career. My husband would like to spend more time with the children, and I would like to be able to spend some time with my career. We don't want to turn our children over to strangers." A mother who works part time as a substitute teacher advocates: "A major issue of the '80s should be the development of good part-time work opportunities. This could include job sharing—one full-time job shared by two people. If Americans truly believe that the strong family is the structure on which society rests, we will all need to work toward strengthening family units. In my opinion, part-time work opportunities will allow parents to more easily fulfill professional needs *and* family needs. Too many educated people, especially women, feel forced to choose between the two. Why does it have to be all or nothing?"

THE DAY-CARE GAP

Numerous letter writers described the difficulties of arranging for good, or even adequate, child care. In some cases, the struggle proved to be too much and the mother gave up her job. One mother, who has quit her job and is now trying to set up a business at home, charges: "In many communities, there is *no* day care for children after sixth grade or after age 11. What are these children supposed to do between the hours of three and six? They are at an extremely difficult age. Left to their own devices, they get into trouble."

How Do You Handle Child Care During Work Hours?

	CHILDREN 5 AND UNDER IN HOUSEHOLD	CHILDREN 6–12 IN HOUSEHOLD	CHILDREN 13–15 IN HOUSEHOLD
Take child(ren) to baby-sitter	46%	22%	6%
Take child(ren) to private or community day-care center	22%	10%	2%
Let child(ren) take care of themselves	1%	29%	49%
Work different hours; an adult is always home	12%	16%	11%
Baby-sitter comes to your home	11%	8%	3%
Take child(ren) to employee-sponsored day-care center	1%	1%	1%
Other[a]	10%	20%	24%

[a]Includes care by a live-in housekeeper, relative, older children, parents whose job hours coincide with school hours, and for a few lucky parents, child care "at Grandma's house."

CARE THAT MONEY CAN'T BUY

Even those with enough income to pay for a full-time housekeeper have problems, as we see in this letter from a couple in Indiana: "My husband and I are both physicians. On our incomes, we can well afford to pay someone to care for the children, clean, cook, etc. Finding that special person who will love and intellectually stimulate the children is the weak link of our existence." And from a 27-year-old college counselor with a young son and a husband who is finishing up work on his Ph.D.: "I quit work last year because I couldn't stand being pulled apart between home duties and work duties. In one-and-a-half years, my son was 'baby-sat' by *seven* different women. Just when we'd find someone good, she would raise the price to more than we could afford, or take on more kids than she could handle. I'm going to stay home with my son until he is in school, then get my own Ph.D., go back to work, and have no more children."

POSTPONING FAMILES: AGONIZING DECISIONS

Paralleling national trends, a much larger percentage (32%) of our respondents under age 35 are childless than are those 35 and over (9%). Many younger respondents who are childless write that they will remain so until they can afford to get by on one salary, or until one of the partners is well enough established in a career to drop out for a while without a major setback. If they have children, they say, they want to care for those children themselves. Otherwise, they will remain childless. "When we married," a frustrated Texan writes, "we planned to wait to have children until my wife could afford to 'stay home with the kids.' The wait gets longer and longer and longer, and time is slipping away."

NEW BREED OF HOMEMAKERS

If you think homemakers feel put down by society and excluded from the mainstream of life, and are worried about financial security, you are in for a pleasant surprise. Among BH&G readers, we see that full-time homemakers, far from bemoaning their lot in life, are unabashedly enthusiastic about their role.

A disproportionately larger number of full-time homemakers attached letters to their questionnaire, and those letters reveal a new breed of homemaker. She is well educated, well prepared for the work world, has had some work/career experience, and is idealistic. (Only a few of the homemakers we heard from are men, but these few seem to have sought and found the same Holy Grail as their female counterparts.) In concert with her husband, she has made the decision to be a homemaker *primarily for the purpose of raising children and sustaining strong family bonds.*

How Do You Feel About Being a Homemaker?

Like it very much	72%
It's OK	24%
Don't care for it	3%
Hate it	1%

What Do You Like Most About Being a Homemaker?

More time to spend with children	73%
Satisfaction of providing for your family's needs	65%
Pleasure of being at home	44%
Having enough time to do household chores properly	41%
Having enough time for leisure pursuits	40%
Creative satisfaction/fulfillment	33%
Your family's appreciation of what you do	16%

What Do You Dislike About Being a Homemaker?

Repetitious, boring, and/or exhausting work	50%
Family takes you and what you do for granted	38%
Not getting out enough	35%
Isolation from other adults	31%
Worry about how you would manage if spouse left you	16%

These homemakers talk a lot about their priorities—family, marriage, and home—and say they are willing to make material and career sacrifices for the privilege and satisfaction of raising their own offspring. Few say they are fearful about starting or resuming careers at a later date when their children are grown. It's clear that all have problems now and then and dislike some aspects of their role. But significantly more homemakers say that they are happy with their job than do employed respondents.

THE IMPORTANCE OF "BEING THERE"

Time and again, letters from homemakers reveal deep satisfaction in "just being there" to raise children. Typical are these comments from a homemaker in Virginia: "Raising our children is the most important career I could have. I am doing the best for our children by being there whenever they need me, and teaching them the values we believe are important. Although there are times when I feel bored, frustrated, alone, taken for granted, I wouldn't give up watching them grow and learn for anything. I guess that is a parent's reward for staying home with the children. Incidentally, my husband would gladly switch places with me."

In General, Are You Happy at Home, or Would You Be Happier if You Were Employed Outside Your Home?

Happy at home	88%
Would be happier employed outside the home	10%
Happy at neither	2%

CHILDREN VERSUS MATERIALISM

In order to have one parent at home to care for the children, many homemakers and their spouses have had to make substantial trade-offs. An under-35 housewife from Washington writes: "I am a registered nurse with a master's degree in psychology and could readily work outside the home. Monetarily we would be ahead if I did work to augment my husband's salary. However, I feel it would hurt the family in far more important ways—ways money can't fix. Acquiring things has become more important than providing time and love for children and spouse. This is unfortunate because it places human relationships a poor second; our children become obstacles to acquiring."

A letter from a working mother underscores the threat posed by materialism: "My working has enabled us to buy extra things for our kids, and that used to alleviate some of my guilt feelings about not spending more time with them. But, to my horror, it is clear that the kids now prefer having the 'things' over spending time with me."

A young mother who has done postgraduate work best summed up reactions of numerous homemakers: "I am a full-time homemaker with four children, a terrific husband, and financial security. I have it made and have every reason to be happy, and I am. Yet I am astonished at the people who expect me to be unhappy, to feel tied down, act like a drudge, hate housework, and who expect that my children will drive me crazy, etc. I'm doing what I'm doing because I like it. I chose it."

Another young mother exults: "I worked for ten years before we had a baby. Now I'm a full-time mother to a 17-month-old child and I'm having the time of my life. I am raising him, not just caring for his needs."

NOT ALL SUNSHINE AND ROSES

Some things do irritate full-time homemakers. For instance, many of these women resent the fact that they shoulder most of the volunteer work load in their community and get little credit for doing so. Others mention that they often find themselves unofficially caring for working mothers' children—carting them to ball games and scout meetings, etc., and often sheltering these youngsters after school.

A small minority wrote that they are deeply dissatisfied with their lives as homemakers. One of the respondents, who managed an art/antique gallery before becoming a full-time homemaker, sums up this group's frustration: "I feel worthless, and my self-respect has dropped to almost nothing. No one says 'What do you think?' anymore, only 'Where are my socks?' "

GOALS AND PRIORITIES

A common thread in letters from numerous respondents is that the questionnaire prompted thoughtful examination of work and family attitudes and priorities. For instance, a couple in New York wrote: "Your questionnaire stimulated family discussion on a number of issues, one of which was that of goals. Work, professional commitments, and child-care responsibilities have left us either too tired or less than adequately organized to consider what it is we really want."

From California, a reader who signed herself "wife, mother, working woman," observes: "Young people need to set goals and work toward them. Not all young married couples are meant to have children and they would be wise to recognize this. But if they do want to have children, then they also should recognize that it means a lot of sacrifice. You cannot go as much, have as much, but it can still be one of the best times of your life."

A teacher in New Mexico says that after examining her priorities, she has high hopes for the future: "I hope my children are gaining an awareness that women's and men's roles are not relegated to either job or home but can be shared, and consequently be more satisfying and involving for both parties." And, finally, this from a reader in Indiana: "Families need love, care, and dedication. These can be provided just as effectively or just as poorly in homes with one or two parents; in homes where one parent or two work outside the home. I work because I have to financially, and for the personal satisfaction it brings me. But I have a home and family for only one reason: I love them."

About the Editors

A. R. GINI is an associate professor of philosophy and adjunct professor in the Institute of Industrial Relations at Loyola University of Chicago. Besides lecturing to community and professional groups, he is a consultant to industry on corporate ethics and employee relations and is regularly heard on WBEZ-FM, the Chicago affiliate of National Public Radio. His published works include essays, articles, and case studies on a variety of problems in American philosophy, philosophical anthropology, and business ethics. He is co-author of *Philosophical Issues in Human Rights* (Random House, 1986).

TERRY SULLIVAN is a former university administrator with over eighteen years' experience. He is currently a free-lance writer and consultant to a number of colleges, universities, and associations. His works, including essays on popular culture, have appeared in *Planning for Higher Education, The Chicago Tribune, GQ Magazine, Washingtonian Magazine,* and elsewhere. He is regularly heard on WBEZ-FM, National Public Radio's Chicago affiliate.